Performance and Posthumanism

"This timely collection explores the theoretical and material complexities of posthumanism that shape recent cultural performances while, conversely, contextualizing the performing arts within the Anthropocene's onto-historical emergence. With its rich array of topics and perspectives, *Performance and Posthumanism* helps us sense the entanglement of climate change, zoonotic viral transfer, and globalized culture and trade that has produced our contemporary COVID world."
—Jon McKenzie, *Professor of Practice, Department of English, Cornell University*

"*Performance and Posthumanism* allows us to understand the relationship between artistic and scientific practices. Questioning anthropocentric perspectives, this book encourages the reader to comprehend how the connections between aesthetics and science intertwine and create the ever-changing character of mutant, nomadic perception. It is an excellent volume that makes one reflect on current artistic practices."
—ORLAN, *Artist*

Christel Stalpaert · Kristof van Baarle · Laura Karreman
Editors

Performance and Posthumanism

Staging Prototypes of Composite Bodies

Editors
Christel Stalpaert
Ghent University
Ghent, Belgium

Kristof van Baarle
University of Antwerp
Antwerp, Belgium

Laura Karreman
Utrecht University
Utrecht, the Netherlands

ISBN 978-3-030-74747-3   ISBN 978-3-030-74745-9 (eBook)
https://doi.org/10.1007/978-3-030-74745-9

© The Editor(s) (if applicable) and The Author(s) 2021
This work is subject to copyright. All rights are solely and exclusively licensed by the Publisher, whether the whole or part of the material is concerned, specifically the rights of translation, reprinting, reuse of illustrations, recitation, broadcasting, reproduction on microfilms or in any other physical way, and transmission or information storage and retrieval, electronic adaptation, computer software, or by similar or dissimilar methodology now known or hereafter developed.
The use of general descriptive names, registered names, trademarks, service marks, etc. in this publication does not imply, even in the absence of a specific statement, that such names are exempt from the relevant protective laws and regulations and therefore free for general use.
The publisher, the authors and the editors are safe to assume that the advice and information in this book are believed to be true and accurate at the date of publication. Neither the publisher nor the authors or the editors give a warranty, expressed or implied, with respect to the material contained herein or for any errors or omissions that may have been made. The publisher remains neutral with regard to jurisdictional claims in published maps and institutional affiliations.

Cover credit: inv. MC 1972/S - Peplophoros davanti a motore diesel – Statue dressed in peplos in front of a diesel engine (Roma, Centrale Montemartini - Archivio Fotografico dei Musei Capitolini, foto Zeno Colantoni) © Roma, Sovrintendenza Capitolina ai Beni Culturali

This Palgrave Macmillan imprint is published by the registered company Springer Nature Switzerland AG
The registered company address is: Gewerbestrasse 11, 6330 Cham, Switzerland

Acknowledgements

This book emerged from two research projects that were funded by FWO, the Flanders Research Council. The first was the FWO research project *Capturing Dance Movements* (2012–2016), which resulted in the Ph.D. dissertation *The Motion Capture Imaginary: Digital renderings of dance knowledge* (2017) by Laura Karreman. This project was supervised by Christel Stalpaert, Marc Leman and Katharina Pewny.

We also extend our sincere thanks to the collaborators on the grant, Marc Leman from IPEM and Katharina Pewny from S:PAM. They brought particular expertise in motion capture and deep insights into the project as a whole.

The second is the Ph.D. mandate by Kristof van Baarle, *From the cyborg to the apparatus. Figures of posthumanism in the philosophy of Giorgio Agamben and the contemporary performing arts of Kris Verdonck* (2013–2018), supervised by Christel Stalpaert, Rudi Laermans and Jean Paul Van Bendegem.

We are also grateful to everyone who participated in the FWO-funded conference, *Does it matter?*, convened at Ghent University, Belgium, in March 2015, and whose inspiring contributions made us realize that the topic of posthumanism and performance was worth pursuing in a publication. We want to extend a special thanks here to curator and researcher Pieter Vermeulen, who was a co-organizer of this conference, and who also played a crucial role in setting up our first plans for this publication.

We thank the authors for enriching this volume with their particular more-than-human perspectives and for responding so willingly to editorial negotiations.

We are also grateful to all photographers who gave us permission to print their work, and thereby helping to convey the rich and imaginative performance practices that are analyzed in this book in such a vivid way.

The editors also offer heartfelt thanks to Sophie van den Bergh, who meticulously scrutinized the texts for editorial details and delivered a carefully proofread volume.

We would like to thank Jack Heeney and Eileen Srebernik from Palgrave Macmillan for the patient guidance throughout this publication process.

Christel Stalpaert would like to thank all researchers at the research centre S:PAM (Studies in Performing Arts & Media) at Ghent University. They are a wonderful crowd, never hesitant to lend a helping hand. Their sparkling dynamism creates a stimulating research environment.

Kristof van Baarle would also like to thank his current colleagues at the Research Centre for Visual Poetics (UAntwerp) for the support while finishing this volume.

Laura Karreman would like to thank her current colleagues at the Department of Media and Culture Studies at Utrecht University, and in particular her co-members of the research group Transmission in Motion, for the unceasing effort they put in creating the conditions for an inspiring research environment.

Contents

Performance and Posthumanism: Co-Creation,
Response-Ability and Epistemologies 1
Christel Stalpaert, Kristof van Baarle, and Laura Karreman

Co-creation with Thingly Matter: Dramaturgies

9 Variations on Things and Performance 51
André Lepecki

Does the Donkey Act? *Balthazar* as Protagonist 61
Maximilian Haas

Latent Performances. *Conditions for Some Things to Happen* 81
Daniel Blanga Gubbay

Aesthetics of Mykorrhiza. The Practice of *Apparatus* 93
Stefanie Wenner

On Composite Bodies and New Media Dramaturgy 111
Peter Eckersall and Kris Verdonck

Response-Ability in Thingly Variations: Politics and Ethics

Decoding *Effet Papillon*, a Choreography for Three
Dancers Inspired by the World of Video Games   127
Mylène Benoit and Philippe Guisgand

The Refrain and the Territory of the Posthuman   137
Aline Wiame

The Right to Remain Forgotten and the Data Crimes
of Post-digital Culture: A Ceaseless Traumatic Event   153
Matthew Causey

The Biography of a Digital Device: The Interwovenness
of Human and Non-human Movements in Production
and Distribution Processes as Thematized in the Artwork
Rare Earthenware by Unknown Fields   171
Martina Ruhsam

Tentacular Thinking-With-Things in Storied Places.
Parliament of Things (2019) by Building Conversation   195
Christel Stalpaert

Posthuman Epistemologies: The Politics of Knowledge Transmission

The Point of the Matter: Performativity in Scientific
Practices   237
Maaike Bleeker and Jean Paul Van Bendegem

Music Notation and Distributed Creativity: The Textility
of Score Annotation   261
Emily Payne and Floris Schuiling

Spectators in the Laboratory: Between Theatre
and Technoscience   287
Mateusz Borowski, Mateusz Chaberski,
and Małgorzata Sugiera

A Hybrid Device to Choreograph the Gaze: Embodying
Vision Through a Historical Discourse on Optics
in Benjamin Vandewalle's *Peri-Sphere*   315
Dieter Brusselaers and Helena Julian

Index   337

NOTES ON CONTRIBUTORS

Mylène Benoit is a French Visual Artist and Choreographer, trained at the University of Westminster in London and at the University of Paris 8 then at Fresnoy, National Studio of Contemporary Arts of Tourcoing. She considers choreography as a choral writing, which is not limited to dance, but extends to the artistic performance as a whole, without distinguishing body, sound material, light vibration, or text. In her performances—*EFFETS PERSONNELS* (2004), *EFFET PAPILLON* (2007), *LA CHAIR DU MONDE* (2009), *ICI* (2010), *WONDER* (2012), *LE RENARD NE S'APPRIVOISE PAS* (2012), *COLD SONG* (2013), *NOTRE DANSE* (2014), *L'AVEUGLEMENT* (2016)—she works on dance as a visual artist. Her company Contour Progress if is supported by Drac Nord-Pas de Calais and Conseil Régional des Hauts de-France in the activity programme.

Daniel Blanga Gubbay is a Brussels-based Curator and Researcher. He is currently the artistic co-director of the Kunstenfestivaldesarts. He has worked as an Educator and an Independent Curator for public programmes, among which: *Can Nature Revolt? for Manifesta*, Palermo 2018; *Black Market*, Brussels 2016; *The School of Exceptions*, Santarcangelo 2016. He has worked as co-curator for LiveWorks and was head of the Department of Arts and Choreography (ISAC) of the Royal Academy of Fine Arts of Brussels. He graduated with Giorgio Agamben at Università Iuav di Venezia and he holds a Ph.D. in Cultural Studies from Palermo and Berlin. Recent articles appeared in *South as a State of Mind* (Athens), *Mada Masr* مدى مصر (Cairo) and *Performance Journal* (New York).

Maaike Bleeker is a Professor of Theatre Studies at Utrecht University. She combines approaches from the arts and performance with insights from philosophy, media theory and cognitive science. Currently, she also leads the research project *Acting Like a Robot: Theatre as Testbed for the Robot Revolution* (NWO Smart Culture, 2020–2025). Her monograph *Visuality in the Theatre* was published by Palgrave (2008). She (co-)edited several volumes including *Transmission in Motion: The Technologizing of Dance* (Routledge, 2016) and *Thinking Through Theatre and Performance* (Methuen, 2019).

Mateusz Borowski teaches cultural studies at the Department for Performativity Studies at the Jagiellonian University, Kraków. He holds a Ph.D. from Johannes Gutenberg University in Mainz, Germany and the Jagiellonian University. He started his academic activities in the field of drama studies and devoted his Ph.D. dissertation to the latest developments in the field of texts for the stage. In 2005, he published his dissertation *In Search of the Real. New Developments in European Playwriting of the 1990s*. Subsequently, he shifted his research interest to the field of performativity studies. Currently, his main areas of interest are the history and sociology of science and counterfactual narratives in historiography and memory studies. He published *Strategies of Forgetting: Memory and Cyberculture* (2015) and, with Małgorzata Sugiera, *Artificial Natures. Performances of Technoscience and Arts* (2017). Together with Mateusz Chaberski and Małgorzata Sugiera he co-edited the volume *Emerging Affinities: Possible Futures of Performative Arts* (Transcript Verlag 2019). He is also active as a translator of literary and scholarly texts.

Dieter Brusselaers is an actor, theatre maker and writer who studied at the University of Antwerp, East 15 Acting School and the Royal Conservatoire Antwerp. He also teaches acting and creative writing. His theatre work centres on revamping themes from art history and the literary canon, such as Baroque aesthetics and poetic justice. He has previously published on topics ranging from Walter Benjamin to *RuPaul's Drag Race* and has worked as a curator for CINEA.

Dr. Matthew Causey is Fellow Emeritus at Trinity College Dublin where he served as Head of School of Creative Arts and Director of the Arts Technology Research Laboratory. He is the Author of *Theatre* and *Performance in Digital Culture* (Routledge, 2009), and co-editor of *Performing Subject in the Space of Technology: Through the Virtual Towards the Real* (Palgrave, 2015) and *Performance, Identity and the Neo-political Subject* (Routledge, 2015). His theoretical writings on digital culture and theory are published in many journals including his essay 'Postdigital Performance' (*Theatre Journal* 68, 2016).

Mateusz Chaberski teaches cultural studies at the Department for Performativity Studies at the Jagiellonian University, Kraków. In 2020, he defended his Ph.D. dissertation on the human experience in the context of the current eco-catastrophe. In 2016, he won a Foundation for Polish Science scholarship for innovative research in the Humanities. His academic interests range from performance studies, affect and assemblage theories to Anthropocene studies. He is the author of over 20 articles and chapters in Polish and international peer-reviewed journals and collective monographs. In 2019, he published *Assemblages, Assemblages. Experience in the Foggy Anthropocene* and in 2015 *(Syn)Aesthetic Experience. Performative Aspects of Site-Specific Performance* with Księgarnia Akademicka, Kraków. Together with Mateusz Borowski and Małgorzata Sugiera, he co-edited the volume *Emerging Affinities: Possible Futures of Performative Arts* (Transcript Verlag, 2019). Together with Ewa Bal, he co-edited the volume *Situated Knowing. Epistemic Perspectives on Performance* (TBP Routledge, 2020). He is also Deputy Managing Director at the Jagiellonian University Press.

Peter Eckersall teaches at the Graduate Center, CUNY and is an Honorary Professorial Fellow at the University of Melbourne. Recent publications include: *Machine Made Silence*, with Kristof van Baarle (2020), *The Routledge Companion to Theatre and Politics*, with Helena Grehan (2019), *New Media Dramaturgy* with Helena Grehan and Ed Scheer, (2017) and *Performativity and Event in 1960s Japan* (2013). He has worked as a dramaturg for more than 25 years and is the co-founder of the Not Yet It's Difficult performance group based in Melbourne.

Philippe Guisgand is professor at the Dance Department of the University of Lille 3. He is a specialist in the oeuvre of Anne Teresa De Keersmaeker, and he wrote his Ph.D. dissertation about her work, as well as numerous articles and three books: *Les fils d'un entrelacs sans fin* (Septentrion, 2008); *Anne Teresa De Keersmaeker* (L'Epos, 2009) and *Accords Intimes: Musique et danse chez Anne Teresa De Keersmaeker* (Septentrion,

2017). He has contributed to the following books: *Approche philosophique du geste dansé* (Septentrion, 2006), *À la rencontre de la danse contemporaine: résistances et porosités* (L'Harmattan, 2009), *Les rythmes du corps dans l'espace spectaculaire et textuel* (Le Manuscrit, 2011), *Passions du corps dans les dramaturgies contemporaines* (Septentrion, 2011) and *Pratiques performatives. Body Remix* (Presses de l'Université de Québec, 2012).

Dr. Maximilian Haas is a theatre/media Theorist and a Dramaturge based in Berlin. He is a Postdoctoral Fellow at the DFG Research Training Group Knowledge in the Arts at the Berlin University of the Arts. Haas studied Applied Theatre in Giessen, Germany and worked for theatres such as Volksbühne Berlin, Berliner Festspiele and HAU Hebbel am Ufer. His Ph.D. on *Animals on Stage: An Aesthetic Ecology of Performance* was published in 2018 with Kulturverlag Kadmos, Berlin. His research interests include the theory and practice of dramaturgy in contemporary theatre and dance, aesthetics of performative arts, methodology and epistemology of artistic research, science and animal studies and the philosophy of post-structuralism, new materialism and pragmatism.

Helena Julian is a Curator and Writer who studied art history and critical theory at the University of Antwerp. She writes for artists, institutions and magazines and teaches at the Sandberg Instituut. She was the Assistant Curator for *If I Can't Dance, I Don't Want To Be Part Of Your Revolution* and organizes solo shows with upcoming artist at several cultural institutions.

Laura Karreman is an Assistant Professor in the Department of Media and Culture Studies at Utrecht University (The Netherlands), where she teaches in the B.A. Media and Culture, the M.A. Contemporary Theatre, Dance and Dramaturgy, and the RMA Media, Art and Performance Studies. Her research engages with epistemological questions about movement, representation and digital technologies and investigates new notions of dance and performance knowledge. Her dissertation *The Motion Capture Imaginary: Digital Renderings of Dance Knowledge* (Ghent University, 2017) examined how dancing bodies are reimagined through emerging practices and applications involving motion capture and other digital capturing technologies. Recent publications include chapters in *Contemporary Choreography* (Routledge, 2017) and *Futures of*

Dance Studies (University of Wisconsin Press, 2020) and several articles in *Performance Research*.

André Lepecki works and researches at the intersection of critical dance studies, curatorial practice, performance theory, contemporary dance and visual arts performance. Selected curatorial work includes Chief Curator of the festival IN TRANSIT (2008 and 2009 editions) at Haus der Kulturen der Welt, Berlin and co-curator of the archive *Dance and Visual Arts since 1960s* for the exhibition MOVE: choreographing you, Hayward Gallery (2010). He also curated the project "The Future of Disappearance" for Sydney Biennial 2016 and co-curated with Adrian Heathfield the symposium *Afterlives of Performance*, at FiAFF and MoMA 2015. He is the editor of various anthologies including *Points of Convergence: Alternative Views on Performance* (MoMA-Warsaw and Chicago University Press 2016, with Marta Dziewanska). His single-authored books are *Exhausting Dance: Performance and the Politics of Movement* (Routledge, 2006), currently translated in 13 languages, and *Singularities: Dance in the Age of Performance* (Routledge, 2016).

Emily Payne is a Lecturer in Music at the University of Leeds. Her research interests include psychological and anthropological approaches to the study of musical performance (particularly of post-war music), creativity, collaboration, embodiment and materiality. Her work has been published in *Contemporary Music Review*, *Cultural Geographies*, *Music & Letters*, and *Musicae Scientiae*. She is co-editor of the *Oxford Handbook of Time in Music* (Forthcoming) and *Material Cultures of Music Notation: New Perspectives on Musical Inscription* (Routledge, Forthcoming). She also holds the role of Assistant Editor of the journal, *Music & Science*.

Martina Ruhsam is a Writer, Lecturer and Artist. Since 2016, she is a Teaching and Research Assistant in the M.A. programme "Choreography and Performance" at the Institute for Applied Theatre Studies at Justus-Liebig-University in Gießen (Germany). From 2006 until 2017, Martina Ruhsam realized numerous performances, interventions, transmedial projects and artistic collaborations (primarily with Vlado G. Repnik) that were presented in various venues in Europe. In 2011, her monography *Kollaborative Praxis: Choreographie* was published by

Turia + Kant. Martina Ruhsam has been giving lectures about choreography and related philosophical and sociopolitical issues internationally. She completed a Ph.D. about non-human bodies in contemporary choreographies that will be published by transcript Verlag.

Floris Schuiling is an Assistant Professor of modern and contemporary music at Utrecht University. His research addresses the role of technology in musical creativity, specifically the relation between notation, performance and improvisation. His book *The Instant Composers Pool and Improvisation Beyond Jazz* was published with Routledge in 2019 and he is currently co-editor of *Material Cultures of Music Notation: New Perspectives on Musical Inscription* (Routledge, forthcoming).

Christel Stalpaert is a Professor of Theatre, Performance, Dance and Media Art Studies of the Art Studies Dept. at Ghent University (Belgium). She is director of the research centre S:PAM (Studies in Performing Arts and Media) and co-founder of the dance research network CoDa (Cultures of Dance). She published works such as *No Beauty for Me There Where Human Life Is Rare: On Jan Lauwers' Theatre Work with Needcompany* (with Frederik Le Roy and Sigrid Bousset, 2006, Academia Press), *Bastard or Playmate? Adapting Theatre, Mutating Media and the Contemporary Performing Arts* (with Rob Vanderbeeken, 2012, Springer) and *The Choreopolitics of Alain Platel's les ballets C de la B: Emotions, Gestures, Politics* (with Guy Cools and Hildegard De Vuyst, 2020, Bloomsbury).

Małgorzata Sugiera is a Full Professor at the Jagiellonian University in Cracow, Poland and Head of the Department for Performativity Studies. She lectured at German, French, Swiss and Brazilian universities. She was a Research Fellow of the Alexander von Humboldt Foundation, DAAD, Institut für die Wissenschaften vom Menschen in Vienna, Svenska Institutet, the American Andrew Mellon Foundation in American Academy in Rome and IASH in Edinburgh, and in the academic year 2015/2016 of the International Research Center "Interweaving Performance Cultures" at the Freie Universität in Berlin. Her research concentrates on performative arts and memory, speculative and decolonial studies, particularly in the context of the history of science. She published twelve monographs, the most recent of which are Nieludzie. Donosy ze sztucznych natur (Non-humans. Reports from Nonnatural Natures, 2015) and, together with Mateusz Borowski, W pułapce przeciwieństw.

Ideologie tożsamości (In the Trap of Opposites. Ideologies of Identity, 2012) and Sztuczne natury. Performanse technonauki i sztuki (Artificial Natures: Performances of Technoscience and Arts). She co-edited four books in English and German: *Fictional Realities / Real Fictions. Contemporary Theatre in Search of a New Mimetic Paradigm* (2007), *Theater spielen und denken. Polnische Texte des 20. Jahrhunderts* (2008), *Worlds in Words: Storytelling in Contemporary Theatre and Playwriting* (2010) and *Emerging Affinities. Possible Futures of Performative Arts* (2019). She translates scholarly books and theatre plays from English, German and French. She is a member of an interdisciplinary expert panel HS5 of the European Research Council (ERC) in Brussels, and of Review Panel expert in the European Cooperation in Science and Technology (COST).

Kristof van Baarle is a Dramaturg and Researcher. He received his Ph.D. in art sciences at Ghent University in 2018, titled *From the cyborg to the apparatus. Figures of posthumanism in the philosophy of Giorgio Agamben and the contemporary performing arts of Kris Verdonck*. Currently, he is Post-doc Researcher at Antwerp University, where he also teaches dramaturgy. Together with Kris Verdonck, he conducts a three-year research project on the convergences between Samuel Beckett and Noh-theatre at KASK - School of Arts. As a dramaturg, Kristof is a long-time collaborator of Kris Verdonck/A Two Dogs Company, and Michiel Vandevelde. He has also worked with Heike Langsdorf, Thomas Ryckewaert and Alexander Vantournhout. Kristof has published about his research and dramaturgical work in various academic and other journals and book chapters, such as *Performance Research, Etcetera* and *Documenta*. He is co-editor, with Peter Eckersall, of *Machine Made Silence. The Art of Kris Verdonck* (Performance Research Books, 2020).

Jean Paul Van Bendegem is at present Retired Professor at the Vrije Universiteit Brussel (Free University of Brussels) where he taught courses in logic and philosophy of science. While strict finitism is still one of his main research projects, the study of mathematical practice has become equally important, viz. to try to understand what it is mathematicians do when they do mathematics. In addition, he closely follows the discussion about the relations between the sciences and religious worldviews and is interested in possible connections between mathematics and the arts. He was furthermore director of the Center for Logic and Philosophy of Science (www.vub.ac.be/CLWF/). In the public realm, he is the author of several books such as *De vrolijke atheist (The cheerful atheist)* in 2012 and *Verdwaalde stad (Wandering City)* in 2017 (both with Houtekiet publishers).

Kris Verdonck studied visual arts, architecture and theatre and this training is evident in his work. His creations are positioned in the transit zone between visual arts and theatre, between installation and performance, between dance and architecture. As a theatre maker and visual artist, he can look back over a wide variety of projects presented internationally in theatres and musea. Just recently, *ACT,* a curated Beckett evening premiered (February 2020), in which Johan Leysen performs *Texts for Nothing*. ACT is part of a three-year research trajectory into the work of Samuel Beckett and Noh theatre, co-funded by KASK-School of Arts. More information can be found on his company's website: http://www.atwodogscompany.org/en/.

Aline Wiame holds a Ph.D. in Philosophy from the Université Libre de Bruxelles (Belgium) and works as an Assistant Professor of arts and philosophy at Université Toulouse—Jean Jaurès (France). She is the author of *Scènes de la défiguration. Quatre propositions entre théâtre et philosophie* (Les Presses du réel, 2016— in French). Her main areas of research regard the interactions between arts and philosophy, contemporary French philosophy and American pragmatism. Her current research project focuses on the cartographical reason and imagination and the reshaping of our mapping modes in the face of the ecological crisis.

Stefanie Wenner is Professor for Applied Theater Studies at HfBK Dresden since 2015 and holds a Ph.D. in Philosophy at FU Berlin in 2001. Since then she works as Dramaturge and Curator in the independent scene, at HAU Berlin and Theater Festival Impulse. In 2014 she established *apparatus*, where she is working on creating better depictions of reality with the means of theatre and art. Currently, she is writing a book as a manifesto for a new landscape theatre.

LIST OF FIGURES

Performance and Posthumanism: Co-Creation, Response-Ability and Epistemologies

Fig. 1 Laurent Liefooghe and Sanja Mitrović, *Daydream House*, 2011 (© Anna Van Kooij)   19

Fig. 2 Steph Hutchison in motion capture suit with optical markers in *Emergence* (2014), created by John McCormick and Steph Hutchison (Photo John McCormick)   35

Does the Donkey Act? *Balthazar* as Protagonist

Fig. 1 David Weber-Krebs, Maximilian Haas, *Balthazar* (© Maximilian Haas)   63

Fig. 2 David Weber-Krebs, Maximilian Haas, *Balthazar* (© Maximilian Haas)   72

Aesthetics of Mykorrhiza. The Practice of *Apparatus*

Fig. 1 *Mykhorriza, an apparatus*, by Stefanie Wenner and Thorsten Eibeler (© Apparatus)   98

Fig. 2 *Mykhorriza, an apparatus*, by Stefanie Wenner and Thorsten Eibeler (© Apparatus)   104

On Composite Bodies and New Media Dramaturgy

Fig. 1   Kris Verdonck, *DANCER #3* (© A Two Dogs Company/Jasmijn Krol)   116

Fig. 2   Kris Verdonck, *UNTITLED* (© A Two Dogs Company/Hendrik De Smedt)   120

Decoding *Effet Papillon*, a Choreography for Three Dancers Inspired by the World of Video Games

Fig. 1   *Effet Papillon*, Mylène Benoit/Contour Progressif (© Mathieu Bouvier/Mylène Benoit)   129

Fig. 2   *Effet Papillon*, Mylène Benoit/Contour Progressif (© Mathieu Bouvier/Mylène Benoit)   134

The Refrain and the Territory of the Posthuman

Fig. 1   Heiner Goebbels, *Stifters Dinge*, 2007 (© Wonge Bergmann/Ruhrtriennales)   140

Fig. 2   Heiner Goebbels, *Stifters Dinge*, 2007 (© Wonge Bergmann/Ruhrtriennale)   148

The Biography of a Digital Device: The Interwovenness of Human and Non-human Movements in Production and Distribution Processes as Thematized in the Artwork *Rare Earthenware* by Unknown Fields

Fig. 1   Unknown Fields Division, *Rare Earthenware* (film still), 2014 (© Toby Smith/Unknown Fields Division)   174

Fig. 2   Unknown Fields Division, *Rare Earthenware* (vases made from the toxic mud), 2014 (© Toby Smith/Unknown Fields Division)   175

Tentacular Thinking-With-Things in Storied Places. *Parliament of Things* (2019) by Building Conversation

Fig. 1   Building Conversation, *Parliament of Things*, 2016 (© Michiel Cotterink)   196

Fig. 2   Postcard of *The Tree That Owns Itself*. Athens, Georgia, 1930–1945 (© The Tichnor Brothers Collection, Boston. Public Library Print Department)   218

Fig. 3 Jean Baptiste de Noter, *Vue d'une Partie du Jardin Botanique de Gand, prise devant la statue de Baccus*, 1816 (© Ghent University Library, BIB. TEK. 004,722)   224

Music Notation and Distributed Creativity: The Textility of Score Annotation

Fig. 1 Example 1: Trial sheet for "Clouds" (bb. 11–14), from "For my Father", by Nick Planas   268
Fig. 2 Example 2: Downer's annotations in response to problematic fingering combinations, section I, "Clouds" (basset clarinet part), from "For my Father", by Nick Planas   270
Fig. 3 Example 3: "Czardas" (bb. 10–18), from "For my Father", by Nick Planas, with Archibald's annotations (basset clarinet part)   270
Fig. 4 Example 4: Instant Composers Pool Orchestra, *Kneushoorn*, Wierbos' copy with "Begin F" in the margins   275
Fig. 5 Example 5: Instant Composers Pool Orchestra, *East of the Sun (West of the Moon)* with trombone positions added by Wierbos   276
Fig. 6 Example 6: Instant Composers Pool Orchestra, *Kehang*   278

A Hybrid Device to Choreograph the Gaze: Embodying Vision Through a Historical Discourse on Optics in Benjamin Vandewalle's *Peri-Sphere*

Fig. 1 *Peri-Sphere*, Benjamin Vandewalle, Dieter Brusselaers and Helena Julian (© Paul McGee)   317
Fig. 2 *Peri-Sphere*, Benjamin Vandewalle, Dieter Brusselaers and Helena Julian (© Paul McGee)   319

Performance and Posthumanism: Co-Creation, Response-Ability and Epistemologies

Christel Stalpaert, Kristof van Baarle, and Laura Karreman

A Genealogy of Posthuman Research

Since it was first used by Ihab Hassan in 1977, the notion of posthumanism has developed, multiplied and proliferated throughout the humanities and the arts. Indeed, the title of Hassan's lecture, "Prometheus as Performer: Toward a Posthumanist Culture", indicated an intrinsic relation between the arts and philosophy in the field of posthumanism. For Hassan, one of the indications of an upcoming posthumanist culture was precisely "the incorporation of technology into the arts, both as theme and form" (1977, 839). In this book, posthumanism is an umbrella concept, gathering artistic and scientific

---

C. Stalpaert (✉)
Ghent University, Ghent, Belgium
e-mail: christel.stalpaert@ugent.be

K. van Baarle
University of Antwerp, Antwerp, Belgium
e-mail: kristof.vanbaarle@uantwerpen.be

L. Karreman
Utrecht University, Utrecht, the Netherlands
e-mail: l.l.karreman@uu.nl

© The Author(s), under exclusive license to Springer Nature Switzerland AG 2021
C. Stalpaert et al. (eds.), *Performance and Posthumanism*,
https://doi.org/10.1007/978-3-030-74745-9_1

practices and ways of (un)doing and thinking that challenge anthropocentric worldviews in which the nonhuman is but a mute, malleable, human-controlled element.

The Anthropocene is a term that was coined by ecologist Eugene Stoermer in the early 1980s, but became popular through Nobel Prize winner Paul Crutzen's famous speech in which he proposed to denote a new geologic time period, one which followed the Holocene. The Anthropocene is the Human Epoch, in which human activity has significant transformative effects and a lasting impact on the earth's geology and its ecosystems. Since the mid-eighteenth century, with the invention of the steam engine and the dictate of progress in the Industrial Revolution, human impact intensified immensely, contributing to "global transformation" (Haraway 2016, 45) and resulting in, amongst others, anthropogenic climate change. The Anthropocene at once centres and decentres the human: human activity—and it should be noted, the activity of a relatively small part of humankind—fundamentally changes the earth system, leading to consequences and insights that displace and decentre the human position based on entitlement and control. Posthumanist theory lets go of anthropocentric privileges, in the sense that it moves beyond the normative (and restrictive) conception of the liberal humanist subject. In liberal humanism, the human is the centre of attention, an individual that maintains control over nonhuman matter in a competitive and hierarchical constellation. Posthuman theory challenges and rearticulates what the human is, how it moves and how it becomes-with matter.

In the twentieth century, the Western humanistic and anthropocentric ideologies, that can be traced back to the Judeo-Christian roots of Western culture (De Mul 2014, 464) and that aligned with progress and human mastery over the world, had undeniably revealed their dark and destructive sides. The category of the human, which with the rise of humanist thinking already proved to be an exclusive notion towards other, non-European human beings, had led within Europe, too, to a genocide executed with industrial and biopolitical precision. The development of new technologies of warfare dramatically revealed the destructive potential of scientific knowledge and technology. In *Hominescence* (2001), Michel Serres called the atomic bomb the first 'world-object' (*objet-monde*), because of the global questions it raised about the survival of the human species. Such questions had been simmering since the First World War, but only then led to a profound crisis in the 'centre' as well.

The posthuman current in philosophy and science demands a fundamental rethinking of the self-confident and arrogant positioning of the human and of the category of 'the human' as such.

Posthumanism Brings Two Tendencies Together

One current in philosophy and science observes a decentring of the human since the Renaissance. Neil Badmington (2000), as well as Timothy Morton, has described how with Copernicus, Marx, Darwin, Nietzsche and Freud, humanism's Man with a capital M has been removed from the centre of the universe, has become a consequence of economic systems, has lost its exceptionality in comparison with other animals, both evolutionary and in terms of religion, and eventually, appeared to have no control over his mind and psyche. What Freud already called the great humiliation of humans only continued throughout the twentieth century (Morton 2013, 16). From the universe to the individual psyche, the human appeared as interwoven and networked, as part of a chain of events and agents, of which many were unknown. Poststructuralist thinkers in the nineteen sixties and seventies, such as Michel Foucault, Gilles Deleuze, Félix Guattari and Jacques Derrida, were an important catalyst in understanding that. Foucault's archaeology of the (human) sciences, *The Order of Things (Les Mots et les Choses)*, appears as the culmination of this, especially his assertion that "as the archaeology of our thought easily shows, man is an invention of recent date. And one perhaps nearing its end" (422).

In posthuman evolutionary terms, Darwin's evolutionary thinking is rethought with matter. Biologists such as Lynn Margulis developed a radical evolutionary theory, considering symbiosis in evolution. She proposed "a symbiotic, interactive view of the history of life on Earth" as an alternative to the typical, competitive view of neo-Darwinian evolution as "an unmitigated conflict in which only the strong survive" (1997, 16). Margulis observes, for example, how the green algal transition to land plants resulted from a merging of the genomes (or genetic material) of a fungus with some aquatic green alga ancestor (1997, 22). In other words, the living together and even the merging of different species of organisms has been crucial to the evolution of life forms on Earth. Acknowledging this, Margulis deconstructs our destructive attitude of ecological self-importance and recognizes evolution as a process based on interdependence and interconnectedness of all life on the planet. Evolution for that matter evolves not through mastery, conflict or submission, but through "the long-lasting intimacy with strangers" (Haraway 2016, 60). Also, evolution is not teleologically predetermined and is rather an involutionary process (Hustak and Myers 2012, 77).

Along with this post-Darwinian thinking, an alternative model for scientific research has been in development. The model of the experimental laboratory, and its idealized model of the disengaged, impartial, scientific observer is now emulating other, alternative models such as the "sensory partnership" with "experimental subjects" (Hustak and Myers after Darwin 2012, 84); or "science art worldings" (Haraway 2016, 64). This demands a scientific inquiry into our becoming *with* the world rather than our being *in* and in control *of* the world. It is an attitude that defies any form of human exceptionalism and entitlement.

Another current in philosophy and science considers the emergence of computer-based technologies from the mid-twentieth century onwards as an important development that has led to posthumanism's momentum. Cybernetics, the scientific field that regards everything—from living beings to ecosystems, to computers and machines—in terms of feedback systems, proclaimed that both living and non-living systems followed the same information logics. This cybernetic view held that there was an information flow between the actor and the environment in order to conduct actions in the hope of achieving goals. As early as 1948, Norbert Wiener observed in his book *Cybernetics* that both animals (biological systems) and machines (non-biological or 'artificial' systems) operate following the same cybernetic principles; they had purpose as they both connected actions with communication. Cybernetics placed human beings, social phenomena, machines and organisms on the same analytical level, providing a strong impetus to decentre the human and to think about life and existence in more relational terms.

Technology is becoming even more omnipresent in our everyday, intimate lives. It is also becoming much smarter to the extent that abilities thought to be uniquely human increasingly have to be 'yielded' to nonhuman machines and algorithms. 'The human' is thus once again losing ground. From another political perspective on technology, many new devices and software have been used by state power and have become intertwined with a capitalist society of spectacle. Technology has the potential for grassroots' and emancipatory roots' communities and actions, but has also led to a large-scale expansion of surveillance technologies and control societies (Deleuze 1992) and the hollowing out of subjects in a process of ever-increasing, objectifying entanglements with desubjectifying apparatuses (Agamben 2009). Hence, technological developments make the human 'less human' in two ways, by copying so-called human faculties, and by enabling human beings to be treated as objects.

These two decentring movements in philosophy, science and technology have influenced the realm of fiction as well. Science fiction has often exposed the consequences of these technological developments. William Gibson, for example, created a cyberspace in 1982 in his short story *Burning Chrome*, in which he described a realm of total-immersion virtual reality in which Man merges with the space of the machine. J.G. Ballard's science fiction stories today read like premonitions of an age in which spectacle, media, technology, politics, violence, stock markets and psychology are instantly intertwined.

A recurring speculative fabulation about the technology of the future was the cyborg. This figure featured in many science fiction novels and films, but it was feminist Donna Haraway who turned it into an iconic posthuman figure in her *Cyborg Manifesto* in 1985. To her, the figure of the cyborg is not a dreadful hybrid, but a constellation full of opportunities, arising out of troubled times, moving mankind beyond the Anthropogenic, as humanism and the human have proved to be exclusive categories, causing harm and suffering, pollution and dependence, power and violence. The cyborg, short for 'cybernetic organism', imagines how technology invades the body and creates docile, lethal, semi-artificial beings as well as new entities that would not be able to be controlled by any form of state power, be it capitalist or communist.

> Cyborgs are kin. (…) In fact, they are not hybrids at all. They are, rather, imploded entities, dense material semiotic 'things' – articulated string figures of ontologically heterogeneous, historically situated, materially rich, virally proliferating relatings of particular sorts, not all the time everywhere, but here, there, and in between, with consequences. (Haraway 2016, 104)

Particularly after the publication of Haraway's seminal manifesto, the cyborg can rightfully be called the dominant conceptualization of the entanglement of human bodies and technology, both in the arts and in philosophy. However, times and technologies change, and following

Hassan's suggestion that the conflation of art and technology will also have consequences for those art practices that do not immediately and concretely show, use or demonstrate (cyber-)technologies, the cyborg as an explicitly technological frame might not suffice for those practices (Hassan 1977, 841). This is not a critique on the cyborg as such, rather a plea to open up the many possible ways of 'being' and 'becoming-with' in a posthuman constellation. In fact, many theoretical tropes in posthuman theory think the entanglement of human and nonhuman matter in a broader sense; from string figures (Haraway 2016), to Actor Networks (Latour), and "cosmic webs" (Hayles) to the collectively-producing system of "sympoesis" (Dempster), and many more.

These many theoretical tropes, however, can be traced back to particular philosophical genealogies. In the field of science and technology studies (STS), sociologist and philosopher Bruno Latour contributed in an important way to attributing agency to 'nonhuman' entities in Actor Networks. Latour showed clearly that phenomena are *not* either human, cultural and social; or nonhuman and natural. It is precisely this split that has led to an inability to read and see how things happen, and moreover, it has led to the idea of a humanity that can control, exhaust and destroy its environment. Latour argues that the idea of 'Nature', in a dual relation with 'Culture', is discursively constructed as a comprehensive unity that is part of reality. This modern divide between the natural world and the social or cultural world is "but *one* idea about nature", however, and an "idea that is fabricated by the Modern Constitution" (Latour 2007, 254). Latour considers the positivist way of thinking about nature to be in line with the modernist project of the nineteenth century. Following positivist science, the relations of living organisms to the external world, their habitat, their customs, etc., could only be observed through carefully controlled, observational-empirical knowledge. Latour exclaims that "positivists were not very inspired when they chose 'facts' as their elementary building blocks to build their cathedral of certainty" (2007, 112). "How could a solid fact be that solid if it is also fabricated?", he wonders (112). Philosopher Lorraine Code similarly observes the obsessive need for control and the 'ethos of mastery' at work in positivist-empiricist epistemologies (2006, 48). Positivist knowledge, she says, is gathered along a "narrow path of linear connections" (48). The confidence in "monologic knowledge claims" gives facts a "universal validity" that has secured a rationalist determination over nature by humans (104, 49).

The "allure of mastery" is deceptive, however, as it depends on classifying and constructing taxonomies, solidifying 'nature' in one coherent identity, detaching it from 'culture' (48; see Stalpaert 2018).

Another field leaving behind the persistent object-subject divide in modern and humanist traditions is that of New Materialism, which was booming in the twenty tens. New Materialist thinkers turn to considering matter as an underexplored, dynamic force. Karen Barad's *Meeting the Universe Halfway* (2007) brought quantum physics into the conversation and implemented the concepts of "agential realism" and "intra-action" in New Materialism. Jane Bennett's *Vibrant Matter* (2010) brought about the proliferation of New Materialism, attributing "thing power" to matter. Elizabeth Grosz shed light on Darwin's evolutionary biology from a New Materialist perspective in *Becoming Undone* (2011). Rosi Braidotti's neo-vitalist theory of matter was developed in *The Posthuman* in 2013. In her latest book, *Staying with the Trouble*, Donna Haraway similarly draws on Darwin to outline her "sensible materialisms of involutionary momentum" (2016, 88). These new materialists build on and stretch the ideas of vitalist thinkers such as Bergson, Gilles Deleuze and Félix Guattari, and Luce Irigaray. It is telling, for example, how Deleuze's concept of becoming is replaced by a "becoming-with" (Haraway 2016, 12) and how Grosz articulates through Irigaray her new ontology of sexual difference that takes materiality seriously.

Another group of philosophers consisting of Graham Harman, Ray Brassier and Quentin Meillassoux initiated the fields of Speculative Realism and Object-Oriented Ontology, experimenting with a nonhuman philosophy and an epistemology that goes beyond the human. This object-thinking has an alienating effect, as it invites us to see 'our human selves', and relations, systems, etc., as objects as well, which in turn inspired thinkers such as Timothy Morton to develop his ecocritical notions in *Hyperobjects* (2013) and *Dark Ecology* (2016). His writings are widely cited in the field of posthumanism, again making clear that posthumanism is not only about the relation between human bodies and societies and technologies, but about how that relation has an impact on and emerges within ecologies, and requires alternative frameworks and concepts to think and act.

The authors in this edited volume all relate in one way or another to these diverse strands of thought. However, a shared attribute of these posthuman thinkers is that for them, 'it' matters.

Does It Matter?

This book is the result of a process that began with a conference entitled *Does it Matter? Composite Bodies and Posthuman Prototypes*. This question is of course rhetorical. Posthuman thinkers repeatedly stated that 'it' matters, that materiality is action, that the actual thing solicits response, that the semiotic cannot be separated from the material. However, we took as a particular point of departure a posthumanist perspective on the performing arts. How does 'it' matter when we adopt the notion of a posthuman community as an entangling mesh of interdependent objects, technologies and beings as the basic constellation of a performance context?

Hans-Thies Lehmann's publication on postdramatic theatre already indicated how within a newly developed aesthetics, posthumanist dramaturgical strategies were emerging and being experimented with. Throughout twentieth-century theatre, Lehmann observed a deconstruction of humanist values and the challenging of a rational, knowing, controlling subject as a basis for characters in the performing arts, as well as of a linear, logical and teleological development of events. Elinor Fuchs's *The Death of Character*, for example, resonates with the collapse of what Hayles termed the liberal subject of humanism. As the previously outlined genealogies also show, posthumanism did not come out of the blue; it represents a shift in thinking and practising that has been developing for decades. Also, in the performing arts, the twentieth century saw a tendency towards human performers becoming-with nonhuman entities on stage: objects, dolls, scenography, machines...

Our hypothesis was that the contemporary performing arts render interesting configurations of what we called composite bodies and posthuman prototypes. The metonymy of composite bonding cancels the subject-object divide and hence challenges oppositional thinking, while the concept of the prototype challenges the utilitarian use of technology. These two concepts were key to the conference and to this publication.

Composite bodies are posthuman entities in the sense that they consist of so-called human as well as non-human composites, bonded in a non-binary constellation. The term 'composite' is used in material science and engineering for describing the way glass fibre and polyester bond into fibreglass. While the individual materials or components of a composite— glass fibre and polyester—also exist in a separate and distinct way, they are no longer discernible within the new composite structure of the glass fibre. Moreover, as Krishan K. Cha observes: "it has characteristics that are not depicted by any of the components in isolation" (2013, 5). The glass fibre is relatively strong and stiff (but also brittle), whereas the polymer is ductile (but also weak and flexible). The composite fibreglass is relatively stiff, strong, flexible and ductile. As such, "composite material systems result in a performance unattainable by the individual constituents" (Cha 2013, 4).

Implemented into the context of posthuman bondings on stage, a composite 'body' denotes a particular bonding of two entities—human and/or nonhuman—into a new entity as third term. The bonding is more than merely relating; it demands an intimate coupling in movement or locomotion and perception (Ingold 2016, 81). Contrary to the verb *to relate*, the verb *to bond* denotes an actual joining of forces. In the realm of performing arts, the figures in Belgian visual artist and theatre maker Kris Verdonck's *END* (2008), for example, could be called *composite* bodies. They are more than a combination of a human body and a non-human element. A new, third term is at stake, with new capacities of movement. As Kris Verdonck explains in his interview with Peter Eckersall in this publication, their bonding entails more than merely making a functional or instrumental use of an object or technology. In performance maker David-Weber Krebs' performance *Balthazar*, discussed by Maximiliaan Haas in this volume, the performers likewise do not relate to the donkey on stage, to avoid anthropomorphism and instrumentality, and to allow the incorporation of the qualities of the animal. The verb to incorporate means to include an 'other' thing into one's own body, as part of a new whole, with the human body acting as a central motor of experimentation. This anthropocentric mode of incorporation does not provide space for the 'other' things' agency in a new, experimental and performative third term. In *Balthazar*, the performers and the donkey bond into a composite body because of their joint forces, their bond in movement, communicating new capacities of movement, of dwelling, and distributing a new mode of temporality together.

It is important to note here that the composite body is not defined in terms of substance or outward appearance, but in terms of the particular bonding and the movement that it generates. In his *Ethics*, Spinoza developed the notion of the "composite body" in order to distinguish bodies "from one another in respect of motion and rest, and not in respect of substance" (2001, 58–59). The new, consistent constellation or the 'certain fixed proportion' therefore only exists *in* the movement. A composite *body* for that matter does not propose a body as new unity or identity. The composite of posthuman bonding forms a consistent (but not compound) body. It is consistent because the components manage to join forces and to move together. They are not compound, as the composite body is always more than the sum of its constituent parts. Following Deleuze's rhizome ontology, a composite body is an extremely mobile entity, an entity in undulatory motion, always in a perpetual state of becoming (Stalpaert 2019).

As such, the composite body can never turn into an exemplum, into a model to be traded for more efficient use. A composite body always remains a prototype, and hence escapes the utilitarian use of technology. With every new performance context—or even, with every iteration of a performance—a new composite of bodies is inaugurated, like a prototype, in the sense that a prototype generates an early sample, a first impression. A prototype is, like a performance, always in a perpetual state of becoming-with. In "The Productivity of the Prototype" film scholar and curator Edwin Carels precisely celebrates this notion of undecidedness; prototypes, he says,

> perform exactly what their etymology promises (from *protos* 'first' and *typos* 'impression' or 'model'). (...) As industrial prototypes, these original creations – no matter how technically clever and refined – are rather useless: too complex, too delicate and too clunky to ever be considered for mass-production. As artistic statements, the main function of these full-scale constructions is to provoke an effect of wonder, alerting the viewer to the ambivalent status of moving images produced by a machine. (Carels 2012, 178)

For the conference *Does it Matter? Composite Bodies and Posthuman Prototypes in Contemporary Performing Arts*, we invited theatre and performance scholars, theatre makers and philosophers to reflect on the diverse constellations of posthuman composite bodies on stage. The call for papers was developed out of converging research lines at the Research Centre S:PAM (Studies in Performing Arts & Media) at Ghent University and the three individual research trajectories of the editors of this volume. Each of us engaged with the performing arts from various perspectives that nevertheless all related to posthumanism and the posthuman.

Each of these three perspectives covers various instances of a performance: co-creative processes and performance analysis of contemporary posthumanist performing arts (van Baarle); the (political and ethical) implications for the response-ability of the spectator, in attunement with a networked conception of performance (Stalpaert); and the evolving politics of knowledge production and transmission in contemporary performing arts and how this knowledge in turn generates new artistic processes (Karreman). These three research lines reappeared in the way we structured the conference programme and also in the way we clustered the contributions in this volume. As such, this publication seeks to unfold the many features of posthuman performance practices along the notions of co-creation (dramaturgies), response-ability (ethics) and knowledge transmission (politics of knowledge).

Posthumanism implies a revision of all aspects pertaining to performance, from the creation process to its performance, reception and (knowledge) transmission. This should come as no surprise, as a posthumanist perspective precisely blurs the boundaries that would isolate the artwork from its creation, reception and transmission, making a pure hermeneutics no longer possible. Or to formulate it in another way: in posthumanism the boundaries upheld in modernity between practice and theory, between input and output, between giving and receiving collapse. Hence, the division in the three clusters is not intended here as a separation. Rather, one flows over into the others and vice versa. Along with this blurring of boundaries various methodological crossovers happen in this volume, of which performance philosophy is one of the most important ones. Posthumanism does not only join dots between science and technology studies (STS)—which Braidotti rightfully called the *analytical* type of posthumanism (2013, 42)—and theatre, dance and performance studies, but there are also many travelling concepts between philosophy and art studies.

However, concepts seeping into or 'travelling' from one field of study to another tend to lose their rigid employability and might suffer from conflation. As Mieke Bal aptly observes, the conflation of different, but affiliated concepts has impoverishing effects (2002, 35). For this reason, this introduction carefully calibrates some terms and concepts before allowing the interdisciplinary network to resonate in the various authors' contributions. In addressing how a posthumanist perspective influences creative processes, performances, spectatorship and knowledge practices, we aim to not only demonstrate the widespread fundamental impact of this paradigm shift, but also to offer a clear toolbox to artists, scholars and audiences. What vocabulary, which theoretical tropes, what theory, which practices and which questions and potential answers arise in our contemporary posthuman condition?

On Things and Objects

A first terminological calibration concerns the use of 'objects' or 'things' in posthuman discourse. It is important to highlight that a 'thing' differs from an 'object' in the sense that an object already implicates a utility-driven or intentionality-driven approach from a human 'subject'. The 'object' refers to the non-human counterpart in the modernist divide. Heidegger regrets the split of things into subjects and objects. He suggested a 'being-in-the-world' (*In-der-Welt-Sein*) as an alternative for terms such as subject and object. As such, a being-in-the-world denotes our being intertwined with other beings and 'presences'. We expand Heidegger's ontological concept to a being-in-a-more-than-human-world, referring to David Abram's phrase coined in *The Spell of the Sensuous* (1996), hence moving beyond an anthropocentric viewpoint. Next to the more-than-human, other theoretical tropes circulate in posthuman discourse, including the "other-than-human, inhuman, and human-as-humus" (Haraway 2016, 101).

From an anthropocentric perspective, human beings animate things intentionally into useful objects. Their living reality is nothing more than a material presence waiting to be animated. In her theory of vital materialism, political theorist Jane Bennett re-values the capacity of things. Her aspiration is to give objects their thing-power back: "to articulate a vibrant materiality that runs alongside and inside humans to see how analyses of political events might change if we gave the force of things more due" (2010, viii). Building on insights from Bergson, Deleuze and Latour, Bennett acknowledges a certain thing-power, a vitality when moving beyond the commodification of objects: "the curious ability of inanimate things to animate, to act, to produce effects dramatic and subtle" (6). Things as such not only enable or prevent human beings to do something, to move or to act, things move and act themselves, "as quasi agents or forces with trajectories, propensities, or tendencies of their own" (viii).

Acknowledging this thing-power startles our habitual ways of perceiving the world, as it outwits the active relationship that human beings believe they have with so-called inanimate objects, also in the performing arts. Drawing on Heidegger and Latour as well, object-oriented ontologist Graham Harman also seeks to unpack the being of what he still terms 'objects'. Objects are withdrawn, have unknowable qualities and are in various kinds of relations that are aesthetic and do not operate according to causal logic (Harman 2011, 104). From a more explicit technological perspective, the agency of things is interwoven with political systems, as for example by Giorgio Agamben—who also draws on Heidegger—and his update of the Foucauldian notion of the *dispositivo*, or apparatus. The same Agamben—in a move that many posthumanist thinkers and artists share—sees potentialities in the agency of things and the decentring and de(con)struction of the liberal humanist subject. Other relations can be explored, in which the self is shared and explores its own thing-ness as a form of life that deactivates existing power structures (Agamben 2014, 46).

In dramatic theatre, things are traditionally considered objects: they are "props, an object or sculpture used on stage" (Lepecki, in this volume). In postdramatic theatre, objects are allowed to exert their thing-power and their intrinsic performativity is explored. As Hans-Thies Lehmann observes, postdramatic theatre has "the possibility of returning to things their value and to the human actors the experience of 'thing-ness' that has become alien to them" (2006, 165). Lehmann refers to the work of Polish visual artist and theatre maker Tadeusz Kantor as symptomatic for a tendency in postdramatic theatre "to valorize the objects and materials of the scenic action" (72). The attention to and the life of objects on Kantor's stage are part of the deconstruction of a traditional dramatic hierarchy "in which everything (and every *thing*) revolves around human action" (72).

> The verbal dialogue of drama is replaced by a *dialogue between people and objects*. (...) a quasi-linguistic exchange between human being and thing. (...) The hierarchy between human being and object is relativized for our perception. (Lehmann 2006, 73)

This thing-power not only refers to so-called inanimate objects, but also to the sphere of machines, mechanics and technology.

> It seems indeed that the ever accelerating technologization and with it the tendency of a transformation of the body from 'destiny' to controllable and selectable apparatus – a programmable techno-body – announces an *anthropological mutation* whose first tremors are registered more precisely

in the arts than in quickly outdated judicial and political discourses. (Lehmann 2006, 165 – italics Lehmann)

Echoing Hassan, Lehmann set the stage for the development of a posthumanist artistic practice. The latter pursues and takes the consequences of thingly agency, the nonhuman, technology, ecology and dehumanizing late-capitalist politics to further, deepened, nuanced levels. This persistence on the nonhuman, in the arts but also in the world, is where the postdramatic veers into the terrain of the posthuman. Whereas academics often speak of a postdramatic aesthetic, we would argue that when it comes to posthumanism, the notion of posthuman dramaturgy seems more apt to describe and analyse artistic practices. Aesthetics as a field is closely tied to modernity (Mignolo and Vazquez 2013) and often implies a distance between the perceiving subject and the object of perception. On stage, within the artwork, the boundaries between humans and nonhumans might be suspended in favour of things and thing-being, but posthumanism requires a fundamental rethinking of all aspects pertaining to performing arts. Creative processes, spectatorship and the transition of knowledge all 'matter'. Dramaturgy then allows for a more open perspective, understood not in the traditional sense as pertaining to the (writing of the) text and language and operating in a linear development or in service of the execution of a concept, but rather as what Belgian dramaturge Marianne Van Kerkhoven called 'new dramaturgy' (1994) in which the process is key, and where concepts are developed throughout the creative practice. Dramaturgy allows us to consider the contexts, audiences, communications, knowledges, practices, networks, concepts.... As the various genealogical lines that have been tentatively drawn thus far show, there is not 'one posthumanism', but there are many posthumanisms. In the same way there is not 'one posthumanist dramaturgy' but there are many. We therefore chose to speak of posthumanist dramaturgies as compositional principle connecting the three clusters of this book: co-creation with thingly matter, response-ability in thingly variations and posthuman epistemologies in arts and sciences.

Realigning Action and Movement on the Posthuman Stage

Posthumanist dramaturgies imply a different position for and conception of agency. Acknowledging 'objects' as to let their thing-power speak and to co-create the performance also realigns the anthropocentric perspective on movement and action, as it has been developed in Aristotle's *Poetics* and hence in classical dramatic aesthetic and the realm of representation. As many authors in this edited volume tackle the notions of action and movement in the posthuman era, a calibration of these terms along a new dramaturgy is needed too.

In a classical dramatic aesthetic, action is produced mainly through the behaviour of characters, impersonated by actors or human actants. It is "a series of deeds and actions which constitute the subject of a dramatic work" (Pavis 1998, 9). Aristotle developed the unity of action in his *Poetics* as the cornerstone of classical dramatic aesthetic. In the Aristotelian paradigm of representation, "tragedy is an imitation of an action, and on account above all the action is an imitation of agents" (12; see also Stalpaert 2010b, 440).

On a narrative level, action is "the dynamic, transforming element that makes the logical and temporal transition from one *situation* to another. It is the logical and temporal series of dramatic situations" (Pavis 1998, 10, italics his). Dramatic action therefore has a teleological principle; there is a clear beginning, middle and end in the linear-successive, causal development of the plot. According to Aristotle's *Poetics*, the ideal of clarity is obtained through the principle of unity of action, based on the analogy of logic. A dramatic aesthetic hence presupposes a paralogical arrangement of the drama, with beginning, middle and ending carefully connected by means of the logical chain of cause and effect, of action and reaction.

On a physical level, it is primarily the human body that *does* the gesturing and acting in a dramatic aesthetic. The movements are telos-oriented and follow the logic of action and reaction, of stimulus and response. Movement as motivated and meaningful action is the key element. In his study on the movement-image (*image-mouvement*), poststructuralist Gilles Deleuze explains the tight connection between perception (*image-perception*) and action (*image-action*) in the realm of representation. The bodily movements of the actor fit what Deleuze defined as the sensory-motor scheme of a classical dramatic aesthetic. The actor moves and acts properly, towards a particular goal, a narrative end or result. He or she assimilates what he or she sees (perceptions, opponents), hears (dialogues) or feels (psychologically motivated emotions) in function of the plot structure of the play. This traditional use of appropriate gestures was prescribed by Aristotle from a dramatic point of view: "for those who feel emotion are most convincing through natural sympathy with the characters they represent; and one who is agitated storms, one who is angry rages, with the most life-like reality" (32; see also Stalpaert 2010a, 365).

Aristotle's dramatic aesthetic hence follows an anthropocentric—albeit divinely influenced—reasoning, both on a narrative and physical level. Following the structure of dramatic action as sensory-motor scheme, what the character/actor sees is tightly connected with a logical, meaningful and targeted action. In this sensory-motor scheme, objects are screened for their usefulness in action: "perceived things tender their unstable facet towards me, at the same time as my delayed reaction, which has become action, learns to use them" (Deleuze 2005, 67).[1]

Also, according to anthropocentric reasoning, the human 'thing' becomes 'subject' through subjectivation. Subjectivity emerges from the clash between the object and the subject. In other words, humans need 'things' in order to become a subject in a more-than-human-world. In a dramatic aesthetic, this means that together with the plot, a subject position evolves from the narration. The story represents the subject, and his or her being-in-the-world. From an anthropocentric perspective, we tend to consider the dual relation between object and subject in terms of human control or mastery, effectiveness or utility, and efficiency. However, as Lepecki aptly points out in his contribution to this edited volume, 'things' are in fact controlling and commanding our becoming-*with*-the-world. "Subjectivity itself is becoming a kind of objecthood", Lepecki claims, following Agamben's reasoning.

In posthumanist performances, the sensory-motor scheme and the process of subjectivation are out of joint. The prop-function that is traditionally attributed to 'things' in dramatic theatre is disturbed. And particularly when it comes to agency, "action is not necessarily emanating from humans" (Blanga Gubbay, in this volume), and movements cannot be reduced to the human body. Nearly all contributions in this volume situate action in a more-than-human, networked mode. The authors analyse entangled human bodies within systems and technological environments; they discuss performance contexts, preparations and experiments that foster agency beyond human control. The thing in itself becomes a material force that unsettles any logical transition from one dramatic situation to another. Things might 'fail' to work at the 'appropriate' time, but they matter. They move in unexpected, unforeseeable ways, but they are response-able; they are capable of response. The response the things solicit is not targeted action, but rather a state of response-ability from the perspectives of both the creating artists, human performers and audiences; a "method alert to off-the-beaten-path practices" (Haraway 2016, 127). The result is a co-creation with reciprocating energies. Performers and artists let go of preconceived notions of what things are supposed to be able to do, and open up to what things evoke, allowing things to matter. Subject and object require each other in unexpected collaborations and combinations in order to move forward in complexity. Or, to put it in Donna Haraway's terms; they "become-with each other or not at all" (2016, 4).

In this constellation of response-ability, the human actors' targeted movements are in fact useless, as the sensory-motor scheme is completely out of joint. The actors simply can no longer perceive to move and to act properly, consciously, towards a particular goal, a narrative end or result. As such, they can no longer be the hero in a salvation tale. The tale of the hero turns into tales of "ongoingness" (Haraway 2016, 125). Composite bodies—in the sense of bonded entities (human and nonhuman)—are engaged in an open-ended exploratory process, in which they have to iterate, deviate and elaborate constantly, which differs clearly from the efficient way of moving forward in the modern concept of progress. The artists' and/or actors' "appropriate gestures" (Aristotle 2003, 32) give way to what Didier Debaise and Isabelle Stengers coined "speculative gestures" (*gestes spéculatifs*), insisting on the possible, not to be pinned down in a plot to follow, and always embedded in relational perspectives (2015, 4).

PART I: Co-Creation with Thingly Matter (Dramaturgies)

In the article "**9 Variations on Things and Performance**", dance scholar **André Lepecki** detects a move beyond the Anthropocene in contemporary performing arts as he observes "a deep link between performativity and thingliness". The article was first published in 2011 in a booklet called *IT, Thingly Variations in Space*, published by the alternative management bureau MOKUM vzw and the artistic research environment A.PASS/A.RC. It explores the position of the object in the works of Lilia Mestre, Joanna Bailie and Christoph Ragg, Laurent Liefooghe and Sanja Mitrović. Lepecki's contribution is re-published in this edited volume, as it provides a conceptual cornerstone for the topic of performance and posthumanism, and hence for this book. Already early on, it largely expands on the matter why for a growing group of performing artists in the twenty tens an object is more tool-driven than a thing.

Lepecki briefly refers to *LivingMachine* (2010) to make his point. *LivingMachine* is an audio-spatial installation by the Belgian architect Laurent Liefooghe that also appeared as the performance space of *Daydream House* in 2011, created in collaboration with the Brussels-based Serbian theatre maker and performer Sanja Mitrović. The installation of *LivingMachine* was originally commissioned by Z33 as part of the exhibition *Design by Performance* that was on display in 2010. When the installation was turned into a performance space for *Daydream House* in 2011, Liefooghe considered the performance space of 'the house' mainly "as an architecture, rather than a décor". Lehmann would say that in *Daydream House* the scenography functions as "visual dramaturgy, (…) freely developing its own logic" (93).

Décor is not décor anymore (Bruno Latour, in van Baarle and Hendrickx 2018, n.p.) in a posthumanist and post-anthropocentric conception of the world and artistic practice. In other words, what is mainly considered to be 'dead' material acquires agency. 'The house' has its thing-power speak and co-creates the performance. Indeed, the coffee machine, the toaster, the curtains seem to have a life of their own. They do not 'act' properly, following the utilitarian use that humans have attributed to them. They have agency in the sense that they solicit other responses than the ones expected in habitual and functional usage. The presence of machines and technologies in our everyday living environment is highlighted (this is before the proliferation of the 'internet of things') and it is suggested that our dwelling, our way of inhabiting, occurs *with* things (Fig. 1).

Since Liefooghe and Mitrović premiered their *Daydream House* and Lepecki's article appeared (both in 2011), many performances have experimented with "thingliness". In the first part of this edited volume, a number of authors investigate the artistic strategies that performances engage with to allow a 'thing' to remain a 'thing'. This means freeing the object of being a mere prop in theatre, freeing the object of being a sign in a logical, human-centred, meaning-making process, but also freeing

Fig. 1 Laurent Liefooghe and Sanja Mitrović, *Daydream House*, 2011 (© Anna Van Kooij)

the performer from habitual expectations of virtuosity, beauty and skill related to classical drama. This has political implications. When things are freed from their 'proper' function as prop in a theatre context, they are allowed to remain merely a thing. In Lepecki's words, the objects are freed from the utility-driven forces in capitalism, from use-value and exchange-value, from the meaning-making process in the realm of representation, regaining their "dispossessive force". The same accounts for the becoming-thingly of performers. The production of objects or 'things', paradoxically also producing 'us', reaches culmination in capitalist times of consumption and commodification, in which 'things' are turned into commodities. As such, "uncovering a performativity in things" questions broader political issues "of obedience, of governing gestures, of determining movements". Conceiving of the object as a thing is a political gesture. Referring to Agamben's notion of the apparatus in *What is an Apparatus?* (2009), Lepecki observes how this political gesture becomes apparent in thingly movement and human becoming in relation to things.

Contemporary Posthumanist Performing Arts

In theatre, as in dance, performers usually display their virtuosity, affirming the importance of personhood and self-centredness, even when moving beyond traditional narrative structures in dance and theatre. In 2011, Lepecki listed Vera Mantero, Boris Charmatz and Xavier Le Roy as theatre makers and choreographers who moved beyond the anthropocentric perspective of virtuosity. The Belgian theatre maker and visual artist Kris Verdonck is another example. In an interview with **Peter Eckersall**, entitled **"On Composite Bodies and New Media Dramaturgy"**, **Kris Verdonck** explains how his theatre work is not only an investigation into the thingly performance of objects, but also, how his particular way of creating demands the performing subjects to move away from "the imperial force of controlling objects, commodities, or apparatuses" attributed to humans (Lepecki, in this volume). Together with his late dramaturge Marianne Van Kerkhoven, Verdonck adopted the notion of 'figure' to indicate both human and nonhuman performers and their conjunction. They were inspired by Agamben's use of the word 'figure' in his *Remnants of Auschwitz*, where it is used to indicate both a state of dehumanization and objectification, as well as a provocative and disruptive form of life on the threshold between life and death, between subject and object, between action and inaction (for a more extensive analysis of the use of the notion of the figure, see van Baarle 2015 and 2018). The marionette-dancers attached to cables in *I/II/III/IIII* (2007), the figures attached to cables, thin wires or body bags in *END* (2008), and the mascot-dancer in *UNTITLED* (2014) are all figures engaged in different sorts of bondings with matter, wires or machines. This demands a particular way of moving, acting and dancing in attunement with matter. Rather than aiming for the excellence of acrobatic movements in hyper-controlled spectacles, seeking perfection and stretching human capacities to overcome forces of gravity, these string figures articulate a particular kind of virtuosity and beauty. Virtuosity for that matter is not about perfection, harmony or effectiveness of technology. It has everything to do with "the courage to connect, with the skill of response-ability, in the sense of accounting for the ability to respond in the attachment within an actor-network" (Stalpaert 2020, 124). The virtuosity lies in the ability of these "string figures" to think-with other beings, including the other-than-human, of "rendering each other capable of unexpected feats in actual encounters", to "enlarge the capacities of all the players", "to render each other capable of mutual trust" (Haraway 2016, 7, 22). This being co-present in the thick, ongoing presence, encountering one's thingliness demands courage, but is very liberating in the end. As Verdonck himself testifies in the interview:

> Just to be there in the moment, is the greatest thing that can happen to a dancer, performer or actor. They all dream about it and when it happens, they say: "Finally I was on stage. I was what I was".

This figural thingliness is both a response to and an affordance of being within a technological apparatus. Verdonck's co-creative method, in which non-human agency is explored and included from the onset of the creative process, and hence able to unfold during the moment of presentation, is characteristic of what Eckersall, together with Helena Grehan and Edward Scheer, has termed 'New Media Dramaturgy' (NMD). NMD is one of many posthumanist dramaturgies, but the features attributed to it by Eckersall et al. are close and familiar to our general understanding of posthumanism and are helpful to analyse agency in a posthumanist constellation. NMD is used to indicate "technologies and techniques of new media in relation to the dramaturgical function of translating ideas into practice and compositional awareness" (Eckersall et al. 2014, 376). "Dramaturgy here thus becomes something that performs a relation between idea/concept/statement and form/enunciation/reception" (375), it 'performs' throughout the composition, the performance and its reception by an audience, and, we would add, in the way knowledge is formed, challenged and passed on in artistic practices. As the notion of the figure also indicates, a dramaturgical approach is not merely analytical—it is ideological and makes power relations visible.[2]

In "**Latent Performances**", **Daniel Blanga Gubbay** further discusses how the becoming-thingly of performers is a matter of creating conditions in which the inherent agency of objects can come to the fore. In a traditional, dramatic *mise-en-scène*, the *décor* illustrates the text. It translates the drama's place of action into meaningful images, "limiting the scenery to a static container for performance" (Pavis 1998, 322). The stage designer carefully selects objects, props and architectural elements that actualize the place of action suggested in the drama text. As such, he renders the place of action visible in the mind's eye of the spectator, mimicking reality or evoking a suitable atmosphere. In his article, Blanga

Gubbay moves away from this imitative or evocative role in function of a pre-existing anthropocentric narrative.

Whereas performance is strongly linked to the activity of the human being, Marina Abramović's state of latency in *Rhythm O* challenges this notion of activity in performance. The actual thing not only solicits a response in itself, without a (performing) body activating it. The silent and still body also appears in its thingly variations, becoming-with the various objects that are displayed on the table in front of her. Drawing on the legacy of the Situationist International, Blanga Gubbay goes on to say that the instructions of the artist turn the space into a prepared space, inciting and overturning the activation of latent performance. Following Guy Debord, it becomes a situation, "a concrete construction of temporary settings of life". In contrast to the spectacle, that landscape of capitalist modernity, this situation incites and overturns all possible actions. The politics lies in the dialectical relation between the preparation of material conditions and the openness to unforeseen behaviour.

As with Verdonck, this is a matter of a dramaturgy of co-creation. Abramović's instruction does not really instruct; the situation opens a complex field of uncertainty. The thingly variations cannot simply be domesticated by goal or functionality. The hyper-controlled functionality of the spectacle gives way to a situation, "designed with the chance for an 'out-of-control'". This means that the stage is no longer limited to what Pavis calls a "performance machinery", where the scenography merely provides "the actors with a space for their movements" (323). This utility-driven function such as in Meyerhold's biomechanical theatre, for instance, is still in service of actors who "build the places and moments of action" (323). This is not the case in *latent performances*. Rather, the prepared elements take a materialist turn. It is as if they have moved beyond the timescape of the Anthropocene and its creed: "only if things work do they matter – or, worse, only if what I and my fellow experts do works to fit things" (Haraway 2016, 4). As such, the figure of the creator is no longer the centre of the performance, as only a withdrawal from agency provides space for unexpected abilities, while being still fully response-able.

A dramaturgy of co-creation challenging the position of the human performer, creator and the notion of action in itself is also at stake in **"Does The Donkey Act?"** by **Maximilian Haas**. In this chapter, Haas explores the politics of 'subjects' becoming-animal. In line with the philosophy of Deleuze, this becoming means that the human neither incorporates nor disappears in the object or the animal. The human rather becomes-with the animal. Through David Weber-Krebs' performance *Balthazar*, in which a donkey is the 'protagonist', the divide between human/non-human; nature/culture is scrutinized and criticized. Placing a donkey centre stage redefines what the function of a protagonist (a centre) is (i.e. the character as hero that steers forward the drama) and how agency unfolds beyond human intentionality. In the binary-hierarchical opposition between humans and animals on the one hand and animals and humans on the other hand, action, in the sense of consciously conducted movement within a sensory-motor scheme, can only be attributed to humans, while action as mechanical assemblage (unintentional movement, habits...) belongs to animals. Haas, however, draws on the Baltic-German zoologist Jakob von Uexküll and the Anglo-American mathematician and philosopher Alfred North Whitehead to observe the notion of agency in animals in *Balthazar* and hence to question and deconstruct the binary-hierarchical opposition between humans and animals, and between nature and culture.

In her contribution, **Stefanie Wenner** similarly moves beyond the nature/culture divide with her notion of becoming-fungi in what she calls an aesthetic of Mycorrhiza. It is no surprise that the theoretical trope of mycorrhiza pops up frequently in posthuman writings. New Materialists drew heavily on Deleuze's observation of the rhizomatic pattern of mushroom spores, and considered its talent for cohabitation a vital model for social organization. Haraway's speculative fabulation of Terrapolis, for example, is "composted with a mycorrhiza of Greek and Latin rootlets and their symbionts" (2016, 11). Its complex network of rootlets and its particular habitat resided well in her theoretical trope of the "com-post", her alternative for the inflated term of the posthuman (2016, 11).

What draws Wenner to the fungi is their intrusive potential in the timescape of the Capitalocene. As biologist Lynn Margulis observed, a general characteristic in the "fungal way of life" is their absorptive heterotrophy; the "derivation of nutrients from the digestion of living or dead tissue" (2009, 381). The fungi therefore erupt with unexpected liveliness and vital infectiveness in blasted landscapes. In *The Mushroom at the End of the World*, anthropologist Anna Tsing likewise observes the fungi in their contaminated diversity in ruins and explores with them the possibilities of collaborative survival in the capitalist ruins that have become our collective homes (Tsing 2015). Tsing's account is characteristic for many posthumanist discourses and practices balancing between dystopian conditions and the utopian alternatives that become visible within them. Becoming-with-fungi for that matter means getting acquainted with "possibilities of coexistence within environmental disturbance" (Haraway 2016, 37).

Wenner's Mycorrhiza project puts into practice a sustainability beyond the journalistic real, in ongoing collectively-producing systems. She gives an account of the trajectory she followed as a curator and researcher over a period of seven weeks in Heizhaus at Uferstudios Berlin in the summer of 2014. Wenner set up a collaborative situation between humans and nonhumans (mushrooms, plants and trees) in a network called Mycorrhiza. She refers to Barad's notion of the apparatus as a performative space, as an underlying dramaturgical framework and as a practice and a situation in which, according to Wenner, "All is matter and all matters". In this performative space, she moves away from the disproportionately large emphasis on power through discourse and seeks to grasp and use the power of matter. "There is action in matter and this is not created by humans speaking about it", Wenner says.

In different ways, posthumanist co-creative practices with thingly matter involve the development of conditions for allowing 'things' to happen, be it the setup of a Debordian Situation (Blanga Gubbay), a precise dramaturgical frame implying an interaction with an object (Verdonck), the initiation of an open-ended performative space that can cultivate relations between various entities and forms of expression (Wenner) or a set of rules of conduct for human performers in relation to animals (Haas). This preparatory phase is dramaturgical and allows not only for 'things' to matter, but also for unexpected collaborations between human and nonhuman, for combinations in "conjoined work" (Haraway 2016, 129) between subject and object. The preparatory work is elementary, but not restrictive. On the contrary, it unleashes "myriad unfinished configurations of places, times, matters, meanings" (Haraway 2016, 1). Time entails a "now, a time of beginnings, a time for ongoing, for freshness"; place is "entangled and worldly" (Haraway 2016, 2, 4). Through his reading of Deleuze and Guattari and Uexküll, Haas connects affects and empathy to the environment, the *Umwelt* of a performing entity. Blanga Gubbay refers to the landscape as a latent field of potential actions, of potential interventions, and Wenner seeks to shape conditions for grassroots inter- and intra-species entanglements. This implies an abandonment of linearity, not only in the sense that postdramatic theatre (Lehmann) has already opened up, but in terms of causality. *The chain of events* is broken. It is the differences between situations that matter. Indeterminacy (Massumi) becomes an important factor of a posthumanist perspective on surroundings and this brings us close to the 'here and now' of performance, albeit this time a condition shaped by nonhuman entities—the random software of a performing robot (Verdonck), the unpredictable behaviour of a donkey (Haas & Weber-Krebs) or the latent actions in a particular setup. This has important political and ethical implications for the response-ability of the spectator, who thinks in attunement with a networked conception of performance.

PART II: RESPONSE-ABILITY IN THINGLY VARIATIONS (POLITICS AND ETHICS)

In posthuman theatre and performance, the stage is no longer limited to the idea of the *décor* as a container of dramatic meaning of events (unity of place of action). In the situations that erupt, materiality is action. Referring to architect Etienne Turpin, Blanga Gubbay points out that the *décor* and the architecture cannot be dissociated from the actions happening within it. In *Balthazar*, questions of acting lead to larger questions of 'action' in a philosophical sense. "How do actions relate to the surrounding milieu? Does the environment shape the action, or, on the contrary, does the action shape the environment?" (Haas, in this volume) How do latent actions in and with objects and environments (Blanga Gubbay) entangle with a Whiteheadian "entelechy", with a potential relation to an environment (Haas, in this volume)? The potential for unexpected collaborations and combinations in conjoined work for that matter also concern the spectator. In the second part of this edited volume, matters of care, response-ability and potentiality erupt. As Silva Benso observed, response-ability is "an ontological attitude whose implications border on ethics in its recognition of the multilayeredness of things, and in its intimation to an act of listening, caring, attention to their alterity" (in Lepecki, in this volume). Rosi Braidotti (2013, 10) indicated how response-ability should be understood as an accountability that is both epistemic and ethical. It is also a matter of producing knowledge.

Let us return for a moment to Liefooghe and Mitrović's *Daydream House* to understand better this notion of response-ability in a performance context. If we might say, following Blanga Gubbay, that performance space is materiality in action, the space in *Daydream House* is a particularly entangled one. It explores in a truly interdisciplinary way the boundaries between a 'real' house to live in (architecture), the act of living, or performativity in a staged house (in the (theatre) performance *Daydream House*) and the display of the architecture's agency in a museum context (the house formerly known as the installation *Living-Machine*). The performance space, displaying a peculiar setup of everyday movements, is situated in-between a "functional" house (a modernist glass house), a theatre-box or black box, and a museum context. The curtains as such shape-shift from functional appliances of a house, to a theatrical device that hides the actors from the spectator's eye, to (automated) objects on display, reclaiming their thing-power in an active space. This active space, rather than being a container in which the action can happen, provokes the action itself.

By accessing this entangled, active space the spectator becomes a participant and co-creator too, becoming-with-the things. As Liefooghe himself observes: he or she "can choose to actively live in the installation, or, simply by his presence, be experienced as 'part of a scene'". The ambivalence in the active space installs a persistent indecisiveness on behalf of the spectator; in the performance context, the sound and light produce a succession of domestic scenes to be 'observed', but the architectural context also gives these 'props' the features of 'real' objects, such as running water, Ikea furniture and a cooker. "The visitor can make coffee or take a shower if he or she feels like it". Or the visitor can respond to the action provoked by the objects, freeing things from their functional, serving role as in a classical drama setup. As linearity and causal relations are abandoned, the performance becomes "vitally infectious" (Haraway 2016, 138), rather than having a calculated effect with preconceived notions on the spectator. After all, posthuman performances entail "sensible materialisms of involuntary momentum" (Haraway 2016, 88).

The blurring of the boundaries between the disciplines of visual arts and performing arts that occurs in Liefooghe and Mitrović's work was already an important feature of postdramatic aesthetic. In posthumanist performances, the confusion between installation and performance is deepened and explored further as a consequence of the in-between time and space that opens up when human performers become thingly and when objects become thingly performers. As Van Kerkhoven already noted, this tendency requires and allows for a *dramaturgy of the spectator* (2009, 11).

French visual artist and choreographer **Mylène Benoit** works on the threshold between visual arts and performing arts disciplines precisely to tackle the way human beings are called to respond to technology. In her contribution, "**The Butterfly Effect**", co-authored with scholar **Philippe Guisgand**, she describes how throughout her practice she explores how a contemporary, fundamentally mediated body, infused by images, functions and looks like. Digital bodies operate in logics of gamification, they become avatars involved in violence, body normativity and data mining. Benoit and Guisgand recount their dramaturgical strategies to give shape to human bodies immersed in environments of simulacra, chased and flattened by their own images. Just as the performers are absorbed by videogame-style imagery, the spectators are included in this game as well. Benoit is connected to Ars Industrialis, an "international association for an industrial politics of the spirit",[3] founded by philosopher Bernard Stiegler. His notion of the pharmakon offers a concept to understand how technology operates on human beings and is constitutive of it, both in constructive and destructive ways, creating a dependency (Stiegler 2010, 161). On the other hand, *pharmacology* suggests a dynamics leading to a cure, as the pharmakon is, like the vaccine, an injection of the sufficient amount of the disease, in order to develop the right antibodies. In her work with technology, as with many posthumanist practices, technology is dealt with in a pharmacological way. Artists use it, re-appropriate it, to understand it, in order to grasp its effects on human bodies and societies, a necessary first step in order to create the conditions for performers and spectators to respond. Pharmacology breaks the short-circuiting caused by omnipresent and invasive technologies, it opens up a space to think, to bend, to unfold. It generates the time and distance that are needed to develop a response-ability.

In "**The Refrain and the Territory of the Posthuman**", **Eline Wiame** takes up the notion of 'landscape' to further explore the active ambivalence of the post-anthropocentric stage. As if endowed with tentacular feelers herself, or having swapped her limited 'human' binocular eyes for "compound-eyed insectile and many-armed optics" (Haraway 2016, 52), Wiame thinks-with the animal's gaze of the territory. From this animal perspective, any fragile centre (on stage) is the beginning of a territory that can be shaped by visual as well as auditory (vocal and rhythmic) means (think of birds claiming their territory by singing). The all too human ocular is no longer the core of perception. Meticulously following the development of Deleuze and Guattari's concept of the territory, Wiame delves into Heiner Goebbels' performance-installation

Stifters Dinge—a piece that interweaves stage and territory, nonhuman and posthuman in a very particular way.

Thinking-with the animal gaze of the territory also has ethical consequences for the spectator, as "one does not establish a territory to remain locked in, prisoner of a lugubrious repetition of what is already known, but to have enough stability for slowly opening the circle to other milieus". This breaking away from a sterile repetition of the 'same' and opening up to the 'other' is also at stake in Goebbels' machinic opera. Its constant urge for deterritorialization moves away from the anthropocentric ideal of the subjection of objects and animals to serve 'higher' human actions. Thinking with the animal territorial perspective for that matter always has political and ethical consequences:

> A machinic deterritorialization thus has political effects, not only because questions of inhabiting and leaving a territory are highly political, but also because the deterritorialization of refrains extracts from them new propositional powers. (Wiame, in this volume)

Goebbels primarily deals with mechanical machines. In **"The Right to Remain Forgotten and the Data Crimes of Post-Digital Culture"**, **Matthew Causey** explores the political and ethical questions concerning digital machines and their particular configuring of past, present and future. He thinks through the ethical compartments of response-ability. In a posthuman sense, the notion of response-ability differs from the traditional crime and punishment discourse. But this does not mean that culpability disappears in the network. Causey asks the pressing questions: "Are we freed from culpability if we are virtually removed (remember the telepresent soldier and his remote-controlled drone) or if we represent only a tiny fraction of the number of users involved in a viral moment?" In the precarious topic of child abuse on the Internet, repetition becomes an unbearable ongoingness, a "ceaseless traumatic event". Without question, the individuals committing the abuse and those documenting the event are to be held accountable in the digital network, but what of those who watch? How do we judge their participation?

The ceaseless reappearance of the traumatizing image touches upon the act of mourning as intrinsic to cultivating response-ability. As ecological philosopher and ethnographer Thom Van Dooren put it, mourning is "not opposed to practical action, rather it is the foundation of any sustainable and informed response" (2014, 24–25). After all, as Hannah Arendt observed in *Eichmann in Jerusalem* (1964), the biggest danger is that of not knowing, of denial and commonplace thoughtlessness, of a politics of sublime indifference. The act of mourning is hence also intrinsic to cultivating "robust response-ability for powerful and threatened places and beings" in ecological matters (Haraway 2016, 71). From a New Materialist perspective, Haraway urges us to stay with the trouble, and not to retreat in confident hubris, dreadful defeatism or sublime indifference. Staying with the trouble, mourning the extinct and showing the stigmata of vexed places are hence necessary practices of the arts of memory (Haraway 2016, 69, 79, 133).

In "**The Biography of a Digital Device**", **Martina Ruhsam** observes the subversive potential of art to mourn blasted landscapes, such as those vexed places. From the perspective of New Materialism, Ruhsam further explores the interwovenness of human and non-human movements in production and distribution processes as thematized in the artwork *Rare Earthenware* by Unknown Fields Division. The members of this nomadic research and design studio function as visionaries and reporters, documentarists, and science fiction lovers, and investigate the Baotou area as vexed space. Its toxic and radioactively polluted environments emerged in response to modern technological production modes and the toxic radioactivity has agential capacities in many (dangerous) ways. Exhibiting vases made from the toxic mud in the area, this artwork implicates the viewer in a particular corporeal way. Being exposed to even a small amount of radioactivity over an extended period of time might have concrete consequences for the human organism. As Timothy Morton designates in his object-oriented ontology: radioactivity functions as "poisoned light" (2010, 130). Radioactive objects are especially haunting examples of his thesis that hyperobjects are always already under our skin. This profoundly embodied ecological practice pulls closer those distant ecological disasters that are too easily dismissed as remote problems. Or, to put it in Latour's terms, the artwork relocalizes the global (Latour 2007, 173–190). We are always already corporeally implicated in ecological matters, how remote they may seem. As such, *Rare Earthenware* makes it evident that agency is a complex phenomenon, and certainly not a purely human privilege.

Because of its complex, boundless character and its enormous, global scale, climate change is likewise all too often and all too easily dismissed as a remote problem. In "**Tentacular Thinking-With-Things in Storied Places**", **Christel Stalpaert** relates her experience of participating in several conversational practices and performances facilitated and executed by the Dutch collective Building Conversation. Since 2016, this collective of artists co-creates several conversational performances. Their *Parliament of Things*, for example, is inspired by the theory of Bruno Latour and rituals of the Aboriginals. In September 2019, Stalpaert invited the Flemish philosopher and theatre maker Peter Aers, also a member of Building Conversation, to the Summer School on Climate at Ghent University. Implementing the conversational practices/performances in a university context, the participants developed alternative ways of thinking through the crises of care wrought by the ecological and environmental challenges that our world faces.

In her contribution, Stalpaert looks into this particular alternative to the usual production of knowledge in university contexts. Rather than finding solutions to climate change problems, the participants of the conversational performances practised what Donna Haraway coined tentacular thinking in an art-science-activist worlding. Stalpaert observes how a tentacular thinking-with-things expands scientific language, providing space for (re)generating or resurging a "grammar of animacy" (Kimmerer 55), allowing things to emerge as mediators of thinking in a parliament of things (Latour 1993, 142). This challenges the scientific model of the laboratory. Allowing things to emerge as mediators in a *Parliament of Things* means to allow 'things' to story the place. Through a speculative and tentacular thinking-with flora on the edge of extinction, Stalpaert herself practised an art of mourning that allowed trees and plants to story the seemingly paradise-like place of the Hortus Botanicus of Ghent University as a vexed place (Haraway 2016, 133), burdened with the economization of nature, and bearing with it a history of colonialism. After all, as anthropologist Tim Ingold observed, every thing is a parliament of lines (5). As such, Stalpaert also observes how a voicing of the endangered and extinct could also call upon an ethics for decolonization (Deborah Bird Rose) on behalf of the spectator/participant. In a final part of her contribution, Stalpaert wonders whether the conversational practices/performances have activist potential. Echoing Hannah Arendt's belief in the world-making potential of interacting through speech, she looks into the pedagogical activism at work in the art-science-activist worldings facilitated by Building Conversation in a university context.

Posthumanism realigns the notion of activism in relation to complex issues such as ecological disasters and climate change. How not to command how to act, but still reach "an inflection point of consequences?" (Haraway 2016, 100). "How to matter and not just want to matter?" (Haraway 2016, 47). The articles in this second part of the publication all directly or indirectly pose these important ethical questions. Moving away from the (impossible) dictum of curing, they suggest new and vital modes of caring in a "resurgent world" (Haraway 2016, 3). In this resurgent world, things not only act, they also generate knowledge and activate. After all, as Latour put it (1993, 142), when things are allowed to emerge as mediators in a parliament of things, they reveal "their crazy ability to reconstitute the social bond". This resurgence differs from the discourse of salvation, restoration or reconciliation. It differs from the all too human, heroic claim to create a better world or to save the world along a preconceived action plan. Posthumanist activism and activation hence also comes with another politics of knowledge production and transmission. This topic is deepened in the third part of this publication, where the premises of modernist humanist doctrines are further deconstructed.

PART III: POSTHUMAN EPISTEMOLOGIES: THE POLITICS OF KNOWLEDGE TRANSMISSION

After looking at co-creative processes and into the ethics of spectatorship, the third part of this volume comes full circle by focusing on the complex collaboration of technological and human agents in scientific and artistic practices. Knowledge transmission is the focal point of the last part of the book. Each in their own way, all essays in this closing part of the book reflect on the relation between performance practices, knowledge representation and the performative role of technologies in both arts and sciences. Knowledge-finding processes in these realms have changed profoundly under the instigation of new technological developments in software, sensor registration and novel notational practices (Karreman 2017a; Leach 2013). These developments involve new methods and new views on the validity and legitimization of knowledge. This, in turn, also leads to new epistemologies because new theorizations of knowledge are prompted by posthuman engagements with our environments. The overarching question of this part of the book is: What could a posthuman analytical approach to knowledge transmission practices in the arts and sciences look like?

From a posthumanist perspective, practices of knowledge sharing and knowledge transmission are performative practices, with a creativity in their own right. On the one hand, these practices acknowledge the agency of the archive, and on the other hand, they explore how alternative modes of sharing knowledge can lead to new co-creative practices. The authors in this part of the book address human beings' entanglements with various types of technologies, such as telescopes, motion capture systems and musical scores. A recurrent theme in these essays is the examination of performative aspects of established knowledge systems, such as the scientific laboratory (Borowski, Chaberski, Sugiera), and the profound connection in Western culture between vision and knowledge (Brusselaers and Julian). The essays also examine specific technologies of knowledge transmission, such as algorithmic tools in dance (Bleeker), notation systems in music (Payne and Schuiling) and mathematical notation (Van Bendegem). How do these technologies shape the way in which human actors make sense of their environments? And how can these processes be understood through a posthumanist lens?

The essays in this section of the book reveal another aspect of posthuman dramaturgies: the way in which performativity is 'found' within scientific practices and the way that scientific practices are recognized within artistic strategies, and the way in which this can disrupt positions and constructions. It does not only influence the principles active within the performance, but also those by which an audience is implied. When it comes more specifically to the transition of knowledge produced through performative practices, this is also dramaturgical in a twofold way. It is a nexus where the dramaturgy 'after' a work, which can take the shape of a score, a text or some other form of residue, transforms into a new dramaturgical impetus, opening up towards new creations, as passed-on knowledge becomes artistic material that, indeed, 'matters'.

"**The Point of the Matter: Performativity in scientific practices**" is an exchange that was set up as a 'thought experiment' between performance scholar and philosopher **Maaike Bleeker** and mathematician and philosopher of science **Jean Paul Van Bendegem**. Speaking from their respective areas of interest and expertise, they discuss various examples of scientific processes that expose performative mechanisms resulting from the entanglement of technological tools and human agency—a dynamic that is a characteristic feature of scientific practices. In their gathering of knowledge-through-dialogue, they observe how in modernist humanist doctrines, "nature is made to perform, and made to perform in such a way as to produce the proof".

Several posthuman thinkers have laid the basis for the deconstruction of such modernist premises. In *We Have Never Been Modern* (1993), Latour outlined how natural philosopher Robert Boyle introduced the empirical style as a new doxa. He relied on "trustworthy, well-to-do witnesses" (read: members with a social status that would sustain their credibility) gathered around an artificially produced experiment in the close and protected space of a laboratory setting to give the results from these experiments credibility. The presence of these witnesses guaranteed the validation of an observation into a matter of fact, even though these witnesses did not necessarily know the true nature of the experiment. As Latour observes, "Boyle did not seek these gentlemen's opinion, but rather their observation" (1993, 18). In this "theatre of proof" (19), knowledge is restricted to "the instrumentalized nature of the facts and leaves aside the interpretation of causes" (Latour 1993, 18). As such, Enlightenment has fabricated the Laws of Nature in the laboratory, consolidating a dominant, but poor repertoire for speaking about nature (Latour 1993, 25, 31). Following philosopher Thomas Hobbes' reasoning, Latour calls this dominant repertoire a limited one: "We live in communities whose social bond comes from objects fabricated in laboratories: ideas have been replaced by practices, apodeictic reasoning by a controlled doxa, and universal agreement by groups of colleagues" (21). The iconic image of Archimedes and his bath, shouting Eureka when he had an enlightened idea, is similarly striking in this context. What we need, Latour argues, is the emergence of the object in a Copernican counter-revolution (79), allowing for Parliaments of Things in which objects turn from intermediaries or instrumental tools into mediators. Several philosophers developed alternatives to the production of knowledge in the experimental laboratory. Donna Haraway, for example, proposes the vital model of the art-science-activist worldings (76). In 2006, before Karen Barad implemented the notion of agential realism and intra-action in New Materialism, Lorraine Code coined those terms in her research into the politics of knowledge, investigating amongst others the potential of intra-actions between objects and agents of observation (see also Stalpaert 2018a).

In the digital era, the objects that are reduced to inanimate, artificial intermediaries in laboratory settings become even more invisible. Wondering whether the Higgs boson exists, Bleeker and Van Bendegem query in their contribution who or what is actually speaking when the scientist speaks. After all, only the dials and the digits inform us that something has happened and that it has been measured by the Large Hadron Collider (LHC), which is the world's largest particle accelerator, based at CERN. Besides, the transmission of this knowledge is largely technologically driven. "The 'raw' material is sent over the 'grid', a network of computers world-wide, making use of existing networks, to perform the most amazing calculations". Who or what is transmitting knowledge then?

As opposed to the other authors in this part of the book, then, Bleeker and Van Bendegem do not only take artistic performance works as their primary objects of analysis, but extend their view by also looking at scientific practices through a philosophical lens. As both authors observe, the philosophy of science has undergone major changes in the twentieth century. "These changes have foregrounded the performativity of scientific practices of knowledge production and transmission and how knowledge production and transmission are grounded in social material practices" (Bleeker). They engage with questions such as: How are practices of knowledge finding and knowledge transmission structured by scientific apparatuses? What does the performative dimension of the sciences reveal to us about their meaning-making strategies? Through their examination of phenomena such as the hunt for the Higgs particle and the teaching process of the Pythagorean theorem, both Bleeker and Van Bendegem reveal the "complex assemblages of actors (human-machine-matter-data) intra-acting with one another in various ways" (Bleeker, in this volume).

Van Bendegem takes as his point of departure *0/10*, the exhibition on the relation between mathematics he presented at the Vrije Universiteit Brussel in 2011, to problematize the complex set of beliefs and conditions that need to be in place to produce convincing mathematical proof. He also questions the logics and stability of mathematical notation and shows how notation as a knowledge system structures mathematicians' practices to "find" proofs.

Bleeker uses John McCormick and Steph Hutchison's performance project *Emergence* to focus attention on contemporary questions "concerning the relationship between human agency and technology, and of technology as itself endowed with agency". *Emergence*, which was also presented at the *Does it Matter* conference, features collaborations between a human dancer (Hutchison) and an artificially intelligent (AI) performing agent. The dancer wears an optical motion capture suit so that her movements can be tracked. Her motion data are processed by an AI agent and its visual output is projected in Stereoscopic 3D. In an earlier reflection on *Emergence*, Laura Karreman described this as a setting that defies clear-cut cause-and-effect relations: "New movement emerges here from an undefined and intangible source, an origin that is nowhere, a distinct 'in-between'" (2017b, 505). Bleeker refers to *Emergence* and also considers other performance works by artists such as BADco, Annie Dorsen and Wayne McGregor. She suggests that "we might understand these projects as contributions to the development of new, posthuman perspectives, where posthuman does not mean the absence or doing away with the human, but refers to a decentring of human agency, and to acknowledging the implications of such decentring" (Fig. 2).

Fig. 2 Steph Hutchison in motion capture suit with optical markers in *Emergence* (2014), created by John McCormick and Steph Hutchison (Photo John McCormick)

Both Bleeker and Van Bendegem's approaches present ideas of how a posthuman perspective may support a deconstruction of traditional scientific endeavours such as 'collecting facts' and 'finding proof'. Throughout their exchange, both authors discover several shared points of reference, including Barad's notion of 'intra-action' and the work of mathematician and philosopher Brian Rotman, who draws attention to the embodied processes that are involved in grasping abstract ideas. Their dialogue also reveals how concepts such as 're-enactment', 'composition' and 'creativity' prompt different meanings and affordances in their separate fields. In closing, Bleeker brings in even more concepts with promising potential for continuing debates in this intra-disciplinary area, such as 'incorporeal materialism' (Foucault), and 'lived abstraction' (Massumi). Without any more room for Van Bendegem to respond, the end of this dialogue fits the topic of their discussion: it is not finite, but open-ended. And it begs for new responses.

In "**Music Notation and Distributed Creativity: The Textility of Score Annotation**", musicologists **Emily Payne** and **Floris Schuiling** analyse annotation practices of music performers as processes of "itineration". They show how the consideration of music notation "in its textility rather than its textuality" decentralizes the predominant conception of the musical score as the main descriptive and prescriptive text, and makes room for the view of the annotated score as but one of the material agents that play a role in "weaving" the piece into practice. The central concepts "itineration", "textility" and "weaving" are all derived from social anthropologist Tim Ingold (2007), whose notion of "bonding" was already referred to in Part I. Ingold uses these concepts to reframe creative processes by shifting the attention to continuous movement, developing social relationships and the material dimension as their core characteristics. This perspective on creative processes is used by Payne and Schuiling in the analysis of the rehearsal process of a musical piece for basset clarinet and piano, composed by Nick Planas and performed by clarinetists Lucy Downer and Margaret Archibald. An ethnographic analysis of this process shows how annotation functions as a tool for problem-solving and "gestural reinterpretations" of Planas' composition. The analysis of the improvisatory strategies of the Instant Composers Pool Orchestra further reveals how annotation functions as a trace of music performers' "embodied relationship to their instrument, their own creative agency and (co-)ownership of the music".

The contribution of Payne and Schuiling thus is a revealing example of emergent musicological research that questions the "sacralisation of texts" (Bleich 2013, 11) and "the occularcentric identification of the score with what the music is" (Cook 2004, 21) in favour of a turn towards performance and attention for the "body language" of texts (Andersen 2015, 122) that understands the creative process as the result of "tangled relationships between bodies, instruments, materials and the environment". Payne and Schuiling also position their research in an interdisciplinary performing arts research context by pointing out the similar interest in annotational practices in contemporary performance research, as exemplified by the recent study of the notebooks of theatre directors Jan Fabre and Jan Lauwers (De Laet et al. 2015).

The discussion of the performative dimension of scientific technologies by Bleeker and Van Bendegem is further examined through a different angle in "**Spectators in the Laboratory: Between Theatre and Technoscience**". In this chapter, **Mateusz Borowski**, **Mateusz Chaberski** and **Małgorzata Sugiera** propose that scientific laboratories are used as a model in contemporary performance practices in order to challenge spectators to rethink their own perceptual patterns.

Borowski, Chaberski and Sugiera recall that when modern science emerged in the seventeenth century, performative practices by spectators during scientific experiments, such as observing, experiencing and witnessing, played an important role in the legitimization of scientific knowledge. They also remind us of several ways in which the arts have functioned and continue to function as a means to explicate scientific methodologies and findings. Conversely, they argue that scientific practices have also inspired a range of 'metonymic' approaches to the theatre as a laboratory. The aim of such laboratory theatre experiments is twofold: "the spectator becomes both the analyst as well as the site where situated knowledge is being performatively produced".

While Emile Zola's drama is briefly referred to in this essay as a theatre laboratory that famously prompted audiences to examine their own social status, and those of others, Bertolt Brecht's *Lehrstücke* receive more attention as a key reference point in the genealogy of a laboratory approach. An analysis of *Der Ozeanflug*, a play by Brecht that features an airplane as one of the main characters and also assigns roles to phenomena such as the 'Voice of the Fog' and the 'Working Engine', reveals how these plays "self-reflexively direct their gaze towards the processes of perception and the way they condition communication between humans and non-humans". Half a century later, in the 1980s, Heiner Müller's "laboratory of the social imagination" was exemplified in works such as *Description of a Picture*, in which, the authors tell us, "it is the onlooker that becomes a laboratory animal, when he/she is confronted with a depicted scene which sets in motion the mechanism of recognition and meaning-making".

These historical predecessors provide a rich context for an examination of performance works that illustrate contemporary examples of laboratory approaches. In each of these examples we recognize the double meaning of the French term *expérience* that Chris Salter recently recalled as "that of experiment or speculation and that of experience, of something that happens to us" (2015, 241). ORLAN's bioart project *Harlequin Coat* challenges perceptual patterns of spectators by presenting a "polyphonic assemblage" (Tsing 2015, 22–4) of growing skin cells. Rimini Protokoll's performance *Situation Rooms* confronts spectators with ways in which technologies such as Augmented Reality and Hand-Held Displays may create stabilizing and destabilizing effects in their sensory awareness. The experience of this performance thus provides tangible support for Christine Ross's statement that "Augmented Reality means in fact a new spectatorial paradigm" (2010, 19). As a final example, Rabih Mroué's performative lecture *The Pixelated Revolution* makes spectators aware of how they can never remain a "mere onlooker", but necessarily become co-creative agents when they engage with war imagery. This performance "puts the spectators in the double role as both the recipients of images and distant analysts who had to question the perceptual schemes, receptive mechanisms and affects occasioned by these images".

This chapter by Borowski, Chaberski and Sugiera builds on Bleeker's and Van Bendegem's dialogue in "The Point of the Matter" because it similarly underlines how sciences and technological instruments mediate our perception of reality. In addition, "Spectators in the Laboratory" focuses our attention on how emerging performance experiments that mix arts and (techno)sciences prioritize a view of spectatorship as essentially participatory and co-creative. These "metonymic theatre laboratories" also deliberately position spectators within a network of human and non-human actors. With the effect, in the authors' words, that "the boundaries between watching and being watched, the observer and the object of study, effectively collapse". This shift in conception of spectatorship, and its relationship to epistemological questions, returns as a central topic of concern in the following, final chapter by Dieter Brusselaers and Helena Julian on the research project *Peri-Sphere*.

In "**A Hybrid Device to Choreograph the Gaze: Embodying Vision through a Historical Discourse on Optics in Benjamin Vandewalle's *Peri-Sphere***", **Dieter Brusselaers** and **Helena Julian** report on their discursive exploration for the research project *Peri-Sphere*. In collaboration with choreographer Benjamin Vandewalle, whose "performative oeuvre is profoundly preoccupied with vision", they investigated a large range of historical and theoretical sources, in order to map specific views on the relationship between vision, optics, spectatorship and corporeality. In this contribution the authors revisit the research of Martin Jay, Jonathan Crary, Elizabeth Carlson, Michael Fried and Laura Mulvey. They interweave a discussion of these theoretical ideas with re-examinations of views of artists ranging from Ralph Waldo Emerson to John Ruskin, and from Bertolt Brecht to Robert Morris.

Brusselaers and Julian show how all of these findings combined have informed the creation process of a mobile performer-operated installation, prompted by Vandewalle's question: "Can we choreograph not for, but with an audience's gaze?". In the resulting performative apparatus of *Peri-Sphere*, technological and discursive layers intersect in many ways. For instance, the 'gestalts' of Robert Morris, such as his sculptural performance *Column* (1962), received special attention as part of *Peri-Sphere* since "the objects proposed in Minimalism have been experienced as resembling the presence of a 'surrogate person'" (Fried 1998, 156). This "corporeal referentiality" and the process of "becoming-object" that Brusselaers and Julian associate with Minimalism, and with Morris' work in particular, proved to be key inspirations in how the ambiguous corporeal presence of the performer in *Peri-Sphere* was constructed and staged.

Another significant discursive influence on *Peri-Sphere*'s performance design came from Elizabeth Carlson's "proposal to connect the emergence of the subjective spectator in the nineteenth century to the era's obsession with mirrors". This idea was incorporated through the assemblage of mirrors used in the installation. This "caleidoscopic strategy" had a deconstructive effect by displacing the performer's body as the dominant focal point in the performance. The performer's body was mostly filtered from the participant's view, even though a 'nearness' of the performer could still be felt.

Through employing these and other strategies, the apparatus in *Peri-Sphere* functioned as a "theoretical automaton" by creating room for reflection on the participant's gaze, and on how this gaze might be employed as choreographic material itself. Moreover, Brusselaers and Julian invite us to interpret *Peri-Sphere* as a prototype for a vision machine that thwarts and challenges dominant representational logics. *Peri-Sphere* asks us to imagine alternatives to established Western "scopic regimes" (Crary), specifically alternatives to Cartesian perspectivalism and the "spectatorial ecstasy" that is associated with it. What would a scopic regime look like that *highlights* instead of *downplays* embodied aspects of seeing? The playful choreography of the gaze that was enacted by the experiential and discursive prototype of *Peri-Sphere* provides us with several imaginative answers to that question.

One additional perspective that is not yet explored in this contribution but offers fruitful future perspectives is the relevance of this project for critical examinations of how scopic regimes operate in virtual realms. Brusselaers and Julian describe *Peri-Sphere* as a "flayed apparatus", since its cables, joints and assemblage of mirrors are clearly visible for its audience. This makes *Peri-Sphere* in its performative appearance an analogue device, almost stubbornly so. However, by presenting us with a multitude of viewpoints that defies occularcentric logic, and through its reflection on the invisible, but still tangible 'nearness' of embodied presence, *Peri-Sphere* also provides us with useful perspectives on open questions in the digital realm. As a "theoretical automaton", *Peri-Sphere* opens up new points of entrance in contemporary debates on topics such as augmented reality, gestural interfaces and presence theory.

In one way or another, all authors in this third and final part of the book discuss how our engagement with instruments and other technologies shapes our findings. Their contributions underline how processes of knowledge creation and transmission can be understood as performative practices. For instance, the dialogue between Bleeker and Van Bendegem shows that the technologies that are used to discern the Higgs particle are not objective capturing apparatuses, but rather function as co-creative agents that define a technological worldview in which such particles may exist.

Another recurring motive of this section of the book is the emphasis on the value of technological experimentation as an essential component of creative and knowledge-finding processes in both the arts and the sciences. Technology is not merely something used by actors in these realms, but is itself a co-creative agent that shapes the meaning-making process of a performance and the generation and transmission of knowledge. This can for example be illustrated by Payne and Schuiling's ethnographic analyses of music performance that reveal the creative dynamics between musicians and scores. Payne and Schuiling's research reveals what happens when we understand music scores as one of several agents in the distributed creativity in music performance, rather than as objective representations of music. It shifts our perception of musical performance of a one-directional, interpretative process, to a more complex layered reality that foregrounds the intra-action of musicians, technologies and their environment. Such a posthuman recalibration of the concept of the score has more potential, as was already addressed by Daniel Blanga Gubbay in Part II of this edited volume. He pointed out that Karen Barad reads the score not as the precise orchestration of something, of how something should be performed, but of performativity; how instructions are imagined, experienced, interpreted, perceived and tested out (Barad 2003), and he also reconnected this with Debord's situationist notion of the term "score", as "an idea of a program for uncertainty" (Blanga Gubbay, in this volume).

"Posthuman times call for posthuman Humanities studies", Braidotti already stated in 2013 (157). The transmission of knowledge found and developed in and through artistic practices is part of this search for what a posthuman humanities field could be and do. The previous clusters have shown how artistic disciplines are mixed and crossed in artistic practices and in relation to spectatorship. Posthuman humanities is about inter—and cross-disciplinary "knowledge practices" (Braidotti 2013, 156), humanities no longer being able to hold onto an exclusive definition of the 'Human', nor to a field that separates soft from hard science, culture from nature. Again, the omnipresence of technology is an important catalyst in posthumanizing the humanities, calling for dialogue and an expansion of fields, for the development of collaborative knowledge practices. If we follow Braidotti's thinking, posthuman humanities are a consequence of a decentred human position in a fundamental relational world, as well as of matter that very much 'matters'. It is a network of 'studies', rather than disciplines, often fuelled by a political or social impetus, that may develop alternative epistemologies of looking and sensing (such as Julian and Brusselaers do), deconstruct power and knowledge structures (such as Borowski, Chaberski and Sugiera do), demonstrate the profound potential of interdisciplinary dialogue (such as Bleeker and Van Bendegem do) or shift our attention to the embodied and material dimension of our interpretation of scores and other texts (such as Payne and Schuiling do).

Coda

This book is the outcome of a project that started in 2015. At the time of finishing this book, April 2020, we find ourselves in the midst of a pandemic crisis caused by a novel virus, bringing into deep *trouble* political and capitalist structures, but also radically disrupting social structures as four billion people (more than half of the world's population) are currently part of what has already been termed the Great Lockdown, confining and separating themselves from many loved ones and other kin by practising 'physical distancing' and *quarantine* measures.

Medical technologies such as image technology, medicine, blood analysis equipment, ventilators for respiration, but also surveillance technologies to monitor infected individuals reveal the importance for a critical stance towards biopolitics within posthumanism once again. A virus, a nonhuman entity, a critter, if you want, disrupts a whole way of life—the good and the bad sides of it—and leads to death. In its expected slipstream, this virus-based crisis will cause the deepest economic recession since the 1930s, which will inevitably wreak havoc in the livelihoods of millions of people around the globe. It makes clear that in the search for a decentring of the human, in the search for a post-anthropocentric, posthuman world, there is always an existential dimension. Developments in politics, technology, ecology and economy are pushing towards a dehumanized, inhuman posthuman condition, whereas within the posthuman humanities and arts, this 'push' is taken as an impulse to rethink the world for the better. As Braidotti reminds us, the posthuman (humanities and arts) needs to give a place to suffering caused by these tendencies (2013, 148). After all, as Haraway observed, "we are all responsible to and for shaping conditions for multispecies flourishing in the face of terrible histories, (…) but we are not all response-able in the same ways. The differences matter—in ecologies, economies, species, lives" (29).

So, as we finish this book, a whole world view seems to be finishing, or at least is suspended, paused. The afterimage of the last time we met in a performance space, in a bar, in a classroom or in any other social gathering in real life is rapidly fading away, with no certain prospect about when this dimension of our lives may be revived. And if it is revived, under what circumstances and conditions will these encounters take place? Who can still afford to be part of communities they identified with when they will? Who will go missing? It feels as if something new, something post- is about to begin, which calls for a continued academic and artistic research into what it might mean to be alive in a world where the process of posthumanization has taken such a leap. For how long will we be living in the CODA of the coronavirus crisis? How (long) will it affect our ways of being-in-the-world and becoming-with together, our means of initiating and maintaining relations, bonds and composites, our modes of knowledge making, of moving about? Might this CODA also be an intro, an overture towards a more-than-human world where things might look the same, but, on a closer look, nothing is left unchanged?

Notes

1. "les choses perçues me tendent leur face utilisable, en même temps que ma réaction retardée, devenue action, apprend à les utiliser" (Deleuze 1983, 95).
2. For an expanded definition of dramaturgy as a *critical process* in relation to ideology, see Eckersall (2018).
3. http://www.arsindustrialis.org/lassociation, last accessed 8/4/2020.

Works Cited

Abram, David. 1996. *The Spell of the Sensuous. Perception and Language in a More-than-Human-World*. New York: Pantheon Books.
Agamben, Giorgio. 2009. *What is an Apparatus? And Other Essays*. Translated by David Kishik and Stefan Pedatella. Stanford: Stanford University Press.
Agamben, Giorgio. 2014. *L'uso dei corpi*. Vicenza: Neri Pozza.
Andersen, Tore Rye. 2015. "'Black Box' in Flux: Locating the Literary Work Between Media." *Northern Lights: Film & Media Studies Yearbook* 13: 121–36.
Aristotle. 2003. *Poetics*. Translated by Malcolm Heath. London: Penguin Classics.
Arendt, Hannah. 1964. *Eichmann in Jerusalem. A Report on the Banality of Evil*. New York: Penguin.
Badmington, Neil, ed. 2000. *Posthumanism*. Houndmills: MacMillan.
Bal, Mieke. 2002. *Travelling Concepts in the Humanities. A Rough Guide*. Toronto: University of Toronto Press.

Barad, Karen. 2003. "Posthumanist Performativity: Toward an Understanding of How Matter Comes to Matter." *Signs* 28, no. 3: 801–831.
Barad, Karen. 2007. *Meeting the Universe Halfway*. Durham: Duke University Press.
Bennett, Jane. 2010. *Vibrant Matter. A Political Ecology of Things*. Duke University Press.
Bleich, David. 2013. *The Materiality of Language: Gender, Politics, and the University*. Bloomington: Indiana University Press.
Braidotti, Rosi. 2013. *The Posthuman*. Cambridge: Polity Press.
Braidotti, Rosi. 2017. "Posthuman, All Too Human. The Memoirs and Aspirations of a Posthumanist." *The 2017 Tanner Lectures*, March 1–2. Yale University.
Carels, Edwin. 2012. "The Productivity of the Prototype: On Julien Maire's 'Cinema of contraptions'." In *Bastard or Playmate? Adapting Theatre, Mutating Media and the Contemporary Performing Arts*, edited by Robrecht Vanderbeeken, Christel Stalpaert, David Depestel and Boris Debackere. Amsterdam: Amsterdam University Press.
Cook, Nicholas. 2004. "Making Music Together, or Improvisation and its Others." *The Source: Challenging Jazz Criticism* 1: 5–25.
Debord, Guy. 2004. "Towards a Situationist International.". In *Guy Debord and the Situationist International: Texts and Documents*, edited by Tom McDonough. Cambridge and London: MIT Press.
Debaise, Didier and Isabelle Stengers, eds. 2015. *Gestes spéculatifs*. Paris: Les Presses du Réel.
Deleuze, Gilles. 1983. *L'image-mouvement*. Paris: Les Editions de Minuit.
Deleuze, Gilles. (1986) 2005. *Cinema 1. The Movement-Image*. Translated by Hugh Tomlinson and Barbara Habberjam. London: Continuum.
Deleuze, Gilles. 1992. "Postscript on the Societies of Control." *October* 59: 3–7.
Deleuze, Gilles, and Félix Guattari. 2004. *A Thousand Plateaus*. Translated byrans. Brian Massumi. London: Continuum.
De Laet, Timmy, Edith Cassiers, and Luk Van Den Dries. 2015. "Creating by Annotating: The Director's Notebooks of Jan Fabre and Jan Lauwers." *Performance Research* 20: 43–52.
Dempster, Beth M. 1998. *A Self-Organizing Systems Perspective on Planning for Sustainability*. MA thesis, University of Waterloo.
Despret, Vinciane. 2008. "The Becoming of Subjectivity in Animal Worlds." *Subjectivity* 23, no. 1: 123–139.
De Mul, Jos. 2014. *Destiny Domesticated. The Rebirth of Tragedy Out of the Spirit of Technology*. Translated by Bibi van den Berg. New York: SUNY Press.
Eckersall, Peter. 2018. "On Dramaturgy to Make Visible." *Performance Research* 100: 241–3.

Eckersall, Peter, Helena Grehan, and Edward Scheer. 2014. "New Media Dramaturgy." In *The Routledge Companion to Dramaturgy*, edited by M. Romanska, 375–80. Abingdon and New York: Routledge.
Foucault, Michel. (1970) 2018. *The Order of Things. An Archaeology of the Human Sciences*. London: Routledge.
Fried, Michael. (1980) 1998. *Absorption and Theatricality. Painting and Beholder in the Age of Diderot*. Chicago: University of Chicago Press.
Grosz, Elizabeth. 2011. *Becoming Undone. Darwinian Reflections on Life, Politics, and Art*. Durham: Duke University Press.
Haraway, Donna J. (1985) 1991. "A Cyborg Manifesto. Science, Technology, and Feminism in the Late Twentieth Century." *Simians, Cyborgs, and Women: The Reinvention of Nature*, 455–75. London: Routledge.
Haraway, Donna J. 2016. *Staying With the Trouble. Making Kin in the Chthulucene*. Durham: Duke University Press.
Hassan, Ihab. 1977. "Prometheus as Performer. Toward a Posthumanist Culture." *The Georgia Review* 31, no. 4: 830–50.
Harman, Graham. 2011. *The Quadruple Object*. Winchester (UK), Washington (USA): Zero Books.
Hayles, Katherine. N. 2018. *The Cosmic Web. Scientific Field Models and Literary Strategies in the Twentieth Century*. Ithaca, NY: Cornell University Press.
Heidegger, Martin. 1970. *What is a Thing?* Translated by W. B. Barton and Vera Deutsch. Gateway: Henry Regnery.
Hiros. n.d. *Laurent Liefooghe*. Accessed 4 September 2018 http://www.hiros.be/en/artists/detail/laurent-liefooghe.
Hustak, Carla, and Natasha Myers. 2012. "Involutionary Momentum. Affective Ecologies and the Sciences of Plant/Insect Encounters." *Differences. A Journal of Feminist Cultural Studies* 23, no. 3: 74–118.
Ingold, Tim. (2007) 2016. *Lines. A Brief History*. London: Routledge.
Karreman, Laura. 2017a. "The Motion Capture Imaginary: Digital Renderings of Dance Knowledge". PhD diss., Ghent University.
Karreman, Laura. 2017b. "How Does Motion Capture Mediate Dance?" In *Contemporary Choreography: A Critical Reader*, edited by Joanne Butterworth and Liesbeth Wildschut, 494–512. London and New York: Routledge.
Krishan, K. Cha. 2013. *Composite Materials. Science and Engineering*. New York: Springer.
Latour, Bruno. 1993. *We Have Never Been Modern*. Cambridge, MA: Harvard University Press.
Latour, Bruno. 2007. *Reassembling the Social. An Introduction to Actor-Network Theory*. Oxford: Oxford University Press.
Leach, James. 2013. "Choreographic Objects, Contemporary Dance, Digital Creations and Prototyping Social Visibility." *Journal of Cultural Economy* 7, no. 4: 1–18.

Lehmann, Hans-Thies. 2006. *Postdramatic Theatre*. Translated by Karen Jürs-Munby. London: Routledge.
Lepecki, André. 2010. "9 Variations on Things and Performance." In *IT. Thingly Variations in Space*, edited by J. Baillie and E. Van Campenhout. Brussels: Mokum.
Margulis, Lynn, and Dorian Sagan. 1997. *Microcosmos. Four Billion Years of Microbial Evolution from Our Microbial Ancestors*. Berkeley: University of California Press.
Margulis, Lynn, and Michael J. Chapman. 2009. *Kingdoms and Domains. An Illustrated Guide to the Phyla of Life on Earth*. London: Academic Press.
Mignolo, Walter, and Vazquez, Rolando. 2013. "Decolonial AistheSis. Colonial Wounds/Decolonial Healing". In *Social Text Online*. Accessed 28 April 2020. https://socialtextjournal.org/periscope_article/decolonial-aesthesis-colonial-woundsdecolonial-healings/.
Morton, Timothy. 2010. *The Ecological Thought*. Cambridge: Harvard University Press.
Morton, Timothy. 2013. *Hyperobjects. Philosophy and Ecology After the End of the World*. Minneapolis: University of Minnesota Press.
Morton, Timothy. 2016. *Dark Ecology. For a Logic of Future Coexistence*. New York: Columbia University Press.
Pavis, Patrice. 1998. *Dictionary of the Theatre. Terms, Concepts, and Analysis*. Translated by Christine Shantz. Toronto: University of Toronto Press, 1998.
Ross, Christine. 2010. "Spacial Poetics. The (Non)Destinations of Augmented Reality Art", Afterimage. *The Journal of Media Arts and Cultural Criticism* 2: 19–24.
Salter, Chris. 2015. *Alien Agency. Experimental Encounters with Art in the Making*. The MIT Press: Cambridge.
Sanja Mitrović. n.d. "Daydream House (2011)." Accessed 4 September 2018. http://sanjamitrovic.com/?cat=29.
Serres, Michel. 2001. *Hominescence*. Paris: Éd. Le Pommier.
Spinoza, Benedictus de. 2001. *Ethics*. Translated by W.H. White and A.K. Stirling. Ware: Wordsworth Editions.
Stalpaert, Christel. 2010a. "On Poet-Dancers and Animal-Thinkers. The Bodily Capacity to Read and Make Sense of Unjointed Time and Intensive Space in Wayn Traub's Maria Dolores (2003)." *Text and Performance Quarterly* 30, no. 4: 356–373.
Stalpaert, Christel. 2010b. "Something is Rotten on the Stage of Flanders. Postdramatic Shakespeare in Contemporary Flemish Theatre." *Contemporary Theatre Review* 20, no. 4: 437–448.
Stalpaert, Christel. 2018. "Cultivating Survival with Maria Lucia Cruz Correia: Towards an Ecology of Agential Realism." *Performance Research* 23, no. 3: 48–55.

Stalpaert, Christel. 2019. "Maria Lucia Cruz Correia's *Urban Action Clinic GARDEN*: Political Ecology with Diplomats of Dissensus and Composite Bodies Engaged in Intra-Action." In *The Routledge Companion to Theatre and Politics*, edited by Peter Eckersall and Helena Grehan, 203–206. London: Routledge.

Stalpaert, Christel. 2020. "Figures Performing Prototypes of Composite Bodies. Kris Verdonck's Ontological Politics of Time and Movement." In *Machine Made Silence. The Art of Kris Verdonck*, edited by Peter Eckersall and Kristof Van Baarle, 118–131. Aberystwyth: Performance Research Books.

Stiegler, Bernard. 2010. *Taking Care of Youth and the Generations*. Translated by S. Barker. Stanford: Stanford University Press.

Tsing, Anna Löwenhaupt. 2015. *The Mushroom at the End of the World. On the Possibility of Life in Capitalist Ruins*. Oxford: Princeton University Press.

van Baarle, Kristof. 2015. "The Critical Aesthetics of Performing Objects: Kris Verdonck." *Performance Research* 20, no. 2: 39–48.

van Baarle, Kristof. 2018. *From the Cyborg to the Apparatus: Figures of Posthumanism in the Philosophy of Giorgio Agamben and the Contemporary Performing Arts of Kris Verdonck*. PhD diss., Ghent University.

van Baarle, Kristof, and Hendrickx, Sébastien. 2018. "Decor as protagonist. Bruno Latour and Frédérique Aït-Touati on theatre and the new climate regime". *Etcetera* no. 155. Accessed on 4/5/2020. https://e-tcetera.be/decor-is-not-decor-anymore/.

Van Dooren, Thom. 2014. *Flight Ways. Life at the Edge of Extinction*. New York: Columbia University Press.

Van Kerkhoven, Marianne. 1994. "On Dramaturgy." *Theaterschrift*, no. 5–6: 8–33.

Wiener, William. (1948) 1961. *Cybernetics: or Control and Communication in the Animal and the Machine*. Cambridge, MA: The MIT Press.

Co-creation with Thingly Matter: Dramaturgies

9 Variations on Things and Performance

André Lepecki

The current investment in objects, and the incredible proliferation of stuff and things that we find in recent works of dance, performance and installation art, characterizes the current art scene. When displacing the prevalence of notions of subject and object, spectator and artwork, what emerges in these pieces is the proposition of a deep link between performativity and thingliness. In what follows, I offer nine preliminary theoretical variations on this phenomenon, which I believe to be less aesthetic than it is political.

This article has originally been published in Lepecki, André, Elke Van Campenhout, Christophe Van Gerrewey and Nele Wynants. 2011. IT, Thingly Variations in Space. Brussels: Mokum.

A. Lepecki (✉)
Department of Performance Studies, Tisch School of the Arts, New York University, New York, NY, USA
e-mail: andre.lepecki@nyu.edu

The Apparatus Variation

In a recent essay, Giorgio Agamben made an intriguing proposition: that the world as we know it, and particularly the contemporary world, is divided into two major realms: living organisms on one side, and "apparatuses"(or *dispositifs*) on the other (Agamben 2009). From the clash between these two realms a third element emerges: "subjectivity". However, in this trinity, apparatuses have the upper hand: "I shall call an apparatus literally *anything* that has in some way the capacity to capture, orient, determine, intercept, model, control, or secure the gestures, behaviours, opinions, or discourses of living beings" (Agamben 2009, 14 [emphasis added]). Oddly powerful, this "anything" endowed with the capacity to capture, to model and to control gestures and behaviours matches quite well the definition of that aesthetic-disciplinary invention of modernity, choreography, which can be understood precisely as an apparatus of capture of gestures, mobility, dispositions, body types, bodily intentions and inclinations for the sake of a spectacular display of a body's presence. But, as Agamben proceeds by listing a series of apparatuses, it becomes clear that his conception of the term goes beyond the notion of apparatus as a general system of control, and approaches instead a very concrete and specific understanding of apparatus as a *thing* that commands. Indeed, Agamben's listing reveals a quasi-paranoid perception of the world, where what predominates is the *omnipotence* of things: "Not only therefore prisons, madhouses, the panopticon, schools, confession, factories, disciplines, juridical measures, and so forth (whose connection with power is in a certain sense evident), but also the pen, writing, literature, philosophy, agriculture, cigarettes, navigation, computers, cellular telephones..." (14).

Variation on the Apparatus Variation

It seems that Agamben's listing of commanding/controlling apparatuses could go on forever, since between pen and cigarettes, computers and cellular telephones, the amount of objects that might be seen as controlling and commanding our gestures and habits, our desires and movements, is limited only by their availability in the world—particularly in "the extreme phase of capitalist development in which we live", characterized by "a massive accumulation and proliferation of apparatuses" (15). In other words: as we produce objects, we produce apparatuses that subjugate and diminish our own capacity to produce non-subjugated subjectivities. As we produce objects, we find ourselves being produced by objects. In the struggle between the living and the inorganic, it is not only as if objects are taking command—subjectivity itself is becoming a kind of objecthood: "today there is not even a single instant in which the life of individuals is not modeled, contaminated, or controlled by some apparatus" (15). It is in this sense that Agamben's definition of apparatus as a controlling thing becomes useful in order to probe the recent emergence and predominance of objects in some experimental dance. Firstly, because it uncovers a performativity in things and secondly, since dance has an intimate relationship to the political and ethical question of obedience, of governing gestures, of determining movements, it is no wonder then that dance (but also performance art, thanks to its openly political verve, and particularly its concern about how objects elicit actions) must itself approach objects—since objects seem to be governing our subjectivity, seem to be subjecting us, under their apparatus-function. But perhaps, there is more to it than just control…

THE COMMODITY VARIATION

Karl Marx noted that if human activity is capable of enacting *corporeal transformations* on matter by turning it into objects of usage (for instance, by turning a block of wood into a table), under capitalism, human activity makes. Objects endure a supplementary, "magical", or *incorporeal transformation*, where anything made for the use of humans turns into "a very strange thing" called a commodity. Guy Debord noted how in this peculiar mode of transformation, "we have the principle of commodity fetishism, the domination of society by things whose qualities are 'at the same time perceptible and imperceptible by the senses'"(Debord 1994, 26). Debord took this principle of domination and used it to define our "society of the spectacle", which is not a society made of spectacles, but one where "the spectacle corresponds to the historical moment at which the commodity completes its colonization of social life. It is not just that the relationship to commodities is now plain to see; the world we see is the world of the commodity" (Debord 1994, 29 [emphasis added]).

The political destiny of the commodity (very close, in a way, to Agamben's apparatus-thing) is then, to complete its total dominance over social life, over the life of things, but also over somatic life, since its dominance inscribes itself deeply into bodies. Indeed, the commodity dominates not only the world of things, but also the realm of the perceptible, the imperceptible, the sensible and the infra-sensible, the domain of desiring, even the domain of dreams. The commodity governs, and so much so it even governs the very possibility of *imagining governance*. Moreover, the commodity governs not only subjects, but also the very life of objects, the life of matter—the life of life and the life of things. Under its domain, humans and things find their concrete openness for endless potentiality crushed or substantially diminished. Even if the commodity is a material object, its power is to make sure that things are not left in peace. The incorporeal transformation of a thing into a commodity corresponds to its entrapment within one single destiny: becoming a utilitarian object attached to an economy of excess, linked to a spectacular mode of appearing, firmly demanding "proper use", bound to capital, and aimed eventually at the trash-bin, preferably within less than six months, when it will become again *a mere thing*, that is, valueless matter for capital. So perhaps, the counter-force of objects lies precisely in merely being a thing.

The Dispossession Variation

Let's propose that objects, when freed from utility, from use-value, from exchange-value, and from signification reveal their utter opaqueness, their total capacity to be fugitives from any apparatus of capture. When free, objects should gain another proper name: no longer object, apparatus or commodity, but simply *thing*. Fred Moten, theorizing on the "resistance of the object" that black radical performance always activates, remarks: "While subjectivity is defined by the subject's possession of itself and its objects, it is troubled by a dispossessive force objects exert such that the subject seems to be possessed – infused, deformed – by the object it possesses" (Moten 2003, 1). I call the dispossessive and deformative force always being exerted by any object, *thing*. Perhaps we need to draw from this force, learn how subjects and objects can become less like subjects and less like objects and more *thing*.

The Decolonizing Variation

How can the performative power of things unleash vectors of subjectification away from Agamben's and Debord's generalized diagnosis of our contemporary *subjectivity* and *objectivity* as existing exclusively under the sign of *subjugation* and *resignation* before the imperial force of controlling objects, commodities, or apparatuses? How do we decolonize the violent suturing of objects and subjects under the rabid violence of colonialism, capitalism, and racism (understood as forces intrinsic to commodity-apparatuses)? Towards the end of his essay, Agamben proposes "profanation" as an act of resistance that would "restore the thing to the free use of men" (18). I find this solution objectionable, with "men" affirming their power over "things" by using them as they wish. The violence in this proposition forecloses the recognition of a radical alterity in things. I see some recent dance recognizing precisely the necessity to enact an ethics of things. Such an ethics implies being with things without forcing them into constant utilitarianism. This is why in much recent dance where objects are central, objects are not used as signifying elements, nor as proxies for the subject of enunciation or for the dancing body, but often objects appear simply to enact purely referential situations, where dancers and stuff remain within a kind of synchronous "along-sidedness" freed from utilitarianism, signification and domination, even freed from being "art".

The Ethical Variation

How does one engage with the ethics, poetics, and politics that a thing's radical alterity proposes? How to enact what Silva Benso called "an ontological attitude whose implications border on ethics in its recognition of the multilayeredness of things, and in its intimation to an act of listening, caring, attention to their alterity" (146)? A possible answer is to say that perhaps a *becoming-thing* might not be such a bad destiny for subjectivity after all. As we look around us, it certainly seems a better option than continuing to carry on living and being under the name of the "human". A thing reminds us that living organisms, the inorganic as well as the organic, and that third produced by their clash called subjectivity, all need to be liberated from that subjugating force named the apparatus-commodity, a force that crushes them all into impoverished, sad, docile, cowardly, limited, or utilitarian modes of living. And a thing (the thingly element in any object and subject) may actually be that which offers us vectors and lines of flight away from the imperial sovereignty of colonizing apparatuses. In order to do so, things would have to be left in peace, allowed to *become-thing* once more—so as to actively counter their subjugation to a particularly detestable regime of the object (the commodity-apparatus regime) and a particularly detestable regime of the subject (the personhood regime) that imprisons both objects and subjects in mutual captivity. Perhaps some recent dance has been preoccupied precisely with this mutual liberation: of things and of bodies, of subjectivities and objects. In this mutual, necessary struggle, maybe we need to follow Mario Perniola's advice and "place our trust not in the divine or the human but in the mode of being of the thing" (Perniola 2004, 110). This mode of being, with its own motions, sounds, and phantasmagorias, is explored in Laurent Liefooghe's *Living Machine*. Space becomes saturated with a presence that—in its absence—reveals autonomous activities and modes of being when things are left alone.

THE ANTI-PERSONHOOD VARIATION

Mark Franko reminds us of the constitutive force of the "personal" in Renaissance dance, a force we can see traversing the whole history of Western theatrical dance: "The dancer's own *person* is the ultimate and single object of praise and dispraise in the dance". This is why "the dancing body must in turn display the admirable *self* for praise and index this display as praiseworthy, elicit praise" (Franko 1986, 22). Consequence of this foundational, constitutive element of personhood and self-centredness in dance: a blocking of the dancer's desire to become thing, to become animal, obfuscated as it is by the emphatic need to constantly affirm and reaffirm its *personhood* and its *self*. In the 1990s and early 2000s, some important experiments, by Vera Mantero, Boris Charmatz, and Xavier LeRoy among others, seem to have privileged a *becoming-animal* as a line of flight for dance. (Butoh had a similar political-performative impetus, becoming-animal as rejection of the human and of the person, Hijikata: "I adore rib cages but, again, it seems to me that a dog's rib cage is superior to mine"). It appears that now a line-of-flight can be found in dance's embracing of a becoming-thing. It is fundamental here to find other devices of visibility, where the object and the person does not occupy a centre—thus other spaces must be invented, involving the viewer, dissolving the stage, scrambling distinctions. One of these new regimes of visibility is the installation in performance, where "the open horizon of the installations" leads exactly to this "spatial dissolution of the work of art" (Perniola 2004, 103), destroying the work as art to reveal the work as a "thing". Here, we can remind ourselves of Heidegger's formulation on the performativity of things: not to be, but to *gather*. We can see this mode of transversal reaching out and inclusive gathering in the operation of the work *C.O. Journeys* by Joanna Bailie & Christoph Ragg, where spectators are placed inside a camera obscura in such a way as to become contiguous to the images, fusing with images, dissolving representation and presence. In a sonic reformulation of the same premise, Lilia Mestre's *Live-in-Room* gathers audience in order to propose ways to be alongside objects in a virtual space of endless modulations: sonic, thingly, imaginary.

THE LINES-OF-FLIGHT VARIATION

Of course objects have always been present on dance stages. Rosalind Krauss once wrote: "a large number of postwar European and American sculptors became interested both in theater and *in the extended experience of time* which seemed part of the conventions of the stage. From this interest came some sculpture to be used as *props* in productions of dance and theater, some to function *as surrogate performers*, and some to act as the on-stage generators of scenic effects" (Krauss 1981, 204, emphasis added). But now it is not *sculpture* created by visual artists that we see appearing on dance stages—but *things, stuff* that choreographers drag into the scene, precisely *not to make a scene*, but to create an environment. Moreover, things are used in ways totally different from how Krauss had described the use of sculptures in theatrical and dance events. Today, objects do appear, but not as "properties" (or "props"— as objects are significantly called in theatre parlance), nor as generators of "scenic effects" or "surrogate performers" (i.e. as puppets). Rather, objects and bodies *take place* alongside each other and…and sometimes little else takes place. This simple act of just placing things in their quiet, still, and concrete thingliness alongside bodies, not necessarily *together* with the dancers, but just *alongside*, effects a substantial event: to underline the thin line simultaneously separating *and* joining bodies and things, to delineate a zone of indiscernibility between the corporeal, the subjectile, and the thingly. This operation is not Duchampian, in the sense that it wants to affirm the everyday object as art, once the object is signed by an artist or brought into an art context. Instead, this operation wants to affirm the object as thing, to liberate the thing captured in the object that had been trapped by instrumental reasoning and artistic apparatuses.

To invest in things, not as proxies of the body, nor as signifying or representative elements of a narrative, but as *co-partners in a sheer, co-determinant, co-presence*—as co-extensive entities in the field of matter—is to activate a fundamental change in the relationship between objects and their aesthetic effects (in dance, theatre, performance art, and installation art). This change is the political activation of the thing so that it may do what it does best—dispossessing objects and subjects from their traps called apparatus, commodity, person, and self. When this dispossession takes place within particularly involving environments called installations, a reversibility takes place where "it is the installation that feels the visitor...penetrates him" (as Perniola would say), turning the visitor then also into a thing. This operation of dispossession, that is also a kind of gathering and repossession, can be found in *Moving You* by Lilia Mestre—a theatrical situation with no characters and no story, but where this baring out is what allows for the creation of a sheer interchangeability between bodies and things, experimenting with an alongsidedness and a kind of gathering where modes of distributing presence are activated by thingliness.

The Final Quote Variation

"Therefore, when I give myself as thing, I do not mean at all to offer myself to the exploitation and benefit of others. I do not offer myself to the other but to the impersonal movement that at the same time displaces the other from himself and allows him in his turn to give himself as thing and to take me as thing" (Perniola 2004, 109).

References

Agamben, Giorgio. 1998. *Homo Sacer. Sovereign Power and Bare Life*, Meridian. Stanford, CA: Stanford University Press.
Agamben, Giorgio. 2009. "*What is an apparatus?*" *and other essays*, Meridian: Crossing Aesthetics. Stanford, California: Stanford University Press.
Benso, Silvia. 2000. *The face of things : a different side of ethics*, SUNY Series in Contemporary Continental Philosophy. Albany, New York.: State University of New York Press.
Césaire, Aimé. 1972. *Discourse on colonialism*. New York and London: Monthly Review Press.
Debord, Guy. 1994. *The society of the spectacle*. New York: Zone Books.

Franko, Mark. 1986. *The Dancing Body in Renaissance Choreography* (c. 1416–1589). Birmingham, AL: Summa Publications.
Johnson, Barbara. 2008. *Persons and things*. Cambridge, Massachusetts: Harvard University Press.
Krauss, Rosalind E. 1981. *Passages in modern sculpture*. Cambridge, Massachusetts: MIT Press.
Moten, Fred. 2003. *In the Break: The Aesthetics of the Black Radical Tradition*. Minneapolis: University of Minnesota Press.
Perniola, Mario. 2004. *The Sex Appeal of the Inorganic, Athlone Contemporary European Thinkers*. New York and London: Continuum.

Does the Donkey Act? *Balthazar* as Protagonist

Maximilian Haas

An ordinary, untrained donkey and half a dozen human performers on a theatre stage, walking and standing, walking and standing at a moderate pace. While the animal moves freely through the space, the people act formalized in a group. Wordlessly, they decide upon the direction and rhythm of the walks they draw diagonally through the entire space. The donkey joins in or follows after a short hesitation. One hears his hooves clatter regularly then. But sometimes he doesn't move at all. He refuses to take part in the game. The people then return to him with a few turns, stand up in front of him and start over. The donkey, now part of the group again, comes along. But sometimes it also seems as if it is not the people who rule the game, but the animal, who deliberately shapes the performance. The donkey takes the artistic direction and leads the way.

This is how all *Balthazar* shows started. *Balthazar* is the title of a performance research project that I developed as a dramaturge together with artist David Weber-Krebs, between 2011 and 2015. It took shape in four productions featuring different performers in different cities (Amsterdam, Hamburg, Brussels, and Berlin), each focussing on different artistic means in the spectrum between performance art, dance, and

M. Haas (✉)
Berlin University of the Arts, Berlin, Germany

© The Author(s), under exclusive license to Springer Nature
Switzerland AG 2021
C. Stalpaert et al. (eds.), *Performance and Posthumanism*,
https://doi.org/10.1007/978-3-030-74745-9_3

theatre. *Balthazar* is also the fictional name of the protagonist of each of these productions, a donkey.[1] The animal is put next to a group of human performers who seek to engage him or her in theatrical action. The donkey is at the very centre of the action, and the pieces affirm the uncertainties that such a decision brings with it. The artistic approach is thus contrary to what one could call the 'circus-paradigm' of animal live performance, where the animal performs perfection in executing predefined tasks. Based on a dramaturgical structure the *Balthazar* shows rather unfold in the interaction between the species. If the human performers can act in this theatrical environment, the donkey can act too.

Yet, what does 'action' mean here? How can we conceive of action without restricting it to the anthropocentric conception of an intentional and purposeful operation on the one hand and the mechanic execution of scripted movement patterns or protocols on the other? How can we thus conceive of action in a way that allows us to describe the performative doings between the human performers and the animal? Following this question, this article unfolds the theoretical propositions that inspired the *Balthazar* project or resulted from it, and offers insight into the development of the performances throughout the years. In doing so, it touches on problems, questions, and arguments that I developed in greater detail in my practice-based dissertation on *Animals on Stage. An Aesthetic Ecology of Performance (Tiere auf der Bühne. Eine ästhetische Ökologie der Performance*, Haas 2018), which is centred around the *Balthazar* project, and makes them accessible in English.

The article sets out with a critique of the dualism of subject and object, nature and culture in modern ontology, then turns to pragmatic approaches to the living by theoretical biology of the early twentieth century, which are lastly conceptually reflected on through the lens of Alfred North Whitehead's pragmatist cosmology. Throughout, the theoretical discourse is compared with artistic practice in these respects. Both the theoretical and the artistic propositions thus pursue a pragmatic perspective, which is focussed on processes, practices, and doings—rather than on categorical dualisms.

According to the historically predominant understanding in Western philosophy, an action is that which is performed by an agent. In contrast to behaviour, which is defined as automatic and reflexive activity, action necessarily involves an intention and a movement made wilfully by the agent. Furthermore, it is defined as purposive, conscious, and subjectively meaningful. Hence, an action is that which is (deliberately) *done by* an

Fig. 1 David Weber-Krebs, Maximilian Haas, *Balthazar* (© Maximilian Haas)

entity, as opposed to that which it (accidentally) *happens to do* or what *happens to it* (i.e. passion).[2] Our Western notion of action is thus based on the distinction between intentionality and instinct, which is also essential to the human-animal divide. Whether as the *zoon politikon*, the *animal rationale* or, in early modern terms, the body-machine that thinks, Man is defined as nature's exception, the categorical opposite of animal (Fig. 1).[3]

THE MODERN HUMAN-ANIMAL DIVIDE

The human-animal divide is a key feature of modern ontology, rooted in René Descartes' exposition of the dualism of body and mind and his conception of the animal organism as a mere machine (1968). It is rendered explicit in Kantian anthropology (2006), as Immanuel Kant as humanist *par excellence* unfolds the ethical ramifications of his critical philosophy of the subject, in which animals are generally assigned to the object side—only humans can be considered subjects. Accordingly, it is only humans who can be regarded as persons, that is, as bearers of moral rights and duties. Animals, on the other hand, are considered things and are therefore subordinate to the human power of disposal.

This touches upon yet another distinction with humanist grounds, namely the distinction between culture and nature.[4] The first category covers all man-made things, including Man himself, while the second covers everything else, from inanimate material to fungus and plants to the great apes. The cosmos is thus divided into two fundamentally different worlds: while, supposedly, culture is created by free subjects, nature contains living objects that are without any consciousness, cognition or will. This reductionist ontology is the outcome of a critical philosophy originating from epistemological precautions, and thus necessarily arriving at anthropological claims—even about the non-human world.

The modern human-animal divide must thus be understood in terms of that which Jacques Derrida described as a binary-hierarchical opposition, a linguistic operation that relates two concepts so that they exclude each other and presuppose each other as opposite: A is what B is not, and vice versa (Derrida 1981). One concept is thereby considered original, while the other is seen as derived from the original. Ultimately the opposition is naturalized, which means that its construction is concealed and appears henceforth as naturally given. The binary-hierarchical opposition is essentially a power operation. Thus, Derrida claims that 'in a classical philosophical opposition we are not dealing with the peaceful coexistence of a vis-à-vis, but rather with a violent hierarchy. One of the two terms governs the other (axiologically, logically, etc.), or has the upper hand' (41).

It is obvious that, in our context, this upper hand is the hand of Man. Biologically an animal himself, ontologically he is a class apart, at least according to modern standards. Whenever the sciences discover a capacity in animals that was formerly only credited to humans (suffering, sign use, social learning, cumulative cultural evolution, et cetera), and whenever the ontological territory of the animal is thus extended, philosophers feel obliged to offer new criteria for anthropological difference. Hence, as Derrida has argued in his influential lecture on *The Animal That Therefore I Am* (2008), the border between humans and animals shifts continually without its function as border being called into question. This ontological tug-of-war expresses a general tendency of modern animal philosophy, namely that it thinks in oppositions rather than commonalities, and it proceeds top-down.

Empirical encounters with animals, however, especially in the intensifying frame of art, draw a very different picture. Here, animals seem to undermine the modern ontology separating the world into human subjects (conceived as self-conscious, self-transparent, intentional agents), and non-human objects including animals (conceived as totally dependent on their power of disposal). When put to the aesthetic test, the linear gap refuses to hold. As numerous artistic approaches to animals show, even in the bleakest hours of modernity and industrialization (violent anthropocentrism), human beings have never been completely immune to experiencing empathy with animals—and this feeling implies some sense of relatedness on the part of those who feel it. Furthermore, in the arts, it is never a matter of something as general as 'the animal'. Aesthetic experience always stems from a relationship with a particular animal, always with just this one. Besides, generally, the realm of animals is much too diverse for it ever to be appropriate to speak of 'the' animal. Only from the perspective of the human (understood as the exception of nature) does the wide variety of creatures between amoeba and chimpanzee appear under this general signifier. The word thus merely designates the living Other of those who call themselves humans. *L'animal n'existe pas.*

'Human nature is an interspecies relationship'(Tsing 2012, 141). This dictum applies to our practical livelihood as well as our theoretical self-understanding as humans. Human life and survival are based on numerous non-human partners, from intestinal bacteria to working animals, which make the thinking subject possible in the first place. But the anthropological self-definition of human subjects, too, is dependent on animals, if only in opposition to or in contrast with them. Humans can only understand themselves in relation to animals. Without the animal there is no human, materially as well as conceptually. The efforts of theorists and researchers associated with the emerging field of animal studies had a profound impact on the nomenclature of the critical humanities: it has become customary here to refer to 'conscious subjects' as 'human animals', and to the sentient beings formerly known as 'animals' as 'non-human animals'. Language and consciousness (i.e. mind or spirit) were formerly emphasized as proof for the exceptional position of the human; now we stress vitality and sensibility (i.e. body) as proof for the human position within the landscape of terrestrial life forms. The exclusive self-understanding has yielded to an inclusive one. Or, as the

American philosopher Donna Haraway—who was an important inspiration in conceiving *Balthazar*—asserts in retrospect: 'We have never been human' (Haraway 2008, 165).[5]

THE *BALTHAZAR* PROJECT

The *Balthazar* project was inspired by Robert Bresson's film *Au hazard Balthazar* (1966), which tells the eventful life story of a donkey: from his early adoption by a human family, through several changes of owners and tasks, until his lonely death, the animal spirals down towards its tragic destiny. The film enacts the dramaturgy of ancient tragedies (especially as understood by Walter Benjamin) and the Christian passion. These two leading Western narratives concern the isolation of a single outstanding and exemplary person—who represents mankind as a whole—and the fulfilment of his destiny.[6] Bresson takes as his central figure an animal that suffers a distressing fate—that most humble of beasts, a donkey. By so doing, he brings animality into the very heart of Western tales that track the course of Man into his very own being.

Unlike in Bresson's movie, the human performers in 'our' *Balthazar* have no names and no specified or stable characterization, and there is no plot. The piece sets up and modifies performative constellations between the donkey and the human performers, thereby pursuing theatrical experiments with notions of animality and the otherness of the animal. *Balthazar* repeats on stage the artistic approach to the animal applied by Bresson in film: the donkey is transferred into an alien artistic context designed for representing humankind—and this transfer has an impact both on the animal and the context. In *Balthazar*, scenes in which the animal is involved in simple constellations and patterns of movement are juxtaposed with scenes in which the human performers influence the situation by superimposing fragments of narration onto it. The piece thus shifts back and forth from performance to theatre, if we schematically define performance as a live, active intercommunication that has an open outcome, and theatre as a specific representation of an absent meaning. It oscillates between provoking a face-to-face encounter between the animal and the spectators, and presenting the animal as an element in a framed image.

The Pragmatic Individuality of Organism and *Umwelt*

In order to better understand the relationship between animals and action, it is helpful to take a look at basic concepts of biology. It is the very notion of the organism that reveals the agential dimension of the respective modes of being. An organism never actually *is*, but always *becomes*: it is an entity that realizes itself in the interaction between body and environment. The organism is the origin and the result of an ontogenetic action that creates and maintains an inner and an outer milieu. Ontogenesis is not primarily understood here as the individual development of a living being into adulthood, but rather implies the elementary transformations through which the being lives: respiration, nutrition, metabolism, renewal of cells, as well as courtship behaviour, cultivation and defence of territory, social interaction, et cetera. Thus, an organism is never simply given, but unfolds in a continuous process of individuation that is coextensive with its life. To consider the 'pragmatic individuality' of the organism, i.e. the ontogenesis of the living individual in and through dynamic relations between body and environment (Haas 2018, 157–196), means to emphasize the role of action in its specific mode of being: how does the capacity to effect or act belong to the organism as such? In what way are actions constitutive for a particular organism? How do actions relate to the surrounding milieu? Does the environment shape the action, or, on the contrary, does the action shape the environment? The pragmatic individuality of the organism stresses the existential relationality and processuality of the living being.

In 1934, German neurologist and biologist Kurt Goldstein formulated a general theory of the organism as a pragmatic unity. This theory emerged from the author's medical practice with soldiers who had returned from World War I with brain injuries. By theoretical analogy he extended his fundamental findings onto higher organisms in general. For Goldstein, the organism is constituted neither by the material that composes it, nor the form and structure of its body parts, nor the functions they perform, but rather its preferred behaviour:

> We can consider an organism at one time, in the usual analytic way, as composed of parts, members, organs, and, at another time, in its natural behaviour; then we find, in the latter case, that by no means all kinds of behaviour, which on the grounds of the first consideration would be

conceived as being possible, are actually realised. Instead we find that only a definite, selective range of modes of behaviour exists. (Goldstein 1995, 266)

Hence, if we define an organism based on that which differentiates it from other organisms, the definition cannot be derived from the analysis of its anatomic structure or physiological processes (*partes extra partes*), but only from the synthetic observation of its individual behaviour as a whole. This view is supported by Goldstein's empirical research, showing that organismic behaviour cannot be dissected into parts, such as reflexes or drives, but unfolds in 'the relationship of each individual performance to the whole organism' (Goldstein 1995, 173). The biologist even claims that the organism essentially *is* the complex of relations between the performances it prefers. Thus, the nature of an organism is not determined by its biologically inherited species being, which shapes its anatomic and physiological condition (or determines possible mates), it is specific to the organism as an individual, which defines itself through the choice of what it does with its body.

Goldstein's contemporary, the Baltic-German zoologist Jakob von Uexküll, developed a whole systematics of nature based on the conception of the organism as an individual subject that realizes itself through action. While Goldstein puts the individual body centre stage, Uexküll's *Umweltlehre* (1909) focusses on the environment. The *Umwelt* is construed here as a system analogous to the organism, which is composed of the factors that are relevant to its normal life practices. Hence, each environment is specific to one particular organism, and consequently there are as many environments as there are organisms, intersecting only partially. This presupposes that the organism is open to external factors; an organism fully enclosed onto itself would not have an environment (and would not be an organism). Organism and environment form a relational assemblage that is constitutive for both sides. Uexküll even considers the *Umwelt* an integral part of the animal, or rather, he regards the higher organism of the body and its environment as the animal: organism + environment = animal. Thus, just as in Goldstein, for Uexküll actions form the essential features of the organism. Yet, while the former considers them as part of the individual, the latter expands pragmatic individuality to the dimensions of the environment.

Uexküll conceptualizes the constitutive interaction between the organism and its environment as a function-circle, a feedback loop between stimulus and responsive action, which is internally processed by almost personal interconnections between sensors and effectors. At the theoretical core of this biology lies a philosophically adventurous extension of (Kantian) transcendental subjectivity onto non-human animals. Based on the assumption that 'All reality is subjective experience,' Uexküll seeks to expand 'in two directions the results of Kant's investigations: (1) by considering the part played by our body, especially by our sense-organs and central nervous system, and (2) by studying the relations of other subjects (animals) to objects' (Uexküll 1926, xv). According to Elisabeth Grosz, this makes Uexküll 'the first animal phenomenologist, with all the irony that entails' (Grosz 2011, 173). The irony would obviously lie in the fact that, by definition, a phenomenology can only be derived from subjective experience, and non-human animals usually do not practise phenomenology (as far as we humans can tell). Yet this does not fully apply to the *Umweltlehre*. Although Uexküll does make use of empathy as a means of zoological speculation, he does so on the grounds of technical knowledge about the sensorimotor apparatus that predetermines the perceptions and actions of a given animal.

Yes, the animal is a machine, but there is someone inhabiting the machine, there is an operator actively producing the particular connection between stimulus and response. Descartes held the view that animals are mere machines, and so are humans, to the extent that they are physical bodies too. Uexküll, on the contrary, argues that since we as humans know that the senses do not deliver just any data, but rather the act of sensing is required to produce certain data, we cannot ignore that there is such agency also in other (non-human) animals, and the same applies to their actions:

> Whoever still holds the view that our sensory organs serve perception and our motor organs serve the production of effects, will also not see in animals simply a mechanical assemblage; they will also discover the machine operator who is built into the organs just as we are into our body. But then he will address himself to animals not merely as objects but also as subjects, whose essential activities consist in perception and production of effects. (Uexküll 2010, 42)

Hence, against the ambitions of its author, the *Umweltlehre* is conceptually anti-Kantian: it is based on the commonalities between humans and animals, not their differences, and it systematizes the diversity of terrestrial life forms with bottom-up logic. To avoid the traps of philosophical anthropocentrism, Uexküll makes strategic use of a speculative anthropomorphism. He applies to other animals the model that conventionally guarantees the exceptionality of modern Man, namely transcendental subjectivity. Non-human animals actively perceive and create a world, just as we do.

Gilles Deleuze and Félix Guattari have taken up the *Umweltlehre* in crucial parts of their neo-vitalist philosophy, crossing it with the Spinozist theory of affect: 'Von Uexküll, in defining animal worlds, looks for the active and passive affects of which the animal is capable in the individuated assemblage of which it is a part' (Deleuze and Guattari 1987, 257). With Spinoza, the authors believe that a body is defined by the actions and perceptions it is capable of, i.e. by what a body can do. Species do not differ primarily in anatomic form or physiological function, but in their capacity to affect and be affected. This principle leads to a peculiar taxonomy of life forms, one that is always situated and provisional, and radically contradicts the worldview of positivist science:

> For example: there are greater differences between a plow horse or draft horse and a racehorse than between an ox and a plow horse. This is because the racehorse and the plow horse do not have the same affects nor the same capacity for being affected; the plow horse has affects in common rather with the ox. (Deleuze 1988, 124)

Thus, Deleuze (and Guattari) locate elements of Spinoza's *Ethics* at the core of the biological discipline that Uexküll inaugurated, *ethology*—and it is this radically pragmatic and non-anthropocentric speculative take on ethology that deeply resonates with the practicalities of interspecies collaboration in performance production as the experiences with the donkeys on stage showed.

Performance Ethology, the Specificity of Donkeys

The *Balthazar* performances were realized with different donkeys in each city. In total, we have seen about fifteen animals, and most of them did not have much more in common than their *taxon*. Furthermore, it was impossible to know in advance how the donkeys would move and behave on stage. They literally developed a stage persona the moment they first stepped onto the planks. We knew very little about a donkey's sensori-motor abilities, capacities and behaviour before we started working. As we later learnt, the positivist findings of behavioural biology would not have helped much given our aim. Performance work emphasizes the individual characteristics and habits of the entities involved, rather than their species being. In the Hamburg performance, for example, the donkey would always come to the front of the stage after he entered the space through the back door. He would stand still for a bit, obviously scanning the space, then walk to the back left corner, piss, and bray loudly. He repeated the same pattern every time he came on stage. After that ritual, he was ready to work with us. We did not witness this behaviour with any of the other donkeys.

The movement patterns that we executed with the donkeys throughout the pieces required a rather specific mode of being on the side of the animals. They needed to be calm but not bored, interested in humans and willing to interact with them. They had to move at an average pace and stay with the action for an hour without being distracted by the food and hay that waited for them behind the back door. It was not unusual that we had to try three or four donkeys at each location to find the one that could meet our expectations. We saw donkeys that were simply too young and male to be interested in anything other than exploring the space or joking around with their owners or companions, and we could not work with them. Maybe a llama or zebra would have done better in the situation—we did not have the means to try. Maybe a llama or zebra, or rather some specific llama or zebra, would have had more in common with the young female donkey that performed so well in Brussels than with the young stallions in Hamburg. If this were the case, it would be because those two different animals have more affects in common than these specimens of the same biological species. These rather speculative thoughts about what one could call 'performance ethology', however, stem from a simple observation: it seems that interspecies performance production is about what Deleuze locates at the heart of his Spinozist reading of ethology: 'the capacities for affecting and being affected that characterise each thing' (Deleuze 1988, 125).

Yet, also Uexküll eventually proved to be a dramaturgical thinker: not only were we unaware of the donkeys's stage persona, neither did we know the stages they were entering, because to them it was not the stages as we perceived them. Something that did not even exist for us could turn out to be an insurmountable obstacle to the donkeys: a black cable

Fig. 2 David Weber-Krebs, Maximilian Haas, *Balthazar* (© Maximilian Haas)

on a black wall, a tiny gap in the floor, or simply frontal light: all these conditions could distract the donkeys so forcefully that we would not be able to get their attention. Only as we observed how the donkeys interacted with the space did we actually see the space in which we had to work as a temporary interspecies performance collective. Performance work unfolds between the individual *Umwelten* of its co-workers, human and non-human. Only when method and dramaturgy manage to account for the individual perspectives of all entities involved can the collective action possibly succeed. There is no such thing as *the* stage (or, from the perspective of reception, it only exists for the spectator), and there is no such thing as *the* donkey on that stage.

However, it is not only the pragmatic modes of relating that shape interspecies interaction in theatre—there are decisive moments of distance and distinction too. In a peculiar way they are connected with a (partly) involuntary reaction of the body: laughter (Fig. 2).

Interspecies Identification in Theatre with Humorous Results

When we encounter an animal in the theatrical function of the protagonist or main performer—especially a vertebrate that stands on stage like a human being, has a face with eyes that look back, and a mouth that expresses a voice—and when we thus encounter the donkey Balthazar, we are tempted to identify with the animal, fully knowing that this fundamental projection by the spectator in conventional theatre—putting yourself virtually in the position of an acting other—is inadequate for the situation at hand. The spectator, accustomed to finding something meaningful in theatre, assigns significant patterns to the donkey's behaviour. This becomes very obvious in one scene of the performance, in which a performer puts a loudspeaker right in front of the donkey, a melancholic piece of music plays, and Balthazar seems to listen carefully. Does he understand that this is music? Does he get the beauty of it? Do we witness the fall of a natural being into culture? Is he amazed by the technical achievement of sounding objects? Or is he merely orienting himself towards the acoustic waves? And what does it mean that the donkey turns away at the most inappropriate moment, in terms of the music, and pisses on the stage?

One cannot help but project a psychological meaning onto the donkey's behaviour: personal experiences, clichés and stories (often children's stories) come into the imaginary play here. Or, on the level of the performative doings, we assign an artistic or anti-artistic purpose to it. We may assume that the donkey is complying with the performance, that he understands and approves of it, and participates intentionally using artistic means. But sooner or later, the moment comes when the progressively constructed expectation is either fulfilled or disappointed, and both options can be funny. Sometimes the animal seems to behave like a human, and the identification temporarily succeeds. Yet in the very next moment, through an unexpected and undue action of the donkey, the illusion collapses and we become aware of the absurdity of our projections. Herein lays the performance's humorous component.

Henri Bergson understood laughter as a psychosomatic reaction to a human body that acts like a mere apparatus, that is, to '[s]omething mechanical encrusted on the living' (Bergson 2008, 24). Thus, comedy laughs about the ontological borderline between human subjects and material objects, between organism and machine. This line runs straight through the animal, as Simon Critchley elaborates in his discussion of the question if humour must be regarded as a marker for the anthropological difference:

If humour is human, then it also, curiously, marks the limit of the human. Or, better, humour explores what it means to be human by moving back and forth across the frontier that separates humanity from animality [...]. Humour is precisely the exploration of the break between nature and culture, which reveals the human to be not so much a category by itself as a negotiation between categories. We might even define the human as a dynamic process produced by a series of identifications and misidentifications with animality. Thus, what makes us laugh is the reduction of the human to the animal or the elevation of the animal to the human. (Critchley 2010, 63–64)

As noted above, the cognitive mechanism that allows one to see the world through the eyes of another person lies at the very heart of the possibility of conventional theatre, which involves the identification of the spectator with the protagonist. 'To identify with' means to put yourself virtually in the position of. Theatre engenders an irresolvable tension between these two modes of experience: a first-hand experience of the theatrical situation, and a second-hand experience through that which provokes identification. The spectator constantly shifts from one perspective to the other, moving back and forth between the position from which she views and the position with which she identifies. Usually this shifting remains unnoticed. More than that, this process of shifting, which constitutes the very mediality of conventional theatre, must remain unnoticed in order to allow for a smooth theatrical experience. Yet, there are forms of theatre (the so-called meta-theatre), where through this process the spectator is elevated to a meta-position, allowing her to reflect on the process of perception and meaning-making between subject and object—an epistemic process that is usually incomprehensible in the purposeful, goal-oriented relation to entities in the everyday. Artistic framing cuts those instrumental relations, thus rendering the mechanisms of relating visible. Furthermore, theatre requires a certain trust or even faith in the entity it puts forward, along with an anthropomorphic charging of whatever it presents. This seems to be a prerequisite for relating, at least in terms of empathy or identification.

Applied this way, theatre can function as an equalizing machine: it levels the ontological differences that precondition our orientation in the world and the way we approach certain entities, living or not living, from humans, to animals, to things. Everything we encounter in the position of the protagonist seems more similar to us than usual, meaning more human. Theatre is thus essentially a humanistic art form, training humans in humanity by means of identification with that which is presented as human. This historical legacy is deeply inscribed into theatrical mechanisms, and it is necessary to negotiate with these mechanisms while staging an animal. The conjunction of animal and theatre as incompatible entities can reveal the (deeply modern) construction of both *animal* and of *theatre*. Impossible identification with the animal is the very motor of this dismantling process. Consequently, theatre can be regarded as an effective means of working through the great divide between subject and object that constitutes its very possibility, defining humans as humans and animals as animals, at least for now. Laughter seems to be a good indicator of the crucial problems, amongst which the problem of action is of utmost importance.

WHITEHEAD'S COSMOLOGY OF ACTION

While this article started by critiquing dualistic ways of thinking the relation between human and animal in modern ontology and then confronted them with pragmatic approaches to organisms in theoretical biology, which foster an inclusive view of the living that covers non-human as well as human animals, I will now turn to a peculiar attempt at a pragmatist cosmology that extends a certain way of organismic thinking also towards the non-living. The English-American mathematician and philosopher Alfred North Whitehead founded a whole experimental system of philosophy on the pragmatic individuality of the organism (1978, 18–60). Reflecting on the eccentric theories of early twentieth-century physics, namely the theories of relativity and quantum mechanics, he formulates a general systematics of nature that contradicts the mechanistic worldview of Newtonian physics in almost every decisive aspect (1948, 96–137). Whitehead's philosophy of the organism is not based on universal laws of nature, but on the empirical realization of natural reality as given in experience (1919,1920). Nature does not consist of inert matter, passively subjected to the laws of motion; instead it consists of entities defined by the relations that they actively maintain with their environment. Each entity pursues individual ends, through which it becomes what it essentially is. Thus, Whitehead regards an entity primarily as an event that unfolds through time—and thus as an occasion for experience. The discrete position of a body in space and its discrete moment in time as maintained by mechanistic physics are mere abstractions from its relational happening. Reality rather unfolds as a process through which natural relations condense into agential entities. Thus, agency becomes the fundamental force in natural reality, regardless of the respective ontological realm.

In Whitehead's cosmological account, the binary oppositions of body and mind (Descartes) as well as subject and object (Kant) are systematically contained. An entity becomes through the realization of its individual end, which the philosopher qualifies as subjective. In doing so, it incorporates the propositions of other entities that enter into its becoming as objective data. Hence, an entity is a subject as long as it becomes, and an object as soon as it eventually is and enters into the becoming of other entities as data. Furthermore, Whitehead characterizes these entities as bipolar: they have a physical and a mental pole. The physical pole is causally determined by the objective data, the mental involves the freedom to realize the subjective ends. Thus, body and mind, subject and object, are not conceived here as ontological attributes that distinguish a specific set or ontological class of entities; they rather characterize the relational position and partial perspective of each entity in its respective situation.

With this cosmology, we can identify a basic misconception of action that is based on the subject-predicate form of thought, which Whitehead traces back to Descartes (1978, 7). This logic presupposes an underlying subject that stays the same no matter what is predicated of it. As the scheme of 'he/she/it does', this logic is deeply inscribed into the Western grammar of thinking. In its syntagmatic structure, it leads to the assumption that an action must be performed by a pre-given agent, which intentionally pursues certain purposes with it. With Whitehead, we can turn this logic upside down by arguing that there is first an agential structure, a situation that enables a certain action, which is then executed by a subject. This subject is not given in advance of the action, but is constitutively subject *of* and *through* that action. Hence, it would be an anthropocentric mistake to say 'I do', since, cosmologically, there is first a certain doing that then constitutes its subject.

The Ontogenetic Dimension of Interspecies Performance Action

Viewed from the objective side and mapped on empirical particulars, the concept of action thus derived from Whitehead's cosmology shows some similarities with Bruno Latour's version of actor-network theory, which defines an actor as 'what is made to act by many others'. It is not an individual entity, but an association of many human and non-human agents that express their affiliation with the actor pragmatically by their participation in it. Thus, an actor is 'not the source of an action but the moving target of a vast array of entities swarming toward it' (2005, 46). It manifests itself by 'modifying other actors through a series of trials that can be listed thanks to some experimental protocol'. This is, according to Latour, 'the minimal, secular, nonpolemical definition of an actor' (Latour 2004, 75).

In *Balthazar,* the donkey is the focus and moving target of every action performed on stage. It moves around, and around it, the constellation of actors and artistic intentions reconfigures time and again. On the level of the artistic concept, the donkey is an object of our intention. On the level of the performance, however, the donkey rules the scene. Every action initiated by a human performer needs to get the attention (and therefore the approval) of the donkey. Human will is only relevant insofar it matches the will of the non-human animal, otherwise it loses itself in irrelevance, or all too human hysteria. Every action requires the active participation of the donkey, and its contribution: action can only happen between actors on stage. Hence, the primary task for the performers is to seduce the animal into the collective action, that is, to mobilize it. If, for example, the animal is bored and simply stands around on stage, losing interest in the performers, the show collapses. The same is true if the donkey is anxious and only wants to leave the theatre space. The medium of the *Balthazar* performances is not so much the theatre stage as it is the active intercommunication between human and non-human animals. It does not happen in the Euclidian container space of the stage, but in the relational process, by which all actors become who they are, at least for now.

Notes

1. The 2011 iteration happened in collaboration with the Mimeschool Amsterdam (AHK), the 2013 iteration was a co-production with Kaaitheater and RITS' acting department (Brussels). In 2013, there was also a version in Berlin, a coproduction with Kampnagel (Hamburg) and HZT (Berlin). The performance was shown in 2015 and 2016 in Berlin (DE), Kortrijk (BE), Polverigi (IT), and Frankfurt am Main (DE).
2. The respective concept of action is rendered explicit in Aristotle's *Nicomachean Ethics* where the author states that the 'first principle of action

[...] is rational choice'. This is the very reason why for Aristotle ultimately 'animals have [...] no share in action' (Aristotle 2004, 104).
3. The definitions of Man as the political or the rational animal have prevailed in different formulations since Plato and Aristotle. The idea of Man as a thinking body-machine goes back to René Descartes' *Discourse on the Method* (1968).
4. The human-animal divide forms the basis of the nature-culture dualism already in its early modern definition in Samuel von Pufendorf's *De jure naturae et gentium* [1672/84], an important reference also for Kant. In recent decades, the nature-culture dualism was reinterpreted from the pragmatist viewpoint of science and technology studies (cf. Latour 1993; Haraway 2008, Barad 2007).
5. Haraway specifies that 'we have never been the philosopher's human' (2008, 165).
6. For Walter Benjamin, the basic structure of the Greek tragedy is the progressive isolation of the protagonist, ultimately fulfilled in his death. This isolation is expressed in language as a becoming silent. The tragic hero forms the ultimate human sacrifice: he is the last subject of the old Olympic right, whose language has exhausted itself, and the first of the coming community, whose language still lies in the future. His death marks a change of epoch. In Benjamin's reading, the tragedy thus shows structural similarities with the Passion of Christ (Benjamin 1998).

References

Aristotle. 2004. *Nicomachean Ethics*. London: Penguin Books.
Barad, Karen. 2007. *Meeting the Universe Halfway*. Durham/London: Duke University Press.
Benjamin, Walter. 1998. *The Origin of German Tragic Drama*. London/New York: Verso.
Bergson, Henri. 2008. *Laughter - An Essay on the Meaning of the Comic*. Los Angeles: Athanasius Press.
Critchley, Simon. 2010. "Is Humour Human?" *Inaesthetics 2: Animality* 61–70.
Derrida, Jacques. 1981. *Positions*. Chicago: University of Chicago Press.
Derrida, Jacques. 2008. *The Animal That Therefore I Am*. New York: Fordham University Press.
Deleuze, Gilles and Félix Guattari. 1987. *A Thousand Plateaus: Capitalism and Schizophrenia*. Minneapolis: University of Minnesota Press.
Deleuze, Gilles. 1988. *Spinoza: Practical Philosophy*. San Francisco: City Lights Books.
Descartes, René. 1968. *Discourse on Method and the Meditations*. London: Penguin Books.

Haraway, Donna. 2008. *When Species Meet*. Minneapolis/London: University of Minnesota Press.
Goldstein, Kurt. 1995. *The Organism: A Holistic Approach to Biology Derived from Pathological Data in Man*. New York: Zero Books.
Grosz, Elisabeth. 2011. *Becoming Undone: Darwinian Reflections on Life, Politics, and Art*. Durham/London: Duke University Press.
Haas, Maximilian. 2018. *Tiere auf der Bühne. Eine ästhetische Ökologie der Performance*. Berlin: Kadmos Kulturverlag.
Heidegger, Martin. 1995. *The Fundamental Concepts of Metaphysics World, Finitude, Solitude*. Bloomington: Indiana University Press.
Heidegger, Martin. 1996. *Being and Time*. Albany: State University of New York Press.
Kant, Immanuel. 2006. *Anthropology from a Pragmatic Point of View*. Cambridge: Cambridge University Press.
Latour, Bruno. 1993. *We have never been modern*. Cambridge/Massachusetts: Harvard University Press.
Latour, Bruno. 2004. *Politics of Nature*. Cambridge/Massachusetts: Harvard University Press.
Latour, Bruno. 2005. *Reassembling the social*. Oxford: Oxford University Press.
Tsing, Anna. 2012. "Unruly Edges: Mushrooms as Companion Species (for Donna Haraway)." *Environmental Humanities* 1:141—154.
Uexküll, Jakob von. 1926. *Theoretical Biology* London and New York: K. Paul, Trench, Trubner & Co.
Uexküll, Jakob von. 2010. *A Foray into the Worlds of Animals and Humans*, Minneapolis/London: University of Minnesota Press.
Whitehead, Alfred North. 1919. *An Enquiry Concerning the Principles of Natural Knowledge*. Cambridge: Cambridge University Press.
Whitehead, Alfred North. 1920. *The Concept of Nature*. Cambridge: Cambridge University Press.
Whitehead, Alfred North. 1948. *Science and the Modern World*. New York: Pelican Mentor Books.
Whitehead, Alfred North. 1978. *Process and Reality: An Essay in Cosmology*, New York: The Free Press.

Latent Performances. *Conditions for Some Things to Happen*

Daniel Blanga Gubbay

The Baudouin/Boudewijn Experiment will take place in one of Belgium's most famous architectural landmarks: the Atomium. Built as the Belgian Pavilion for the 1958 World Fair in Brussels, the Atomium imitates the structure of an atom, and is made up of nine spheres connected by tubes. In the Brussels and European Conference Rooms, situated in the central sphere, a space will be set up to accommodate 100 people who are invited to spend twenty-four hours in the space, stepping out of their usual, productive lives for one day. From 10AM on 27 September until 10AM on 28 September 2001, the space will be closed to the outside world. Public access will be denied, and the inhabitants will be allowed to cease their normal activities. They will do nothing at all, and they will do it collectively. *The Baudouin/Boudewijn Experiment* will not be documented by means of film or video; the only recordings will be the memories of the participants, and these will be disseminated through the stories they may tell after the event. The experiment will thus be completely unscientific, since objectivity is not the aim. Rather, it will be a unique opportunity to experience together the possibilities of escape from one's daily routine, to participate in a unique event with an unclear outcome. (Hoffmann et al. 2001)

D. Blanga Gubbay (✉)
Kunstenfestivaldesarts, Brussels, Belgium
e-mail: daniel@kfda.be

© The Author(s), under exclusive license to Springer Nature Switzerland AG 2021
C. Stalpaert et al. (eds.), *Performance and Posthumanism*,
https://doi.org/10.1007/978-3-030-74745-9_4

The event took as its point of departure an incident during 1991 when the late King Baudouin of Belgium abdicated for a day to allow an abortion law of which he did not approve to be passed. (Bishop 2006)

In June 1957, Guy Debord wrote the *Report for the Construction of Situations* as one of the preparatory texts for the July 1957 conference at Cosio d'Arroscia, Italy, during which the Situationist International was founded. In this text Debord writes:

> Our central purpose is the construction of situations, that is, the concrete construction of temporary settings of life and their transformation into a higher, passionate nature. We must develop an intervention directed by the complicated factors of two great components in perpetual interaction: the material setting of life and the behaviors that it incites and that overturn it. (Debord 2002 [1957], 44)

While Debord is most known for his analysis of the spectacle, we can take advantage of the gap between the spectacle and the situation as an entry point to analyse the notion of performance in a post-human landscape. Indeed, in recent years the question of post-humanism frequently emerged in performance studies, a discipline strongly linked to the human body. In the wake of a desire to overcome the association of the post-human with the bodiless (as proposed among others by N. Katherine Hayles [1999] in her call for the preservation of embodiment), this article constructs a genealogy of the relation between post-humanism and performance, starting precisely from the legacy of the Situationist International and the possibility of unpacking the definition quoted above.

1—In a recent interview in Tourette Journal, Jakarta-based architect and philosopher Etienne Turpin articulated the relation between the architecture of a city—that which we might consider the *decor*—and the desire it might produce in its inhabitant: "I must admit that when I feel attracted by a real space it tends to be because it frames the possibility of an encounter, or the play of desire, but never just in and of itself. I can't understand or respond to architecture in isolation from the social relations and practices of liberty it makes possible" (Turpin 2014).

Turpin's impossibility to dissociate the decor from the behaviours it implies, stands here as a starting point to question their relation. At first sight, it would be easy to install a logical and temporal—and hence hierarchical—relation between the two elements: there is (first) a decor, which might (then) activate some encounters. However, Turpin's refusal to isolate architecture from social relation questions, whether it would ever be possible to consider the decor completely independent from behaviours: Is not the decor nothing but a sum of possible behaviours?

While pronouncing this question, the words echo with a resembling reflection that preceded this one on the relation between decor and action. They resonate with the words with which seventy years ago Jean-Paul Sartre, in the attempt to complicate the modern and Cartesian division of subject and object, was describing the landscape in front of him while writing. "Although we are surrounded by presences (this glass, this inkwell, this table, etc.), these presences are inapprehensible as such, for they release whatever it may be of them only after a gesture or an act projected by us – that is, in the future"(Sartre 1956, 509). Although we are surrounded by presences (this glass, this inkwell, this table, etc.), these presences are not understandable as such, since they explain nothing of themselves, if not for a gesture or a future action projected by us on them.

To put Sartre's analysis into practice, I might focus on the glass leaning on the table in front of me while writing this article. I might in a while bring it to my lips, or I might leave it on the table, as well as I might accidentally move it and break it by letting it fall on the ground. Suddenly, the glass before my eyes does not simply appear in its physical presence as a passive *object*, but rather in all the possible actions present and emerging from it. There is no logical or temporal hierarchy: the object and its materiality do not pre-exist the possibility of projecting an action onto it. The glass is filled already with possible actions, and through its form (which among others allows to contain a liquid) and material (the fragility of glass), it suggests with its presence all the actions that I will or will not do in a moment.

While moving my eyes from the glass to the rest of the room, a second question emerges. Are there actions that I might do, which are not embedded in the sum of objects in front of me? Suddenly I cannot think about doing something that is not already written in the objects in front of my eyes. To be under the illusion of doing something unexpected—to take the landscape off guard and feel again myself as the owner of my own actions—I could think of destroying the glass. But if this happens, it is simply because the action was already intrinsic to the glass, in its possibility to be destroyed. Hence I will again find myself as the one who can act among a basin of possibilities already held in potential by the world of objects. Again, with the purpose of escaping these objects that know everything about my future, I can stand and leave the room. But the action was already there in the form of the object-door ready to be crossed, and once outside I will just find myself in front of new objects, vessels of new actions. The world stands in front of me as a landscape which jealously preserves in itself the entirety of my possible actions in latency. The possible appears as a property of the landscape and, full of latent actions, the world in its entirety is vibrating in front of us.

Similarly, when entering Studio Morra in Naples in 1974, where Marina Abramović was presenting *Rhythm 0*, the participants might have had a clear picture of this latency of actions. In what became one of her most famous actions, Abramović stood naked and impassive for six hours while a set of objects, with which the spectator was invited to potentially act on her body, was displayed on the table in front of her. A brush, a knife, a pair of scissors, a gun and a bullet: each object was placed there, silently looking at us to reveal the possibility of future actions that might occur during the night, and that are already present in the landscape of the room—and in the object—in a state of latency.

The space of Studio Morra invites us to rethink the notion of performance present within it: if the term is usually strongly linked to the activity of the human being, suddenly the performances appear as inscribed, as potential, in the world, with a latent life independent from the bodies that will activate them. The space discloses the image of a non-human performativity, where the notion of *performance* is present in latency, namely the state of something ready to emerge.

2—Still, when going back to the definition of the situation, what is then the difference between a landscape and a situation? If the world is uninterruptedly filled in all its details with latent performances that might—or might not—be activated, what would justify the term proposed by Debord?

To understand the gap between the landscape and the situation, one might go back and re-read the description of the situation and the choice of Debord's words. By speaking of a "concrete construction of temporary settings of life", Debord marks a clear distance with the daily landscape of life. We are in front of a prepared space (that to which the word *décor* alludes), an albeit minimal artificial intervention that transforms the landscape; a reality in which the modification of some conditions—such as the adding of a single detail—changes the temperature of the landscape and incites a behaviour.

In *Rhythm 0*, we are in front of a prepared set of objects, and of a last element—a sign—left by the artist and that turns it into a situation (*Instructions/There are 72 objects on the table that one can use on me as desired/Performance/I am the object/During this period I take full responsibility*, [Abramović 1974]). Sometimes, the threshold between the landscape and the situation can be overstepped with the addition of a single element. One might imagine an abandoned piece of luggage in the landscape of a public space. The landscape is already filled by pre-given conditions, such as time, space and the political situation, but is only in the moment in which the luggage is abandoned, that the concrete construction of a temporary setting of life is achieved, inevitably inciting behaviours: someone might walk (?) faster; someone might point at it; someone might call the police; the whole range of latent performances foreseen by the situation.

We are, then, in front of a detonator that, once added, turns the landscape into a situation, and that once there, triggers and—according to the words of Debord—incites the activation of latent performance. If the situation is a constructed space, filled with previous narratives and hence alluding to a new possible latent performance, the detonator is the element that activates the allusion.

With the incitement—with the introduction of the allusion—Debord's situation reveals its future heritage in something that would later be explored through the experiences of Object-Oriented Philosophy (OOP): the allure (Harman 2005) and the agency of the object. More than a passive latency, the situation is defined by its active agency. There is nothing cold and aseptic in this constellation of objects; and if the landscape was already looking at us to suggest its potential, the situation actively vibrates full of narratives in front of us. While speaking about post-human performances in a situation, we are not simply in front of human performances kept in latency within the object (as in kept in custody until the only possible owner arrives), rather it is a performance of the very object, which incites to do.

For this reason Turpin was using, as a continuation of his sentence, the metaphor of BDSM (sadomasochistic sexual practices) to explain the interaction of buildings and behaviours: "The pleasure one feels, for example, as the restraint begins to tighten is certainly proper to the object (i.e. the type of restraint), but this property is indistinguishable from the capacity for pleasure that is unfolded in the mental and physical subspace made possible by the form of restraint. One responds to the object because it anticipates pain and pleasure, because it primes the body to receive its stimulation without reserve" (Turpin 2014).

3—Nevertheless, in front of the agency of the landscape and the triggering presence of the detonator a question suddenly emerges. In his writings, Debord creates an ideal opposition between the spectacle and the situation, but was not already the spectacle precisely that which incites behaviours? While determinately criticizing the spectacle and its use in capitalist modernity, Debord seems apparently to fall in the trap of not recalling some of its strategies: Is not the landscape of capitalist modernity precisely the one built on the allure of advertisement, the one that triggers people, seducing to do things? Was Debord not describing a society of spectacle—something that would exponentially increase in the following decades—in which humans are more and more pushed to buy, to say, to interact? While seeming to be an act of resistance, does the situation risk ending up living in a close proximity with the spectacle, in sharing its strategies?

While returning to the definition of Debord ("we must develop an intervention directed by the complicated factors of two great components in perpetual interaction: the material setting of life and the behaviours that it incites and that overturn it") a word ("overturn") might clarify this point. It resonates like a small crack between the two terms—the spectacle and the situation—that might, however, eventually spread a gap between them. If in the spectacle of modernity the material setting of life might incite some behaviours, in the situation the former does not simply incite the latter, but rather is overturned by them.

The situation is still characterized by an allure, by a voice. However, it is a voice that does not form intelligible words; it does not instruct. The latency of the situation is not simply a not-yet–activated instruction, but rather it is something that is saying without being said. The material setting of life incites some behaviours, which might in turn overturn the very setting in an unpredictable way. We are not in front of a chain of events, where one thing leads to the other in a linear way, but rather in a situation that opens a complex field of uncertainty. In the situation, the landscape appears in a different way, in a way in which it is not simply domesticated by goal or functionality. We stand in front of the landscape and for the first time we do not hear the voice we previously gave to it, but rather we hear its silent voice.

But this is only the silence before the storm: in this silence the situation capsizes like a ship in the storm, overthrown, reversed, overturned. Debord chooses a term, *bouleverser*, which is tautologically composed of *bouler* taken in the sense of *renverser*, *abattre* (to overturn, to tear down) and *verser* (to tip). Turning and turning. The situation overturns and is overturned. Everything becomes unpredictable; the instructions are lost, disclosing a field where one can act otherwise. The singularity of the instruction leaves the space to a multiplicity of possibilities. In the construction of the situation, the linear determinacy is hence abandoned to make way for a shapeless collection of uncertainties. We are not creating the condition for *something* to happen, rather for *some things* to emerge (for the distinction between the two terms, cfr. Spångberg 2015). The creation of something is overcome by the creation of a non-human space ready for the emergence of some unspecific things to happen. The situation invites to act, but it doesn't say how, suddenly revealing a world that is emptied of its instructions.

It is now clear how the shift between the spectacle and the situation is not so much on the level of the proximity, rather it is on that of its uncertainty. The situation might be defined as a space for indeterminacy, the opening of the unexpected, a space for potentiality.

4—In *Sensing the Virtual, Building the Insensible,* social and architecture theorist Brian Massumi uses some words that might be fundamental to continue the analysis of the uncertainty opened up by the situation: (abstract) spaces have to be "actively designed to integrate a measure of indeterminacy" (Massumi 1998, 17). In a world that has turned towards the hyper-controlled functionality of the spectacle, the possible can no longer be thought as an empty space, rather it is a space that has to be constructed with conditions for the unforeseen to happen. The possible itself is not an empty space, it is a space filled with conditions for some things to happen, designed with the chance for an "out-of-control". In a world that has turned towards hyper-control, the possibility of the unforeseen needs the greatest precision in its preparation: it has to be a prepared space, where the highest precision works for the greatest uncertainty to happen. This is the reason why Debord was speaking about *scores*, in the apparently oxymoronic idea of a programme for uncertainty.

For this reason, we can imagine two different performances in the situation, its preparation and its experience. We can understand the idea of preparation as form of performance from the perspective Karen Barad offers on the notion of performance, in a 2003 paper on *Posthuman Performativity*: "Performativity, properly construed, is not an invitation to turn everything (including material bodies) into words; on the contrary, performativity is precisely a contestation of the excessive power granted to language to determine what is real" (Barad 2003, 802). Barad concentrates on the score that would free the landscape from its pre-given certainty; that would free a world occupied by instructions, and points at the necessity of making room for uncertainty. The first performative act—the preparation of the situation—is an act of liberation of the world from its certainty to open an opaque pond of uncertainty; an act of rescue of the landscape from its anthropocentric utility (that would open up the posthuman perspective), where things appear in a new and unforeseen way. The world does not simply vibrate in front of us, but rather it vibrates in its un-functional materiality, freed from an anthropocentric imperialism.

The fundamental opposition of precision and uncertainty hence mirrors the two distinct moments and performances of the situation—its preparation and its experience—and allows to see emerging in them two distinct figures. On the one side, we have those (whom Debord calls *pre-situationists*) who constructed the situation, who accurately took into account its preparation, filling the space with latent performances; on the others these (whom we can call the *activators*) who will activate it, who will actualize the latent performances. On the one side, the preparation of the objects in Studio Morra, on the other the ones who will activate some of the latent performances. On the one side, she who leaves the luggage and goes away; on the other the ones who—ignoring it, running away, alerting others—will perform one of the latent performances embedded in the situation.

5—More than simply allowing to dissect the structure of the situation, the emergence of these distinct positions discloses a crucial question on the figure of the creator. If the contemporary ontology of performance art sees the artist as the centre of the performance, in the situation and its activation she might be already absent. She might resign from any active role, as Abramović did; she might conceive the performance as that which happens before the arrival of the audience; she might conceive performance to be no longer in action, rather as given in potential to the audience. She withdraws, knowing that only a withdrawal from agency leaves open the space for contingency, for the unforeseen. This is the sense of the words with which in a 2013 interview with Japan Time, Francis

Alÿs analyses the tension between the engagement in the pre-situation and disengagement in the moment of the situation:

> I am interested in seeing how a certain situation can develop with potential accidents. (...) I am very clear about the rules of the game, but once it's launched I don't intervene at all. Whatever development it takes is valid. Sometimes it leads to failure; sometimes it leads to a different outcome. I am not even a participant, I retrieve and I watch. (Alÿs in Jack 2013)

In the landscape of the situation, we are in front of a withdrawal of the creator; more than simply a physical absence (or a completely passive position) we witness a withdrawal from the position of the artist as the one who masters the situation; a withdrawal from certainty and genius— masculine categories linked to the notion of the artist. A withdrawal allows the landscape to speak for itself, to allude and allow the emergence of some things. This is the crucial use of post-humanism in latent performance, where post-humanism does not start with the end of the human being, but rather with a withdrawal of the human being from a dominant position.

Often the post-human has been simplistically associated with the absence of men. If the figure of the air-drone might appear here as an example, we can keep this figure above our heads as a crucial reminder of the necessity to bend our idea of post-humanism.

If the figure of the drone suggests an idea of post-humanism where the human being is remote, but her/his human agency still present, the model of the situation invites to reverse the position. Post-human performance might not always imply a performance without human beings, rather one in which the human agency disappears, to disclose a new contingency; it is the creation and abandonment of a space filled with unforeseen possible discourses.

In the last image of this abandonment of a prepared space, a final question emerges about the position of the artist in these post-human landscapes, and more particularly the threshold between responsibility and agency: how does this act of withdrawal from agency affect the (artistic) responsibility? And what is the relation here between agency and responsibility? In the situation, the artist withdraws from mastering the performance, but she nevertheless prepared the conditions for unforeseen performances to happen. This contingency is not to be seen as a non-affirmative space, of which an artist would not hold responsibility; the analysis of the situation suggests how the creator is fully responsible for opening the situation without having control over its outcome. In the same way, Carsten Höller is still responsible for *The Baudouin/Boudewijn Experiment: a deliberate, non-fatalistic, large-scale group experiment in deviation;* and eventually Baudouin himself was responsible for his withdrawal from agency. The act of withdrawing is a withdrawal from agency and not from responsibility. The performance of withdrawing consciously opens up a post-human empty space, and within this space filled with latent performance, some things will happen.

The Latent Performance Lexicon

While closing the article, I retreat and watch, leaving to the words the agency to allude. I am responsible for the writing, without mastering the performances that will be activated by it. Maybe the tool of a glossary at the end of the article might also no longer be perceived as a retrospective tool to grasp *something*, but rather as the material elements from where *some things*, yet unknown, will emerge; once I close the article, will they become the seeds of different reflections, better articles, unforeseen behaviours? Or maybe, once alone, they will follow the suggestion of Karen Barad, vibrating and alluding to the possibility to empty each word from its given meaning to eventually invent new ones.

Situation: a constructed space, filled with latent performances. A situation is composed both by given and constructed conditions (among which a detonator).

Detonator: the specific element that changes the temperature of the situation, that incites latent narratives, that alludes to possible performances, that suggests to be activated.

Activator: the one (or those) who will actualize a latent performance existing in the situation.

Pre-situationists: the one (or those) who constructs the conditions for a situation, by taking care of its preparation without taking care of its result.

References

Abramović, Marina. 1974. *Rhythm 0*. Naples: Galleria Studio Morra.
Barad, Karen. 2003. "Posthumanist Performativity: Toward an Understanding of How Matter Comes to Matter." *Signs* 28, no. 3 (Spring): 801–831.

Bishop, Claire. 2006. "The Social Turn: Collaboration and Its Discontent." *Artforum*, February: 179–85.
Debord, Guy. 2002 [1957]. "Report on the Construction of Situations and on the Terms of Organization and Action of the International Situationist Tendency." In *Guy Debord and the Situationist International: Texts and Documents*, edited by Thomas F. McDonough. Cambridge and London: MIT Press.
Harman, Graham. 2005. *Guerrilla Metaphysics: Phenomenology and the Carpentry of Things*. Chicago: Open Court.
Hayles, N. Katherine. 1999. *How We Became Posthuman*. Chicago: The University of Chicago Press.
Hoffmann, Jens, Carsten Höller, and Barbara Vanderlinden. 2001. "Roomade Presents." *Nettime*, 8 September. https://nettime.org/Lists-Archives/nettime-bold-0109/msg00168.html.
Jack, James. 2013. "Replaying people's actions with a twist." *Japan Time*, interview with Francis Alÿs, 9 May. http://www.japantimes.co.jp/culture/2013/05/09/arts/replaying-peoples-actions-with-a-twist/#.V-VhmqJ97-k.
Massumi, Brian. 1998. *Sensing the Virtual, Building the Insensible*. In *Hypersurface Architecture*, edited by Stephen Perrella. *Architectural Design* 68, no. 5/6 (May–June) 16–24
Sartre, Jean-Paul. 1956. *Being and Nothingness*. Translated by Hazel E. Barnes. Abingdon: Routledge.
Spångberg, Mårten. 2015. "Lecture Dance Conference." *MDT*, Stockholm, October. https://vimeo.com/151532717.
Turpin, Etienne. 2014. "What Do Cities Tell Us About Their Inhabitants' Desire?" *Tourette Journal* 1.1, WideOpen Turin.

Aesthetics of Mykorrhiza. The Practice of *Apparatus*

Stefanie Wenner

AGAINST ABOUTNESS

Imagine going to a theatre. You are invited to see a show, a critical examination of the miserability of the world. This night it is about climate change. Climate change as the source of all kinds of evil, not only the destruction of the world we can inhabit in the short or long term, but as the cause of wars, of mass migration, hunger and so on. The story is told effectively, you are immersed in the situation, you are confronted with being part of this system, of capitalism, you learn about companies and governments involved, playing their tricks with *gezinkte* cards. You

---

APPARATUS is the name under which Thorsten Eibeler and Stefanie Wenner develop their shared practice. The term is borrowed from Karen Barad, who coins it to formulate her agential realistic philosophy. We agree with Barad 's notion of the apparatus in which human and non-human bodies intra-actively realize a situation. For a definition of the term apparatus in Barad please check: Barad, Karen. *Meeting the Universe Halfway. Quantum Physics and the Entanglement of Matter and Meaning*. For an overview of apparatus activities please check www.apparatus-berlin.de.

S. Wenner (✉)
Hochschule für Bildende Kunst Dresden, Dresden, Germany

© The Author(s), under exclusive license to Springer Nature Switzerland AG 2021
C. Stalpaert et al. (eds.), *Performance and Posthumanism*,
https://doi.org/10.1007/978-3-030-74745-9_5

are shocked and fall silent. After the show, the evening continues with other audience members, who drink and talk about what is going wrong in the world. While going home, you consider starting to avoid plastic and consuming products of the companies mentioned as global players in the monopoly of climate change. When the next day you go to work, you go by bike, since you have become eco-conscious. In Summer, and maybe in Winter too, you board a plane to fly to the beach. You buy your clothes in normal stores. You never look where they were produced, which ways they took to get to you. Standing in the supermarket, every once in a while you remember this show you saw, and then you decide against one product or for another for ecological reasons. You think this really had an impact. This was political theatre. You never ask yourself: how did they do it? How was this show produced? How did this come together? How did it reach my town, how does the production tour?

In speaking, we frequently say something about something or about somebody. This does not seem to be problematic at all. We speak about the weather, knowing very well that speaking about the weather is safe ground. There is not much to discuss, when we are complaining about too much rain or not enough rain. Or so it seemed. It seemed to be the perfect topic to speak about when you did not have a lot to talk about. What we were saying when we were talking about the weather, was that there was not a lot we shared with the people we communicated with, or that we were avoiding problematic fields. So besides being a container for the content about weather, this conversation would in itself be understandable in a completely different way. Stephen Yablo wrote a whole book about aboutness (2014), discussing different levels of truth dimensions in language that talks about something. According to him, it is evident and understood in everyday language, that talking about something is not *doing* what one is talking about. For example, if I am talking about enlightenment, I might not at all be enlightened. Or, if I am talking about yoga, I might never have practised yoga, so my talking about yoga will not be yoga itself. Still, what I say about yoga might be applicable or even be true. For example, I might say that Patanjali was a scholar from India and the author of Yogasutra. The difficulties begin right here, as there are many legends around Patanjali. Adding to the obvious criteria of difference between speaking about something and the object of the talk, we have to add the criterion of truth. Yablo uses the example of his daughter, who complained he never bought her ice cream. But when the day before, they did go to have ice cream together, this did not count from the perspective of the daughter, as it was her birthday.

We now seem to be very far away from the theatre event about climate change that was mentioned in the beginning. Quite obviously, books are about topics, just like portraits are of people, says Yablo in the opening chapter of his book: "Aboutness is the relation that meaningful items bear to whatever it is that they are in or of, or that they adress or concern" (2014, 1). Yablo is a philosopher of language in the tradition of Clemens Brentano, but he also refers to Edmund Husserl and the materialists, who saw aboutness in natural regularities, as well as Rudolf Carnap, who thought about physical objects and their identity over time (1). *Aboutness* in philosophy today seeks to close the gap between what is considered truth and partial truth. There is a relation here that can be discussed using the article "Truth about Jones" by Joseph Ullian and Nelson Goodman, in which it is argued that a blunt lie reveals the truth about the liar (1977, [333]). Language is not as simple and neither is truth. A piece about climate change might tell a completely different story than it seeks to. That could maybe be considered *the truth about* documentary theatre.

Theatre is about aboutness. That is, European theatre in general is about aboutness. As we saw, aboutness in philosophy is a notion defining the quality of being about something. It is used in philosophy of language to avoid the phenomenological notion of intentionality and the notion of the subject, which is considered imprecise. Another example: a close connection exists between the word *autism* and what it is about. Words like *an*, or *or* have less aboutness. Metaphors have a very specific kind of aboutness frequently used in theatre. Aboutness in theatre is used in order to create what generally is referred to as political theatre. Climate change, the genocide in Rwanda, Donald Trump, the Middle East, you name it, anything that a show can be about will be staged in a critical approach. Ten years ago Pieter de Buysser and Jacob Wren were discussing critique as the sofa cushion of the bourgeoisie in their "Anthology of Optimism", which premiered at Kunstenfestivaldesarts in May 2009. Wren and de Buysser talk about people going to a politically critical show in a theatre nearby, they are shocked and then have a nice glass of red wine and go to sleep. This is affirmative action; others are much worse off than we are, so let's continue, keep going, hoping to stay on top. *Aboutness* thus could be described as a reactionary way to keep the system going through implementing not aesthetic experiences of otherness, potentiality and imagination, but by documenting the horror of the real. Realism is being used here as a static reference that leaves no option for (imagining or creating) other realities.

My use of the term aboutness is not very specifically defined in this essay; I am merely using it to describe a way to produce narratives that are regarded as relevant for contemporary audiences. The words *contemporary* and *audience* in the previous sentence refer to notions that are highly problematic, but still in use, especially in Germany, where I live and work. They are problematic from a decolonizing and a class perspective in a rather heterogeneous society. The term *contemporary* has been critically discussed as it frequently refers to art practices rooted in Europe, prolonging the long history of neglecting to realize that we are living in one world, with different aesthetics, practices and expectations confronting art and theatre.[1] The term *audience* has been critically discussed because of its narrowness, as the threshold to enter the field of art is rather high and whether or not you are able to enter that field depends on social class, among others factors. Still, the quest for artists is frequently to find a topic that would be regarded as worthwhile for a contemporary audience and thus worthwhile giving money to. The domination of the system of state and city theatres in Germany with its hegemony of interpretation of (repertoire) texts is accompanied by the precarious system of independent theatre and its production places that are dependent on funding granted by juries who—broadly speaking—grant money to productions with relevant topics, including a high sense of aboutness.

Climate change definitely is such a topic, but while there is an ethics of paying at least minimum wages even in the theatre scene in Germany, there is no such thing when it comes to practising what you preach on stage. You can tell the story of climate change, be highly successful with it and tour the world, and not even come close to one thought about the materials being used, the waste being produced, not to mention sustainability. Sustainability itself has a *deus ex machina*-like story that I cannot go into detail about here, but I am not quite convinced that it is the perfect term to describe what I am aiming for. Not only because the state and city theatres in Germany with their restrictions and fire protection necessities already create so many obstacles for any kind of aesthetics that are not developed strictly from within the frame of the architecture of this institution, and we do not need more guidelines to prohibit aesthetical experiments, but less. Not only because the term "sustainability" was invented in economic contexts of harvesting trees in forests, which would be a way to work more effectively for more profit, again taking less care of the environment that is destroyed by this. Not only because the discourses of ecology and sustainability are also part of the history of racism and colonialism and thus need to be reviewed in not only a deconstructive, but also a decolonizing perspective.[2] Each of these points alone discredits this fashionable term, but that is not my reason to dismiss it. My reason is purely and simply an aesthetic one.

My argument in the following will develop an aesthetic against aboutness. I am convinced that aesthetics are highly underestimated in contemporary theatre practices in Europe, and that they as well pretend to be a universal category introducing colonial structures into the field of the arts in the twenty-first century. The way theatre is frequently used as a prolongation of journalism or documentation is not merely a pragmatic choice nor a clear decision towards the delimitation of theatre, but rather a decision against aesthetics and art. I am not going to defend the old bookish idea of the art of theatre as the art of interpreting texts, but I am analysing a tendency against an aesthetics in contemporary [sic!] theatre practices, that feed themselves into the realm of enlightenment. I am following Silvia Federici and her analysis of enlightenment as a factor in the primitive accumulation as it was described by Karl Marx (Federici 2004). This does include documentary theatre using performance and telling a story about, for example, a traumatizing situation on stage that is or is not, in a traditional understanding, text-based. The success of these pieces is using *aboutness* in accordance with the system rather than creating collective aesthetic experiences. But it is also telling a truth about themselves, which goes beyond the actually told story.

Against aboutness and sustainability, I am coining the aesthetics of Mycorrhiza, which we have been working on in the different endeavours of the *apparatus* project launched so far (Fig. 1).

Mycorrhiza: An Apparatus

Theatre in Europe today can easily be regarded as an apparatus. An etymology of the word apparatus, dating back to the 1620s, tells us that it was "a collection of tools, utensils, etc. adapted as a means to some end", from the Latin noun *apparatus*: "tools, implements, equipment; preparation, a preparing", formed by the past participle stem of apparare, "prepare", from ad, "to" + parare, "make ready".[3] By theatre I mean not only the building located in the city, but a specific art form that is closely

Fig. 1 *Mykhorriza, an apparatus*, by Stefanie Wenner and Thorsten Eibeler (© Apparatus)

related to *theoria*, which is even older than philosophy and has to do with a specific kind of gaze on rituals.

Theatre still closely links itself to the tool-side mechanical idea of apparatus instead of following the intra-active agential-realistic perspective on "apparatus" as a world-making machine, as it was defined by Karen Barad (2007). While the field of aesthetics, since the early twentieth century, discusses the dissolution of the limitations of the arts, including theatre, genres remain discrete in their economies and distribution of resources. Funding will mostly be directed towards either theatre or visual arts and transgressions create all kinds of resistance from critics and audiences. The institutional apparatus of theatre nourishes anthropocentrism. European theatre traditions have been using the nature/culture divide for their narratives. Theatre is about aboutness and aboutness is about humans. The fabulations in theatre are tightly connected to the human psyche. Since its European beginning in Ancient Greece, theatre has historically been indebted in various ways to political interest. German theatre history is linked to the becoming of a nation state. Theatre was used here to create narratives that attract bourgeois audiences, actors were supposed to speak "High German" in order to help create one language for one nation. Territorializations as well as colonizations have been realized by means of theatre. We are just at the beginning of the process of decolonizing this institution. Leaving the idea of the genius artist/director behind has proven to be less easy than some would have expected. Even if the visual arts Berlin Biennial 2018 chose "We Don't Need Another Hero" as its title, "heroes" tend to be reconstructed as main figures over and over again. So the question remains as to how we can leave these structures behind and follow the path that Donna Haraway proposed for science, which she defined as better ways of depicting reality (1985).To ask for sustainability will not create other ways of world-making in theatre. And creating other ways of world-making is exactly what Thorsten Eibeler and I started out to do with *apparatus*,[4] beginning with "Mykorrhiza: An apparatus", in 2014.

We were looking for ways not to feed into the market of theatre and performance or dance as it has been established in the independent scene over the last two decades. We wanted to curate from the side, so to speak, taking what in festivals usually remains unseen to be the centre: the process, materiality, communication, growth, but also the wasting, loss and failures. The focus was not to create a glossy surface conveying whatever kind of content, but searching for modes of making process accessible not only for those who are sharing it. If form and content are performatively and intra-actively one, and need to be one, how can that be realized? If theatre is problematic as it is staying within the frame of representation and representation is a source of so many problems, how can this be resolved? Using the term *apparatus* in order to describe what we were setting up, rather than calling it a lab or a workshop, was aiming to create awareness of the world-making part of any kind of artistic process, ours included. Using the notion of apparatus also aimed to recognize our being part of the material world rather than standing opposed to it in a distanced, describing position. It is less a reflection on the machine quality of theatre-making or on our time in general, than the necessity to open our perception to what we can do, what we are constantly doing, being actants in this world that we are co-creating.

We decided to invite mushrooms into the space, as they seemed to be masters of a theatre of illusion, with their small fruiting bodies, hiding a big body that has so much impact. Mushrooms will save the world. Even if we are facing the end of the world as we know it, they will be fine. After centuries of not knowing much about these organisms that are neither plants nor animals, consisting mostly of the same material as the shell of turtles, quinine, which makes them rather hard to digest by humans, the research on mushrooms is flourishing. To avoid chemical detergents, spores are used in washing powders to clean our clothes without creating new chemical waste. There are mushrooms that can digest plastic. They are edible, so I hear. Mushrooms are used to clean beaches that were flooded by oil. Mushrooms contain important nutrients for humans. And they made life on earth possible. Long before the Internet, a "network" between plants and mushrooms developed, which is called mycorrhiza, which not only transfers nutrients, but also exchanges valid information. Only through mycorrhiza was it possible to grow plants on the land. Mycorrhiza is frequently referred to as *Wood Wide Web*. While the metaphorization in technological terms seems to be rather twenty-first century and discussable, the fact remains that the entanglement between mushrooms and trees reaches far. So far as to make it seem a good idea to grow a *Great Green Wall* assisted by mycorrhiza in the Sahel Zone. The trees would not survive without mycorrhiza in the desert. Thus mycorrhiza is used in order to help build a wall of trees against the expansion of the Sahara. We could even say that plants are masters of the theatre of illusion. They create an impressive, visible surface, they are immobile and seem not to be able to defend themselves. But the opposite is the case. They are not only passively receptive, but completely active. Firmly rooted, they are nonetheless in the position to communicate with one another. Through a cluster of underground roots and fungal fibres, plants connect with one another, communicating in a highly efficient way. For instance, acacias can warn each other about predators such as antelopes within minutes; they even caused the death of 3000 antelopes in South Africa that had eaten from them, after sending out the poisonous substance that the plants use to protect themselves. For some time now it has been known that plants communicate through clicking sounds—the science of how the so-called *Wood Wide Web* works is, however, relatively young. Plants cannot only inform one another through their roots, they also organize their defence and support their relatives through intensive networks of fungal threads—mycorrhiza. Botanists and ecologists are currently investigating how plants exchange important information through the fungi at their roots. It is debatable as to whether one can speak of intelligent behaviour, but there is no dispute that the alliances between plants and fungi are targeted and goal-oriented.

Looking for modes of exchange beyond humans, mycorrhiza was to be our partner in creating a research-based collaborative situation between human and non-human bodies in a shared space over a period of seven weeks in the Heizhaus at Uferstudios Berlin in the Summer of 2014. We received funding and invited artists to be residents. Thorsten Eibeler, my partner in apparatus and in life, developed a set-up for the space; we started to collaborate with Colin Hacklander and Farahnaz Hatam of NK, formerly a project space for experimental music in Berlin Neukölln, for the curation of experimental music. All went well, but mycorrhizal mushrooms cannot be cultivated. They cannot be harvested; they can only be foraged and found. They cannot be used in an installation of whatever sort, unless the installation takes place in the forest and the places they live in. All experiments so far to cultivate truffles, for example, have failed. Since the apparatus was not possible with mycorrhizal mushrooms, we invited cultivatable mushrooms such as oyster mushrooms into the space. One part of being a resident artist in the space was to take care of the mushrooms. It was hot, they needed a lot of water, and you had to harvest them regularly. There was a strong smell in the room, some considered it unbearable. Other elements in the set-up were exercise balls, white styro cubes and hay to sit on, cupboards in which the mushrooms grew, a laboratory tent in which the cultivation of mushrooms was practised, baby pine trees in glass frames containing earth in which you could see the growing net of mycorrhiza. Outside was the *Spores Bar*, offering vegan meals and drinks. The curatorial aim was to co-create a robust but porous environment of interweaving entangling practices between species. Besides inviting artists and musicians, mushrooms and plants, we developed a loose organisation of open house situations that would be hosted by the residing artists. Annika

Tudeer, Kate McIntosh, cobratheater.cobra, Quast & Knoblich, Hacklander/Hatam and Orthographe were inviting each other and the public to share their process.[5] There was always free admission. Thorsten Eibeler invited the action *Himmelfahrt*, including families and kids. There were huge events with a lot of guests, like the situation cobratheater.cobra created for the neighbourhood, with a bouncing castle, a dinner cooked of leftovers, performances and a party. And there were smaller interventions like the one by Kate McIntosh who invited Eva Meyer-Keller to work together and both of them told us about their experience. It was Kate who gave the hint for the follow-up apparatus and a core idea of what was special about the apparatus in general; you enter and you are never in an empty studio, like a black box with a theatre machine to serve you, or a white cube challenging your needs. You are immediately confronted with vibrant matter, to quote Jane Bennett, leftovers of artists and others, smell and sound of other beings and space, space being one body just as the other bodies. Annika Tudeer gave us the gift of a vivid and even close to violent discussion on questions of collectivity and work, economy and commons hosted by Kai van Eikels and led between Florian Feigl, Ilia Papatheodorou of She She Pop and many more. Orthographe invited kids into a workshop to create a show in their *Camera Obscura*.

This first *apparatus*, as we since then have been calling the format we developed including a set space, invited artists and hosted situations, was documented only with photographs; there was no video of the discussion, there were no sound files. The space was its own very temporary performing archive, an apparatus limited in time. Apparatus then not only seemed to be the right term to borrow from Karen Barad for this situation, but for our project in the larger frame of the field of performing arts as well. Barad speaks about apparatus in reference to Niels Bohr (2007, 19–30), and I am paraphrasing her in the following. Apparatus, in context of the situation of the laboratory, is not only the set-up in a clean space, the machines and so on, it is broadly speaking anything that creates the situation the experiment takes place in: the place in the world, a city, a university, the weather of the day, the human beings setting up the experiment, the exact materials that are involved. All is matter and all matters. Nature is not timeless, it has a history. While language was treated scientifically from all kinds of sides in the twentieth century, matter was neglected; but if you look into matter, matter is not passive, but active, there is tension and motion going on. Barad leaves the dualism of subject and object behind and speaks of agential realism and intra-action as a new way to phrase causality. Apparatuses thus are not mere instruments to observe something, but practices to create new borders in order to materialize specific material (re)configurations of the world. And this is exactly what we set out to achieve with *apparatus*: not interpreting the world, but creating new configurations of it. And we were taking cues by mycorrhiza to do so. Very special was the series of musical Thursdays curated by Hacklander and Hatam. Visiting the space at the beginning of the development of the project we realized it had an amazing reverb and that porosity of the space was mostly experienced through sound. Cars coming and going, people passing by talking, dogs barking, airplanes starting and landing. Standing in the Heizhaus, it was all there at once. So it was not only a reference to John Cage being a mycologist to invite musicians into the space, it was a level of mycorrhizal interacting that we were trying to invite. With remarkable results. The musical Thursdays developed an own audience, coming in especially for this, but then starting to join for other occasions as well. Musicians used the whole space, creating sound with and next to everything that was there, creating resonance and amplifying what was there. Hacklander and Hatam had mostly curated accoustic sound artists, who delicately treated the apparatus with their means and enriched the process largely (Fig. 2).

Mycorrhiza: An Aesthetic Following Mushrooms

Anna L. Tsing, professor of anthropology at the University of California, Santa Cruz, and Niels Bohr Professor at Aarhus University in Denmark, where she co-directs the Aarhus University Research on the Anthropocene (AURA), researched one of the world's most sought-after fungi, Matsutake, the most valuable mushroom in the world. In "The Mushroom At The End Of The World" (Tsing 2015), she presents her investigation into the relation between capitalist destruction and collaborative survival within multispecies landscapes. Her research is an eye-opener in many ways. She begins with a critical approach towards the idea of nature planted by enlightenment in Europa, with an economic interest, as being a "backdrop and a resource for the moral intentionality of Man, which could tame and master Nature" (vii). This misunderstanding of an exceptionalist position of Man, opposing nature, created the vast destruction of the world we live in, now referred to as the Anthropocene. The anthropocene, claims Tsing, is thus a misleading term, since its timeline does not begin with our species, "but rather with the advent

Fig. 2 *Mykhorriza, an apparatus*, by Stefanie Wenner and Thorsten Eibeler (© Apparatus)

of modern capitalism, which has directed long-distance destruction of landscapes and ecologies" (19).Jason W. Moore claimed it would make more sense to speak of the Capitalocene, since capitalism, with its strong belief and reliance on growth and progress, created the consequences now discussed under the term Anthropocene (2015).

Aesthetics acknowledging that we are living under the condition of the Anthropocene are confronted with distinct necessities. *Aboutness* in the arts may use a moral club to point out some disasters far away. It is beating the drum of disasters worldwide, or it may point out how somebody nearby is creating a political problem. But this showing of something is mostly done in such a way that it creates other problems. The credibility of the arts suffers if we are not practising what we preach. If relational aesthetics focused on the communal aspect and enforcing exchange, mycorrhizal aesthetics focuses on what we share: matter. Matter matters as we are all matter and form matter intra-actively. If artists become part of the jet set and travel the world, however precarious, we still need to start a discussion about what that does. Nobody wants more restrictions in art-making, but if we take the notion of performativity seriously, we need to face what we create through our performative actions. This is just the beginning, but there are thinkers and terms which can help to start making art in a different way.

Donna Haraway, for example, prefers not to use the term Anthropocene, but coined her own notion, which is the *Chthulucene*, another neologism. Haraway borrows one part of the term from the name of a spider, Pimoa cthulhu, using her web in order to envision interweaving life as opposed to the hierarchy we are used to referring to, seeing man as the crown of creation. And she borrows the term *hózhó* from Navajo language, which translates as peace, harmony or balance. Symbiosis between humans and their technology is compared to interspecies symbiosis in Haraway's writing. There is no return to nature, as there is always only ways to speak and to interweave in order to co-create entangled life (Haraway 2016, 31, 76).

Aboutness, as a key function of the age of representation, creates interpretations of the world. To talk about something is also to create that something. This is one of the main findings of twentieth-century theory in performance, following Austin and others. According to Barad and Haraway, however, there is more than this. There is action in matter and this is not created by humans speaking about it. There is entanglement, intra-action and co-creation, you name it, the world is not a clean room in which we enter covered in plastic. We all are the world. The world is us. This is also what Anna L. Tsing focuses on in her book: "This book argues that staying alive – for every species – requires livable collaborations. Collaboration means working across difference, which leads to contamination. Without collaborations, we all die" (Tsing 2015, 28). It is no use to keep phantasizing about the border between humans and other bodies in the world. In fact, I would even consider it a dangerous fetishization of an outdated worldview. We are part of the *Milieu* that is not surrounding us, but is deeply intra-actively rooted in our bodies. As co-creators of that Milieu, our perspective needs to shift from users to collaborators, from spectators to actants. It is not the earth that is in a precarious situation, we are. "The problem of precarious survival helps us see what is wrong. Precarity is a state of acknowledgement of our vulnerability to others. In order to survive, we need help, and help is always the service of another, with or without intent" (Tsing 29). Mycorrhiza is not the only example of that kind of help, with or without intent, but it is a strong one. One which can give us cues into ways of *worlding* in times of trouble—which is the notion introduced by Donna Haraway in "Staying with the trouble". Mycorrhizal aesthetics as I am developing it here is creating better depictions of reality and is staying with the trouble. We have been following this development in our works *Apparatus, Mykorrhiza, Dirt* and *Pharmakos/n*, that were inspired by fungal interweavings with plants, from the beginning, but in the following years, our return to the format of *apparatus* was enriched with further information. Our aim has been to use a rather broad idea of theatre to establish *fabulations*— another term by Haraway—of interspecies interaction and dependency. As Anna Tsing puts it, species interdependence is a well-known fact, except when it comes to humans:

> Human exceptionalism blinds us. Science has inherited stories about human mastery from the great monotheistic religions. (…) The idea of human nature has been given over to social conservatives and sociobiologists, who use assumptions of human constancy and autonomy to endorse the most autocratic and militaristic ideologies. What if we imagined a human nature that shifted historically together with varied webs of interspecies dependence? (Tsing 2012, 144)

We tend to see human actions of subjects in a frame of independently created matters of free choice. In contrast to the general idea of domestication, it is not a one-way road. Grains have been domesticated and societies stopped their nomadic life as foragers of cereals and other nutrients, starting to plant fields in order to harvest them in the end. But a field needs a lot of caretaking and humans taking care of cereals necessarily change their lives in order to do so. According to Tsing, cultivation costs more human labour than foraging (2012, 40). However, what Anna Tsing is explaining about cereals not primarily and only having been domesticated by humans, but also having domesticated humans themselves, is something that can also be said about theatre. Nation states have an interest in cultivation and domestication of any sort; the cultivation of grains as well as the cultivation of theatre and art in the spirit of domestication of humans themselves. The theatres that were built in Germany two hundred years ago formed an apparatus of human and non-human actants. There are contracts involved, buildings that need to be maintained, labour that is keeping this system intact and that cultivates any kind of theatrical artistic production. The same can be said about the system of the visual art world, with its museums, galleries and auctions. Bodies at work, a working body. This workforce is evaluated in productive terms, in terms of effectiveness and influence. This system is hiding perfectly well what it is doing. It is, as any medium, about itself and nothing else. And this aboutness tells us the story of destruction, consumption and wasting in order to create a perfect image, a non-troublesome surface, whose highest aim is domestication. Domestication has been described for animals as a process of taming that makes them usable for human profit and unfit to survive in the wild. The dependency thus developed is again not a one-way road, but leads both ways. Conventional theatre is domesticated by the law with all the safety rules that force the theatre of the *as if* to work with unburnable material in order to create a perfectly safe environment to tell the next story about the destruction of the environment. Artists and theatre makers have been historically constructed as a counterpart of society. The problematics of this conception of theatre when it comes to their productivity have been widely discussed. Theatre on markets used to be nomadic and anarchic until it was domesticated into theatre houses in the cities, which created their own narrative. Theatre about humans was creating that human being as a bourgeois individual, a process that was made use of at the time. The story about climate change that is told on stage follows a perfectly wrong narrative, as the environment is not around us, but in our bodies, we are deeply entangled and interdependent. A deeply wrong narrative such as this domestication is realized by using material that is toxic. And as aboutness is about aboutness, this theatre is toxic, as it does not change itself. No camouflage will be able to last so long as to prevent the interdependency to find ways to finally make itself visible in our bodies.

Mycorrhizal aesthetics work along the cracks of this system and invite dependency, interdependency, entanglement and failure. Mycorrhizal aesthetics invite co-creation and the mess of noise. However, human players in the system tend to want themselves domesticated in it for success. Visibility is an important goal in a system of rotating artists, importing and exporting them all over the world as a basis to make a living. That was one major experience of failure we experienced, which is one reason for leaving the curatorial score behind, as *apparatus*' goal is not to help artists start their careers, but rather shift ideas about art-making itself. A misunderstanding was that we were providing a platform for emerging artist to develop, merely using New Materialism as a theme. But we were looking for different ways of working together, not being leaders of a pack. Following again the cues of mushrooms: mycorrhiza finds its paths, it does not have a third communicator between plants and fungi, it is shared tissue of mycelium, which is the main part of the mushroom, and roots. At the moment of writing this, Autumn 2018, after realizing three apparatuses (*Mykorrhiza, DRECK, Pharmakos/n*) in three years, *apparatus* is currently in a phase of transition, foraging in a nomadic form, with no set goal, no house, no company. After the format of apparatus, *apparatus* will find a new form, most likely in ferment, still following the spirit of mycelium, mushroom, mycorrhiza and spores. Our new series will then be launched as *FERMENT* in the beginning of 2019.

A sci-fi fungus—travelling between fiction and seeking to become reality—might guide the way. *Prototaxites Stellaviatori* is a fungus that has a short but intense career, having featured in Star Trek Discovery. It is used for transport that should better not be called that way. It is fast and it works in ways that are hard to describe. Transport is realized through the mycelium, that is spread in spores all over the universe. The task is to find a way into the mycelium in order to use it to get somewhere else. May the spores be with all of us, always!

Notes

1. *Kampnagel* in Hamburg dedicated a whole festival around this question, that has been critically discussed in dance, performance and also visual arts: http://www.kampnagel.de/we-dont-contemporary/.
2. Highly informative in this respect is Anker, Peder. *Imperial Ecology. Environmental Order in the British Empire, 1895–1945.*
3. https://www.etymonline.com/word/apparatus, last accessed 26/5/2020.
4. For detailed information and an archive of our apparatus please check www.apparatus-berlin.de.
5. The program and our blog of Mykorrhiza: Ein Apparat can be found online here: http://apparatus-berlin.de/en/mykorrhiza-ein-apparat/.

References

Anker, Peder. 2001. *Imperial Ecology. Environmental Order in the British Empire, 1895–1945.* Cambridge, MA: Harvard University Press.
Barad, Karen. 2007. *Meeting the Universe Halfway. Quantum Physics and the Entanglement of Matter and Meaning.* Durham and London: Duke University Press.
Federici, Silvia. 2004. *Caliban and the Witch: Women, the Body and Primitive Accumulation.* London: Autonomedia.

Haraway, Donna. 1985. "A Cyborg Manifesto: Science, Technology, and Socialist-Feminism in the Late Twentieth Century." *Simians, Cyborgs and Women: The Reinvention of Nature*. New York: Routledge, 1991.
Haraway, Donna. 2016. *Staying with the Trouble: Making Kin in the Chthulucene*. Durham: Duke University Press.
Moore, Jason W. 2015. *Capitalism in the Web of Life. Ecology and the Accumulation of Capital*. London: Verso Books.
Tsing, Anna Lowenhaupt. 2012. "Unruly Edges: Mushrooms as Companion Species." *Environmental Humanities* 1: 141–154
Tsing, Anna Lowenhaupt. 2015. *The Mushroom at the End of the World. On the Possibility of Life in Capitalist Ruins*. Princeton University Press.
Ullian, Joseph and Nelson Goodman. 1977. "Truth about Jones." *The Journal of Philosophy*, 74, no. 6: 317–338.
Yablo, Stephan. 2014. *Aboutness*. Princeton and Oxford: Princeton University Press.

On Composite Bodies and New Media Dramaturgy

Peter Eckersall and Kris Verdonck

INTRODUCTION

This dialogue between the artist and performance maker Kris Verdonck and performance scholar Peter Eckersall aims to explore the dramaturgical significance in Verdonck's work of the invention of composite bodies, prototypes and machinic objects. Verdonck's particular constellation of objects and performers is often termed as "figures" and "actors" (Eckersall 2012; van Kerkhoven and Nuyens 2012; van Baarle 2015) that are agents to express poetic sensibilities and an uncanny politics that questions our existential relationships and our sense of place in the world. As Eckersall phrases in this conversation, Verdonck's work aims to "ask what…objects and machines can tell us about what they do". How are they organized, and what clarity or discipline of agency or effect might arise in encountering his installations and performances?

P. Eckersall (✉)
The Graduate Center, City University of New York, New York, NY, USA
e-mail: peckersall@gc.cuny.edu

K. Verdonck
A Two Dogs Company, Brussels, Belgium
e-mail: kris@atdc.be

With reference to Maurizio Lazzarato, Eckersall and Verdonck consider if composite bodies are machines for desiring; are they "the assemblage of human and non-human flows, [made] from a multiplicity of social and technical machines" (2014, 51)? If so, what is the significance of this for artistic practice and for what Lazzarato terms "the production of subjectivity" (2014, 51)? The following conversation is an extended version of the conversation, beginning at the *Does It Matter? | Composite Bodies and Posthuman Prototypes in Contemporary Performing Arts* conference (Ghent University, 17–19 March 2015) and continuing via Skype, recorded on 29 February 2016.

Eckersall: The conference *Does It Matter? | Composite Bodies and Posthuman Prototypes in Contemporary Performing Arts* invited us to consider a number of questions around the idea of making connections between humans and non-human forms. Discussion about these composite bodies is perhaps giving us an understanding of a new way of being: to consider the possibilities of how our subjectivity and our personhood have been changed because of the presence of objects in our lives and of machines. In the title of the conference, there is an astute wordplay on the term "matter" pointing to the materiality of things and the consequences of this. The theme is playing on the meaning of the question of something mattering as in being an ethical or political question about composite forms, from science, technology and the animal world, as well as art and politics. And then the meaning of matter in relation to the conference is also a focus on material matter, the theory of vibrancy associated with Jane Bennett (2010). These discussions around objecthood and questions of material culture are strongly expressed in visual and performing arts.

Another theme at the conference was a concern to bring a certain kind of focus on historical materialism back into the conversation and how this might happen. What is historical materialism in relation to understanding the power dynamics in the twenty-first century? What does this look like? Thinking about your work: what objects and machines can tell us about what they do and, to think a little bit more broadly, how might that relate to the construction of the social world, or the material world, or the human and non-human world. Can we also think about how that changes our understanding of subjectivity, humankind, social development and so forth?

These are some prefacing remarks to start our conversation.

More concretely, I could refer to a comment of yours in relation to one of your earlier works, *BOX* (2005), where you stated that humankind has become a stranger to its own environment.

Verdonck: First of all, I'm starting to think that maybe the whole of my work is about this comment. We're getting more and more estranged. And in a very broad sense there are not so many animals we know that relate to their own environment as much as our species does. We create environments that are literally dangerous for ourselves. And we create them because we have the technical means to do so. We invent tools that are stronger than our hands and things that go faster and produce more energy, that are capable of a whole spectrum of things that we would love to do but that we cannot. So we invent machines, such as cars, to do that kind of work for us. The dark side of this is that they *are* stronger and faster and produce more energy than we can do on, for example, our bicycle. And so, we deal immediately with something that is dangerous for our own health and our own environment, because we sculpt our environments by these machines, using these tools. But then at the same time, we become more responsible for this environment because we have to live in it. And there we are at last, in this constant dilemma. Probably the best example of an invention in that sense is the atomic bomb.

Did we have to invent this or that particular machine or application, yes or no? We cannot say, apparently. So we invent it anyway and then we just see the results of our invention. Sometimes it's very difficult for us to see in the long-term. Midterm is also difficult. Very short-term, we have a slight idea. I think that with these inventions, it's very difficult for us to predict the results. So, we suffer by our own inventions. And it is these inventions that have a huge influence on the whole planet at this moment.

We are also estranged from our own environment on a practical, everyday level. For example, somehow we think bread is still a natural product, but it hasn't been that 'natural' for a long time. Apart from the grains, bread contains chemical dough conditioners, added artificial flavouring, and even chemical bleach. Thus we get strange kinds of diseases and we have to invent new machines to clean this up. For example, patients suffering from cancer die of the chemotherapy, not of the cancer they have. However, at this point in time, chemotherapy is the only weapon we have against this disease. It appears that we would rather die of our own invention than die of the cancer we probably produced by ourselves by polluting our environment.

What conditions us in our daily life are these environments: the political, social, technological environments we created for ourselves and don't acknowledge. We don't even think we created any of it.

Eckersall: Why do you think that we have this paradoxical relationship to machines? On the one hand our relationship is quite dystopian, as you have outlined, but we also seem to have an enormous faith and willingness to trust machines. We trust them to do some very complicated tasks whether they're flying airplanes or conducting operations inside our bodies. In environmentalist discourse there is also a pushback from a certain sector of the community – and very much from (techno-elites in) the scientific community saying – well, we will invent machines to clean the air or to reverse climate change: to transform the dystopian realities of the machine age. What do you think of this faith in the possibility of the machine?

Verdonck: It's one of the things I'm really thinking about a lot – how come we trust these machines and these inventions? I guess we don't have something else to place our confidence in, nor a different way of thinking. If the wheel or fire allowed us to make a distinction between the human and other animals that are running around on this planet, then it is also by these machines and these inventions that we maintain this distinction. These inventions determine who we are and so we have to trust them – and vice versa. And *that* is what we call progress. In other words, our whole evolution and our whole thinking and everything we claim we 'are', everything that defines us, depends on the tools we invented.

The thought experiment of asking the question about what would have happened if we had not invented a tool to make fire or the wheel would be a very interesting one. We destroy the whole planet by means of machines. They are what we can and hence will use and we don't have any other option.

Eckersall: Can I add the notion of complexity here? Imagine that you are trekking in Nepal and you come across a really dilapidated cable bridge. It's a machine, it's a form of technology and you don't trust it. You say: "Well, it's too rusty," or: "It's got too many holes." But we're quite willing to trust a computer-controlled elevator in a 60-floor building where we have no understanding of how the machine works. There's an argument about how we tend to trust complexity in these situations.

Verdonck: Yes, and the mystery continues to increase. Why does everyone trust their car, for example? As soon as it seems complex, we trust it more because apparently we can't estimate if it's safe or not. It's a closed box. It's complicated, so it must be good. On the other hand, I guess if you lived next to this bridge in Nepal, then you would say: "But we use this bridge every day. There's no problem whatsoever." Or you would say: "Well, this bridge will stay good for a couple of years and then we'll have to change it." There is a whole social element in the influence these machines have on us. Our daily connection with them is one of trust. We trust the things we know – these elevators, cars and airplanes – because they are familiar to us. We see them every day. But that is also the only reason. The more complex they get, the more we need to have faith in them, because we do not have the knowledge to verify this.

I was once in Tanzania on a boat and the captain said: "Actually the sea is rough today; we shouldn't go." But he was paid to cross the sea, so we went off and one of the passengers drowned. I couldn't read that environment. I couldn't read the danger. While in a city, in our daily life, we can somehow read our environment and understand how to survive in this technological environment we created. I guess it's also a real survival relationship we have with machines – victim and killer – especially when they're so strong, as cars, elevators or airplanes are (Fig. 1).

Eckersall: In recent human history, do you think we have changed from *not* expecting machines to work perfectly to expecting them to work perfectly all the time?

Verdonck: I'm almost convinced that if we would consider the wheel as a high-tech invention, then basically we have always had the same relationship with technology: "Oh, my wheel is broken and oh, I can or cannot fix it." Now, of course, we can no longer actually *see* our technology. Then again, we are also so used to not knowing our technology anymore that I like the idea that we know that if we restart our machine it will 'make' itself. That is a nevertheless a big novelty in the history of technology. Before, it was not as if you could stop your chariot for a moment and relaunch it so it would run better, while that is what computers and mobile phones do. If you have a problem with your mobile phone, what do you do? You relaunch the thing and it makes itself better again. This is a crazy idea if you think about it: machines fix themselves.

Apart from that, I think that we basically always had the same relationship with technology. It gets more complex, of course, and in our daily life, this influence cannot be underestimated.

Eckersall: I want to shift the conversation to the work that you make by picking up from when you were talking about the fatality of machines.

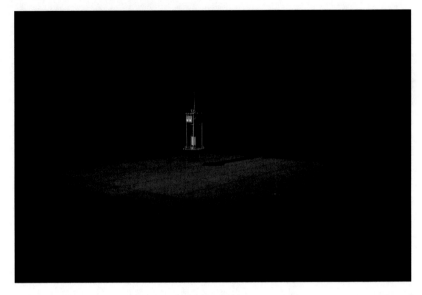

Fig. 1 Kris Verdonck, *DANCER #3* (© A Two Dogs Company/Jasmijn Krol)

When a plane crashes or when a car stops at the wrong time, people say, "It has to do with human error." Human error is a huge problem in this scenario: the machine is telling us that we are going to crash but in this catastrophic moment, we don't trust it, so we do crash. Where is the human error located in your work?

Verdonck: I consider human error and machine error as equal. In my work, it is more about both of them understanding each other and both of them trying to have a dialogue from an equal point of view, with their errors and their problems. I think machines make errors all the time, but then we are so kind to say that we made a mistake and try to fix the machine, because we believe that they will be perfect at some point. And then they still don't do it. We adapt to this situation and say: "You're not perfect but it's okay. *We* will adapt until we think you are perfect." Human error is not my first problem. It is rather the question: do we need to construct this machine? Do we need to fly around the world constantly? Is this a basic need? It's all about the dialogue between species, machines and human beings and their problems and communication.

Eckersall: In her dramaturgical notes on *END* (2008), dramaturge Marianne van Kerkhoven talked about how the performers' relationship to the machine was symbiotic and how this enabled the performer to have an unmediated moment with a machine; what she called sheer presence. I am wondering what this kind of presence is. The performers in *END* also testified of how they partnered with the machine (in elements of the performance) and developed a sense of intimacy with their particularly mechanic activity. Does intimacy equate with presence?

Verdonck: Absolutely, yes. The dialogue between species, machines and human beings has to do with representation and presence. And while this argument might be a bit too simple, I would like to run with it for a moment: an object represents itself. You go to a museum to visit an object and it represents itself. It is what it is. Basically, it doesn't lie. A table is a table. You can exchange it of course (to refer to Marx's dancing fetish table), but it represents what it is – it is 'present' (see Marx 2005, note 26a).

By definition theatre is the mirror to society as it represents society. However, we humans have a very complicated agenda and even languages are constructed in a way that it is most of the time very difficult to communicate something in an unambiguous way. From the start, communication is complicated because our language cannot even cope with reality. It is very complex; we ourselves don't even know each other, and so forth. That is the whole tragedy of theatre and, especially, of course, of the actor. The highest thing to realize on a stage is just to be. Just to be there in the moment, is the greatest thing that can happen to a dancer, performer or actor. They all dream about it and when it happens, they say: "Finally I was on stage. I was what I was."

Imagine what could happen if we have the two languages of visual arts and performance clash (the object and the actor) and we ask machines to slowly lie, or to try to act – this is a very difficult and fundamental thing. The other way is a little easier to imagine; to ask a human to have a dialogue with a machine; a dialogue in the sense that the machine proposes some kind of movement and the actor or the dancer follows this. This is for example what happens on stage in *END*. The audience sees the actor having a complex problem with these machines and at the same time, these performers are not pretending to do something else than having their real physical dialogue with objects. As a result, the performers start to become a bit like an object. They start to have a similar language. They are closer to the object and they are not pretending anything else than the reality of struggling with this machine. By the way, struggle is a difficult word for me, it is too psychological; it is by having a dialogue with an object that these performers come much closer to this thing-like way of being.

Interestingly, this is not a question of audience perception. Whether the audience was there or not, actually, it would not make any real difference. It would probably be more or less the same show. This is also the case in a museum. You put the lights on, you walk around but, basically, the objects are always the same.

Eckersall: This touches upon the possibility for action and transformation. There is an idea of being in a moment of clarity in a performance that performers are seeking. Certainly, part of that is a kind of hyperkinetic awareness of space and a sense of being connected to it and connected to the agency of theatre. However, there is a paradox at the heart of this idea, because it is both a singular momentary experience and also something that is moving through time. Many of your machines are engaged in a process of gradual transformation. The act of transformation seems to be something that is being performed. Whether it is a transformation from visible light to light that is so bright that we cannot see (in *BOX*, 2005) or the figure of an engine blurting out its CO_2 (*DANCER #2*, 2009) or the robots that are performing unproductive labour (*DANCER #1*, 2003; *DANCER #3*, 2010), these examples can all be read in a very transformational kind of way.

Verdonck: This transformational idea was also central in *IN VOID* (2016) – a work in which we filled a theatre building with living machines, with the spectators as the only human presence. I wonder now, if we presented this work in a museum rather than a performance space, if the feeling about these objects will be different, or if the audience will look differently towards these objects, than if they were presented in a theatre. What I am suggesting here is that because most of the time we present these living machines in a theatre, they also become performative. I am also looking at my own objects in that sense, to see how performative they are. Anyway, that wasn't really the question, I think.

Eckersall: Well, I guess it's pointing to a question. You have used the word feeling a number of times in talking about your work. It's an age-old question to ask if machines feel. But there is a particular feelingness that is associated with objects that I think your work explores. It relates to the question of projection too – the transfer of feeling onto an object. You have spoken about the human need to project onto something. Clearly, empirically, an object does not have any sense of feelingness. It is just an object. It just does what it does. But at the same time, in your work objects very much manifest certain emotional states or connections to human desire.

Verdonck: In *IN VOID*, and also for myself, language-wise – I try to speak as much as possible about this in the sense of "they don't like to do this, this machine likes to do that", and so on. I really try to humanize them as much as possible, trying to see them, regardless, as living creatures. As animal-like – yes, as creatures.

At one point, somebody asked the question: "But if one of your machines broke," – say, the engine – "what would you think about it or what would you feel about it?" I don't feel anything about it. Nothing. Because we just take another engine, we turn it on and then there it goes again. Or we solder things, or we make a second version. Even the most lively ones, like the jumping robot *DANCER #3*; I really fundamentally don't care about the objects themselves. But what they provoke, this interaction and the amount of things people project on them, that's actually what it's all about. We project so much onto these machines and objects in our daily life that our emotions and relationship to them become very blurry. From the first thing you invented, or the first object you own, suddenly it gets emotionally attached to us because of our projection of emotions. Think about the feelings you projected onto the teddy bear you had when you were three or four years old.

We constantly project life onto them – yet, machines are not alive. In fact, it is very difficult *not* to see ourselves in these objects and *not* to project. You can compare it to a biologist who has to follow rules in order to prevent himself from projecting their own imagination on the chimpanzees they are watching. This is one of the most difficult exercises, because in this situation you don't have a point of reference but yourself. If I allow the audience to see a transformation in these machines, then the process of empathy and theatre and lying is suggested. And this of course is my playground: creating machines that allow people to project onto them as much as possible.

Eckersall: I want to explore this a little further. In an essay with Kristof van Baarle and Christel Stalpaert (2013), you discussed how our connections to machines have a way of leading to confusion about our subjectivity and we experience alienation. I think we saw this convincingly in *UNTITLED* (2014), where, essentially, a human dressed in a mascot costume is engaged in a machine-like acting out of unproductive labour and then ultimately gets discarded for the machine. The way that *UNTITLED* stages the relationship to the machine as one of alienation and a loss of subjectivity is very powerful. I would also like to explore with you something about what we might call a subjectivity of objects and how different objects might produce different encounters with the spectator, different feelings. The mascot in this performance is hapless and gains our sympathy, but his work – if we can call it that - is an act of cruelty forced upon him as the reality of work. The objects that replace him, the dark column and the silver flower, are more sinister. I am interested to think about perhaps the way in which objects become symbols of a totalitarian society – just as we might think of racing cars, or of machine guns, as objects that are associated with violence and extreme forms of behaviour (Fig. 2).

Verdonck: I guess that alienation is first of all a fact. I try not to have a moralistic idea about what we do with the planet. My opinion about

Fig. 2   Kris Verdonck, *UNTITLED* (© A Two Dogs Company/Hendrik De Smedt)

engines and about all the inventions that we make is, in itself, not very interesting. It is a very boring thing to tell people what I think about the mobile phone. The exercise is to try not to do this and, at the same time, to try to discover the objects and try to see what they are.

For me this encounter can be a very harsh thing. In *UNTITLED*, the performer Marc Iglesias, inside 'his object', the mascot suit, knows that basically what I do is I pay him to go into a suit and entertain people. And this is what he does. That's his job. That's it. It's harsh for both of us. The mere establishment of this relation – my paying him to do this – Marc also uses it in discussions with other dancers. People criticize him, or say, "Oh, that has to be so hard to be in this puppet, or this mascot." And he then replies: "Well, I get paid for it." This became an important point between us – to really acknowledge this.

We also saw so many interviews with people who are in these mascots – and actually they like it a lot. Sometimes they like it because they can do things that they cannot do in everyday life. In one interview a mascot said: "I can hug every woman in town if I'm dressed up as a bear or as a dragon." And indeed, he could. I am talking borderline sexual violence here. He could go for it as long as he was in this dragon thing. But if he was out of this doll, well, reality hits. Actually, this mascot was liberating for this particular guy.

So there again you have a seemingly horrible thing – to disguise yourself to the point where there is no more human being to be seen in this whole *UNTITLED* project. But that statement alone would not be an interesting thing to say. The most compelling thing is looking at this situation as harshly or as nakedly as possible. I pay him and he does the job – in French they have a beautiful word for it: *assumer*, which means to take on the burden, to assume and think the situation through to its more radical extent, however unpleasant this is.

I place the performer and myself within a dramaturgical frame and do the exercise of making an installation or performance inside this frame, not leaving it anymore. Questioning the frame is, once again, not very interesting. The more stimulating question is what kind of struggles we put ourselves into – and trying to delve into this problem as deeply as we can. That's when we get to places where we are strangers in the environment we have created. As a director, and for the performers, we find ourselves sometimes in places where we think: is this really where we want to be? But the frame brought us there. We got there because we didn't question the frame. By this way of working, we arrive in places where sometimes I don't even know anymore what we are doing, except for trying to understand the frame we are working on. To delve into this frame this profoundly gets us to places where it's really strange. Sometimes people ask me how I invented this or how I got onto this idea. Well, I didn't. I just created a frame that would produce this environment. And we just stayed with it. Is that an answer to the question of alienation?

Eckersall: I think what you are saying makes a lot of sense. There is a tendency, including in my own work, to read a performance for its metatheatricality. For example, we might look at *UNTITLED* and see that the question of acting is foregrounded alongside the question of the actual activity that is being performed. But what you are saying is that, in terms of the process, you are very much involved in performing the action and not necessarily stepping back and thinking about that in relation to its reading. You don't want to overdetermine the possible readings of that action. Is that fair?

Verdonck: Yes, absolutely. We work with whatever the dramaturgical frame implies, whatever the result of this may be: there is no other choice.

This is also a very nice feeling for me as a director. I am always *with* my performers and with my machines because we all are in trouble. I do create the problems and I define the frame, but from that moment on it becomes a problem we wish we hadn't caused for ourselves, because there are always a lot of difficulties that follow from it. Consequently, the actors, machines and myself – we have the same enemy, the obnoxious frame that I invented. Nevertheless, we don't question it any more. If we questioned it, then we would have an even bigger problem. If you start questioning the frame itself, everything is again open and so everything is lost. If the idea is good enough, then it produces imagination and adventures. If it's a bad idea, then we get stuck and we have to throw away the whole concept. That's why I sometimes work for two years on one idea: because it has to be good. Otherwise it will not survive our research on the frame, or we can't dive into it because there's nothing there.

Eckersall: I want to shift focus again and ask you about your relationship to particular texts, especially texts by Samuel Beckett, Heiner Müller and Daniil Kharms. These are all texts that seem to draw on certain aesthetic regimes, also relating to history in particular ways.

Verdonck: I think these texts form one line in history. An important starting point for me is Heinrich von Kleist's *On the Marionette Theatre* (1810), followed by the works of Franz Kafka, and then you get to Kharms, to Müller, to Beckett, and so on. Probably this was something I adopted from Marianne Van Kerkhoven. She always saw one line of thinking in these writers. First of all, there is an existential aspect in all of them. This existential aspect has a lot to do with society – society as a rigid system. In all of these writers' works, there is a very fundamental clash between the living "us" – the organism, something organic – and something rigid. And that leads to the fundamental questioning about what we do on this planet. I think this is a key theme with all of these writers.

Secondly, there is their use of language. In all of these writers' texts – with the exception of Kafka, although he plays with it – the language is very clear. If they can write a shorter sentence, they will absolutely do it to make their point. In their treatment of language, they almost objectify it. Especially Beckett, he reaches a level where text almost becomes an object.

Eckersall: Text as object. I think that is a crucial relationship. I am also wondering about the aesthetics of failure that permeates the work of most of these writers, sometimes in a humorous way; there is always a focus on a certain kind of circularity and inevitability of failure.

Verdonck: Of course there is the idea of Beckett and failure, but he sees it as a way to progress. This makes it more complicated. Heiner Müller's perspective is a very difficult but interesting one in respect to failure. At one time Alexander Kluge asked him how he would describe the First World War, especially the effects of the gas attacks. Müller replied that in a way it had the feeling of a complete artwork in that all of the senses were engaged. Everything was one. Then he gave the example of a Disney World rollercoaster with its immersive projection and speed and where you are inside of a whole environment. He would compare this with gas attacks in the First World War. He continued with something funny about how strange it was that the Germans invented gas bombing because actually the Germans were coming from the East and most of the winds blew their way. They had to wait until there was no wind to throw the gas, otherwise they would have suffocated themselves. I don't think this is cynicism. It's much more complicated and I think Müller is convinced of the need to talk about the war like that. The failure lies in how people can invent gas bombs while the wind is always blowing in their direction. So you throw it in your own face and that would be it.

However, there is a sense that we *need* to do these kinds of things. The failure is also telling us something about us and our urges. It tells us

about our condition and about the way we invent things. Again, here we are, we are our own victim while doing these kind of things...
I think all these writers that I like play with things we do to ourselves. However, they describe how we do it actively and with a lot of joy. That tells us something about the nature of our absurd condition that makes us human beings so incredibly interesting. What we invent makes our lives so horribly complicated – but the energy with which we invent things is absolutely amazing.

References

Bennett, Jane. 2010. *Vibrant Matter: A Political Ecology of Things*. Durham: Duke University Press.

Eckersall, Peter. 2012. "The Locations of Dramaturgy." *Performance Research: A Journal of the Performing Arts* 17, no. 3: 68–75.

Lazzarato, Maurizio. 2014. *Signs and Machines: Capitalism and the Production of Subjectivity*. Los Angeles: Semiotext(e).

Marx, Karl. 1867. *Capital a Critique of Political Economy Vol. 1*. https://web.stanford.edu/~davies/Symbsys100-Spring0708/Marx-Commodity-Fetishism.pdf. 2005. Accessed August 21, 2018.

van Baarle, Kristof. 2015. "The Critical aesthetics of Performing Objects." *Performance Research: A Journal of the Performing Arts* 20, no. 2: 39–48.

van Baarle, Kristof, Christel Stalpaert, and Kris Verdonck. 2013. "Virtual Dramaturgy: Finding Liberty in the Virtual Machine." *Performance Research: A Journal of the Performing Arts* 18, no. 3: 54–62.

Van Kerkhoven, Marianne, and Anoek Nuyens. 2012. *Listen to the Bloody Machine: Creating Kris Verdonck's 'End'*. Utrecht: Utrecht School of the Arts.

Response-Ability in Thingly Variations: Politics and Ethics

Decoding *Effet Papillon*, a Choreography for Three Dancers Inspired by the World of Video Games

Mylène Benoit and Philippe Guisgand

CONTEMPORARY BODIES

Mylène Benoit

> You can call my body 'matter' or you can call it 'image'; the word is of little importance.—Henri Bergson

Having trained as a visual artist and videographer, I founded the company Contour Progressif in 2004. After working with images for quite some time, I felt the need to take a leap and to consider contemporary representation techniques from the perspective of another medium. I was both worried about the proliferation of images as well as the way they 'choreograph' us and careful not to adopt a naïve attitude towards technology.

See http://www.contour-progressif.net/projets/spectacle/effet-papillon for more information and a video.

M. Benoit (✉)
Contour Progressif, Lille, France

P. Guisgand
Dance Department, University of Lille, Lille, France

© The Author(s), under exclusive license to Springer Nature Switzerland AG 2021
C. Stalpaert et al. (eds.), *Performance and Posthumanism*,
https://doi.org/10.1007/978-3-030-74745-9_7

I went in search of visual devices in which the image and the body could interact with and interrogate each other, essentially and substantially. In my first performances, I used the concept of dance and the space of the stage to heighten the artificiality of bodily representations in our mediated society. These pieces confronted the body with the image in various contexts: that of video games in *Effet Papillon* (2007), war imagery in *La chair du monde* (2009) and the scopic double in *ICI* (2010; created with Olivier Normand). The *leitmotiv* of these creations was: how do images affect/distort our bodies? Contrary to being pure or immune to contamination, our bodies are porous, impressed (in the photographic sense) by images.

Dance seemed to me the best tool to investigate the codes that shape us and that create new definitions of the contemporary body. Indeed, dance allows you to embody certain issues, to inextricably link physical and mental exercise, to establish a tactile connection between the realm of thought and that of the body. My creative work thus becomes a way to hypothesize and, through dance, to share my thoughts with others. For *Effet Papillon*, I imagined the performers' bodies as cabins, as vessels for fleeting images, potentialized, virtual body shells, the avatars of a video game. Indeed, *Effet Papillon* rests on the conviction that the images that choreograph us, do so by simultaneously acting upon the body and the mind: these images fascinate and collectively shape us; they constitute our shared bodily memory. Our minds absorb them, we incorporate them into our flesh and symptomatically regurgitate them as behaviours and feelings, as the ways we hold our bodies.

Yet our bodies and the subjective forms in which they appear are involved in a historical process of change that is announced by the appearance of new types of images: the image perceives, learns, conducts itself, acts. Images are no longer produced to be looked at, but to become associated with certain deeds. Digital interactive images contribute to the projection of gesturality and the body. The contemporary body expands and perishes in and through the image. It is mediatized, deterritorialized, modelled.

So, *Effet Papillon* attempts to question, through dance, the symbolic and technological origins of video game imagery, particularly of avatars[1] (think of Lara Croft, Prince of Persia, or the characters of GTA/Vice City), which arise from a series of abstractions that generate archetypes and invent a corporeality. In a risk-free world and in the context of an obsessive denial of danger, responsibility and death, the bloody combat taking place in video games compensates for, and offers respite from, the death drive. Fighting against nothing, fighting against images or against the machine, in a vacuum, is a clean way to feel triumphant, to risk your life and redirect your aggression… Yet avatars give us a mediatized me-body, unaffected by time or gravity, an ideal body, ultimately, that contrasts sharply with the subject's body and the experience of dance itself.

In *Effet Papillon*, the performers' bodies function as echo chambers, as image-flesh. And it is the fallibility that the dancing bodies bring to our attention, their ontological reality, their humanity, that allows us to question these images. It is as if dance instantly gives voice to an intuitive, phylogenetic knowledge, relentlessly reminding us where we came from and what we are made of (Fig. 1).

> It goes without saying that the sea you hear in the distance is not contained in the shell you press to your ear, so hard it turns red and starts to burn. However, you are not wrong to think such a thing. There's a phylogenesis that has been flowing from the bottom of your body since the dawn of

Fig. 1 *Effet Papillon*, Mylène Benoit/Contour Progressif (© Mathieu Bouvier/Mylène Benoit)

time. The sea got lost in your ear, like the dance got lost in the other world.—Pascal Quignard, *L'origine de la danse*

Effet Papillon—Creation Process

The choreographic language is based on the rigorous analysis and the systematic reproduction of avatars' gestures by the piece's three performers, Barbara Caillieu, Laure Myers and Lilou Robert. They had to identify the 'animation path', the key images, the breaks in intensity and the simplifications of gestures necessary to model bodies reduced to signs. Slowing down, retracing your steps, taking breaks and coming to life again: the incorporation of simulacra that encourage the belief in a perfectible body, immortal and omnipotent, does not happen without a struggle, both in terms of skills and ethics, with the physicality of the dancers' bodies (which are all too real). In a matter-movement moulded from pixels rather than flesh, colliding trajectories, looping gestures, circular kicks and other Kungfu tricks have been stretched to the limit and appropriated to conjure up an unpredictable, dehumanized and virtualized activity.

We have created the conditions for images aspiring to become flesh, as if the wonderful adventures took place in the bodies themselves, in their architectures, and as if the surface activity, somnambulistic and opaque, was the 'useful' manifestation of these interiorized agitations. Bodies argue with and against the space, in themselves, by virtually assimilating powers and opposing intensities.

This rigorous process of incorporating images and their artefacts, getting into the skin of avatars for hours on end, and reducing that specific vocabulary (by slowing down, stretching, sequencing) enabled the creation of new, never-seen-before bodily activities in the body's becoming-virtual. A body that appears as a flux, a displacement, never really dead, never really immobile yet nevertheless completely absent to itself.

> The virtual is a spectacle, allowing you to evolve while in a mode of analogue existence, in a universe that is extremely reliable, even down to the worst dangers. (…) Entailing a logical contradiction that is both fascinsating and disturbing, the virtual proposes a mode of existence without existing, as well as–conversely–an existence modelled and modalized, and

hence existentially completed.—Gilles Benham, *Le virtuel, la présence de l'absent*

Sensors and Computer Programming: Towards a Dramaturgy of Simulacra

In video games, space is continuously calculated, actualized, in function of the avatars' movements. Inspired by the graphic engines and sensors typical of the universe of virtual reality, the scenographic installation of *Effet Papillon* encourages a constant interaction between dance, space, light and sound. The performers are outfitted with sensors that turn their steps, their jumps and their fights into sound: while dancing, the dancers create sound effects, their weapons generate light flashes and their enemies cry out. The sensors and computer programming are entirely at the service of the dramaturgy of the potentialized body: operated by a joystick, they connect images (of light and sound) to corporeal acts. Their heightened gestures give the dancers the air of weightlessness, speed and power that is so characteristic of virtual bodies, thus opening up new territories for dance.

Credits

Concept and staging: Mylène Benoit
Assistant: Annie Leuridan
Performers: Barbara Caillieu, Laure Myers, Magali Robert
Choreographic research: Mylène Benoit, Barbara Caillieu, Laure Myers, Magali Robert
Scenography: Xavier Boyaud
Lighting design: Annie Leuridan
Sound design, programming: Laurent Ostiz
Sensors, real-time programming: Cyrille Henry
Costumes: Carole Martinière
Scenic design: Alain Le Beon, Thomas Ramon, Frédérique Bertrand
Electronic development: Interface-Z, Cyrille Henry
Administration: Angeline Barth
Director: Pierre-Yves Aplincourt
Technical director: Maël Teillant
Stage director: Aurore Leduc

Partners

[[ars]numérica,
Atelier d'Art 3000 - Le Cube, Issy-les-Moulineaux
Le manège.mons/maison folie
Le manège.mons/cecn
Le Vivat - Armentières
Les Fous à réaction [associés]
DRAC Nord-Pas-de-Calais
ADAMI
Fondation Beaumarchais
Ministère de la Culture et de la Communication (DICRéAM)
Conseil Régional Nord-Pas-de-Calais
Le manège.maubeuge
Didascalie.net
Centre National de la Danse, Danse à Lille, Danse Création and La Condition Publique, who generously offered studio space

Winning project of "Bains numériques # 1" of the Centre des Arts d'Enghien.

On Their Wings

Philippe Guisgand

In the context of its key movement 'Real-Virtual', the Vivat dance festival in Armentières staged a piece called *Effet Papillon*, created by Mylène Benoit and her company Contour Progressif, on 15 and 16 December 2006. In this piece, Benoit, who trained as a visual artist, examines our relationship to the virtual universes of video games, more specifically to the avatars that inhabit them (like Lara Croft) and how they influence the way we move. Over a two-year period, the choreographer and her three dancers explored the pixelated movements of the characters from blockbuster games like *Prince of Persia*, *GTA* and *Tomb Raider*. The text that follows will start from its author's thoughts on the premiere to establish the main issues of this choreographic piece that explores a surprising theme in the field of contemporary dance.

The scenic space is closed off by a large white screen that extends into a pristine strip at shoulder height. The clinical contours of this glass universe contain three diagonally suspended screens that, thanks to clever lighting, are transformed into a translucent maze brimming with reflections. From the outset, the frontal position that gamers typically assume when playing seems to have exploded, setting free—through malice or neglect—the virtual heroes, who are nevertheless obliged to venture into that frosty decor and into the remains of a sound field filled with disquieting echoes. Three characters appear, dressed in grey and white outfits that are halfway between *Star Trek* and the soldier monks of Shaolin: they are set on fighting, but the enemies seem to have disappeared, together with the decors that would give them a sense of context. The three warriors take up their positions, make martial arts movements or adopt resting postures; they draw virtual sabres or fight with their bare hands. At times they collapse and slowly come back to life, without apparent logic. Sometimes amplified by whistling sounds—which in the context of games are synonymous with efficiency and power—the martial movements alternate with breaks, hesitations, steps backwards, and moves that are all the more pointless because none of the three heroines seems to acknowledge the existence of the other two; three isolated figures at the mercy of the hesitating joystick of a newbie gamer, or one that is totally confused (Fig. 2).

A cold universe, hence an icy performance? Quite the contrary! As a spectator, you do not expect to be won over by these strange movements that are rendered superfluous, but you are; they fold back on themselves and transform into a dance that is surprisingly contagious. The result is reminiscent of Édouard Lock's *Amélia* (2002), in which a tiny digital ballerina (a kind of Lara Croft—her again!—in tutu) appeared on screen to give a moment's respite to the performers of this Canadian choreographer's frantic dance. The aphorism that she proposed, ever so softly, made her seem almost more real—to the spectator exhausted by the energy spent on stage—than the performers with their superhuman speed. But here, the contamination increases because the virtual is made real, allowing us to better explore the figurines that we were previously merely manipulating in another context—one of entertainment and fun. The figure of the avatar is no longer a disembodied extension of ourselves; it is welcoming and embracing us, enabling the genetic manipulation of a new genre.

Fig. 2 *Effet Papillon*, Mylène Benoit/Contour Progressif (© Mathieu Bouvier/Mylène Benoit)

Furthermore, the piece steers clear from projecting images (without which, it seemed at the time, most so-called technological spectacles failed to impress): if the virtual, digitized, pixelized, corrected, perfected, deformed body—in short, the adaptable body—is often a body that disappears in favour of its image, Mylène Benoit shows us the exact opposite: the image makes way for a real body, albeit one with increased sonorous and luminous powers. It was a daring gamble, but the artist pulled it off because of the confidence she placed in dance, her new medium—one that is at ease in 3D environments. *Effet Papillon* prefers to evoke imaginary landscapes and adversaries that we see only in our minds, rather than imposing on us a universe filled with supplementary images of which we already see more than enough in our daily realities.

So, what ultimately constitutes that 'butterfly effect' whereby a series of small causes turns out to have large effects? An insightful look at the impoverishing effects of a rampant pixelization? A playful take on the consequences of a future dominated by video games? Or an exploration of a virtual bodily state that transforms into empathy thanks to the grace of the dancers' interpretation; an exploration of a density that is all too real this time, even being transmitted onto the spectators? Let's keep the first two options on the table, referring as they do to themes clearly addressed by the performance. Without a doubt, they go a long way to explain the success of this creation and the adolescent audience it so often targets, whose members are more inclined to spend their time in front of game consoles than to go and watch a live performance.

Yet the last hypothesis seems to me to transcend that question and to open up another, bigger one, namely that of the issue of corporeality tackled by the performance. It is not the first time that a dance piece draws heavily on images: think of hip hop, which was originally inspired—especially the Smurf—by the visual effects made possible by using a remote to control a VCR; it was not so much about being inspired by the contents of videotapes than by the possibility of fast-forwarding them, pausing them, rewinding them or playing them frame by frame. The result was a fragmentation and reconfiguration of movement that expanded the corporeal and rhythmic vocabulary of what was considered 'dance' in the early eighties. But speed and virtuosity have led these practices towards a dance of effects, often remarkable in its innovativeness, but which the non-practising spectator has difficulties identifying with: he cannot project his own corporeality onto it. He admires the physical prowess, but from a distance, staying outside of it. In *Effet Papillon*, the coldness evoked by the scenography gradually gives way to kinaesthetic empathy. And it is to the credit of the performers slash captivators that, having abandoned all attempts at mimesis and having become 'empty forms', they manage to become creatures, thus sharing with us—from the inside—that unsubstantial skeleton, those gestural redundancies, those blank movements, that corporeality that is left hanging, those purposeless sprints, those leaps into the stage decor, those inhuman standby modes.

We have all had the experience, however briefly, of being immersed in a video game—pretending to drive a car, to ski down a slope, to fly an aircraft or to crawl into the skin of a heroic fantasy character. At that moment, our perceptual habits treat our body to all kinds of feelings: of touching things, accelerating, losing our balance, getting tense or dizzy. Kinaesthetic empathy, which the American dance critic John Martin (1991, 28) referred to as metakinesis in the early thirties, was backed up neurobiologically by the work of Rizzolatti and Sinigaglia (2008). What is key here is that this kinaesthetic sharing, this corporeal contamination caused by mirror neurons, offers us a shared world based on the things we sense: seeing a certain movement means becoming the movement itself. And that's how that movement makes sense.

At this point, it is worthwhile to note the dancers' anxiety, leaving the stage at the night of the premiere, that perhaps they had given the audience an experience in which it no longer regarded them—or recognized them—as dancers. That anxiety was touching insofar as the audience, on that particular night, had not at all experienced mimetic gestures summoning up the imagery of video games; rather, *Effet Papillon* gave the genre of dance the opportunity to venture into a new range of movements that it did not inhabit before. Having stepped into the bodies of the performers, at that point we shared the sensations of a body with an ethereal consistency, gesturing smoothly and airily, or, on the contrary, sharply and intensely. We relativized the space–time, playing around with the objective limits of the stage; we experimented with different gravitational densities in a constant interplay of forms. And all of this took place, not in the pixelated universe we find when face to face with our computer screens or game consoles, but rather in the utopian reality/real utopia hosted on stage. If that is not dance, I do not know what is!

And if, even embracing a logic resembling that of a Nelson Goodman, we ask ourselves not *is this dance?* but *has there been dancing?* the answers seem to be the same, bringing us back as it does to the approach taken by choreographer and dancer Meg Stuart (2000, 49)—which might resonate with the audience of *Effet Papillon*: "it seems to me that dance is something that is related to what we call the 'intimate', and that it happens every time a body reveals its self to itself".

Note

1. Derived from the Sanskrit word *avatāra*, which refers to extra-terrestrial beings descending to earth in various guises.

References

Martin, John. 1991. *La Danse moderne*. Translated by J. Robinson and S. Schoonejans. Arles: Actes Sud.
Rizzolatti, Giacomo, and Corrado Sinigaglia. 2008. *Les Neurones miroirs*. Paris: Odile Jacob.
Stuart, Meg. 2000. "Chorégraphier." *Mouvement* 10: 49.

The Refrain and the Territory of the Posthuman

Aline Wiame

The notion of "posthumanism" I intend to use throughout this paper encompasses both the assemblages of human and nonhuman components and the critical tool that posthumanism can be. Indeed, posthumanism addresses two problematic situations facing humanism as well as the humanities today. On the one hand, historically, humanism has often identified itself with imperialism—the universal Human as a norm shaped according to the image of the Western, white, Christian, heterosexual, upper-middle-class male. On the other hand, the development of biotechnologies and artificial intelligence, as well as the development of systemic and environmental modes of thought—all types of knowledge that lead to thinking in terms of life milieus rather than of isolated individuals—have made obsolete the possibility of studying humankind as a species separated from other life forms, whether they are organic or artificial (see for instance Haraway 2004; Braidotti 2013; Nayar 2014).

If "posthuman" figures, because of their important place in our contemporary societies, affect numerous propositions elaborated upon within the performance arts, I am particularly interested in the way they affect the postdramatic *stage*. What can the stage, that space which

A. Wiame (✉)
Université Toulouse - Jean Jaurès, Toulouse, France

was once supposed to remain hidden in order to allow the showing of inter-human relations, become when it is overwhelmed by a whole assemblage of nonhuman components? In *Postdramatic Theatre*, Hans-Thies Lehmann tackles this question with Gertrude Stein's concept of "landscape-play": instead of the continuous tension required by a drama always situated in a specific time between the past and the future, we should be able to watch a play just like we contemplate a landscape. What comes first then is the effects of defocalization and equal status for all parts, which are inherent to the contemplation of a landscape: the spectator's attention is no longer focused on the progression of a human drama represented on stage (Lehmann 2006, 62–63), but the gaze can now wander freely around the different elements presented on the stage. Theatre and its stage thus become, according to Lehmann, post-anthropocentric:

> They are aesthetic figurations that point utopically towards an alternative to the anthropocentric ideal of the subjection of nature. When human bodies join with objects, animals and energy lines into a single reality (as also seems to be the case in circus – thus the depth of the pleasure it causes), theatre makes it possible to imagine a reality other than that of man dominating nature. (81)

In the following pages, I will develop on some propositions about this post-anthropocentric stage and its connections to the staging of the posthuman. It requires a first shift, a step to the side, away from the concept of landscape-play. Rather than thinking with landscapes—defined by and for a human gaze—I want to examine the outcomes of an animal point of view on space, on the shaping and appropriation of space, through the concept of *territory* such as it is approached by Gilles Deleuze and Félix Guattari in the "Refrain" chapter of *A Thousand Plateaus*. But even before going into the characteristics of such a territory, an important issue raised by this point of view must be underlined. There are, of course, some similitudes between a territory and a stage, beginning with the way both are traced—let us think, for instance, of the famous chalk circle. However, if Deleuze and Guattari's concept of territory allows for a direct account of the assemblage of human and nonhuman elements, its connection to the question of the posthuman remains more difficult to describe. For this reason, I will proceed step by step with an articulation of Deleuze and Guattari's territorial propositions and Heiner Goebbels' performance-installation *Stifters Dinge*—a piece that interweaves stage and territory, nonhuman and posthuman. Echoes and passages between *A Thousand Plateaus* and *Stifters Dinge* will allow for an evaluation of the relevance of the concept of territory to thinking the stage of the posthuman, in a reciprocal communication rather than in a vain exercise that would apply philosophy to theatre.

Let us begin with a few words about *Stifters Dinge*. Initially known for his collaborations with Heiner Müller as a stage designer and music composer (his first specialty), Heiner Goebbels, born in East Germany, has long been interested in the relations between theatre, opera and politics and has worked on texts from Jean-Jacques Rousseau, Gertrude Stein, Paul Valéry, Samuel Beckett and Maurice Blanchot—to name a few. First shown in 2007 at Théâtre Vidy, Laussanne, *Stifters Dinge* (literally "Stifter's stuff", derived from the name of Austrian writer Adalbert Stifter, who lived in the first half of the nineteenth century) is one of Goebbels' major successes: the piece has been performed more than 350 times on four continents. Goebbels describes *Stifters Dinge* as a "a composition for five pianos with no pianists, a play with no actors, a performance without performers – one might say a no-man show" (2008a). What the audience is facing on stage is indeed a nonhuman device: five mechanically activated pianos; three pools that will allow for the development of textural plays with water, ice and vapour; visual projections and sound effects (Fig. 1).

Such no-man shows entertain obvious connections to the question of the nonhuman: besides the fact that the star of the show is a mechanical device that plays with "natural" elements such as water, the music composed by Goebbels is conceived as discordant with harmonies familiar to our human ears[1]—or at least to what the Western world has shaped as "humanity". But the posthuman question is also present; the presentation of *Stifters Dinge* in the press kit concludes with the famous last lines of Michel Foucault's *The Order of Things* about the historical and transitory character of the dispositions that have allowed the constitution of the humanities:

> If those arrangements were to disappear as they appeared, (...) then one can certainly wager that man would be erased, like a face drawn in sand at the edge of the sea. (2005, 422)

Fig. 1 Heiner Goebbels, *Stifters Dinge*, 2007 (© Wonge Bergmann/ Ruhrtriennales)

This erasing of "man"—one would rather say "humanity"—is omnipresent in *Stifters Dinge*. The performance makes us read and listen to extracts of Stifter's *My Great Grandfather's Portfolio* in which the writer crafts meticulous accounts of a forest immobilized and frozen. In Stifter's text, any human point of view is already exceeded by some kind of "natural" estrangement. When this text itself is taken into Goebbels' assemblage and combined with an old traditional Greek song in chromatic scale, antiphonal singing by Columbian Indians, interviews with and readings by Malcom X, Claude Lévi-Strauss or William Burroughs, then our usual representations of what a human is, become, indeed, similar to a face drawn in sand about to be erased by a rising tide.

With Goebbels' proposition for a post-anthropocentric stage, let us turn now to the concept of territory developed by Gilles Deleuze and Félix Guattari in the chapter "The Refrain" and proceed by means of three propositions.

Proposition 1: The constitution of a territory is a performative practice that does not represent anything but that makes other ways of feeling and thinking exist

Hans-Thies Lehmann himself underlines that the notion of "landscape" is only suitable for thinking about the post-anthropocentric stage if, from the usual values attached to the idea of the landscape, we draw instead on a defocalization that gives equal status to all parts of the landscape. Indeed, other aspects of the notion of landscape can only refer to a nature shaped by and for humans and their gaze; it is not a mere coincidence if, among the different types of art, the pictorial scheme is the most commonly associated with landscapes—and especially with the classical, very well-known genre of landscape painting. Opposed to this pictorial predominance, the whole of *A Thousand Plateaus* is underpinned by a discrete but consistent valorisation of music as an expressive component able to create material and conceptual beings without any need for a humanist kind of representation. This function of music throughout the book is at the heart of the "Refrain" chapter, which opens with the evocation of a child lost in the dark who tries to conjure away the chaos that surrounds him by singing a song that will give a rhythm to his walking:

> A child in the dark, gripped with fear, comforts himself by singing under his breath. He walks and halts to his song. Lost, he takes shelter, or orients himself with his little song as best he can. The song is like a rough sketch of a calming and stabilizing, calm and stable, center in the heart of chaos. Perhaps the child skips as he sings, hastens or slows his pace. But the song itself is already a skip: it jumps from chaos to the beginnings of order in chaos and is in danger of breaking apart at any moment. There is always sonority in Ariadne's thread. Or the song of Orpheus. (Deleuze and Guattari 1987, 311)

Vocal components, rhythms, accelerations, interruptions are all risky attempts to organize a fragile but stable centre withdrawn from chaos—and this fragile centre is the first sketch of a territory (311–312). Every territory is an act that affects milieus and rhythms, that territorializes them (313). A territory is not created by the shaping of an image-landscape but by rhythmic assemblages of heterogeneous components: a recurring theme of the "Refrain" chapter is, in fact, birds' songs which create a territory through purely vocal and rhythmic means.

Goebbels' stage is certainly not that different when it affirms its post-anthropocentric character with intentionally out-of-tune pianos that contradict the common rule of equal temperament tuning and thus "display a certain rebellion against the sound of human control" (Bell 2010, 155). For its part, with its description of the sound constitution of a territory, with its insistence on the fact that a territory does not *represent* anything but rather *makes exist* stable centres withdrawn from chaos, *A Thousand Plateaus* clearly echoes the idea that contemporary theatre is characterized by a break from the pictorial scheme, which dominated representation in the Italian theatrical apparatus (Hénin 2003), to a musical scheme—an idea that can be found, between others, in Saison (1998, 72–73) or Lehmann (2006, 91–93).

If relations between *A Thousand Plateaus* and a form of contemporary theatre such as the one shaped by Goebbels can be established so easily, it is also because Deleuze and Guattari explicitly connect the drawing of a territory with the question of the emergence of art. In fact, for the two philosophers, an artist's work is defined by the withdrawing of untreated, expressive materials in order to add her signature; she thus transforms those untreated materials into elements of her own territory ("readymades" are territorial acts—see Deleuze and Guattari 1987, 316). Deleuze and Guattari continue:

> And what is called *art brut* is not at all pathological or primitive; it is merely this constitution, this freeing, of matters of expression in the movement of territoriality: the base or ground of art. Take anything and make it a matter of expression. The stagemaker practices *art brut*. Artists are stagemakers, even when they tear up their own posters. Of course, from this standpoint art is not the privilege of human beings. (316)

Beyond the assertion that art does not begin with human beings, another remarkable point deserves to be noticed; the equivalence between the movement of territoriality, stagemakers, and artists. Would making a stage be a territorial practice close to *art brut*? There is no doubt that a clear equivalence between territory-making and stage-making would delight the author of this article, but things are more complicated than that. "Stagemaker" is the English translation for a word that the French, original version of *Mille plateaux* gives in Latin: *scenopoïetes*. Obviously, *scenopoïetes* can literally be translated as "stagemaker", but Deleuze and Guattari use the Latin and not the French (they could have written something like "faiseur de scène", after all), for a reason. *Scenopoïetes dentirostris* is indeed the name of a bird living in Australian mountain forests and commonly called the tooth-billed bowerbird (or, in fact, "stagemaker bowerbird") in English.[2] This bird is particularly interesting for Deleuze and Guattari (1987, 315 and 331) as its varied song, including imitations of other birds' songs, is produced during amorous parade season, from a branch called *singing stick* that sits on top of a "stage" (*display ground*) made of leaves laid out with their pale underside face up. By affirming that a *scenopoïetes* makes *art brut*, by affirming that an artist is a *scenopoïetes*, Deleuze and Guattari are not simply establishing an analogy between the (human) making of a stage and the (animal) making of a territory: they actually argue that both the stage and the territory are parts of the same process—a process that is in no way exclusively human. "Of course, from this standpoint art is not the privilege of human beings (1987, 316)." Drawing a territory does imply the making of a stage, but that stage is not drawn by a human artist-creator; it is an element of a nonhuman, expressive assemblage.

Proposition 2: A territory is made of nonhuman gestures and affects whose machinic becoming shapes the post-anthropocentric stage

Let us go back to our "stagemaker" artist. Her motto could be: from anything, make an expressive material. "Indexes" from any milieu then become pretexts for a territorializing refrain, whatever the kind of indexes—"materials, organic products, skin or membrane states, energy sources, action-perception condensates" (Deleuze and Guattari 1987, 315). It means that, although the musical paradigm remains central in the constitution of a territory (notably in regard to the importance of rhythm in the process), every type of "refrain" can be constitutive of a territory—whether it be an optical, motor or gestural refrain (323). In the act of making a territory, something very singular then happens: there is a disjunction between the territory-in-the-making and the code inherent to the species of the animal shaping its territory (322). This can be explained with the case of a territorializing bird: while territorializing, the bird is *decoding* its innate reflexes and abilities, which are no more mere products of an internal necessity but are adjusted to the refrain required by the territory to make. Moreover, the bird territorializes its acquired abilities by adjusting them to the expressive materials of the territory rather than to external stimuli. Those disjunctive operations allow for the creation of novelty, beyond the code of the species: one does not establish a territory to remain locked in, prisoner of a lugubrious repetition of what is already known, but to have enough stability for slowly opening the circle to other milieus.

In *Stifters Dinge*, Stifter's texts, the projection of classical paintings, non-Western musical songs, and speeches by Malcom X, Burroughs or Lévi-Strauss are not mere expressive materials, prisoners of a technical device that runs idle; on the contrary, they are assembled with out-of-tune pianos, elevated to other powers which make us see another milieu, a milieu that is really "posthuman". While humans and their creations used to master and organize this milieu, they are now mere cogs in a more-than-human machine they cannot comprehend. This is actually one of Goebbels' goals: staging "a confrontation with the unknown: with the forces that man cannot master" (Goebbels 2008b; quoted in Bell 2010, 154). *Stifters Dinge* could then very well be what Deleuze and Guattari call a *machinic opera*:

> If a quality has motifs and counterpoints, if there are rhythmic characters and melodic landscapes in a given order, then there is the constitution of a veritable machinic opera tying together orders, species, and heterogeneous qualities. What we term machinic is precisely this synthesis of heterogeneities as such. Inasmuch as these heterogeneities are matters of expression, we say that their synthesis itself, their consistency or capture, forms a properly machinic "statement" or "enunciation". The varying relations into which a color, sound, gesture, movement, or position enters in the same species, and in different species, form so many machinic enunciations. (1987, 330–331)

In *Stifters Dinge*, actual machines—whether they are mechanical or digital—allow for this synthesis of heterogeneities. What we are facing is an accurate performance of the way Deleuze and Guattari describe what happens when one leaves the territory, when it is deterritorialized: "Whenever a territorial assemblage is taken up by a movement that deterritorializes it (whether under so-called natural or artificial conditions), we say that a machine is released" (333). On Goebbels' stage, those machines are actual machines, but they have to be thought of as a particularly striking exemplification of a broader device that can be of a totally other type, as Deleuze and Guattari define a machine as "a set of cutting edges that insert themselves into the assemblage undergoing deterritorialization, and draw variations and mutations of it" (333). In *Stifters Dinge*'s case, the machine is less exemplified in physically present on-stage pianos than in the overpowering rhythm of the music they produce, with all its unanticipated rhythmic accents (one can think of a musical thriller; see Bell 2010, 151).

A machinic deterritorialization thus has political effects, not only because questions of inhabiting and leaving a territory are highly political, but also because the deterritorialization of refrains extracts from them new propositional powers. For instance, when a speech by Malcom X is assembled with *Stifters Dinge*'s machinic rhythms, elements related to the race question highlight the arbitrary, false binary of the boundaries that separate races, humans, things, and their normative relations (Bell 2010, 155): by deterritorializing the elements and their relations, the device has already raised them to another power, showing the vacuity of normative boundaries.

Proposition 3: The stage-become-territory is an experimental plane with regard to political questions of the Natal, the Earth and the people

A Thousand Plateaus is a political book, haunted by the question of fascist tendencies of desire and its lines of flight.[3] The "refrain" chapter is no exception and gives an important part to German Romanticism, to *Lieder*, to Hölderlin and to the specific operations that this movement effectuates on the territory around the theme of the "Natal":

> The Natal is the innate, but decoded; and it is the acquired, but territorialized. The Natal is the new figure assumed by the innate and the acquired in the territorial assemblage. The affect proper to the Natal, as heard in the lied: to be forever lost, or refound, or aspiring to the unknown homeland. (Deleuze and Guattari 1987, 332)

According to Deleuze and Guattari, the Natal opens the question of territoriality onto the cosmos. With Romanticism, artists abandon *de jure* universality, which was claimed by Classicism, and they reterritorialize; they reclaim the Earth:

> The earth is the intense point at the deepest level of the territory or is projected outside it like a focal point, where all the forces draw together in close embrace. The earth is no longer one force among others, nor is it a substance endowed with form or a coded milieu, with bounds and an apportioned share. The earth has become that close embrace of all forces (...). (338–339)

The territory is the requisite to know the Earth but there always is a disjunction between them—"The territory is German, the Earth Greek" (339). In the German Romanticist notion of territory, Deleuze and Guattari write, the attraction–repulsion movement between the Earth and the territory happens between the One-Alone of the soul and the One-All of the Earth: "The hero is a hero of the earth; he is mythic, rather than being a hero of the people and historical" (340). What is missing, then, is the people, according to Paul Klee's famous formula that would become one of the leitmotivs of Deleuze's *Cinema II. The Time-Image* (1989, 215–224). Paul Klee claims a deterritorialization, a flight from the Earth, but the One-Alone of the soul is not enough to accomplish such a thing; the "One-Crowd" is needed (Deleuze and Guattari 1987, 341). "We still lack the ultimate force… We seek a people. We began over there in the Bauhaus… More we cannot do", says Klee (1966, 55; quoted in Deleuze and Guattari 1987, 337–338). The problem of a missing people is all the more political, given that it is also musical, Deleuze and Guattari add (1987, 341): the romantic opera is a confrontation of the subjectified voice of the hero, which is full of "feelings", with an instrumental and orchestral whole that mobilizes non-subjective affects. The political character of a romantic opera depends on its *composition*—a composition similar to the textual, sonic and visual polyphonies in *Stifters Dinge*: what voices can emerge when assemblages deterritorialize the forces that were framed by a territory?

In German romantic operas, Deleuze and Guattari argue, orchestration and instrumentation both separate and unite sound forces and assign the hero's voice a part according to earthly forces, forces from the One-All. The musicological question is thus political: as the Natal can be thought of according to the Earth or according to the people, as orchestration can manage—or not—to individuate a people, connections of voices to peoples able to populate a territory can vary drastically. A people fed by the forces of the Earth does not individuate in the same way as a people drawn by the forces of the crowd. Such differences in musical composition could very well explain why fascism used Verdi much less than Nazism did Wagner (341).

The problem of Romanticism, although essential because it shows how territoriality can become an active agent in the process of artistic creation, is nevertheless no longer ours. Why would we think of art from the viewpoint of territory today? And what could a post-anthropocentric stage bring to the debate when it is approached as a special kind of territory?

Actually, the question of the Earth and of the people, even if reconfigured nowadays, remains crucial. For Deleuze and Guattari, we are facing a "deterritorialized", "open" Earth as well as a "molecularized" people, a people that cannot be contained in any organized form or institution as it is made of pure forces and intensities:

> The earth is now at its most deterritorialized: not only a point in a galaxy, but one galaxy among others. The people is now at its most molecularized: a molecular population, a people of oscillators as so many forces of interaction. The artist discards romantic figures, relinquishes both the forces of the earth and those of the people. The combat, if combat there is, has moved. (345)

Art then can, and must, propose new forms of perception (with perception referring to all the senses, including seeing and hearing); art has to work on new territorial assemblages to work on our thresholds of perception, our thresholds of discernibility. "All history is really the history of perception" (347), Deleuze and Guattari write, refusing to see a structural evolution in the succession of classic, romantic and modern ages. Modes of perception, the way some beings and some people of the Earth are (or are not) perceptible, are the real agents that determine territories and links to the forces of chaos and cosmos.

By bringing face to face the inhumanity of the Earth and the inhumanity of machines, by tackling Western and non-Western harmonies, by mixing the theme of humanity's disappearance with racial and postcolonial questions, Goebbels' *Stifters Dinge* is composing a stage territory that makes us perceive an open Earth, populated by "posthuman" beings in the critical sense of the term. Those beings are the ones about whom Donna Haraway writes that they "can call us to account for our imagined humanity, whose parts are always articulated through translations" (Haraway 2004, 60). Humans and nonhumans, those beings staged and articulated by Goebbels, play a part in what Rosi Braidotti qualifies as a redefinition of subjectivity when faced with the stakes of posthumanism and post-anthropocentrism: "The relational capacity of the posthuman subject is not confined within our species, but it includes all non-anthropomorphic elements", which makes us feel "the virtual possibilities of an expanded, relational self that functions in a nature–culture continuum" (2013, 60–61). A molecular people for a deterritorialized Earth: such is the aim of a stage-turned-territory for diverse human and

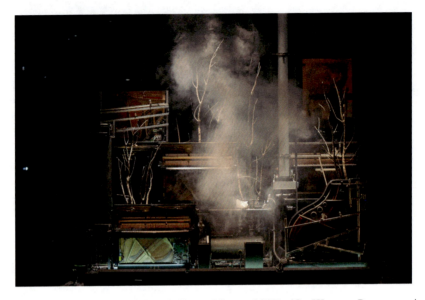

Fig. 2 Heiner Goebbels, *Stifters Dinge*, 2007 (© Wonge Bergmann/ Ruhrtriennale)

nonhuman components assembled to compose a new refrain towards the cosmic (Fig. 2).

Conclusion: The Climate Crisis and the Precarious Creation of the Unknown

The representations of *Stifters Dinge* in New York coincided with the failure of the United Nations' summit about climate change in Copenhagen in December 2008. Goebbels commented on that coincidence by stating that the ecological politics that can be deduced from his play did not arise from a predetermined position but resulted from what the materials themselves were requiring (Schaefer 2009; quoted in Bell 2010, 156). In other words, working on the invention of a posthuman stage-become-territory can only bring posthuman, ecological propositions regarding new ways for species and artefacts to inhabit and interact on the Earth. With that in mind, we should not underestimate Goebbels's statement about the absence of a predetermined (political) position regarding the ecological crisis: the precarious, uncertain factor that could connect posthuman assemblages to climate change-related concerns is key. It is the precarity of our attempts, the uncertainty of the decoding process, that allows for the irruption of yet unseen perceptions of the interwoven futures of many kind of lives on Earth.

Currently, the Anthropocene—and what this strange insertion of human activities in the inhuman geological strata of the Earth tells us about the disjunction of today's human societies and the temporality of a more-than-human Earth—urges us to reconsider the importance of stage propositions that work on the territory-to-Earth connections as well as on the kind of assemblages that can populate that Earth. In that respect, to end this article, I want to insist on the path shown by Goebbels' *Stifters Dinge* as a way to develop artistic creation towards interwoven ways to elaborate new perceptions of the Earth.

Actually, the question of creation is central to Deleuze's and Guattari's view on the task of arts and philosophy regarding the future forms of the Earth and its peoples.[4] In *What Is Philosophy*, they explicitly present creation as a tool of resistance to the present in order to produce a new people for a new Earth:

> We lack creation. We lack resistance to the present. The creation of concepts in itself calls for a future form, for a new earth and people that do not yet exist. (...) Art and philosophy converge at this point: the constitution of an earth and a people that are lacking as the correlate of creation. (Deleuze and Guattari 1994, 108)

Here, creation, whether artistic or conceptual, must be understood as the precarious invention of the unknown, as opposed to the pseudo-inevitability of the "it is what it is" kind of resignation—arts and philosophy create forces against stabilized forms. But what would "the constitution of a new Earth" mean? What does it mean when the two authors write that, in the process of creation, we are lacking an earth, whether it is a creation of concepts or of art? After all, don't we rather have too much of it, too much of a fantasized "mother" earth, too much of an earth to appropriate and exploit, too much of an earth that we have spoiled to the point that it could actually kill us? That is a point recently made by Claire Colebrook (2014, 72): we should not forget that the figure of the globe—the Earth as a globe—is only a way through which "'we' give a world to ourselves through our own recuperating imagination". We probably have too much of this kind of Earth, seized and measured for Man, and that is precisely the reason why the Earth is lacking—the "open earth" Deleuze and Guattari are calling for, the unmeasurable Earth that cannot even be understood in terms of organic life. This resistance opposed by the Earth to any attempt to stamp it with the tools of human thought is precisely the reason why Deleuze and Guattari associate the theme of the Earth with the question of creation: we are not only lacking an earth and a people, we are also lacking tools to think and create them.

The propositions *Stifters Dinge* elaborates on may not be those lacking tools per se but they are assemblages pointing towards those tools. They are not trying to represent the Earth on a stage; they escape from the landscape-play logics to experiment with expressive rather than representative means. The territory that those propositions create can thus only exist outside of a strictly human gaze and requires multilayered, interwoven interactions between all kinds of living species *and* mechanical, sometimes uncanny, forms of existence. The people-to-come suggested by such a stage-become-territory can only be described as revolutionary as it exceeds any classical, humanist definition of the people—those kinds of State-centred definitions that can only lead to deceptive results as the one of the United Nations Copenhagen summit in 2008 did.[5] Yet, thinking-with and acting-with those uncanny peoples could very well be the best option to inherit an Earth both devastated by climate changes induced by anthropic activities and defiant towards any will of human mastery.

In line with Deleuze's and Guattari's call for creation as means to resist the paralysed forms of the present, *Stifters Dinge* creates a process, a becoming that indicates a way beyond pessimism, cynicism, and desperation: those "posthuman" performative experiments may be our chance to create new modes of thought and perception, new philosophical, artistic and political ways to engage with becoming.

Notes

1. For this fact about *Stifters Dinge* as well as many others mentioned in this paper, I rely on Bell (2010).
2. In Massumi's English translation of *A Thousand Plateaus*, the *scenopoïetes dentirostris* is introduced as the "brown stagemaker" (315), just one page before the quotation discussed here.
3. See for instance the chapter "Micropolitics and Segmentarity", 208–231.

4. I develop those questions, articulated with the concepts of geophilosophy and fabulation, in Wiame (2018).
5. On the insufficiencies of a Nation-State-based model for negotiations around climate change, see Latour (2015, 329–373).

REFERENCES

Bell, Gelsey. 2010. "Driving Deeper into That Thing. The Humanity of Heiner Goebbels's Stifters Dinge." *The Drama Review* 54, no. 3: 150–158.
Braidotti, Rosi. 2013. *The Posthuman*. Cambridge, UK and Malden, MA: Polity Press.
Colebrook, Claire. 2014. *Death of the Posthuman. Essays on Extinction Vol. 1*. Ann Arbor: Open Humanities Press.
Deleuze, Gilles. 1989. *Cinema II: The Time-Image*. Translated by Hugh Tomlinson and Robert Galeta. London: Continuum.
Deleuze, Gilles, and Félix Guattari. 1987. *A Thousand Plateaus. Capitalism and Schizophrenia*. Translated by Brian Massumi. Minneapolis and London: University of Minnesota Press.
Deleuze, Gilles, and Félix Guattari. 1994. *What Is Philosophy?* Translated by Hugh Tomlinson and Graham Burchell. London: Verso.
Foucault, Michel. 2005. *The Order of Things. An Archaeology of the Human Sciences*. London and New York: Routledge Classics.
Goebbels, Heiner. 2008a. "Press Kit on *Stifters Dinge*." n.d. http://www.heinergoebbels.com/en/archive/works/complete/view/4/texts.
Goebbels, Heiner. 2008b. "Why I Made Stifter's Dinge." *Artangel*, n.d. www.artangel.org.uk//projects/2008/stifter_s_dinge/heiner_goebbels_on_stifter_s_dinge/heiner_goebbels_on_stifter_s_dinge.
Haraway, Donna. 2004. "Ecce Homo, Ain't (Ar'n't) I a Woman, and Inappropriate/d Others: The Human in a Post-humanist Landscape." In *The Haraway Reader*, 47–61. New York and London: Routledge.
Hénin, Emmanuelle. 2003. *Ut Pictura Theatrum. Théâtre et Peinture de la Renaissance italienne au Classicisme français*. Genève: Librairie Druoz.
Klee, Paul. 1966. *On Modern Art*. Translated by Paul Findlay, introduction by Herbert Reed. London: Faber.
Latour, Bruno. 2015. *Face à Gaïa. Huit conférences sur le nouveau régime climatique*. Paris: La Découverte.
Lehmann, Hans-Thies. 2006. *Postdramatic Theatre*. Translated by Karen Jürs-Munby. London and New York: Routledge.
Nayar, Pramod K. 2014. *Posthumanism*. Cambridge, UK and Malden, MA: Polity Press.
Saison, Maryvonne. 1998. *Les théâtres du réel. Pratiques de la représentation dans le théâtre contemporain*. Paris: l'Harmattan.

Schaefer, John. 2009. "Soundcheck: Heiner Goebbels." *WNYC*, 16 December. http://www.wnyc.org/story/42977-heiner-goebbels/.

Wiame, Aline. 2018. "Gilles Deleuze and Donna Haraway on Fabulating the Earth." *Deleuze and Guattari Studies* 12, no. 4: 525–540.

The Right to Remain Forgotten and the Data Crimes of Post-Digital Culture: A Ceaseless Traumatic Event

Matthew Causey

In no other manner are the ethics of spectatorship, digital surveillance and the performance of data-subjects, or data-doubles, more challenging than within the presence and exploitation of child sexual abuse imagery and non-consensual sexual imagery on the Internet. As I argued elsewhere, victims of this phenomena find the original abuse to be only the beginning of a ceaseless victimization and a resultant non-delusional paranoia in which the digital circulation of the images of the event of abuse and trauma are exploited and distributed. The "extra/ordinary" body of the victim re-embodied digitally and circulated electronically creates a bio-virtual exchange in which the original trauma is replicated, re-animated and virtually re-enacted. The past is circulated as the present, which leads

---

An earlier version of this chapter appeared as "The Right to Be Forgotten and the Image-Crimes of Digital Culture" in *The Performing Subject in the Space of Technology: Through the Virtual Towards the Real*, eds. M. Causey, E. Meehan, and N. O'Dwyer (London: Palgrave, 2015), 69–81.

M. Causey (✉)
Trinity College Dublin, Dublin, Ireland
e-mail: causeym@tcd.ie

© The Author(s), under exclusive license to Springer Nature Switzerland AG 2021
C. Stalpaert et al. (eds.), *Performance and Posthumanism*,
https://Doi.org/10.1007/978-3-030-74745-9_9

to a new understanding of performativity, presence and historicity while accelerating new lived-experiences of abuse, victimization and trauma. How do the experiences of the abuse victims figured in the ongoing, virtual life of these traumatic events exemplify identity in digital culture?

How are our data-doubles, our data-subjectivity, which are farmed and harvested from our own self-surveillance and personal marketing, implicated and influenced in the reconfigured virtual spaces wherein chronological histories and temporal models take place in a ceaseless (eternal) recurrence of the same (only different)? Do the traumatic scenes of abuse, which are taking place (again and again), present a useful proposition, a showing of the things as they are in a post-digital, bio-virtual culture? Are our performances of the self and the other in every day digital life a resistance or do they acquiesce to the late-capital ideologies of the data-doubles? And finally, how are our models of what constitutes historically relevant contemporary art practices affected in this bio-virtual situation?

THE RIGHTS OF THE DATA-SUBJECT

In considering the performativity of the data-doubles of digital culture, it is important to delineate what agency, autonomy and rights we subscribe to these entities. Is a data-double a mere electronic prosthetic to one's material continuity, or an autonomous agent whose existence although appearing virtual creates "real world" effects? Or is the model of doubling inadequate to articulate the models of subjectivity in digital culture? Instead of the doubling, we might consider hybrid identities of folding virtual and material presentations that establish the uniqueness of subjectivity in digital culture. It is not one or the other, virtual or real, data-based or organic, or even a matter of doubling, it is rather that digital culture subjectivities are *hybrid*, or *bio-virtual*, and have been named *homo digitalis*, or even *posthuman*. It is what Rosi Braidotti has termed *the posthuman predicament*, which,

> (...) is such as to force a displacement of the lines of demarcation between structural differences, or ontological categories, for instance between the organic and the inorganic, the born and the manufactured, flesh and metal, electronic circuits and organic nervous systems. (Braidotti 2013, 89)

If we are to understand the posthuman as a subject position within the situation of digital culture which affords the individual the opportunity to forward models of identity that are monistic (in which object, animal, inorganic matter, earth and human are conceived and organized with equanimity), post-anthropomorphic and transsexual, what are the rights to be ascribed to the posthuman? It is the theoretical construction of the posthuman that admits the inevitability of data-subjecthood and digital-doubling. But, as theatre and performance practices and theory have moved away from a foregrounding of the uncanny representations of the mediated doubles, so within a posthuman context the hybrid nature of identity is seen as always-already a hybrid of material and immaterial identities. In less utopic terms, my point is that the rights we would ascribe to the material continuity of the human are the rights which can be reasonably transferred to our extended identities in virtual environments.

What has become increasingly clear during the nascent days of digital culture are the zones of indistinction that exist between the virtual environments and the material world. Simply put, what happens in the virtual does not stay in the virtual, and it is clearly demonstrated that the actions within the virtual have "real world affects". Whatever border was imagined between the virtual and real, or material and cyberspace, was/is an illusion. Data-subjects live life in a blended experience of virtual and real, in which each modality drives the other, spills out over into the other, creating a complex sense of space, time and identity. Politics, art, love and science as the essential modes of communication are rearticulated and reconfigured and human experience is extended across these domains. If these suppositions are correct, how are rights ascribed within these hybrid identities and environments? This short paper considers the developing phenomena that define the identities and subjectivities within digital culture and the essential rights which might be afforded to the data-double or data-subject, although I will draw the notion of the double down to the singular categories of *homo digitalis* and *posthuman*. Subjects of digital culture are not doubled digitally. Data-subjects are digital.

Philosopher and cultural theorist Byung-Chul Han has articulated many of the issues arising in subjectivity in digital culture and argues that amongst the *digital swarm* citizenship is compromised by consumerism, auto-exploitation merges with the panopticon, the act of seeing functions as surveillance, decision processes are reconfigured as operations, thinking itself is compromised as a process of calculations, and truth is devalued as transparency (Han 2017). The subject has become project to be exploited by the individuals themselves as consumer and product simultaneously. What are the rights of those that exist (the human, posthuman or inhuman) within the virtual states of exception of electronic communications? How do we account for the bodies, which are "no-bodies", stateless, outside the law, and which "do not matter" as they do not materialize? What are the rights of the posthuman?

Within the Internet Folds of Social Media

The questions introducing this chapter are not a matter of aesthetics, that is, what technology is most seductive or attractive to watch, which projection narrates the story most accurately, or how the interface illustrates the concepts underlying the practice. Rather they are an attempt at a grounding theory of the culture that for many people exists in digitized societies, taking into account the manner in which their identities and subjectivities are constructed, negotiated and, in some cases, exploited and abused. This chapter examines how experiences of identity and trauma are altered by the ceaseless circulation of material within the folds of social media, the obscurity of the Darknet, the coded disguises of crypto-anarchism, the removable media of the sneakernet and the commercial appropriation of identity through Google, Facebook, et al.... This chapter investigates where there might be a shared experience between the electronic performance of the self both on-stage and online, the forfeiting of the private to the narcissism of a virtual public, and the most controversial examples of image crimes taking place in the possession and distribution of data contained in revenge porn (RP) and child sexual abuse images (CSAI).

I realize that there is a great gap between the processes, motivations and goals of the producers and users of RP or CSAI and the aesthetics or technologies of representation found in the different models of digital art production and the performance of the self in online environments. Yet, there is a shared mode of communication in which the past is circulated as the present, which leads to a new understanding of performance, liveness and presence while facilitating new experiences of abuse, victimization and trauma. So, these questions are not a matter of equalizing or sharing blame, but rather of considering the shared spaces of subjectivity that resonate and illuminate an understanding of the other. I will subsequently explore several lines of thought regarding the right to be digitally forgotten, the neo-authenticity of digital documentation, and mnemotechnologies (memory machines), before drawing them together in a consideration of RP and CSAI.

Droit à l'oubli (The Right to Be Forgotten)

Droit à l'oubli, or the right to be forgotten, is now a privilege that can be availed of by the citizens of the European Union. "Data subjects" (as they are referred to by the EU Court of Justice) are allowed to request that links from search engines such as Google to "inadequate, irrelevant or no longer relevant"[1] (EU Court of Justice 2014) websites be deleted or digitally forgotten. At the date of this writing over 90,000 requests to Google have been filed. In August 2014, the first removal of a link from Google search to a Wikipedia entry was scheduled to take place. The *droit à l'oubli* law is designed to allow a measure of control of the digital representations of one's identity. Of course, there is no manner for full erasure of any digital information that has been circulated on the Internet. Deletion is only a type of masking of the remnants of the digital, a burial of the ruins of the virtual, which are easily excavated and exposed. Digital data never disappears and remains only partially absent.

The right to be forgotten shares a central concern of contemporary identity politics that are summed up nicely by Chelsea Manning, a transgendered person formerly known as Private First Class Bradley Edward Manning. Manning, who was a prominent leak of classified documents for Julian Assange's *WikiLeaks*, was invited to be Grand Marshall of the 2014 San Francisco Gay Pride Parade. Chelsea was found guilty of charges stemming from her revealing confidential material to *WikiLeaks* and was serving a thirty-five-year prison sentence at the time and thus unable to attend the parade.[2] Instead she invited Lauren McNamara to stand in her place. McNamara, writing in *Freethoughts.blog*, stated that Chelsea asked that she emphasize that as transgendered people, "we have the right to exist as our genuine selves, that we are the only ones who can define ourselves, and that we should stand and make ourselves visible" (McNamara 2014). Chelsea Manning argues for a life in which she can present herself as the person she feels/knows she is. Her gender is performative but her identity as her sense of self appears to be certain. She seeks a truth, or at least, a correlation or accuracy between self and presentation. During her struggles with being a transgendered person serving in the military, Chelsea supplied *WikiLeaks* with documents that included strategies of the US government and military regarding the Iraq and

Afghanistan conflicts. The "truth", or a version of the truth, is revealed in the documents. The truth, or a version of the truth, is revealed in Ms. Manning's performance of her self. Each version is a reaching towards authenticity, genuineness and truth.

The collisions of ideologies, more or less similar in outcomes, found in the goals of this transgendered woman and *WikiLeaks* is intriguing. *WikiLeaks* claims to combine "high-end security technologies with journalism and ethical principles" to bring the "unvarnished truth out to the public" (WikiLeaks 2011). It is a passion for authenticity, truth and freedom that we see run throughout the actions and goals of Chelsea Manning, *WikiLeaks* and individuals such as Edward Snowden. It is the linkage between the virtual presences of digital culture and the concurrent demand for authenticity, the right to know and the right to be forgotten that is of interest.

To be forgotten "as was" and to exist "as is", or "as if", as one's genuine self seems to beg the question "does history matter", or to put it less melodramatically, what is our relation to history within digital culture. And to follow this thread to an illogical end, do facts, acts, events become irrelevant through a resistance to, or a forgetting of, their presence? Who judges? If I decide on or discover my genuine self do the facts of my past, or my disingenuous self, lose validity? Or is it just a matter of choice? In other words, I will present myself through the digital traces of myself in the manner I choose and the gaps between the past and the present, the private and the public are reconfigured. Further down this path, do we have a right to know everything or do we have the right to be forgotten as well? Either/or, or both/together?

As the means for representing one's identity within electronic communications slips from one's control and is dispersed amongst other individuals, corporations and state controls, attempts to reclaim that identity are practised. The authentic self finds itself either a commodity in a capitalist exchange or shaped by forces outside the individual's control through wiki-posts, tweets, Facebook updates and so on. One's actions are now not the controlling factor in identity, as one is constructed by a careless commodification through a targeting of identity to a micro-level so that one's desires and interests are tracked, marketed and sold. However, this is not just a struggle of power and agency as there is another psychological or psychic level to the situation. In one sense, the right to be forgotten might be interpreted as the desire to be forgiven. But, there is no virtual confession,[3] although we might fashion a theory of the social network as just that. It may be said that within digital culture nothing is ever truly forgotten and therefore nothing is ever truly forgiven, as the event is taking place in a continual "now". Is it possible that Anthony Weiner, United States House of Representative from New York who was at the centre of a sexting scandal, will ever be unrecognized as the politician who exposed himself on phone photographs? Or more seriously, will journalist James Foley be remembered outside the horrific video of his beheading at the hands of a soldier of the Islamic State of Iraq and Syria?

It was during the Rodney King riots in Los Angeles that protestors called out the phrase "the video doesn't lie, the video doesn't lie". In more ways than one that phrase is true. The video, the image, the text, does not lie, its truth lies in its inexhaustible presence that continues to exist and supersede the subject. Moments of embarrassment, acts of folly, victimizations and violence are ceaselessly replayed in an always-already virtual now. The events documented have the potential to exist in the manic newness of the Internet, unrelenting and recurrent.

However, there are competing interests in the debate of forgetting and knowing. Free speech advocates are concerned over the EU *droit a l'oubli* law and other restrictions on electronic communications. Perhaps one is seeking the right to be forgotten so that one's genuine self might more sharply appear, while conversely there is a concern for the free flow of information. Perhaps one wishes to challenge the random and universal surveillance of contemporary western democracies, but nonetheless demands to know the details of state business. The EU Court of Justice in its directive states the following:

> The Court holds that a fair balance should be sought in particular between that interest [freedom of information] and the data subject's fundamental rights, in particular the right to privacy and the right to protection of personal data. The Court observes in this regard that, whilst it is true that the data subject's rights also override, as a general rule, that interest of Internet users, this balance may however depend, in specific cases, on the nature of the information in question and its sensitivity for the data subject's private life and on the interest of the public in having that information, an interest which may vary, in particular, according to the role played by the data subject in public life. (EU Court of Justice 2014)

The right to be forgotten (*droit à l'oubli*) collides with the right to know (*WikiLeaks*). Obviously, the state and the individual, like Creon and Antigone, exist under different laws and what an individual chooses to reveal and what the state attempts to hide follow separate ethical imperatives. So, what do we have the right to know, what has the right to be forgotten?

The Authenticity of the Virtual (The Techno-Memory of Drones and the Selfie)

When the first steps of cyberspace were taken in the eighties and nineties, it was commonplace to argue that the electronic communication system provided a platform for a liquid and liberated identity with users enabled to perform a variety of characteristics, some fictional and fantastical, some based on more real representations. There was a clear and steady move towards virtuality in which a resistance against the material and an exploration of an absent otherness were seductive.[4] The advent of digital avatars and a world wide web of communication heralded a new consciousness and new identities. However, the flip side of the semi-utopian model of the Internet has in the meantime been exposed and laid bare. There are now many possibilities for recurrent victimization through the tyranny of the digital image and the replaying of traumatic events. The misreading, or partial reading, of the seated human with a computer interface of keyboard, screen and virtual environment (with only the gesture of fingers) as a figure for liberation was short-lived.

Alternatively to a model of virtual communications as progressive, the Internet enacts an ethics of virtual spectatorship that allows telepresent interactions of being both there and not-there that encourages anonymity and invisibility. The divisions between virtual and real existence are no longer clearly defined. The ontologies of the virtual and real are not considered to be autonomous or discrete but interface in a bio-virtual experience. For example, in military installations in the state of Colorado in the United States, soldiers living at home commute to work and enter battle zones in the Middle East via telepresent interactivity, allowing them to control drones or Unmanned Aerial Vehicles (UAVs) and fire on enemy combatants from the relative comfort of a military control room. Interestingly, even though these soldiers remain removed and distant from the field of battle, interacting in a virtual interface, they have the potential to develop cases of post-traumatic stress disorder. As Julian Dibbell demonstrated in "A Rape in Cyberspace" (1996) decades ago the effects of the virtual on the material is one of substance. Interactions in virtual environments have real consequences to the user and the neat division of real/virtual is an erroneous division.

As the absence of the avatars, be they graphic or alphanumerical, has become more or less a central component in the lives of many inhabitants of digital culture, a likewise strong impulse towards authenticity can be charted. To mask the absence of presence, a new passion for personal documentation is prevalent in social media and across the Internet. Gabriella Calchi Novati, in an essay titled "Documentary in the Age of Digital Biopolitics", writes that "the performance of the self, in the age of digital biopolitics, strive[s] to conceal such an absence with self reflexive signifiers such as photographs, online-chats and text messages" (2012, 5). There are many examples of this digital need for recognition through documentation, but perhaps it is the phenomenon of the "selfie" which most sadly encapsulates the passion to document the self and distribute the remains across digital environments so that the memory of the event is recognized and made real through its virtual presence. The quick response to the selfie would be to note its narcissistic construction, its neediness for recognition, and its representation of an existential despair. However, the sticking point of the selfie, and the drone for that matter, is that this digital documentation extracts a cost in the form of relinquishing elements of our memory to machines. In a manner, our memory capacity atrophies, and our relation to history is fundamentally altered. The more we rely on technological memory the less we remember. We forget things, or we forget some things, easily. It is only with the advent of new memory machines, which have problematized our relation to the past so effectively, that we come more detached from our history. Bernard Stiegler writes in that context:

> We exteriorize in contemporary mnemotechnical equipment more and more cognitive functions, and correlatively we are losing more and more knowledge which is then delegated to equipment, but also to service industries which can network them, control them, formalize them, model them, and perhaps destroy them – for these knowledges, escaping our grasp, induce an "obsolescence of the human", who finds itself more and more at a loss, and interiorly empty. (2007, n.p.)

Like a society of Citizen Kanes, our basements, now digital and located in the clouds, are filled with the objects we have misplaced or forgotten, now consigned to a Facebook timeline, or confined to a de-activated online profile. Before digital culture, if a version of a particular history was written, then we might assume a degree of critical reflection shadowed by its own transparent ideology, no doubt, but constructed as a reflective narrative. We can imagine a time when there was a critical distance between any event and its representation. Currently, events can be taking place while simultaneously represented (streaming media and 24-hour news cycles). In some cases, the representations may even precede the event. We now have a new form of history (100 years old?) structured on recordable media and digital data that can be mined and organized with computational accuracy and speed. What is the ideology inscribed in any search code or software? What deals do we make with the machines for their services? Stiegler suggests:

> [T]he more we delegate the execution of series of small tasks that make up the warp and woof of our lives to the apparatuses and services of modern industry, the more vain we become: the more we lose not only our know-how but our know-how-to-live-well: the only thing left for us is to consume blindly, a kind of impotence, without these saveurs (savours) that only savoir – from *sapere* – which is knowledge, can provide. We become impotent if not obsolete – if it is true that knowledge is what empowers humanity. (2007, n.p.)

If, as Stiegler has suggested, we have forfeited some of our humanity to the machines, if our relationship to history and our temporal/spatial constructs of our world are fundamentally changed, if we are led to seek authenticity in the virtual and struggle to appear real within the world, then what about the most vulnerable amongst us who suffer within the chasm of abuse potential in digital environments?

Image Crimes

A report to the US Congress from the United States Sentencing Commission on the subject of child pornography states:

> It is unknown how many victims of child pornography exist worldwide. The National Center for Missing and Exploited Children ("NCMEC") has reviewed over 57 million images and videos of child pornography (many of them duplicates) and has assisted law enforcement in the identification over 4,103 individual victims. It is estimated that there are over five million

unique child pornography images on the Internet and some offenders possess over one million images of child pornography. The number of identified victims represents only a small portion of the victims whose images are in circulation. (US Sentencing Commission 2012)

Nowhere is the ethics of spectatorship more challenged than with the presence of child pornography on the net. The term "Internet Child Pornography" (ICP) has the potential to indicate a degree of consent or participation, and thus the terms of child sexual abuse images (CSAI) and child physical abuse images (CPAI) seem more accurate. Children of this process find the original abuse to be only the beginning of a ceaseless victimization and a resultant non-delusional paranoia in which the digital circulation of the images of the event of abuse and trauma are exploited and (re)distributed. The body of the victim remembered digitally and circulated electronically creates a bio-virtual exchange in which the original trauma is replicated and re-experienced. In 2011, a young woman suing for restitution as a result of the circulation of the CSAI in which she appeared wrote in her victim-impact statement:

> I live every day with the horrible knowledge that many people somewhere are watching the most terrifying moments of my life and taking grotesque pleasure in them. Unlike other forms of exploitation, this one is never ending. They are trading around my trauma like treats at a party and it feels like I am being raped all over again by every one of them. (Arsenault 2013)

This young woman testifies of a "never-ending trauma" that results in a feeling of "being raped all over again". This results not only from the perversity of the perpetrators but also by the particular constellation of the technological communications of peer-to-peer (P2P) networks which evade recognized Internet servers. The technology is not the cause, but it does exacerbate the sufferings that arrive from the original abuse. The trauma is not a matter of history, but of constant presence. The machinic temporality exceeds human memory with its ability to re-enact the trauma with exact repeatability.

The US Supreme Court case "Paroline v United States", which was argued on 22 January 2014, involved "Amy", an eight-year-old child at the time when an uncle sexually abused and raped her. The abuse was photographed and circulated on the Internet and offenders worldwide collected and circulated the images. In her victim-impact statement, she wrote: "How can I ever get over this when the crime that is happening to me will never end? How can I get over this when the shameful abuse I suffered is out there forever and being enjoyed by sick people?" (NCMEC 2014). The question that the court was asked to consider was how much restitution should each offender be responsible for considering the number of individuals who had circulated, copied, stored and traded the images of "Amy". If restitution for pain and suffering, loss of earning potential, and psychiatric care was of a certain amount, say three million, should each offender be responsible for the full amount or a portion? The Supreme Court ruled on April 24, 2014 that a person convicted of child pornography is only required to a pay a portion of the total damages that victims can seek in restitution. In an issue termed "aggregate causation", each individual/offender is responsible for only a portion of the overall damages. Of course this places the onus of claiming the restitution, through multiple court cases and multiple offenders, on the victim. If perhaps thousands, if not tens of thousands of people traded or downloaded the images the situation is challenging for the victim, to say the least.

The dilemma of victims of CASI in seeking restitution for a crime that is ongoing and whose perpetrators are many is an illustrative situation and pressing concern when translated to the commonplace usage of the Internet. What is our stake in the blame, or how much is our response worth, when we contribute to any massive-user network, be it commercial or social? Are we freed from culpability if we are virtually removed (remember the telepresent soldier and his remote-controlled drone) or if we represent only a tiny fraction of the number of users involved in a viral moment?

"Revenge Porn" is another recent, abusive and traumatic phenomenon in which explicit video or photographs, which may have been created with consent from the data subject or exist as a "selfie" circulated through sexting, are uploaded online without the consent of one or more of the subjects of the images. An ex-partner who has been jilted or a bullying peer group generally perform the uploading and find revengeful satisfaction in the posting of the highly personal material. As noted in *The Economist* there are over 3,000 websites that include Revenge Porn imagery (2014). Revenge Porn is another coarse and misleading name (not unlike ICP) for an extreme form of abuse, bullying and invasion of privacy. The effects of the abuse can be understandably traumatic with a substantial number of suicides attributed to the victimization of the circulation of the images. In Brazil, a seventeen-year-old woman, Julia Rebecca, committed suicide "after a sex tape of her with a male and female, also minors, was posted online" (Burger 2013). In California, fifteen-year-old Audrie Pott killed herself after photos of gang abuse at the hands of her peers circulated through her high school (Burleigh 2013). Laws have been passed in a handful of countries and a number of states in the United States, but prosecution and even the removal of the material remain difficult, costly and slow. Once the images or videos are published, circulated and distributed online there is no way to contain their further circulation, distribution and duplication. The right to be forgotten has little currency in the Darknet and P2P networks. But as of yet the law provides little protection to the rights of those violated. "Section 230 of the Communications Decency Act effectively means that no Internet provider can be forced to take down content for invading a person's privacy or even defaming them" (Burleigh 2013).

Without question, the individuals committing the abuse and those documenting the event are to be held accountable, but what of those who watch? How do we judge their participation? If any individual watches, or more importantly, downloads and distributes a video of CSAI or Revenge Porn, are they contributing to the crime and participating in the abuse? Some free speech advocates would argue for an anarchic freedom that suggests viewing falls on the side of free speech and only the act of the abuse counts. Would we suggest that watching a policeman kill a young black man, or the footage of a journalist's execution, is participating, encouraging or creating a demand? It may be that we would.

In the *New York Times Magazine*, Emily Bazelon writes about two young women who are facing a history (and a future) of child sexual abuse. One of the women stated that knowing that so many men have witnessed and taken pleasure from her abuse has been excruciating, commenting that "[y]ou have an image of yourself as a person, but here is this other image (...) you know it's not true, but all those other people will believe that it's you — that this is who you really are" (2013). How can the data subject actually be her "genuine self" as Chelsea Manning described, when the images are present in the public domain? In the same article, forensic psychologist Joyanna Silberg stated:

> Usually, we try to help survivors of child sexual abuse make a very strong distinction between the past and the present (...) The idea is to contain the harm: it happened then, and it's not happening anymore. But how

do you do that when these images are still out there? The past is still the present, which turns the hallmarks of treatment on their head. (2013)

This situation is central to my argument. When the present/past/future are collapsed and identity frozen in a traumatic *cul de sac*, we witness one of digital culture's more disturbing phenomena in the hell of an eternal circle of the same. "I'm scared but I think this goodbye is forever" (quoted in Burger 2013) was Julia Rebecca's last text before ending her own life.

Conclusion

The question bears repeating. Does our shaping of digital culture around "flawless" mechanical memories, our sacrifice of the private for a virtual public, our engagement and simultaneous resistance to surveillance, derive from the same impulse that can exacerbate and sustain many sufferings and traumatic events? In this chapter, I have considered the technological rememberings of trauma as performed by users of child pornography, the ceaseless virtual (but nonetheless real) victimization of the abused, and how participants of digital culture engage in this electronic and panoptic space.

Is there a useful link to be made between these problems of the subject in the space of technology and the practices of digital performance? It must seem, I should think, to the reader that it is a callous comparison to make. And yet, if the medium is the message then there is a shared system of communication that shapes our actions and thoughts. Are the manipulations and commercializations, victimizations and abuses of people, the destruction of privacy and the redefining of the self, replicated in the introduction of the absence of the virtual into the presence of the stage? Our world is no longer private, we are no longer forgotten or forgiven, and our passion for recognition has turned in on itself. When we are watched and watching, engaging and accepting of surveillance, forwarding and retweeting, we partake in a careless conflation of daily life and virtual existence in which rights to privacy and personal space are radically reduced. There is a porous gap between the virtual and the real, each embedded in the other, altering their course and configuring the subjects, users and abusers. While forgetting Auslander's claim that a techno-performativity redefines what we mean by the live,[5] or remembering Phelan's here and now theory of performance,[6] is it too precious to suggest that performance (or, to put a finer point on it, the theatre) is a place of forgetting (of forgiveness), which might resist the ceaseless image-saturation of digital culture? Is the proscenium arch substantially different from any other screen, be it electronic or otherwise? Or, is this situation similar to Derrida's reading of Artaud's Theatre of Cruelty[7] where at the ends of representation, representation reappears? Here, in the folds of the Internet, the image persists. Here, the image of thought meets its logical ends in the electronic consciousness of the Web. Images are models of thought and the anxiety of their proliferation is a historical problem, which is already known as the new normal.[8]

Notes

1. The Court of Justice of the European Union Press Release No. 70/14 of Luxembourg, 13 May 2014, states that, "An Internet search engine operator is responsible for the processing that it carries out of personal data which appear on web pages published by third parties (…) thus, if, following a search made on the basis of a person's name, the list of results displays a link to a web page which contains information on the person in question, that data subject may approach the operator directly and, where the operator does not grant his request, bring the matter before the competent authorities in order to obtain, under certain conditions, the removal of that link from the list of results".
2. Chelsea Manning was pardoned in 2017 by then President Barack Obama.
3. Of course, like most things, there actually is a virtual version. See http://www.absolution-online.com.
4. For example, see Benedikt (1991), Stone (1995), Turkel (1995).
5. See Auslander (1999).
6. See Phelan (1993).
7. See Derrida (1980).
8. These last few sentences, although obscure and perhaps even obscurantist, are meant to condense the problem addressed, which is the proliferation of Internet data (video, photos, etc.) and their interruption and reconfiguration of the temporal-spatial field of contemporary digital culture. The images are how we think digitally and the resistance to their proliferation cannot last. Thus we need new strategies for exploring the potential for genuinely new models of experience while negotiating their capacity for serious harm.

References

Arsenault, Mark. 2013. "Child Pornography Trader Pays Restitution to Victim." *Boston Globe*, 16 December. Accessed 22 August 2014. http://www.boston globe.com/metro/2013/12/16/child-pornography-trader-pays-restitution-rape-victim-groundbreaking-case/2UtGaeTaZKLubxwB0q1vPP/story.html.
Auslander, Philip. 1999. *Liveness: Performance in a Mediatized Culture*. New York: Routledge.
Bazelon, Emily. 2013. "The Price of a Stolen Childhood." *New York Times Magazine*, 24 January. Accessed 22 August 2014. http://nyti.ms/VuxRy8.
Benedikt, Michael. 1991. *Cyberspace: First Steps*. Cambridge, MA: MIT Press.
Braidotti, Rosi. 2013. *The Posthuman*. Cambridge: Polity Press.
Burger, Miriam. 2013. "Brazilian 17-Year-Old Commits Suicide After Revenge Porn Posted Online." *BuzzFeedNews*, 20 November. Accessed 22 August 2014. http://www.buzzfeed.com/miriamberger/brazilian-17-year-old-commits-suicide-after-revenge-porn-pos.
Burleigh, Nina. 2013. "Sexting, Shame and Suicide: A Shocking Tale of Sexual Assault in the Digital Age." *Rolling Stone Magazine*, 17 September. Accessed 22 August 2014. http://www.rollingstone.com/culture/news/sexting-shame-and-suicide-20130917.
Calchi Novati, Gabriella. 2012. "Documentary in the Age of Digital Biopolitics." *Cinemascope: Independent Film Journal*, no. 17: 1–6. Accessed 20 February 2020. https://www.academia.edu/1370113/Documentary_in_the_Age_of_Digital_Biopolitics_Catfish_and_the_Aesthetics_of_Amphibology_.
Causey, Matthew. 2015. "The Right to Be Forgotten and the Image-Crimes of Digital Culture." In *The Performing Subject in the Space of Technology: Through the Virtual Towards the Real*, edited by Matthew Causey, Emma Meehan, and Neill O'Dwyer. London: Palgrave.
Derrida, Jacques. 1980. "The Theatre of Cruelty and the Closure of Representation." In *Writing and Difference*, translated by Alan Bass, 232–250. Chicago: University of Chicago Press.
Dibbell, Julian. 1996. "A Rape in Cyberspace; or How an Evil Clown, a Haitian Trickster Spirit, Two Wizards, and a Cast of Dozens Turned a Database into a Society." In *High Noon on the Electronic Frontier: Conceptual Issues in Cyberspace*, edited by Peter Ludlow, 375–396. Cambridge, MA: MIT Press.
EU Court of Justice. 2014. "Press Release 70/14: Judgment in Case C-131/12 Google Spain SL, Google Inc. v Agencia Española de Protección de Datos, Mario Costeja González." 13 May. Accessed 22 August 2014. http://curia.europa.eu/jcms/upload/docs/application/pdf/2014-05/cp140070en.pdf.
Han, Byung-Chul. 2017. *In the Swarm: Digital Prospects*. London: MIT Press.
McNamara, Lauren. 2014. "Why I'm Representing Chelsea Manning at SF Pride." *Zinnia Jones: Secular Trans Feminism*, 26 June. Accessed 22

August 2014. http://freethoughtblogs.com/zinniajones/2014/06/why-im-representing-chelsea-manning-at-sf-pride/.
NCMEC. 2014. "Paroline v. United States: A Case for Restitution." *National Center for Missing and Exploited Children*. Accessed 22 August 2014. http://blog.missingkids.com/post/74183786414/paroline-v-united-states-a-case-for-restitution.
Phelan, Peggy. 1993. *Unmarked: The Politics of Performance*. New York: Routledge.
"Revenge Porn: Misery Merchants." *The Economist*, 5 July. Accessed 22 August 2014. http://www.economist.com/node/21606307/print.
Stiegler, Bernard. 2007. "Anamnesis and Hypomnesis: Plato as the First Thinker of the Proletarianisation." *Ars Industrialis*. Accessed 20 February 2020. http://arsindustrialis.org/anamnesis-and-hypomnesis.
Stone, Allucquére Rosanne. 1995. *The War of Desire and Technology at the Close of the Mechanical Age*. Cambridge, MA: MIT Press.
Turkel, Sherry. 1995. *Life on the Screen: Identity in the Age of the Internet*. Cambridge, MA: MIT Press.
United States Sentencing Commission. 2012. "Victims of Child Pornography." *Federal Child Pornography Offences*. Accessed 22 August 2014. http://www.ussc.gov/sites/default/files/pdf/news/congressional-testimony-and-reports/sex-offense-topics/201212-federal-child-pornography-offenses/Chapter_05.pdf.
WikiLeaks. 2011. "About." *WikiLeaks.org*, 7 May. Accessed 22 August 2014. https://www.wikileaks.org/About.html.

The Biography of a Digital Device: The Interwovenness of Human and Non-human Movements in Production and Distribution Processes as Thematized in the Artwork *Rare Earthenware* by Unknown Fields

Martina Ruhsam

Rare Earthenware is the title of an artwork by the nomadic research and design studio Unknown Fields Division. As visionaries and reporters, documentarists, and science fiction lovers, the members of the collective attempt to investigate the consequences of emerging ecological and technological scenarios in their artistic works.[1] In several expeditions to locations on various continents, they did research on alternative worlds as well as alien landscapes and industrial ecologies in order to show how the hidden narratives of these localities are intricately and intimately interwoven with the everyday life of the urban population. For every expedition, Kate Davies and Liam Young, the leaders of the collective, assemble a team of experts around them: photographers, filmmakers, journalists, scientists, artists, designers and specialists in aerial

M. Ruhsam (✉)
Institute for Applied Theatre Studies, Justus-Liebig-University, Gießen, Germany
e-mail: Martina.Ruhsam@theater.uni-giessen.de

© The Author(s), under exclusive license to Springer Nature Switzerland AG 2021
C. Stalpaert et al. (eds.), *Performance and Posthumanism*,
https://doi.org/10.1007/978-3-030-74745-9_10

drone photography and film. Each of them documents the expedition in a specific way and reflects on it. *Rare Earthenware* is one project of a series of photographs, films and artefacts with the title *Summer 2014_A World Adrift (Part 02)* developed in the context of a journey to China in 2014.[2] Over the course of this expedition, Unknown Fields investigated remote ecological, social and economic realities that have emerged in response to modern technological production modes. Liam Young, a trained architect, comments on his work with Unknown Fields in relation to questions of urban architecture: "It all stems from this idea of trying to understand the city in a new way...by looking at the landscapes that are fundamental to producing it" (Young 2016).

Unknown Fields Division has tracked the history of electronic devices by tracing back their process of production to their origins in the mines of Baotou. The industrial city of Baotou is the largest settlement in Inner Mongolia Autonomous Region in the north of the People's Republic of China—also known for having the world's biggest refinery for the extraction of rare-earth elements.[3] As these metals are essential components in high-end electronics and are used for the production of magnets, camera lenses and batteries, they are among the world's most sought-after materials and demand for them continues to rise. Every smartphone has components made of around eight different rare-earth metals; laptops and iPods contain even more. Furthermore, and somewhat ironically, rare-earth elements are also required for the production of certain "green" technologies such as components for wind turbines and electric cars. Neodymium is a rare-earth metal used in large quantities (up to one kilogramme) for the production of electric vehicles. Waste products and residues from neodymium extraction are not only toxic but also contain traces of radioactive uranium and thorium. The production of one tonne of rare-earth metals leaves behind more than eight-kilogramme fluorine, 75 cubic metres of toxic wastewater, and approximately one tonne of slightly radioactive mud. These residues are pumped into tailing ponds, and, due to lack of pollution control regulations in China, they then seep into groundwater with severe ecological consequences in Baotou and the surrounding region. For this reason agricultural activities have become impossible in several areas in the vicinity of Baotou mainly due to increasing contamination of the Yellow River. The dimensions of these barely liquid, radioactive tailings can best be imagined by recalling that 95 per cent of global demand for rare-earth metals are mined in China, half of which are extracted in the open-pit mine of Bayan Obo in the vicinity of Baotou. Through a combination of wage dumping, the exploitation of regions with a high concentration of resources, and low production costs connected to the extraction and processing of rare-earth metals, also as a consequence of lax environmental controls, China has monopolized the rare-earth metal extraction industry in the beginning of the twenty-first century. Whereas there are relatively strict regulations concerning the storage of toxic waste in the United States, several mines in China are operated either illegally or are barely subject to state control. The fact that the US imports rare-earth metals from China even when their own resources are sufficient to satisfy worldwide demand is also a result of the relative cost-efficiency of the Chinese model of extraction (Lohmann and Podbregar 2012, 10).[4]

Unknown Fields did not gain access to the Bayan Obo mine legally. For this reason, the expedition team found it necessary to apply strategies learnt from investigative journalism. Those involved in the expedition impersonated a group of interested investors and potential purchasers of the mine. In this way, they gained admission to the factory site where they then filmed with hidden cameras. They were not shown the area where the tailing ponds are located. With the help of GPS data and satellite imagery, however, Unknown Fields were able to discover not only which road led to the tailings, but also when the security teams guarding the entrance to the area changed shifts. In the short time taken for one shift of guard personnel to be replaced by the next, they managed to gain access to the tailings in order to film and photograph these toxic lakes, and to collect a small quantity of toxic mud. They remained unnoticed by security staff. Laboratory tests indicated that the level of radioactivity of the mud was three times higher than usual background radiation (Figs. 1 and 2).

In response to what they had seen in Baotou, Unknown Fields developed an artistic work consisting of three vases and a short film.[5] The three vases are of three different sizes and were made from the toxic mud (with binding material) collected from the tailing pond at Bayan Obo. Each vase represents precisely the amount of radioactive mud produced as a by-product of the manufacturing process for a smartphone, a laptop and the batteries used in an electric car, respectively. The term "representing" is a misnomer in respect to the vases, as, in fact, they do not just *represent* the toxic mud, but consist of it.

Fig. 1 Unknown Fields Division, *Rare Earthenware* (film still), 2014 (© Toby Smith/Unknown Fields Division)

The vases are material-discursive hybrids[6] that are "active" in many and varied (risky) ways, that is to say, they are equipped with various agential capacities. Even if their radioactivity does not exceed the maximum safety limits set by museums for objects in their collections, being in contact with large amounts of this material or being exposed to it over an extended period of time might have concrete consequences for the human organism.

Furthermore, those production and distribution networks in which the vases are involved are also "active" in the artefacts themselves—even when they are placed in a museum (as is visible in the film that is exhibited next to them). *Rare Earthenware* makes it evident that agency is a complex phenomenon and certainly not a purely human privilege. It is instead distributed among diverse actors and actants[7] that are entangled in every instant, just as Jane Bennett has depicted in her writings (2010, ix, 21, 38).[8] In her recent book *Vibrant Matter. The Political Agency of Things* (2010, Preface, X) she writes:

> (...) I try to bear witness to the vital materialities that flow through and around us. Though the movements and effectivity of stem cells, electricity, food, trash, and metals are crucial to political life (and human life per se),

Fig. 2 Unknown Fields Division, *Rare Earthenware* (vases made from the toxic mud), 2014 (© Toby Smith/Unknown Fields Division)

almost as soon as they appear in public (often at first by disrupting human projects or expectations), these activities and powers are represented as human mood, action, meaning, agenda, or ideology. This quick substitution sustains the fantasy that "we" really are in charge of all those "its" – its that, according to the tradition of (nonmechanistic, nonteleological) materialism I draw on, [they] reveal themselves to be potentially forceful agents.

Timothy Morton, who is very involved with object-oriented ontology, designates radioactivity as "poisoned light" (2010, 130) and considers radioactive objects as especially haunting examples of his thesis that hyperobjects are always already under our skin: "We think of "objects" as passive and inert, as "over there". Just by existing, this hyperobject affects living tissue. Radioactive materials are already "over here", inside our skin, as Marie Curie discovered to her cost" (ibid.). According to Morton, whose background is in ecocriticism, humans are implicated in hyperobjects with which they form a "mesh"—which "extends inside beings as well as among them" (2010, 39). Hyperobjects are, according to his definition, (co)produced by human beings and occur massively in time and space. They are characterized by their viscosity, and, even if some of them are invisible, they stand out due to the extremely intimate relationship they maintain with human beings. Climate change, black holes, the biosphere, oil fields, all the nuclear material on Earth, toxic lakes in China and elsewhere, and styrofoam are all examples of hyperobjects that stick to the human body, from which they are indissociable, and which embody a temporality that is radically different from the temporality of a human lifespan (Morton 2012).

In respect to the three vases that Unknown Fields fabricated, Morton's assertion that hyperobjects have to be considered as the real taboos in our society is especially relevant (2010, 132). At a time when nudity, promiscuity and the depiction of violence have ceased acting as taboos in the so-called West, Unknown Fields smuggle artefacts into an art institution that seem, on first glance, utterly traditional, but which are in fact connected to processes that the recipients of contemporary art—as users of high-end electronics—like to ignore. The by-products and ecologies that emerge in the course of manufacturing digital devices, the consequence of their distribution, what happens to those gadgets as soon as they are discarded…these manifestations constitute a kind of collective unconscious of a digitalized society living to the rhythm of the buy-and-discard cycles imposed on it by Late Capitalism (constantly accelerating). The storage of the resulting waste and residues is outsourced as much as possible to other countries and thus disappears from the view of the European or North American urban consumer. Liam Young believes that the potential of aesthetic practices, performances and narrations lies precisely in their capacity to make the unseen connections and entanglements between the things we encounter a subject of discussion (2016).

Donna Haraway highlighted the nexus of inheritance and embodiment when posing the question: "In how many ways do we inherit in the flesh the turbulent history of modern capitalism?" (2015, 24). In regard to those human beings who live in the vicinity of radioactive tailing ponds in Baotou—and in consideration of the non-human beings that do *not* live there any longer—her question attains an utterly concrete significance. Toxic lakes are a paradigmatic "new materiality", hyperobjects that we are compelled to deal with—just like the thawing permafrost in the Arctic and Antarctic that is emitting carbon dioxide and methane, or the Great Pacific Garbage Patch, a conglomeration of plastic bags, bottles, toothbrushes, lighters, CD covers and other household items, which is estimated to cover an area twice as big as Germany (Folkers 2013, 28). These new materialities have also led to the emergence of new philosophical movements such as Object-Oriented-Ontology, Speculative Realism and New Materialism, all of which strive to attribute a new role and status to the non-human in philosophical and political debates. In this text I will mainly refer to concepts that are subsumed under the umbrella term "New Materialism"—despite the (huge) differences in respect to their claims and concepts.

Already, before the advent of these movements, individual humanities scholars were concerned with the status of nature, materials and the materiality of things. The philosopher Félix Guattari was one such scholar who developed an "ecosophy" in order to reflect on the interaction of the environment with social and psychological processes (2008). Together with Gilles Deleuze he later wrote about the relevance of assemblages (*agencements*) and de-territorialized material flows without a human workman (1980). I agree with Susanne Witzgall when she writes that, in fact, New Materialism is not that new. Nevertheless—as Witzgall pointed out in a German publication with the title *Macht des Materials/Politik der Materialität* (Power of materials/Politics of materiality)—in consideration of current developments, New Materialism does indeed pursue a new qualitative orientation that justifies the term "New" Materialism in relation to recent attempts both in science and art (Witzgall and Stakemeier 2014, 150). New Materialism rejects conceptions of matter that predominated in the history of the humanities: matter as either the "other" of culture or imagined as a passive context for human actions.

Reconfigurations of the Real and the Possible

In the context of the human sciences, materiality and nature have often been thematized as passive carriers of cultural inscriptions or meanings, as given environments, or as conditions of production—even if Titus Lucretius Carus, Félix Guattari, Gilles Deleuze or Michel Serres, among others, have proposed a different understanding of matter and non-human actors. New Materialism considers itself a counter-movement to linguistic constructivisms and the linguistic strand of poststructuralism that was entirely focused on the analysis of semiotic systems and disregarded all materiality—with the exception of the materiality of the sign. As Andreas Folkers pointed out, the problem with those linguistic constructivisms that replace the acting subject by de-centred networks of discourses, speech acts and communicational flows was not their reproduction of the Cartesian dualism, but rather the fact that, as a linguistic monism, this theoretical movement bracketed out issues of materiality completely. Here, matter was not the passive other of active subjectivity, but was actually thought to be a product of discourses (Folkers 2013, 20). In contrast to such an overdetermination of discourses, feminist and natural scientist Donna Haraway emphasised the activity of the world:

> One must surely tell of the networks of sugar, precious metals, plantations, indigenous genocides, and slavery, with their labor innovations and relocations and recompositions of critters and things sweeping up both human and nonhuman workers of all kinds. The infectious industrial revolution of England mattered hugely, but it is only one player in planet-transforming, historically situated, new-enough, worlding relations. (2016, 48)

Following Haraway's attempt to counter the neglect of the dynamic quality of matter and to emphasize the fact that matter can no longer be regarded as a given environment or a stable context for human actions, feminist and particle physicist Karen Barad wrote: "(…) matter is not situated in the world; matter is worlding in its materiality" (2007, 180–181). Barad developed the concept of intra-action, which basically states that there is no subject and no object that would pre-exist as such, that is to say, prior to the encounters or intra-actions between specific human and non-human others. Entities do not have fixed or inherent properties; they are but the products of specific intra-actions. An additional goal of this concept is a rethinking of traditional notions of causality and agency in order to show that nature does not simply comply with the laws of causality. This form of agential realism takes the intra-actions of human and non-human actors, as well as of the material and the discursive, into account as a permanent reconfiguration of the real and the possible (Barad 2007, 182). Barad deems all those involved in this permanent reconfiguration to be neither deterministic, controllable, nor malleable at will. Therefore, the toxic mud that forms the raw material for the vases fabricated by Unknown Fields cannot be merely regarded as a resource for human construction or as a carrier of cultural inscriptions. Even the cameras used by Unknown Fields to capture the footage for their film are not neutral instruments, but are instead deeply involved in processes of meaning-making and subjectification. Furthermore, they are materially entangled with the footage they recorded. As soon as human beings see or touch something, they become enmeshed in complex assemblages incorporating human and non-human bodies. All of them are hybrids of nature and technology, artefacts between materiality and discourse, agglomerations of capitalism and its refractions (Volkart 2016, 29).

Emerging Landscapes at the Point of Intersection of Terraforming and Material Autonomy

(...) the universe is agential intra-activity in its becoming. The primary ontological units are not "things" but phenomena – dynamic topological reconfigurings/entanglements/relationalities/(re)articulations. [...] Agency is not an attribute but the ongoing reconfigurings of the world. (Barad 2003, 818)

The film *Rare Earthenware* focuses on the itineraries of three vases made by Unknown Fields and displays the entanglement of the history of these artefacts with socio-economic relations, the dictates of the maximization of profit, international divisions of labour (that are neutral with respect to neither gender nor race) and the consumption needs of an urban population. Moreover, it becomes apparent in the film that the history of the vases is interwoven with a specific ecological afterlife that will outlive the lifespan of the vases as well as those who produced them. Future and past are inextricably interlinked with one another.

The vast tracts of land in Baotou occupied by radioactive tailing ponds testify with great conspicuousness to the impossibility of drawing up a frontier between past, present and future, as well as between nature and culture. They are material manifestations of the conception of nature as raw material for capitalistic enterprise. If such a conception prevails, Donna Haraway assumes, then nature is either "appropriated, preserved, enslaved, exalted, or otherwise made flexible for disposal by culture in the logic of capitalist colonialism" (1991, 198). Haraway compares this imaginary of nature with gender theories that conceive of biological sex merely as (passive) material for the enactment of gender (respectively, active culture). Her conclusion in respect to such theoretical approaches is that a conception of gender as the cultural appropriation of a biological sexual difference is problematic as it blanks out the active role of matter and makes the acknowledgement of bodies/matter as agents instead of resources impossible (Haraway 1991, 200). (It also conceals the construction of the sexual difference itself.) As early as the beginning of the 1980s, Haraway challenged binarisms without "eliminating their strategic utility" (1991, 199). She insisted on the interwovenness of nature and culture and proposed the term "naturecultures", which should undermine the modernist, ontological distinction between nature and culture (2015, 8).[9] In 2003, she wrote: "I want to convince my readers that inhabitants of technoculture become who we are in the symbiogenetic tissues of naturecultures, in story and in fact" (2015, 17).

Video recordings of the lakeland area in Baotou trigger images from science fiction and remind us that "we have been terraforming Earth all along" (Morton 2010, 133). Liam Young considers the fascination that springs from these lakes as an effect of the technological sublime. An ambiguous experience of both fascination and repulsion, the sublime was traditionally connected with the overwhelming forces and phenomena of nature. The lake scenery in Baotou is both natural and artificial/technological, sensational and awful—just like the vases made of toxic mud, which are beautiful and horrific at the same time. Young explains:

> It's quite spectacular when we are able to get into these places and document them and reveal them. It's this idea of what we describe as the technological sublime. So, we used to stand on a mountain top or the edge of the Grand Canyon and marvel at the power and beauty and scale of nature. Now, we get that same feeling when we stand at a massive mine site which, in many ways, is just as large as the Grand Canyon. But it's been made by explosives and diggers and drills as opposed to millennia of river erosion and wind. (Young 2016)

The work of Unknown Fields is based on the documentation of industrial and ecological realities but what is recorded actually resembles science fiction. Hence, "it seems that the more fantastic our image of matter becomes, the more real it becomes (and vice versa)" (Barad 2007,

354). In regard to the black, radioactive lakes—"a landscape ambiguously natural and crafted" (Haraway 1991, 149)—one may indeed wonder if the border between social reality and science fiction is just an optical illusion, as Haraway put it (ibid.).

THE BIOGRAPHY OF THINGS

In their short film *Rare Earthenware*, Unknown Fields depicts fragments of the production and supply chain of their three vases in reverse chronological order. The film begins with images of a huge container port in Shanghai from which goods are packed in boxes and shipped across the world. It then shows a Chinese electronics store where gadgets such as mobile phones, iPads and drones are being sold, followed by images of a workers' dormitory in the Guangdong factory in Dongguan. It shows workers assembling electronic devices in the factory, and then the Bayan Obo mine where the neodymium used in these same gadgets is extracted. Recordings of a man wearing a gumshield, collecting toxic mud on the waterfront of a tailing pond, are followed by images of the laboratory in which the radioactivity of the mud was assessed before it was placed onto a potter's wheel and made into a vase. Finally, the film closes with a man wearing a face-mask packaging the vases for shipment. As the film is shown in reverse every movement runs backwards. In galleries and museums, the vases, created on the model of Chinese Ming vases, are always exhibited in combination with the short film.[10] Unknown Fields superimposes quantitative data on almost every person as well as non-human entity that appears in the short film. Constantly, black digits appear on the human as well as on the non-human bodies, indicating that the latter are but one element of a bigger quantity. As such, the collective confirms the tendency of "datafication" of the world. A consequence of this is that both persons and things are more and more often conceived of, and represented as, quantifiable units of a statistically calculable set. In times of biocapitalism characterized by access to human life and the commodification and commercialization of forms of life, body images, cells, seeds, minerals, rare earths, etc., times in which the human body has become an object of speculation as well as a carrier of genetic information, capital value is not only contained in living beings and non-human material things, but first and foremost in the value of information connected with biodata. In *Rare Earthenware*—featuring several phases of the cultural biography of the vases—persons and things appear to be nodal points in complex networks. The continuous overlay of quantitative data makes a container shown on screen into one representative of the approximately 3.6 million containers that are in motion worldwide at any given moment. An electronic store represents one quantum of all the Chinese stores of this kind, which, if relocated side by side, would cover 175 football fields. A factory employee is but one individual out of 58.5 per cent of factory workers who suffer from depression, while the rare-earth elements are but a fraction of the 100,000 tonnes mined at Bayan Obo every year.

In 1929, Sergei Tret'iakov, a Soviet writer, advocated for a new literary genre that he called the "biography of things" (2006, 57–62).[11] In contrast to the biographical novel that focuses entirely on the virtues of a hero, this new literary genre was intended to "put the novel's distended character in his place" (Tret'iakov 2006, 61). As a consequence of his contempt of the story centred on a human protagonist, Tret'iakov attempted to shift the attention of the reader from the sovereign subject (also the central figure in new proletarian realism at the time) and its feelings, to the act itself, which he considered to be distributed among various actors and actants:

> While it takes considerable violence to force the reader of a biographical novel to perceive some quality of the hero as social, in the "biography of the object" the opposite is the case: here the reader would have to force himself to imagine a given phenomenon as a feature of a character's individual personality. (Tret'iakov 2006, 61)

In traditional novels, the personality of the hero seemed to condition things and their influences whereas in the "biography of the thing" persons appeared to be conditioned by those things. Hence, according to Tret'iakov, it was not the individual person moving through a system of objects, but the object proceeding through the system of people that he favoured as the methodological device of a more progressive literature.

In regard to Unknown Fields, one can recognize a withdrawal of the figure of the author in the collective, but also the negligence of the personalities of the individuals that are visible in the short film in favour of the representation of the genealogy of the thing—entirely in line with Tret'iakov's assertion that the artist should not proceed from a given fable to the required material, but from the given material to the required story. Of course, Tret'iakov was—in contrast to the collective Unknown

Fields—under the spell of a socialist revolution. The social conditions in the Soviet Union as well as socialist industrialization and collectivization had a profound impact on his work. Tret'iakov's insistence on a new genre of narration characterized by a revaluation of the factual has to be considered in the context of debates about the subject matter and method of socialist literature, and was connected with the wish of an inversion of determinisms. The story should not be centred on a delineation of characters, but rather on a description of the sphere of production. Ultimately his aim was to establish the affinity of the writer with the working class and their allies. He was convinced that politics was based on economy and "that there is no single second in a person's day uninvolved with economics or politics" (Tret'iakov 2006, 62). He therefore pled for books such as *The Forest, Bread, Coal, Iron, Flax, Cotton, Paper, The Locomotive* or *The Factory* that were unwritten at the time. His ideas were closely related to Karl Marx's thesis that the human being is not an abstraction but can only be understood as an ensemble of social relations (Marx 1990, 5).

The emphasis on the factual and the fact that the artist is producer and documentarist in personal union are significant characteristics of the work of Unknown Fields as well. In comparison with historical materialists and socialist artists, however, Unknown Fields is not merely thematizing production processes and social relationships, but is also reflecting on an active and processual reality of materials. Furthermore, Unknown Fields is exhibiting ecological transformations that are triggered by production and delivery processes. Workers in the Bayan Obo mine not only contribute to the establishment of specific power relations and social realities, they also induce geological changes—as do the purchasers of digital devices.

When Barad defines the thing as a "congealing of agency" (2007, 183–184), she is expressing an agential capacity significant for actors and actants alike. This is at the core of the difference between historical and new materialists. For Barad, everything is the product of intra-actions and of material-discursive contextures and is never simply given. For this reason, she is especially interested in genealogies and the entanglements of matter and meaning that they comprise. Young considers the backtracking of the cultural itineraries of the vases as a form of cultural archaeology: "Actually all the objects that we surround ourselves with have stories and they are manifestations of the extraordinary cultural archaeology that has produced them" (Young 2016). Whereas the production processes depicted by historical materialists were mostly situated in a specific geographical region—in the premises of a particular factory or enterprise for example—the production and distribution chains traced by Unknown Fields are spatially and temporally extended. *Rare Earthenware* focuses on the diverse locations to which electronic devices are distributed by the choreography of production and distribution. Unknown Fields uses the term "choreography" explicitly in order to describe networks of production and distribution that characterize a global supply-network which is increasingly displacing Earth whilst interweaving materialities all over the Earth. In this context Young talks about "a choreography of planetary scale":

> (...) in their very material they [the vases] embody what we describe as a planetary scale choreography or a planetary scale performance – that stretches from the Apple store in Oxford Circus in London all the way back to the hole in the ground in Inner Mongolia. So the film is really about plotting that journey that is embodied in those objects. We use the drawing language from a choreographic notation, from the early days of photography – mapping movement like Maybridge. But we are also influenced by the motion studies and the studies of efficiency by Frank Gilbreth – when he was looking at the performance of the body in the production line. (2016)

What notion of choreography is discernible in this statement? It has become popular to involve non-human entities in the stories that we tell about ourselves (Ingold 2014, 66). Which tale is told when, in times of neoliberal capitalism, the production and distribution sequences of a technological device are denominated as a choreography of planetary scale? Such a choreography does not take place for one or more spectators. It is the result of highly organized and efficient processes that are perfectly coordinated with one another for the sake of maximizing profits. If these processes (production of raw materials and components, their assembling and packaging, pooling of fright, delivery, etc.) that are geared to interlock with and support each other are referred to as a choreography, the choreographic is first of all linked to an organizational and logistical effort or performance. The reference to Fred Gilbreth hints at such an understanding of choreography. Gilbreth was the pioneer of an efficient organization of work routines. As an author of publications such as *Motion Study: A Method for Increasing the Efficiency of the Workman* (Gilbreth 1911) or *Applied Motion Study* (Gilbreth and Gilbreth 1917), co-authored with Lillian Moller Gilbreth, his studies on the efficiency of workflows highlighted the reduction of unnecessary movements. In comparison with Frederick Taylor, he thereby considered the well-being of the worker in his theories. The choreography of movement patterns, primarily in terms of their synchronization and coordination in regard to maximum efficiency (*qua* monetary profit) and the acceptance of the alienation of the worker who is condemned to repeat monotonous sequences of movements, can be termed the Choreography of Taylorism. However, by depicting the highly coordinated workflows of a globalized business, isn't the short film of Unknown Fields in accordance with a longing for efficiency and proficiency? Wouldn't it be more progressive to highlight movements that are considered to be unnecessary or inefficient in such processes? In fact, the radioactive mud in the shape of the vases embodies a perturbation of this kind. The vases are the embodiment of a disturbance that is implied from the agential capacities of their materiality.

The film *Rare Earthenware* makes visible that which is routinely unseen in the urbanized context of the present day—especially that of the European or North American consumer: the industrial fabrication of items that the average European or North American depends on—when being occupied with so-called immaterial works like data ascertainment, data analysis, customer service, sales assistance, public relations work, sales promotion, research, (continued) education, etc. Since the turn of the millennium, many European enterprises appeared to have been guided by the motto "Profit without Production"—striving to outsource industrial production processes to low-wage countries, primarily in Asia. Also, since the global financial crisis, it is primarily the service sector that has boomed in Europe and North America in the era of Post-Fordism. Here, the subject is not fabricating things; it is the subject itself that is increasingly becoming the product of its own work. Modes of capitalist exploitation in Post-Fordism are less linked to a certain reification than to a sort of de-reification. Cultural theorist Diederich Diederichsen wrote (from a "Western" point of view):

> So what we experience today is the sublation of the old distance between reified labor and alienated laborer, but not by way of a reconciliation between living work and dead product: instead, the product has come to full life just as the worker has been transformed into the product itself. (...) The worker is the object of her own subjective labor, which is nothing but her self, which is nothing but a product. (Diederichsen 2012)

Due to globalization and the outsourcing of industrial production processes, the material things that the average European is in contact with every day are characterized by ever more complex and indiscernible itineraries that usually involve actors and actants from diverse countries and cultural contexts and entail a planetary choreography of commodity flows, labourers and means of transport.

If the term "choreography" is detached from the figure of a sovereign human choreographer, the confrontation with an audience that oversees this choreography, and from a temporality that is related to the dimensions of a human lifespan, then it might be possible to track and describe the movements of human and non-human entities by reference to non-anthropocentric assemblages and to investigate their intra-actions. Such a political ecology would first of all not be concerned with the question who (which subjects?) or what economic or political system (the ghost of capitalism?) is governing certain processes, but would instead explore those concrete transformations that the specific intra-actions of heterogeneous actors and actants effectuate. It would also explore what human beings do with things in those specific, situated and embodied assemblages that they form with non-human actants, and what non-humans do with human beings in these networks—in respect to human and non-human forms of existence and not in regard to a reversal of determinisms. If—following Barad's concept of an agential realism—the fabric, the mine, the container port, the museum, etc. are considered as apparatuses of bodily production (of human as well as non-human bodies) and thereby figure as conditions of possibility for human and non-human bodies, they are all products of intra-actions that are engaged in terraforming to some extent. In this case, an expanded notion of choreography could help analyse the entangled movements of human as well as non-human actors/actants in extended spaces and temporalities. It would also enable one to take into account movements that cannot be observed by a single human individual as they do not unfold in a space (or time) that is easily graspable.

THE MATERIAL BACKBONE OF DIGITAL CULTURE

Unknown Fields track back through the processes that a laptop or camera underwent before landing in the office or living room of a European consumer. Paradoxically, Unknown Fields is also reliant on precisely those items of which they are attempting to thematize their history. The cameras with which Unknown Fields recorded the mine and lakescape at

Bayan Obo and the laptop with which they edited the film are characterized by the very genealogies that the film highlights. It is also possible they contain components of rare-earth elements that were mined from Bayan Obo. As such, the film is not a representation *of* the world but rather a constructed approach *to* the world with material-semiotic effects in terms of the nexus of self-construction, embodiment and relation to the world (cf. Haraway 1991, 27).

> In Madagascar we went to the place where the nickel is mined that is used in digital camera batteries. And we took a photo of it with the camera that – as we know – is powered by a battery that came out of that very mine. So we kind of completed the circle again. And the machine that becomes an agent in the redemption of this landscape when we expose it to the world is also the machine that produced this same landscape. That's the irony of contemporary consumption. (Young 2016)

Cameras and laptops are material-discursive actants that are implicated in intra-actions with other actors and actants with which they engender things, bodies and processes.

In respect to the relationship of human beings and machines, it is therefore not possible to determine "who makes and who is made" (Haraway 1991, 177). Radioactive lakeland areas in Inner Mongolia that emerge as a consequence of the extraction of neodymium are a paradigmatic example for the material backbone of digital culture. Huge areas have been transformed due to the exploitation of resources that are required in order to manufacture and power those communication and information technologies that are oftentimes (ironically) associated with "the immaterial". The hegemonic narrative of the immateriality of computer technologies and those work processes that are based on them is a persistent capitalist myth that obfuscates the materiality of digital technologies as well as the material repercussions of their manufacture. In both theory and art, one can observe a counter-movement to the theoretical engagement with the immateriality of work processes (in the context of semiocapitalism[12]) that was prominent in the late nineties. By foregrounding the materiality of (digital) things and processes, this movement strives to push ahead a certain politics of materiality.[13]

This tendency is even recognizable in those art disciplines that specialize in the exploration of digital media. Media theorist Jussi Parikka introduced the term "medianatures" in order to hint at the fact that digital media are also constructed from crude materials and minerals (cf. Parikka 2011, 2013, 527–544). Not only are crude materials necessary for the production of technological devices, these technological operations have also long since formed that which was once called "nature". The question of what happens with actants such as hard drives, smartphones and computers when they are discarded is also political insofar as illegal e-waste from Europe and the USA is often dismantled under miserable circumstances in Africa (for instance in Ghana), where plastic is incinerated and precious metals are removed from the items again in order to be further processed (cf. Volkart 2016, 29). We are constantly entangled with digital items such as computers, phones and cameras in everyday life. They are not "the other" of the human, neither are they controlled by human beings, nor do they control us. Processes of subjectification are implicated in machinic ecologies. Due to the entanglements of politics, capitalism, and what was called nature and the corporeal world, the delimitation of an inside world (of the individual subject and his organism) and an outside world (politics, economy, "nature") becomes obsolete.

> At first glance, the outside boundary of a body may seem evident, indeed incontrovertible. A coffee mug ends at its outside surface just as surely as people end at their skins. On the face of it, reliance on visual clues seems to constitute a solid empirical approach, but are faces and solids really what they seem? In fact, an abundance of empirical evidence from a range of different disciplines, considerations, and experiences strongly suggests that visual clues may be misleading. What may seem evident to some is not simply a result of how things are independently of specific practices of seeing and other bodily engagements with the world. Rather, it has become increasingly clear that the seemingly self-evidentiary nature of bodily boundaries, including their seeming visual self-evidence, is a result of the repetition of (culturally and historically) specific bodily performance. (Barad 2007, 155)

Polluted air as the result of media economies leads an intra-action with human organisms to specific consequences. So too do body-related ideologies and body images that are disseminated in digital media contribute, on their part, to the development of specific forms of living and embodiment.

The term "ecology" as tackled by *Rare Earthenware* does not designate the environment as such, it refers in an extended sense to the intra-actions of natural-cultural, economic, political, historical and media phenomena that condition, measure, survey, represent and discuss biospheres and thereby materially transform them.[14] New technologies and digital devices have co-produced and shaped the human body and its proficiencies. They are not "opposed to" the body, but rather have to be considered as aspects of the human body schema (Witzgall, Stakemeier 2014, 191). Increasingly, they co-constitute the human organism, as is evident in regard to artificial pacemakers, hearing aids, etc. that are less of a prosthetic extension of the body but are rather implied in the dynamics of mutual engendering and pervasion, the result of which is the human body as a composite of the organic and the inorganic. Or as Haraway encapsulated it: "Post-cyborg, what counts as biological kind troubles previous categories of organism. The machinic and the textual are internal to the organic and vice versa in irreversible ways" (2015, 15).

The visualization technologies and tools used by Unknown Fields constitute an apparatus of bodily production as well—in this case it is an apparatus for the production of digital, visual material. Crucially, the apparatus does not merely comprise instruments of observation, but also the practices of drawing boundaries that are specific material (re)configurations of the world, which materialize and thereby gain relevance. Barad has shown convincingly that "apparatuses are not merely about us. And they are not merely assemblages that include non-humans as well as humans. Rather, apparatuses are specific material reconfigurings of the world that do not merely emerge in time but iteratively reconfigure spacetimematter as part of the ongoing dynamism of becoming" (2007, 142).

Notes

1. Cf.: Unknown Fields. n.d. Accessed May 18, 2016. http://unknownfieldsdivision.com.
2. *Rare Earthenware* was realised in collaboration with Toby Smith (film and photography), Kevin Callaghan (London Sculpture Workshop) and Christina Varvia (animation assistant).

    On the website of Unknown Fields the series *Summer 2014_A World Adrift (Part 02)* is described in the following way: "This year we travelled East to ride the waves of massive container ships and trace the shadows of the world's desires along supply chains and cargo routes, to explore the dispersed choreographies and atomised geographies that global sea trade brings into being". Cf.: Unknown Fields. n.d. Accessed November

14, 2017. http://unknownfieldsdivision.com/summer2014china-aworld adriftpart02.html.
3. The term "rare-earth element" is misleading in so far as occurrences of these metals are not rare in the Earth's crust. They are, however, spread over vast areas. Regions with a very high concentration of rare-earth elements, in which the extraction of the latter is profitable, are relatively rare.
4. Cf. also: Hurst, Cindy. 2010. "The Rare Earth Dilemma: China's Rare Earth Environmental and Safety Nightmare." *The Cutting Edge*, November 15 2010. http://www.thecuttingedgenews.com/index.php?article=21777.
5. The film *Rare Earthenware* is accessible on Vimeo: Unknown Fields. n.d. "Rare Earthenware." Accessed July 29, 2016. https://vimeo.com/124621603. British newspaper *The Guardian* published a documentation of the whole project: The Guardian. 2015. "Rare Earthenware: A Journey to the Toxic Source of Luxury Goods." April 15, 2015. https://www.theguardian.com/environment/gallery/2015/apr/15/rare-earthenware-a-journey-to-the-toxic-source-of-luxury-goods.
6. Donna Haraway mostly employs the term "material-semiotic actors" for non-human entities in her writings whereas Karen Barad prefers to use the term "material-discursive phenomena" for non-human things.
7. The term "actant" was introduced by Bruno Latour and is used in order to denominate concrete but non-human entities that are not mere metaphors or significants but nevertheless bustle about in discourses that they transform while being transformed by them. They do not represent the abilities, ideas or views of human beings, but may have specific effects for other persons and non-human entities. In specific networks that they form with certain people and non-human entities, they enable specific activities, actions and social bonds, while rendering others impossible. In comparison with actants, Latour labels as "actors" those who are endowed with a character and who are normally anthropomorphic. Latour considers actants neither as subjects nor as objects, but rather as mediating and mediated, translating and translated hybrids that are at times human and sometimes non-human, but most of the time an association of both. The term stems from the structural semiotic and narratology developed by Algirdas Julien Greimas in 1979 who used the term in order to substitute the word "person" or "*dramatis personae*" when writing about the non-human protagonists of a story. Latour deduces the competence of an actant from its performance. He does not consider actions in relation to experiences as Niklas Luhmann did, but instead focuses on the relation of acting and the effects and efficiencies of the action (cf. Bellinger and Krieger 2006, 33, 488 as well as Latour 1993, 85–86 and Greimas 1982).

8. Cf. Jane Bennett's concept of a "distributive agency", conceived of as a collaboration of heterogeneous human and non-human actors/actants. I have explained Bennett's concept of "emergent causality" in relation to the performances *Pulling Strings* by Eva Meyer-Keller and *The Artificial Nature Project* by Mette Ingvartsen in an essay with the title "The Agentic Capacity of Things". Both performances foreground the activity of non-human agents and the movements of human performers that stem from the activity of the latter. The protagonists are silver confetti (in Ingvartsen's piece) and ordinary objects that mostly inhabit the theatre, but are usually kept to the sidelines (in Meyer-Keller's performance.) Cf. Ruhsam, Martina. 2017. "The Agentic Capacity of Things." *SCORES °6 no/things*: 104–113.
 9. Haraway refers to the anthropologist Marilyn Strathern and her critique of the binarism of nature and culture (2015, 8).
10. Ming vases are iconic objects of exceptionally high value. Unknown Fields produced the vases in the style of traditional Ming vases as they were fabricated during the Chinese Ming Dynasty (fourteenth until seventeenth century) in order to point out that what is considered to be a luxury item alters drastically according to the historical and geographical context. The title *Rare Earthenware* hints at this subject as well. The earthenware produced by Unknown Fields is rare, not due to its design or method of manufacture but rather because of the materials they are made of. *Rare Earthenware* was first exhibited on 22 April 2015 in the Victoria and Albert Museum in London in the frame of the exhibition *What is Luxury?* Later, both the vases and the short film were exhibited in Shanghai and in this way returned (in a different context) to the approximate geographical origin of their manufacture.
11. Sergei Tret'iakov originally published the article with the title "biography of things" in 1929. In the 1980s the essay was translated into German. In 2006, a large part of the text was published in the magazine *October* in English translation (with the title "The Biography of the Object"). Igor Kopytoff also uses the notion "biography of things" in his essay "The cultural biography of things: commoditization as process" (Appadurai 1986, 64–95).
12. "Semiocapitalism" is a term introduced by the Italian philosopher and activist Franco Berardi ("Bifo") who was a prominent figure in Italian leftist politics in the seventies. He was closely affiliated with the movements of *operaismo* ("workerism") and *autonomia* ("autonomy"). His theory of semiocapitalism is based on the analysis that in the current stage of capitalism—often referred to as cognitive capitalism—affects, attitudes, attributes and ideas are increasingly turned into products. Bifo writes about the precarious working conditions and the psychopathologies of cognitive workers who are employed in order to produce highly

abstract, semiotic artefacts and who are mostly involved in intense digital networking.
13. Cf. for example: Goll, Tobias, Daniel Keil, and Thomas Telios, eds. 2013. *Critical Matter: Diskussionen eines neuen Materialismus*. Münster: edition assemblage Cf. also: Coole, Diana, and Samantha Frost, eds. 2010. *New Materialisms. Ontology, Agency, and Politics*. Durham and London: Duke University Press; and Witzgall, Susanne, and Kerstin Stakemeier, ed. 2014. *Macht des Materials/Politik der Materialität*. Zürich and Berlin: diaphanes.
14. In respect to a rethinking of ecology, compare Timothy Morton's concept of an "ecology without nature" and an "ecology without environmentalism" (Morton 2010, 2012).

References

Appadurai, Arjun. 1986. *The Social Life of Things: Commodities in Cultural Perspective*. Cambridge: Cambridge University Press.
Barad, Karen. 2003. "Posthumanist Performativity: Toward an Understanding of How Matter Comes to Matter." *Journal of Women in Culture and Society* 28, no. 3: 801–831.
Barad, Karen. 2007. *Meeting the Universe Halfway. Quantum Physics and the Entanglement of Matter and Meaning*. Durham and London: Duke University Press.
Bellinger, Andréa, and David J. Krieger, eds. 2006. *ANThology. Ein einführendes Handbuch zur Akteur-Netzwerk-Theorie*. Bielefeld: transcript Verlag.
Bennett, Jane. 2010. *Vibrant Matter. A Political Ecology of Things*. Durham and London: Duke University Press.
Coole, Diana, and Samantha Frost, eds. 2010. *New Materialisms. Ontology, Agency, and Politics*. Durham and London: Duke University Press.
Deleuze, Gilles, and Félix Guattari. 1980. *A Thousand Plateaus*. London and New York: Continuum, 2004.
Diederichsen, Diedrich. 2012. "Animation, De-reification and the New Charm of the Inanimate." *E-flux-Journal* #36 (July). http://www.e-flux.com/journal/animation-de-reification-and-the-new-charm-of-the-inanimate/.
Folkers, Andreas. 2013. "Was ist neu am neuen Materialismus? - Von der Praxis zum Ereignis." In *Critical Matter. Diskussionen eines neuen Materialismus*, edited by Tobias Groll, Daniel Keil, and Thomas Telios, 17–34. Münster: edition assemblage.
Gilbreth, Frank Bunker. 1911. *Motion Study: A Method for Increasing the Efficiency of the Workman*. New York: David Van Nostrand Company.

Gilbreth, Frank Bunker, and Lillian Moller Gilbreth. 1917. *Applied Motion Study. A Collection of Papers on the Efficient Method to Industrial Preparedness*. New York: Sturgis & Walton Company.
Goll, Tobias, Daniel Keil, and Thomas Telios, eds. 2013. *Critical Matter: Diskussionen eines neuen Materialismus*. Münster: edition assemblage.
Greimas, Algirdas Julien, and Joseph Courtés. 1982. *Semiotics and Language: an Analytical Dictionary*. Bloomington: Indiana University Press.
Guattari, Félix. 2008. *The Three Ecologies*. London and New York City: Continuum.
Haraway, Donna Jeanne. 1991. *Simians, Cyborgs, and Women. The Reinvention of Nature*. New York and Oxon: Routledge.
Haraway, Donna Jeanne. 2015. *The Companion Species Manifesto: Dogs, People, and Significant Otherness*. Chicago: Prickly Paradigm Press.
Haraway, Donna Jeanne. 2016. *Staying with the Trouble. Making Kin in the Chthulucene*. Durham and London: Duke University Press.
Ingold, Tim. 2014. "Eine Ökologie der Materialien." In *Macht des Materials/Politik der Materialität*, edited by Susanne Witzgall and Kerstin Stakemeier, 65–73. Zürich and Berlin: diaphanes.
Latour, Bruno. 1993. *We Have Never Been Modern*. Cambridge, MA: Harvard University Press.
Lohmann, Dieter, and Nadja Podbregar. 2012. *Im Fokus: Bodenschätze. Auf der Suche nach Rohstoffen*. Berlin and Heidelberg: Springer.
Marx, Karl. 1990. "Thesen über Feuerbach." In *Marx-Engels Werke*, vol. 3, 1–7. Berlin: Dietz Verlag.
Morton, Timothy. 2010. *The Ecological Thought*. Cambridge: Harvard University Press.
Morton, Timothy. 2012. *Hyperobjects. Philosophy and Ecology After the End of the World*. Minneapolis and London: University of Minnesota Press.
Parikka, Jussi, ed. 2011. *Medianatures. The Materiality of Information Technology and Electronic Waste*. Open Humanities Press.
Parikka, Jussi. 2013. "Media Zoology and Waste Management: Animal Energies and Medianatures." *Necsus – European Journal of Media Studies* 2, no. 2: 527–544.
Ruhsam, Martina. 2017. "The Agentic Capacities of Things." *SCORES* °6 *(no/things)*: 104–113.
Tret'iakov, Sergei. 2006. "The Biography of the Object." *October* 118 (Fall): 57–62.
Volkart, Yvonne. 2016. "Müll zu Gold? Über die schmutzige Materialität unserer Hightechkultur." *Springerin* 1 (Spring): 26–32.
Witzgall, Susanne, and Kerstin Stakemeier, ed. 2014. *Macht des Materials/Politik der Materialität*. Zürich and Berlin: diaphanes.

Young, Liam. 2016. "The project *Rare Earthenware* and the Work of Unknown Fields Division." Interview by Martina Ruhsam. May 30, 2016. Unpublished.

Tentacular Thinking-With-Things in Storied Places. *Parliament of Things* (2019) by Building Conversation

Christel Stalpaert

Building Conversation is a collective of artists that creates dialogical art. The collective performs conversations together with participants all over Europe. From 2016 onwards, they co-created several *Parliaments of Things*. This conversational performance is inspired by the theory of Bruno Latour and rituals of the Aboriginals. In September 2019, I invited the Flemish philosopher and theatre maker Peter Aers, also a member of Building Conversation, to the Summer School on Climate at Ghent University. Students of diverse fields, ranging from performance studies and sociology, to literary studies, to engineering and bio-engineering, participated in the week-long 'workshops'[1] of various conversational practices, leading up to a conversational performance of *Parliament of Things*. Participating in this dialogical art practice, we tackled crises of care resulting from the ecological and environmental challenges facing our world. However, rather than finding solutions to climate change problems, the commissioned conversational practices became what Donna Haraway coined "art-science-activist worldings" (Haraway 2016, 79)[2] (Fig. 1).

C. Stalpaert (✉)
Ghent University, Ghent, Belgium
e-mail: christel.stalpaert@ugent.be

© The Author(s), under exclusive license to Springer Nature Switzerland AG 2021
C. Stalpaert et al. (eds.), *Performance and Posthumanism*,
https://doi.org/10.1007/978-3-030-74745-9_11

Fig. 1 Building Conversation, *Parliament of Things*, 2016 (© Michiel Cotterink)

In this contribution, I observe how the different conversational practices/performances in general and the *Parliament of Things* in particular function as "art-science-activist worldings" that offer an interesting alternative to the usual production of knowledge in university contexts.

First, I observe how the conversational practice of *Impossible Conversation* expands scientific language. The scientific field of botany, for example, is known for its precision of botanical lexis and rigid categorization. Drawing on the writings of American environmental and forest biologist Robin Wall Kimmerer, who was inspired by the production of knowledge in Native American traditions, I describe the participants' experience of *Impossible Conversation* during the summer school as a wordcraft experiment, through which 'lost' words are resurged and "a grammar of animacy" (Kimmerer 2013, 55) is developed.

Second, the conversational practices/performances also convincingly brought forward that the production of knowledge is not (and never will be) the product of an individual. In *Impossible Conversation* and *Thinking Together—An Experiment* the participants are relaying knowledge in creative uncertainty. They cannot proceed with mechanical confidence towards solutions, but have to cultivate response-ability through what Haraway named "tentacular thinking" (31–34). This tentacular thinking resonates with David Bohm's vision on "participatory thought". The American quantum physicist developed this notion as a valuable alternative to the "authoritative structure" in scientific knowledge (48). His book *On Dialogue* was a direct inspirational source for Building Conversation's *Thinking Together—An Experiment*.

Third, the art-science-activist worlding at work during the conversational practices/performances in general and the *Parliament of Things* in particular differ from the scientific model of the laboratory. Following Latour, a laboratory installs "a Parliament of Mutes", which treats things as instrumental tools or artificial intermediaries in a theatre of proof (1993, 142). A *Parliament of Things* allows things to emerge as mediators, hence providing an ally for tentacular thinking-*with-things*. Allowing things to emerge as mediators also means that 'things' are allowed to story[3] the place. During the summer school, the conversational exercise *Impossible Conversation* took place in the seemingly paradise-like place of the Hortus Botanicus of Ghent University. Through a speculative and tentacular thinking-with flora on the edge of extinction, I practised an art of mourning that allowed trees and plants to story the botanical garden as a "vexed place" (Haraway 2016, 133), burdened with the economization of nature, and bearing with it a history of colonialism. As such, the endangered and extinct were voiced, an act that calls upon an ethics for decolonialization (Rose 2004).

In the final part of this contribution, I reflect on the impact of these conversational practices/performances. Taking into consideration that Building Conversation is also inspired by alternative ways of conversing and generating (ecological) knowledge in the traditions of Indians, Congolese oldsters, Inuit chieftains, Maori and Aboriginals, etc. I wonder whether these conversational practices also call upon an ethics for the decolonization of knowledge? Do the conversational practices facilitated by Building Conversation truly have activist potential in the world at large? Echoing Hannah Arendt's belief in the world-making potential of interacting through speech, I observe the opportunities of and limitations to the new modes of activism at work in the conversational practices/performances as art-science-*activist* worldings facilitated by Building Conversation.

FACILITATING CONVERSATIONS AND CO-CREATING CONVERSATIONAL PERFORMANCES WITH BUILDING CONVERSATION

Building Conversation is a steadily expanding collective of artists and people all fascinated by what happens when one meets in conversation. It facilitates conversations in 'workshop' settings and also co-creates conversational performances.[4]

On the Building Conversation website, seven conversations can be booked. *Time Loop*, for example, is inspired by the practice of Indians from the great Lake District in Canada and seeks to counter the short-term thinking that rules the capitalist world. Participants are invited to look at current dilemmas and problems from various perspectives in time: by looking far ahead in time, or, conversely, by reflecting on the deep past. The collective hence hopes to develop a way of extending a sense of time in tackling the current challenges our world is facing (https://www.buildingconversation.nl/en/#conversations/time-loop).

A second conversation is called *General Assembly* and tests out forms of speaking in public, while relating to the city and to each other as one speaks. It is inspired by the conversational practices of the Occupy movement (such as hand signals, 'human' microphone and open space technology) as well as "the idle chattering of oldsters sitting beneath the shade of a tree in the centre of a village in Congo" (https://www.buildingconversation.nl/en/#conversations/general-assembly).

Other conversations that can be booked are *Thinking Together*, a conversation experiment inspired by the writings on participatory thought by Bohm, and *Conversation Without Words*, a performance that explores the intensity of silence, and was inspired by the annual gathering of Inuit chieftains who sit together in complete and utter silence for hours in order to connect well with one another. *Impossible Conversation* follows the practice of Jesuits to speak in personal terms when tackling very complex and abstract topics such as (the belief in) God. The *Agonistic Conversation* tests out the possibilities of disagreement between adversaries and is inspired by Chantal Mouffe's political philosophy and the elaborate practices of Maori conflict 'management'. A seventh conversation that can be booked is the *Parliament of Things*, inspired by the theory of Latour and rituals of the Aboriginals.

A conversation can be booked by diverse agents and hence takes place in very diverse locations[5]: Zinnig Noord, an open community in Amsterdam seeking a more profound spiritual approach of life, commissioned an *Impossible Conversation* to talk about different religious beliefs in De Ark in Amsterdam, while *Conversation Without Words* was performed in the Hazira Theatre in Jerusalem in 2015. *General Assembly*, *Parliament of Things*, *Time Loop* and *Agonistic Conversation* were held, amongst other, at the Ganz Novi Festival in Zagreb and the *Burning Ice #10* Festival in Kaaitheater Brussels in 2016.

Likewise, the *Parliament of Things* adopted many different guises. Not only did it hit the stage at the *Burning Ice* #10 Festival in Kaaitheater Brussels in 2016 and the *Holland Festival* in Amsterdam in 2017. On the occasion of Latour's visit to Amsterdam in November 2017, and the presentation of his book *Facing Gaia*, Building Conversation executed a *Parliament of Things* at the Veem House for Performance Studio. In April 2019, it was commissioned by GreenTrack, a Ghent non-profit organization and "think-and-do tank" that represents all the major cultural organizations in Ghent that are seeking to "co-create a long-term sustainable future" (https://greentrack.be/gent/pages/fr-en). The *Parliament of Things* also knew a cross-generational edition. *Parliament of Things 6 +* is a co-production by Building Conversation, Theater Artemis, a Dutch children's theatre company, and Theatre Festival Boulevard. The Dutch theatre maker Lotte van den Berg and visual artist Daan't Sas created a space for sharing time, space and words, "challenging parents and children to take the perspective of a thing", including picnic and cake afterwards (https://artemis.nl/en/art-projects/the-parliament-of-things-6/).

The border between conversational practices and conversational performances is deliberately blurred[6]: commissioned 'workshop' settings turn into performances while co-created conversational performances also entail a 'workshop' character in the processual way of performing. Over the years, Building Conversation set up and staged conversations with local organizations, international arts festivals and in city theatres. Next to these pop-up events, they also explored long-term residencies. Since 2019, Building Conversation frequently resided in a specific place over a longer period of time in order to "truly create time and space" for "conversations between people". As such, long-term conversational projects were set up in the city of Amsterdam (Stadstraject), in secondary schools (Scholentraject) and in cultural institutions, universities and academies.[7]

For the week-long summer school on Climate in September 2019, I invited Building Conversation member, Flemish philosopher and theatre maker Peter Aers to facilitate some conversational exercises, culminating in the co-created conversational performance *Parliament of Things*.[8] Commissioned in the context of the summer school on Climate, the conversational practices/performances were inevitably, in a direct or indirect way, dealing with ecological crises. For the students and me, these practices offered an interesting alternative to the usual production of scientific knowledge on this hot topic.

In what follows, I observe how the conversational practices/performances in general and the *Parliament of Things* in particular function as art-science-activist worldings that offer an interesting alternative to the usual production of knowledge in university contexts: it expands speaking and thinking, providing space for (re)generating or resurging a "grammar of animacy" (Kimmerer 55) and "tentacular thinking" (Haraway 31–34), allowing things to emerge as mediators of thinking (Latour 1993, 142).

Resurging[9] 'Lost Words' in Conversational Practices/Performances

According to an open letter on 12 January 2015 signed by 28 authors—amongst them Margaret Atwood, Andrew Motion and Robert Macfarlane—our Western language is moving away from nature (https://www.caughtbytheriver.net/2015/01/letter-oxford-university-press-atwood-macfarlane/). In 2007, the Oxford Junior Dictionary featured new words such as 'broadband', 'blog' and 'attachment', indicating an expanding vocabulary after the digital turn. However, the introduction of new words demanded a dropping of other words. The petitioners of the open letter protested against the loss of words such as 'acorn', 'buttercup' and 'conker'[10] in favour of words such as 'attachment', 'broadband', 'blog' and 'chatroom'. They regretted that words associated with the natural world had to make way for words newly introduced in the digital era. The loss of around fifty words connected with nature and the countryside not only reflected a shift in vocabulary. The authors were particularly alarmed that the new words also reflected the increasingly "interior, solitary childhoods of today". The protest was more than mere romanticism, painstakingly clinging to "the rosy memories" of a lost childhood. The shift in words testifies to a symptom of a detached relation with and understanding of nature. The writers asked the publisher to restore some of the most important nature words in a next edition, as an important "cultural signal and message of support for natural childhood".

The words were not retrieved in a next edition. The head of children's dictionaries at OUP replied that environments change and that the dictionary reflects that change. The petitioners of the open letter objected that the Oxford Junior Dictionary "should seek to help shape children's understanding of the world, not just to mirror its trends". Macfarlane argued that "we do not care for what we do not know, and on the whole we do not know what we cannot name". Motion observed that the dropping of the words denied the children "a vital means of connection and understanding".

It seems that our language supports our evolution towards disconnected individuality in the Anthropocene. In *Braiding Sweetgrass*, Kimmerer comes to the same conclusion. She reflects on the effects of botany—the language that is used to speak of plants. The precision of botanical lexis and categorization is very efficient in constituting a common ground for communicating knowledge about what is observed, she admits. However, its language of objectification and distancing "polishes the gift of seeing" (2013, 48), with the risk of missing something that unfolds beneath a finely faceted surface. It creates a short-sightedness that prevents us from acknowledging life in a more-than-human-world, and it prevents us from acknowledging "the unseen energies that animate everything" (49). "To name and describe you must first see. (…) In scientific language, our terminology is used to define the boundaries of our knowing, what lies beyond our grasp remains unnamed", Kimmerer says (49).

The thousands of botanical names and scientific terms she learnt as a botanist did not cover the vocabulary she gradually became acquainted with in Potawatomi, the Native American language that was stolen from her grandfather (2013, 50). Kimmerer marvels at the discovery that the technical vocabulary of Western science has no words that hold the mystery of fungi, for example. The way mushrooms push up from the earth overnight is called *puhpowee* in Potawatomi, but has no English equivalent (54). It is as if these marvellous energies are neglected. Kimmerer herself tries to be mindful of these Potawatomi words when she's doing fieldwork with her students, raising their awareness of the limits of botanical lexis and scientific terminology. She hopes to revalue the animist relation of the words to which they refer. But how to encounter the more-than-human world through lost words then? It seems that there is still a lot of wordcraft to be done...

A meticulous wordcraft experiment was conducted by the British writer Robert Macfarlane, in the children's book *The Lost Words*, for which he collaborated with Jackie Morris. She made watercolour paintings to a number of lost words that Macfarlane hopes to (re)generate in the English language. The lost words are common words that are falling from common usage, a symptom of a growing detached relation with nature in a world where the virtual worlds of Pokémon and Minecraft have moved decisively to the centre of childhood experience. The book is a spell-book, trying to spell the words back into language, conjuring back the species that are steadily disappearing from children's everyday environments. The poetic text enchants animals such as the otter and the raven, resurging the 'lost words' in children's stories, dreams and playing. The otter's spell, for example, that "subtle slider", urges children to experience the exhilarating feeling of swimming in rivers and pools:

> Ever dreamed of being otter? That utter underwater thunderbolter, that whimmering twister?
> Run to the riverbank, otter-dreamer, slip your skin and change your matter, pour your outer being into otter – and enter now as otter without falter into water. (Macfarlane and Morris, no page numbers)

One could say that Macfarlane is a wordsmith, like the main character in Patricia Forde's young adult novel with that same name. In this book, wordsmith Letta is charged with the task of collecting and archiving words in the post-apocalyptic city of Ark, in an era after the Melting, caused by global warming. This speculative fiction story uncovers the impoverishment of life when language is suppressed and when people are robbed from the entangling power of speech. In Ark, language is severely restricted to the use of words that are on the List, art and music are banned, and outcasts are thrown to the wolves. The story reveals how a restrictive use of words affects not only communication, but also relationality.

Building Conversation cultivates a big love for words, as words reflect our relation with our environment and with each other. On their website, Haidar Hamdani is quoted:

We declare love with words, we start wars with words, and we raise our children with words. From the first day until the last day, a person uses approximately eight billion words. We read and hear five times more. We use 4.400 sentences daily, during 21 conversations. Human culture is all about conversation and speaking. Europe is a conversation, the Netherlands is a conversation, we are a conversation. (https://www.buildingconversation.nl/en/)

In the conversational practice/performance *Impossible Conversation*, Building Conversation urges the participants to try to find words for the unthinkable and unspeakable. It is inspired by a practice that the Jesuits follow and departs from the urge to speak of very complicated, abstract themes, such as God, in personal terms, hence avoiding a detached manner of speaking. In a way, Building Conversation invites the participants to become wordsmiths, to resurge words from a relational perspective, to try to find words for complex and seemingly remote matters. 'Climate change' and 'nature' can be considered similarly abstract themes. Climate change is easily dismissed as a remote problem because of its complex, boundless impact on an enormous, global scale. Our narrow scales of time and space rarely exceed one generation. They are too narrow to think through the global climate change impacts for future generations. As I wrote down elsewhere, paraphrasing performance scholar Una Chaudhuri in her keynote lecture at the Psi conference in Stanford in 2013: "the logic of climate change is a very complex one, having no clear spatial boundaries, and not even a spatial logic. It is dependent on numerous choices in numerous different parts of the world simultaneously" (Stalpaert 2018, 48). It is no surprise, then, that this ecological crisis is usually headlined with adjectives such as 'unthinkable', 'unprecedented' or 'unimaginable'. Novelist Amitav Ghosh—acclaimed for addressing climate rupture—added the subtitle *Climate Change and the Unthinkable* to his latest book *The Great Derangement* to denote the limits of human thought and language when it comes to speaking and writing about environmental catastrophes. Ghosh calls it "the broader imaginative and culture failure that lies at the heart of the climate crisis. (…) The Anthropocene presents a challenge not only to the arts and humanities, but also to our commonsense understandings and beyond that to contemporary culture in general" (8).

While the unimaginable scale of climate change renders us speechless, populist discourse seeks to squeeze the impossible climate change whodunnit in a binary logic of crime and punishment, trying to separate 'those who are to blame' from 'those fighting the enemy'. But this is a futile endeavour, as all human beings are in numerous ways implicated in the current environmental crisis. Building Conversation urges us to stay with the trouble of speaking and to persist in trying to find the appropriate words to imagine or think the unimaginable and unthinkable. During the conversational practice/performance of *Impossible Conversation*, we were asked to write about a personal experience that relates to the abstract and complex theme of 'nature', feel a personal connection with it, and from that connection, read aloud and share what we had written. Stumbling and stuttering through words, linking personal memories with raised attention and recalibrated vocabulary, we explored our diverse and ambivalent relations with 'nature' in the current context of climate change. "Re-localizing the global" (Latour 2007, 173–190) in a particular, personal context, we traced matters of concern from our particular relationship with a specific, local environment. We relayed knowledge in creative uncertainty, as we could not mechanically proceed from scientific facts, which would have provided us with rhetoric confidence.

Reading out loud and listening to what we had written was a performance in itself. Listening to the manifold word-struggles to describe an ecological stance that is experienced within the personal everyday, and the diverse ordinary doings of the participants, we "let go of nature" (Latour 2004, 9), in the sense that we let go of the abstract, romantic idea of one, lost ideal order of nature. Instead, Latour would say, we provided mental space for the "*progressive composition of one common world*" (2007, 254, emphasis Latour). Sharing particular contexts with the participants of the *Impossible Conversation*, we generated an ever-ongoing constitution or composition of the world as nature-culture, resurging speech in the unspeakable.

Developing a Grammar of Animacy in the Wood Wide Web

The above-mentioned word-resurging endeavours are valuable rechargers of our oblivious mind. However, the wordsmith's lexical resurgence—resurging words from oblivion or from abstract dismissal—will not suffice to acknowledge the animacy of the more-than-human world. The way we relate to our environment through language not just happens at the level of individual words, but also at a deeper level of grammar and syntax. Macfarlane observes that it is the poor underland of our language, including grammar and habits of speech, that betrays our poor relation to one another and to other matter.

> The real underland of language is not the roots of single words, but rather the soil of grammar and syntax, where habits of speech and therefore also habits of thought settle and interact over long periods of time. Grammar and syntax exert powerful influence on the proceedings of language and its users. They shape the ways we relate to each other and to the living world. Words are world-makers – and language is one of the great geological forces of the Anthropocene. (113)

Kimmerer agrees: "the language (is) a mirror for seeing the animacy of the world, the life that pulses through all things, through pines and nuthatches and mushrooms" (55). And English is a 'poor' language in terms of animacy: it "doesn't give us many tools for incorporating respect for animacy" (56). What is striking, for example, is that "in English, you are either a human or a thing. Our grammar boxes us in by the choice of reducing a nonhuman being to an *it*, or it must be gendered, inappropriately, as a *he* or a *she*" (56).

Taking a closer look at the Native American language of Potawatomi, Kimmerer is struck by the abundance of verbs.[11] This use of verbs indicates that Potawatomi attributes life and agency to all matter—human and so-called non-human (53). Whereas English is a noun-based language, Potawatomi is a verb-based language, assigning no gender differences to nouns, and using the same word 'it' to address all matter in the world, human and other-than-human (55). Paging through the Ojibe dictionary, Kimmerer was surprised to discover words covering all kinds of things "with verbs": "to be a Saturday", "to be a hill", (...) "to be a long sandy stretch of beach", "to be a bay" (54). Not only trees, plants and animals are animate, but also rocks, mountains, water, fire and places. This has nothing to do with attributing magical qualities to inanimate things, but to accept that the water in a bay, for example, can *do* other things than lying there between the shores that are constructed by humans.

> A bay is a noun only if water is *dead*. When *bay* is a noun, it is defined by humans. Trapped between its shores and contained by the word. But the verb *wiikwegamaa* – to *be* a bay – releases the water from bondage and lets it live. 'To be a bay' holds the wonder that, for this moment, the living water has decided to shelter itself between these shores, conversing

with cedar roots and a flock of baby mergansers. But it could be otherwise – become a stream or an ocean or a waterfall, and there are verbs for that too. (55)

To adopt this animate perspective in language, Kimmerer says, is to speak "the grammar of animacy" (55). This grammar of animacy has all too often disrespectfully been discarded as 'primitive' spiritual imagination. It is no phantasy; however, it is the acknowledgement of a deeper, interconnected reality. Also, retrieving the grammar of animacy does not mean to learn to speak an Anishinaabe language such as Potawatomi, or Hopi or Seminole. As Kimmerer herself says, it is adopting another perspective of being in the world, opening up to other habits of speech and other ways of categorizing and attributing names to 'things'. It is becoming acquainted with a language that "reminds us, in every sentence, of our kinship with all of the animate world" (56).

Kimmerer considers it our work "to learn to speak the grammar of animacy, so that we might be truly at home" (58). This learning of another language is more like an awakening, a remembrance, or, as Anna Tsing would put it, a "persistent resurgence", "a regeneration" (2015, 179), moving away from "nostalgia-driven reconstructions" (187). After all, Potawatomi as a language might be in danger of extinction,[12] but the habits of speech it embraces have not disappeared.

A first step in learning to speak the grammar of animacy is to acknowledge the existence of a language that does speak in animate terms and to respect its beneficial qualities. It also means to acknowledge the limitations and barriers of the English language. As Kimmerer put it: "speaking English, thinking in English, somehow gives us permission to disrespect nature. (...) we put a barrier between us (...) opening the door to exploitation" (57).

> Saying *it* makes a living land into 'natural resources'. If maple is an *it*, we can take up a chain saw. If a maple is a *her*, we think twice. (...) The arrogance of English is that the only way to be animate, to be worthy of respect and moral concern, is to be human. (57)

This acknowledgement might animate an awakening, an awareness of interconnectivity with the more-than-human-world. "Maybe a grammar of animacy could lead us to whole new ways of living in the world, (...) a world with a democracy of species, not a tyranny of one" (58).

Like Kimmerer, Macfarlane wishes for a language that recognizes and advances the animacy of the world. He formulates this, in dialogue with biologist and writer Merlin Sheldrake, as a "need to speak in spores" (Macfarlane 2019, 111). This of course does not mean that we literally learn the language that spores speak. It means that we acknowledge the way spores interconnect, evolve and communicate with trees in a "wood wide web" (87), that "mysterious buried network, joining single trees into forest communities" (88). When Macfarlane is exploring the understorey of woods with Sheldrake, he is mind-struck by the way trees interrelate with fungi and with each other: "when one of their number was sickening or under stress, they could share nutrients by means of an underground system that conjoined their roots beneath the soil, thereby sometimes nursing the sick tree back to health" (87).[13] To speak in spores is in other words to acknowledge the benefits of interconnectivity at work in the mycorrhizal symbiosis.

The wood wide web provides an interesting posthuman counterweight to the human-centred network of the world wide web, this system of linkages, putting human beings in different parts of the world into almost instant contact with other human beings, through an instrumental use of computers, modern technology and satellites. While the World Wide Web claims to be democratic, it is not; it confirms and even deepens economic and political divisions. People in poor countries and authoritarian regimes do not benefit from connectivity through the network. And even within similar political and economic systems, divisions are made. The term 'generation gap' betrays a pattern of a precarious distribution of digital literacy, referring to the weaker ability of the older generation to be digitally connected. This is in contrast with the kind of world-making performed in the wood wide web, in which the oldest trees are connected the most to the fungal system, taking care of smaller trees in their resource distribution.[14]

Research on the understorey of forests and below-ground ecology has boomed, especially with the development of new technologies of detection and deep mapping. But as early as the 1990s, Canadian forest ecologist Suzanne Simard was fascinated by the "curious correlation" in the understorey of logged temperate forests in north-west British Columbia (in Macfarlane 2019, 88). She discovered how the pale, superfine threads known as 'hyphae' that fungi send out through the soil interconnected to create a network of astonishing complexity and extent

(89). They were not only masters in mutualism, these 'hyphae' proved to be very beneficial in maintaining a balance in underland ecology.

Simard's discovery was astonishing, as for centuries, fungi were considered to be harmful parasites, causing dysfunction and diseases to plants and other living organisms. Further research also pointed out that fungi were masters in subtle mutualism. "The hyphae of these so-called 'mycorrhizal' fungi were understood not only to infiltrate the soil, but also to weave into the tips of plant roots at a cellular level—thereby creating an interface through which molecular transmission might occur" (in Macfarlane 89). Simard called this subtle mutualist interweaving of fungi with plants and trees "an underground social network" (in Macfarlane, 89), thereby indicating that our society could learn from this magnificently intricate subterranean system. Macfarlane couldn't agree more. What he hoped for was that the kind of world-making these fungi perform, this collaborative system with an unexpected intricacy of interrelations, could maybe inspire us to evolve "from a fierce free market to something more like a community with a socialist system of resource redistribution" (91). Fungi are experts in "making kin", as Haraway would put it, practising a horizontal transfer of genetic material, and hence constituting a non-hierarchical network between species. Other biologists such as Lynn Margulis and Merlin Sheldrake, and anthropologist Anna Tsing, further researched these collaborative compound organisms and were all amazed to find out that these mycorrhizal 'superheroes' reshape our vertical, evolutionary understanding of kinship and descent, and even annihilate our categories of gender.

> They reshape our ideas of community and cooperation. They screw up our hereditary model of evolutionary descent. They utterly *liquidate* our notions of time. Lichens can crumble rocks into dust with terrifying acids. Fungi can exude massive powerful enzymes *outside* their bodies that dissolve soil. They're the biggest organisms in the world and among the oldest. They're world-makers and world-breakers. What's more superhero than *that?*" (Sheldrake in Macfarlane, 94)

Moreover, they not only proved to be very resilient themselves[15]; they are also the key to "future forest resilience", as recent studies have indicated that fungal-networked trees have a much higher chance of adapting faster to the climate transformations our world is experiencing (Macfarlane 103).

Animating a Grammar of Animacy in Conversational Practices/Performances

But how to animate a "grammar of animacy"? How to practise a speaking in spores? Kimmerer herself tries "to be bilingual between the lexicon of science and the grammar of animacy" (56), struggling with verbs, sometimes hardly being able to speak at all. Macfarlane refers to the poetry of Jeremy Prynne and his poetic "mammal language" to practise a relationality of animacy (in Macfarlane 2019, 112). The strategies differ, but in all cases, it will have to come with conversational practice. And this is exactly what Building Conversation seeks to do. It is their conviction that to facilitate conversation practices and performances is to create possibilities for resurgence of a lexicon and grammar of animacy. They regret that in our society, we hardly practise our thinking and talking together. We have grown accustomed to functional check-ups and maintenance contracts for machines, various maintenance exercises for our physical condition and even architectural conservation and maintenance strategies for preserving historical structures, but we rarely speak of communication maintenance.

On their website, Haidar Hamdani continues his declaration of love for words with the following observations and invitation:

> How do we speak? (...) We maintain our car, our house, our body. We exercise, follow diets, plan major cleaning and home remodeling. We get our car MOT checked yearly. But when do we pay attention to the way we speak, to the way we connect with the people around us?
> Building Conversation does exactly that; give attention to the way we speak. Outside our daily reality, free from existing tensions, free from our striving towards expedience, we create a space in which we can practice conversation. We invite you to join. (https://www.buildingconversation.nl/en/)

The conversational practice/performance *Thinking Together—An Experiment* does exactly this: it urges the participants to give attention to the way we speak and to practise conversation. *Thinking Together—An Experiment* is based on the writings on participatory thought by Bohm, who is likewise surprised that we maintain so many things—our body, machines and systems—except our dialogical and conversational skills. In his book *On Dialogue*, he expresses an urge for conversation maintenance, proposing very concrete exercises for practising creative dialogues. Bohm believes that conversation is the place where people can investigate and (re)animate practices of thinking with each other. Only in this manner, he says, will we be able to cope with the complex crisis our world is facing. Building Conversation implements his practical manual into their artistic practice, inviting those who are interested in a deep engagement with dialogue.

The conversational practice/performance *Thinking Together—An Experiment* that I participated in on another occasion,[16] gathered a group of approximately thirty[17] people that voluntarily convene in a circle, for a considerable long period of time. Bohm himself prefers a period of at least three hours, Building Conversation sometimes installs shorter periods. Time is in fact the only pre-set condition of the conversational practice/performance: a timer with an alarm is set, out of sight of the participants, which will carefully keep track of time and indicate the end of the conversation with a sudden, interrupting noise. The participants are oblivious of the clock-time during the performance, as they are asked to set aside their watches and mobile phones before starting the conversation.

After the participants have been welcomed with tea, each individual volunteer is asked to take a chair and to take place in a circle, in the middle of a room that was selected for its 'neutral' appearance. The room should have as few distracting elements as possible, and eyecatchers such as posters, paintings, furniture or design should be removed. Each individual is asked whether he or she wants to participate in the conversational practice/performance; hence, the volunteer is 'contracted' to become an engaged participant. The group is requested to pick up, in a random order, small cards that are all spread out on the floor, and to read out aloud the text written on them. Alternatingly, and without a given order, the participants inform each other about practical and procedural matters of the dialogue process, as well as about the theoretical underpinnings of this conversational gathering, which is Bohm's dialogical world view. We hear, for example, that there is no moderator, and no pre-set agenda or topic. The group is to chart its own course.

During this initiation, some key concepts by Bohm are mentioned, stretching our understanding of the possibilities of a conversational practice. One of these key concepts is "suspension" (Bohm 1996, 83–95). A text on the card explains how Bohm urges us to suspend our assumptions in the context of a dialogue. The example on the card reads as follows and is derived from Bohm's practical manual:

Suspension. Bohm introduces this concept as follows:
It is possible to suspend the impulses that arise from your own assumptions and basic values. When for example you have the feeling that someone is an idiot, 'suspending' means that:
a) you refrain from declaring this out loud and
b) you simply accept the thought, without telling yourself that you shouldn't think such things.
In that way, the effects of your thought that 'he is an idiot' (anger, frustration, irritation) are free to go their own way. But in such a manner that you can perceive these effects and impulses, without entirely identifying with them. In other words, 'suspending' an impulse and a reaction means that you do not suppress that reaction, but you also do not immediately carry through with it. What you do is give it your full attention.
You can picture 'suspension ' like letting something that happens to you hang about half a meter in front of you.
And the more intensively your entire body reacts, your entire body participates. These intense reactions are precisely what we can learn from. What does it mean when I react so strongly? That's also why it's so important for Bohm that we don't suppress these impulses. You must let them be, but in a way that you can look at them. Not only at the content of the thought, but also at the process that has evoked it. As individuals, we do this through 'suspension'. But in Bohm's vision, we also do this as a group. Perhaps you will find a way to present an intense impulse like 'you are an idiot' to the group and investigate it with them. (Building Conversation, *Prologue Thinking Together*)

After this introduction/initiation, the dialogue starts.
A very, very long SILENCE fills the space.
Proceeding into an undirected inquiry without a pre-set topic is confusing and unsettling to me, and probably to the other participants as well. The group remains silent for quite some time. The absence of a pre-set agenda or a pre-established purpose or topic has everyone in the group hesitate to speak up. However, the silence is also beneficial. Indeed, the 'unnatural', long silence in the room with barely other meaning-making material triggers my senses. The stretched scales of time and space nurture my attention and awareness. Only in this state of heightened awareness can I trace the subtle implications of my own assumptions in conversation, while sensing similar yet different assumptions in the group.
Suspension does not mean that one has to suppress the awareness of anger, frustration or eagerness to oppose an idea, but to linger at the obstacles that prevent us from saying what we just suspended. Bohm's

strategy of "suspending assumptions" (Bohm 1996, 22–24) is a matter of suspending judgement in order to become fully open to the legitimacy of others' ideas, even if they are different from our own ideas. As such, I become aware of my own reaction of hostility when confronted with other ideas. Instead of instantly countering or going against proposed ideas, I allow the thought to be suspended for a moment, feeling what blocks my suspended assumption. I do not suppress it, but I also do not proceed with it, giving my full attention to this feeling of hostility. I realize that scientific thought is too often guided by individual ambition, with feelings of flattery blocking true intelligence in co-operative endeavour. I remember how Bohm observed that scientific research is often infected with personal ambition, in a way that the emotion of flattery often blocks an openness to the legitimacy of others' ideas (72). It leads to "fragmentation" (10) in our perception of the world, breaking things up which are not really separate, including—I become aware of— our entanglement with things in a more-than-human-world, preventing us from truly participatory thought. Bohm's *On Dialogue* is hence also a critique of the "authoritative structure" in scientific knowledge (48).

Time allows for frictions to emerge between contrasting ideas and values in *Thinking Together—An Experiment* and, more importantly, to trace these frictions back to assumptions that are active in the group, including my own. Experiencing the presence of these assumptions and giving these thoughts my full attention, I also acknowledge the obstructing nature of my own thought-process: my defensive posturing, for example, which is grounded in scientific thought. Rather than talking *about* something, for example climate change, the conversation gradually becomes something else; an "awakening of some other sense of what thought is" through genuine attention (86). I realize that I tend to do scientific research by defining a problem and a method of how I wish to deal with the problem, systematically working towards a solution. In this *Thinking Together—An Experiment*, knowledge exists in the realm of relationship. In this undirected conversation, the group charts its own course. I cannot maintain any position during the conversation. No one can. This also upsets my assumptions about what art should be. In fact, Peter Aers—the artist I commissioned—does very little. As a "facilitator" (Bohm 1996, 51), he does not talk much and he delivers no arguments, he only makes subtle interventions from time to time, indirectly reminding us of the framework of the conversation that we agreed on as a group. During the sustained time span, social conventions of speaking begin to wear thin. In this free-flowing experiment suspending my preconceived assumptions, I cannot hold on to my fixed position of a professor, a scholar, an instructor or a scholar. In fact, nobody does or can, not even 'the artist' Peter Aers, and I experience a new kind of mindset. Letting go of any fixed position, I also let go of my urge to constantly defend my position. Slowly, I allow meaning and knowledge to develop from constant transformation in the process of dialogue. A new dynamic relationship unfolds beyond the 'fixed' positions of 'artist' and 'spectator', 'student' and 'teacher', engaging the group in another kind of conversation, and I enjoy experiencing the possibilities of dialogue in transforming the relationship between people.

This feels as a way out of the conversational dead-lock I often experienced during the heated debates when discussing solutions for climate change. During the *Thinking Together—An Experiment* I do not experience my 'self' to be positioned in opposition to another person, nor do I experience my 'self' to be interacting with like-minded thinkers. I rather experience my 'self' to be participating in a constantly developing and changing network of thought and meaning. Thinking through the dissensus of the group, we tolerate and accept each other as adversaries, moving beyond any fixed position of an opponent or enemy to be destroyed or silenced. Bohm calls this the practice of a "creative dialogue", seeking to unfold the potential of creativity to reveal the deeper structures of conversation practices. Acknowledging these obstacles is in his view a first step in unfolding a "participatory thought" (Bohm 96–109), practising our ability to listen and speak freely. To listen and speak freely is to engage in thoughts, paying attention to the dialogical process and not only to the content of what has been said. Scientific thought too often works at the expense of curiosity and creative participation.

Resurging Knowledge Through Tentacular Thinking-With-Things

Another very important claim of Bohm's is that you never think alone and that your thinking is always related to the thinking of others. In *On Dialogue*, he says: "A key assumption that we have to question is that our thought is our own individual thought" (Bohm 1996, 59). Once the *Thinking Together—an Experiment* is over—or rather, once the conversation is ended by the signal of the alarm clock—we are not provided with clear-cut answers to a pre-set problem. Rather, we rise anew from a "pool of knowledge" (Bohm xiii) about our perception of things, people and the world, how we assign meaning to events, and how we tend to be stuck in individuality. This knowledge is participatory, tacit and overt.

Bohm's idea of participatory thought, overt or open conversation and tacit knowledge resonates with Haraway's concept of tentacular thinking, who also seeks to turn scientific individual thought into an intelligent, co-operative endeavour. First, tentacular thinking does not pretend to emerge from one source of thinking. It is a co-creative thinking "outside the premises of modernist humanist doctrines" (Haraway 2016, 177, fn 26). A myriad of tentacles is needed, with many appendages, for the art of tentacular thinking. They make "attachments and detachments; they make cuts and knots; they make a difference" (Haraway 31). What Bohm called "participatory thought" is such a kind of tentacular thinking: it is "a mode of thought in which discrete boundaries are sensed as permeable" (Bohm 1996, xvi).

Second, the Latin *tentare* refers to the verb to try, indicating that tentacular thinking is also tentative thinking, in the sense of speculative thinking. As Haraway put it, the myriad of tentacles in tentacular thinking "weave paths and consequences, but not determinisms; they are both open and knotted in some ways and not others" (2016, 31).

Third, the Latin *tentare* also refers to the verb to feel. The etymology of the word 'tentacle' hence entails a double meaning, also referring to a tacit 'production' of knowledge. The Latin *tentaculum* refers to 'feeler', indicating that the tentacular are not disembodied figures. As such, tentacular thinking is "a hugely consequential, mind-and-body-altering sort of commitment" (Haraway 34). In the participatory thought at work in *Thinking Together—An Experiment*, there also is a "proprioception of thought" (Bohm 1996, 27–29), pointing at the tacit knowledge produced. In proprioception, the body is provided with immediate feedback about its own activity, for example, our embodied memory allows us to climb stairs in a confident manner. Bohm wants the movement of thought to become proprioceptive, much as the body does. This proprioception of thought actually happens in the moment of suspension. When I suspend an impulse of frustration in dialogue, I actually feel my body responding with increased muscular tension, providing me with feedback on my actual thought. I learn that I become impatient when faced with long silences, becoming aware of a subtle fear for thoughts that are not part of a designed research plan.

But there is more to tentacular thinking when it comes to cultivating an awareness of interconnectivity in a more-than-human world. Animating a language of animacy also entails a tentacular thinking-*with-things*. The grammar of animacy, Kimmerer observes, should also remind us of "the capacity of others as our teachers, as holders of knowledge, as guides" (2013, 58). And these 'others' might as well be fungi, trees, algae or a bay.

> But imagine the possibilities. Imagine the access we would have to different perspectives, the things we might see through other eyes, the wisdom that surrounds us. We don't have to figure out everything by ourselves: there are intelligences other than our own, teachers all around us. Imagine how much less lonely the world would be. (Kimmerer 2013, 58)

Simard similarly observed that, instead of seeing trees as individual agents competing for resources, one should consider the forest "a 'co-operative system', in which trees 'talk' to one another, producing a collaborative intelligence (…) described as forest wisdom" (Simard in Macfarlane 2019, 90–91).

Is it possible to resurge knowledge from things through conversational practices? Building Conversation thinks it is. Animating a *Parliament of Things*, this collective provides an ally for things to emerge as mediators.

THINGS EMERGING AS MEDIATORS IN A *PARLIAMENT OF THINGS*

Latour made his call to summon the Parliament of Things in *We Have Never Been Modern* in 1991. One might say that Building Conversation has accepted his challenge. Since 2016, they have organized several *Parliaments of Things* as conversational performances. It is a form of conversation in which the participants practise themselves in speaking on behalf of things. It urges the participants to distance themselves "from anthropocentric thinking, which places man in the centre of the universe", and in which "the relation between ourselves and things" is investigated (https://www.buildingconversation.nl/en/#conversations/parlement-van-de-dingen). The first meetings of Building Conversation's *Parliament of Things* was led by the Dutch theatre maker Lotte van den Berg and visual artist Daan 't Sas. The ongoing question was: Is it possible for humans to talk on behalf of things and animals around us? Since then, the

Parliament of Things was set up and experienced by many people in many different parts of the world, which makes a case for the right, autonomy and agency of objects and raising opportunities for tentacular thinking-with-things. The basic question that runs through every parliament of things, be it Latour's theoretical argumentations or Building Conversation's practical set-up, is the following: When we agree that people who are affected by decisions have a right to have a say in making the decisions, do things have the same rights? This seems an awkward question. We are used to hearing people speak on behalf of themselves and only *about* other entities: heaven, the rain forest, animals, the city, and so forth.

However, worldwide there are practices that voice 'things' and that acknowledge rights, autonomy and agency of 'nonhuman' entities, and 'nature' in particular. In Ecuador, for example, 'nature' has official rights. It was the first country to recognize the Rights of Nature (or Pacha Mama) in its Constitution in 2008.[18] Instead of treating 'nature' as a property under law, Article 71 in Chapter 7 of the Constitution acknowledges that nature, in all its life forms, "has the right to integral respect for its existence and for the maintenance and regeneration of its life cycles, structure, functions and evolutionary processes. (…) All persons, communities, peoples and nations can call upon public authorities to enforce the rights of nature" (https://pdba.georgetown.edu/Constitutions/Ecuador/english08.html).

The Whanganui-river in New Zealand got a legal voice in 2017. The Awa Tupua Act (Whanganui River Claims Settlement) dictates that "the Whanganui River is a living entity and a legal person with rights that can be judicially enforced by the Te Pou Tupua, the appointed guardians of the river" (Argyrou and Hummels 2019, 752). It is the guardians' duty to act and speak for and on behalf of the Whanganui River, to uphold the river's recognition and values as a legal person, to protect the river's interests as a living entity, and to perform (legal and other) actions to fulfil this duty.[19]

In June 2018, the North Sea Embassy was established in The Hague, the Netherlands, with similar aims, appointing representatives of the North Sea as an independent entity, giving a voice to things, plants, animals and people in and around the North Sea. It was a joint initiative by many organizations,[20] amongst them Building Conversation and Partizan Public, a Dutch think and action tank led by Joost Janmaat and Thijs Middeldorp. Since 2004, this organization has been devoted to the exploration, production and implementation of social, political and cultural instruments that generate positive and sustainable change to people and their environment. In view of the development of a Dutch policy plan for the North Sea for the period up to 2030, Building Conversation considered it important to make "as many voices, ideas and insights as possible: what would the North Sea itself say? What are the interests of fish, birds and algae? What do windmills, fishermen and ports say?" (https://www.buildingconversation.nl/en/ambassade-van-de-noordzee/). Or, as Thijs Middeldorp of Partizan Public explains:

> Whatever happens: we will have to judge the interests of the North Sea from a broader scope than that of economy, or even sustainability, alone. We will have to take the wellbeing of the Sea itself into account. It will demand of us to see non-humans as autonomous actors with their own pace and their own value-systems. (https://theparliamentofthings.org/lon gread/parliament-new-public-space/)

In the more remote past, too, 'things' such as trees were attributed autonomous rights. The most famous one is *The Tree that Owns Itself*, a white oak with that name in Athens, Georgia. In the nineteenth century, so the story goes, an American colonel was so grateful when seeing the familiar tree in front of his house when returning home from the civil war, that he decided to draft an act in which he assigned the plot of land on which the tree stood to the tree itself. The granted plot of land was eight feet (2,5 m) in radius by its owner. The memorial stone says (Fig. 2):

> For and in consideration of the great love I bear this tree and the great desire I have for its protection for all time, I convey entire possession of itself and all land within eight feet of the tree on all sides—William H. Jackson

The topic that came up during the temporarily raised *Parliament of Things* during the summer school on Climate in September 2019 also concerned 'Trees'. It took some time before the group agreed on the topic of the parliamentary question, or rather before the things themselves decided what they wanted to talk about. After discussing whether we (in the sense of we voicing things) should choose one Tree, or a Forest, we decide that 'Trees' embraces both the autonomous agency of one tree, and the interconnectivity in a forest. The parliamentary question hence became: Should Trees obtain legal rights?

Fig. 2 Postcard of *The Tree That Owns Itself*. Athens, Georgia, 1930–1945 (© The Tichnor Brothers Collection, Boston. Public Library Print Department)

But before formulating and tackling this parliamentary question, we had to prepare something together: we had to decide what we would invite to the parliament. It's up to the group to decide which things will speak. We had to select our quasi-objects, the things that have to be represented while discussing this question, and with whom/which the *Parliament of Things* gathers henceforth. After all, when we agree that things have the same right as people, we also agree that, like people, those who are affected by decisions have a right to have a say in making the decisions, also things. Again, the parliamentary question does not tackle a particular climate case, it tackles a general question of attributing rights to 'Trees', and in which other quasi-objects have a say. Instead of focusing on the content of the debate, it is again the conversational that lies at the heart of this practice/performance.

Parliament of Things is inspired by Latour, who in *We Have Never Been Modern* uttered the idea of organizing a Parliament of Things in order to move beyond Anthropocene thought. The idea is that 'speechless' non-humans, things and other entities are voiced through their representatives, allowing for a debate to unfold in the (represented) presence of all those who are in a way implicated and involved. As such, not only objects, but also more abstract entities such as the meteorology of the polar regions, the chemical industry, the State, etc. might be represented:

> Let one of the representatives talk, for instance, about the ozone hole, another represent the Monsanto chemical industry, another the voters from New Hampshire, a fifth the meteorology of the polar regions; let still another speak in the name of the State, what does it matter, so long as they are all talking about the same thing (…). (Latour 1993, 144)

These quasi-objects have "properties" that "astound us and whose network extends from my refrigerator to the Antarctic by way of chemistry, law, the State, the economy, and satellites" (Latour 1993, 144). As such, the question whether 'Trees' should obtain legal rights, is in 'our' *Parliament of Things* tackled by 'furniture', represented by a wooden plank, 'underground insects', represented by a weird, undefinable plastic worm-like object, 'humans', represented by money, 'Time' represented by a clock, 'the State' represented by a *'tricolore'* or the Belgian national flag, 'Air' represented by an open, glass bowl, turned upside down, etc. 'Optimism' represented by sunglasses with pink glasses, etc. 'Trees', demanding legal rights, is of course also voiced, represented by a huge branch brought along by one of the participants. These representatives of quasi-objects are selected from a table on which the participants displayed the objects they brought with them, as requested by Peter Aers, the facilitator of this *Parliament of Things*. These objects were brought into the performance space by the participants because of their strong, personal bond with 'it', and were chosen without knowing the parliamentary question to be dealt with beforehand. After displaying the objects, and explaining their personal bond with 'it', and before appointing the representatives, the participants could remove the objects if they felt that the object was too close to them. All the things that we have invited get a stool. When the parliament starts, every one of us chooses one of these stools, or rather chooses one of these things, taking it in our hands, and giving voice to that thing. As there are more things than participants, we can shift places and hence can shape-shift between different several thingly representations.

When the displayed objects become representatives of quasi-objects, my mindset is recalibrated. These objects carry with them a personal story that they share with their owner, but they also have a story of their own, and in my mind unfolds an endless network of interconnectivity. The quasi-objects shock me "into recognition of the inescapable interdependencies and shared contingencies between our species and the millions of micro- and macro-organisms with which we share both a gene pool and a planetary ecosystem" (Arons and May 2012, 6). The stone on the table, for example, not only 'functions' as a holiday *souvenir* of one of the participants, it also presents itself as departed from a rock, unfolding a deep time that scatters the narrow scales of time I am accustomed to. I think of Macfarlane's words, in his book *Underland*, which I had been reading the weeks before:

> We tend to imagine stone as inert matter, obdurate in its fixity. But here in the rift, it feels instead like a liquid briefly paused in its flow. Seen in deep time, stone folds as strata, gouts as lava, floats as plates, shifts as shingle. Over aeons, rock absorbs, transforms, levitates from seabed to summit. Down here, too, the boundaries between life and not-life are less clear. (Macfarlane 2019, 37)

The storytelling-with-things also traces my own "fundamental *nonseparatedness* from the more-than-human-world*"* (Arons and May 2012, 5, emphasis theirs).

> We are part mineral beings too – our teeth are reefs, our bones are stones – and there is a geology of the body as well as of the land. It is mineralization – the ability to convert calcium into bone – that allows us to walk upright, to be vertebrate, to fashion the skulls that shield our brains. (Macfarlane, 37)

Even though 'Trees' did not speak for itself, the *Parliament of Things* provided an opportunity for listening to the trees' stories, even if I had forgotten how to hear their voices. Acknowledging our reciprocal relationship in a more-than-human world, I opened up to the arboreal language. Throughout the *Parliament of Things*, I was struck by 'Trees'' generosity in their entanglement with the-more-than-human world ('Trees' provided oxygen to 'Air', shade to 'Soil', nutrition to 'Underground Insects', wood to 'Furniture', etc.) and by their kindness in relating to the other, respecting the other's ecological space (so many other quasi-objects were sharing the space with Trees, including other trees). It was only later that I learnt that this kindness has a botanical term, also known as the phenomenon of crown shyness, "whereby individual forest trees respect each other's space, leaving slender running gaps between the end of one tree's outermost leaves and the start of another's" (Macfarlane 2019, 99). I still find it hard to imagine these arboreal giants in terms other than tenderness, generosity and even love.

I no longer consider 'Trees' or other 'Things' as mere instrumental tools or artificial intermediaries. In Latour's words, this *Parliament of Things* allows objects to emerge as mediators, side-stepping their usual instrumental function in "a theatre of proof" (1993, 19). This animates another production of knowledge. Following Latour, a laboratory installs "a Parliament of Mutes", while the art-science worlding of the *Parliament of Things* allowed things to emerge as mediators, revealing "their crazy ability to reconstitute the social bond" (Latour 1993, 142). Despite the fact that we were gathering in the context of a Summer School, with experts in diverse fields such as performance studies, sociology, literary studies, engineering and bio-engineering, the parliament never resulted in a defence of scientific knowledge *about* an object, as we quite easily adopted the perspective *of* that object. Looking through what Haraway calls an "art-science worlding" lens, (bio)engineering, philosophy, sociology, etc. integrates with art. This art-science worlding is more than mere interdisciplinary scientific research, as another production of knowledge is at stake. It is rather a resurgence of knowledge through a tentacular thinking-with-things.

The conversational practice/performance *Parliament of Things* was a mind-bending journey that expanded my habits of listening and my habits of speech, enabling a dazzling, vibrant journey into a miraculous web of interconnectivities and intra-actions. It had me looking deeper, paying in-depth attention to thingly intra-actions (Stalpaert 2019a, b; Code 2006). Looking again, trying to see how something *is*, how it really *is* and *acts*, not how I thought 'it' looks like, the understor(e)y of my life resurged.

Tentacular Thinking-With-Flora in the Storied Place of the Botanical Garden

My experience of this *Parliament of Things* accumulates with my experience of the *Impossible Conversation* earlier that week. Before joining the conversational practice/performance at the Botanical Garden at Ghent University, I stroll around the winter houses, as I am too early for my appointment with facilitator and artist Peter Aers. The information leaflet of the Ghent University Botanical Garden is proud to present its botanical treasury, offering "breath-taking views throughout the seasons", and inviting the visitor to "enjoy the spring foliage and the wealth of flowers in summer", to "treat your senses with the spectacular display of colour throughout the autumn". I am considering the benefits of this tranquil place—indeed, it plays an important role in encouraging a connectedness of citizens with nature, if offers education and research opportunities that are crucial for plant conservation, etc.—when I spot a plate explaining that sugarcane, also known as *Saccharum officinarum*, is a cultivar that is native to New Guinea. Its instrumental use for the production of sugar (and rum) generated a whole sugar industry that culminated in the sixteenth century, with African slaves being shipped to the Caribbean to work in the sugar industry. The story of Sugarcane is, in other words, linked to the introduction of slavery in America.

This accumulation of thoughts hits me like a bolt from the blue. Why was the history of colonialism completely absent from 'our' *Parliament of Things*? Voicing things, we touched upon so many ecological layers. The way things are voiced is of course largely dependent on the choice of the participants. The *Parliament of Things* suddenly strikes me as a 'white' gathering, oblivious of the more remote history that things carry with them. It seems that our narrow time scales—again—prevented us from exceeding one generation. They are too narrow to think through the slow violence of slavery and colonialism. We failed to read the thick presence of things. After all, as anthropologist Tim Ingold observed, every thing is a parliament of lines (5). Could a storytelling-with-things also trace the (colonial) lines things bear with them?

In *Pour une écologie décoloniale* (2019), political philosopher Malcolm Ferdinand develops a decolonial ecology. Exploring the relation between current ecological crisis and the colonial history of modernity, he points at the importance of integrating ecological and decolonial discourses. I start wondering. What if plants were able to story their witnessing of the slow violence of slavery, colonialism and the transplanting of species for economic purposes? What about the significance of empire in the rise of botany as a formal science? In fact, in the early modern world, botany was big business, supporting colonial profits,[21] but what about this place? What were the priorities of the work of botanical institutions such as the Botanical garden in Ghent in researching the (colonial) plant world? What were the associated political and economic interests to these scientific endeavours?

Since the garden's foundation in 1797, botanists have collected plants from all over the world, especially in Africa, Central America and China. The Botanical Garden now proudly possesses around 10,000 plant species, and hence plays a major role in plant conservation. It is proud to provide a safe haven for various endangered species such as *Ceratozamia robusta*, *Dracaena umbraculifera* and *Hyophorbe verschaffeltii*. I recognize these nearly extinct species by the special sign next to the plant. This botanical garden now appears to me as storied by the plants in it, and reveals itself as a "vexed place" (Haraway 2016, 133), burdened with the economization of nature, and bearing with it a history of colonialism. Mourning the extinct,[22] I observe the layered complexities of living in times of extinction. The endangered and extinct are voiced, calling upon an ethics for decolonialization (Rose 2004). Through a tentacular thinking-with these flora on the edge of extinction, also in the context of the history of colonialism and its entanglement with the economization of nature, I practise an art of mourning that reveals the cracks in the seemingly paradise-like place of the Hortus Botanicus of Ghent University. Ecological philosopher and ethnographer Thom Van Dooren would call this alternative storytelling a powerful attunement to storying in flora multimodal semiotics (2014, 63–86).

However, these colonial issues again failed to be raised during the subsequent *Impossible Conversation*, which took place in the outdoor surroundings of the Botanical Garden. The place is primarily experienced as a place full of beauty and peace, shielding us from the hectic life and traffic noise in the city (Fig. 3). Not only the participants of the conversational practices/performances, but also the participants taking part in the Ghent University summer school and the visitors in the Botanical Garden suddenly strike me as a 'white' gathering, oblivious of the storied place that the botanical garden really is. This makes me wonder about yet another issue. How can a small, 'private' gathering like the conversational performance of the *Parliament of Things* affect or change our 'public' actions in 'real life'?

Fig. 3 Jean Baptiste de Noter, *Vue d'une Partie du Jardin Botanique de Gand, prise devant la statue de Baccus*, 1816 (© Ghent University Library, BIB. TEK. 004,722)

NEW MODES OF ACTIVISM: SILENT REVOLT OF INTERCONNECTIVITY THROUGH ART-SCIENCE-ACTIVIST WORLDINGS

In her manifesto *A Conversation as an Artwork*, Lotte van den Berg wrote down her ambition to turn theatre into a place of action, rather than watching. She wrote the following:

> We use theater to not just watch but act, to face the conversation. It takes courage to participate. We ask the audience/the participant a considerable engagement. And I think this engagement is ultimately necessary nowadays. To engage and to participate. To be there. And not just watch. (https://www.lottevandenberg.nu/english/news/item/?page=nieuws&news_id=110)

Does this active engagement unfold a new mode of activism? The conversational exercises in attentive thoughtfulness changed my understanding of my being and becoming-with-things. The *Parliament of Things* in particular opened an ally for resurgence, it provided a key to understanding my entanglement with things and matter, changing my understanding of how life works. The thingly point of view provided an exhilarating change of perspective, throwing my preconceived notions of individuality and even 'human' intelligence into question. The *Parliament of Things* recalibrated my mindset, my understanding of the more-than-human-world, and the often-overlooked *doings* of 'things' in it. In accumulation with my other experiences of conversational practices, such as *Impossible Conversation* and *Thinking Together—An Experiment*, it was an exercise in embodied thinking together in a thick presence, with tentacles towards a (colonial) past and a (precarious) future.

But, can these conversational practices/performance really *change* things in the future? Or, to put it in Haraway's terms, how not to command how to act, but still reach "an inflection point of consequences" (2016, 100). "How to matter and not just want to matter?" (Haraway 2016, 47).

On the website of the collective Building Conversation, a quote reads: "The way we speak influences the future we create" (https://www.buildi ngconversation.nl/en/).[23] It echoes Arendt's belief in the world-making potential of interacting through speech. This quote gives rise to a final question: Do the *Impossible Conversation*, *Thinking Together—An Experiment* and *Parliament of Things* have world-changing potential? In what follows, I will observe the new modes of activism at work in these conversational practices/performances as "art-science-*activist* worldings" (Haraway 2016, 76).

There are reasons to believe that change does not/will not occur. Bohm's practical manual of practising participatory thought in conversation does not guarantee an instant result. As he himself indicates, the movement of a dialogue group is rarely from point A to B (1996, ix). Also, the dialogues do not proceed with convincing, self-confident reasoning and argumentation, as we often find ourselves stuttering. This feels like a relief in comparison with the endless theorizing and speculation in scientific thought, but the conversational practices/performances also do not seem to be 'serious' business. They are rather brimming with infectious joy and curiosity, at the same time unsettling and exploratory, truly experiencing adventure in thinking. On other occasions, time seems to be 'wasted' when words fail. However, it is only this "relaxed" production of knowledge (Bohm, xviii), that allows time for non-judgemental curiosity, with a profound impact on seeing and listening freely. While we are used to scientific thought effectively moving forward, this participatory thought seems to circle around. Another tempo, another movement, is at work here. As Bohm aptly observes, the group dialogues are in fact "recursive movements", "with unexpected dynamic shifts following periods of frustration, boredom, and agitation, in a perpetual cycle" (Bohm 1996, ix). The revolt of connectivity is a slow revolt. It unfolds slowly, but insistent, "staying with the trouble, yearning toward resurgence" (Haraway 2016, 89), sticking to the stuttering thickness of the present. "In a time of accelerating abstractions and seamless digital representations, it is this insistence on facing the inconvenient messiness of daily, corporeal experience that is perhaps most radical of all" (Bohm 1996, xi).

And this does have an accumulated effect. The collective of Building Conversation keeps expanding, with a growing number of facilitators forging alliances with many different institutions and people in many different parts in the world, unfolding a slow, silent revolution of connectivity. The conversational practices/performances are spreading like a virus. "The accumulated experience of many people in many different parts of the world shows that this unfolding can in fact occur", says Bohm (1996, ix). An example of this unfolding slow revolution through connectivity is an Amsterdam-based initiative of the Parliament of Things initiated by Building Conversation and Partizan Publik, amongst others. This Parliament of Things was installed in view of the publication of the report *Nature in Modern Society Now and in the Future*, written by prominent scholars such as Latour, Roger Scruton and Matthijs Schouten. The report was written in The Hague in 2017, for the Dutch Environmental Agency, a national institute for strategic policy analysis in the fields of the environment, nature and spatial planning. An important project unfolding in the aftermath of this Parliament of Things is *Wild Amsterdam*, imagining the city of Amsterdam as a city housing not only 863 000 humans, but trillions of inhabitants in a more-than-human-world. Almost 80 experts and city council members were involved, resulting in an action plan that was presented in spring 2020 (https://www.partizanpublik.nl).

Facilitating conversational practices and performances, Building Conversation holds open space for "practices for resurgence" (Haraway

2016, 82), and for "speaking resurgence to despair (...) in the face of extermination" (Haraway 71, 76). This entails the resurgence of 'lost' words and a grammar of animacy (Kimmerer 2013) in the case of *Impossible Conversation*, the practice of tentacular thinking (Haraway) or participatory thought (Bohm) in *Thinking Together—an Experiment* and the giving voice to things in a *Parliament of Things* (Latour). However, tentacular thinking-with-things in storied places also and primarily demands the resurgence of indigenous ecological knowledge. The concept of a Parliament of Things is not new. Building Conversation stipulates, also in the introduction to the conversational performance, that *Parliament of Things* is not only inspired by Latour, but also by a ritual of the Aboriginals, who relate to plants, clouds or mountains as if they were their ancestors. In fact, indigenous ecological knowledge always practices a tentacular thinking-with-things. It is indeed no coincidence that the Ecuadorian acknowledgements of the Rights of Nature in its constitution are initiated by a claim of the indigenous communities.

In her environmental and forest biological research, Kimmerer has botany dialogue with the production of knowledge in Native American traditions to restore human curiosity. Being a botanist and a member of the Citizen Potawatomi Nation herself, she brings together the two lenses of knowledge to awaken our ecological consciousness and to seduce us into "land stewardship" (2013, 190) instead of the current exploitation of land. Most of the conversational practices/performances that one can book on the Building Conversation website also bring together these two lenses of knowledge, echoing Bohm's words that this participatory knowledge, this tentacular-thinking with-things "moves independent of any individual, or even any particular culture" (Bohm 1996, xiii). With creative consultant Obiozo Ukpabi recently joining Building Conversation, the collective is currently critically assessing the particular 'use' of their inspirational sources and seeks how to avoid an 'exotic' recuperation of indigenous conversational practices.[24] Provided that the content also reflects its format, the conversational practices/performances by Building Conversation triggers our awareness of our entanglement with things and matter, raising not only ecological matters, but also the entanglement of colonialism and ecocide.

Notes

1. I deliberately put the term workshop in quotation marks, as Building Conversation avoids this term as it is too often considered an aim in itself. They prefer notions such as 'exercises', 'practices', 'experiments' or 'trajectories'. They do not offer 'workshops', but they sometimes do work in a workshop setting. With the term 'workshop' setting, I refer to the processual way of working during the commissioned conversation practices.
2. Donna Haraway introduces this term in different ways throughout her book *Staying With the Trouble*. She talks about "science art worldings" (64, 67, 69, 71, 86, 97) as "an alternative to the experimental laboratory" (64) and about "art science worldings" as "sympoietic practices" (67), swapping places between 'art' and 'science' (69). "Science art activist worldings" (71, 76) are "science art worldings for staying with the trouble" (71). Occasionally, she uses the concept "art-science-activist worldings" with hyphens (79). I prefer the hyphenated term, as it indicates that these worldings do not refer to an interdisciplinary scientific methodology. It requires a resurgence of knowledge in relationality, in tentacular thinking. Knowledge is no longer produced in one of the fields of the 'arts', 'science' or 'activism', with the other field functioning as a auxiliary science. It is in the hyphens that knowledge resurges.
3. I deliberately use the verb 'to story' instead of 'to narrate', as Haraway's concept of a vexed place is building on Thom van Dooren's theory of storytelling, developing "a nonanthropomorphic, nonanthropocentric sense of storied place" (in Haraway 2016, 39; see also van Dooren 2014, 63–86).
4. The concept of the conversations was developed and realized by Lotte van den Berg and Daan 't Sas, in collaboration with Peter Aers, Andreas Bachmair, Ewout Bomert, Bart van Capelle, Antwan Cornelissen, Katja Dreyer, Adelijn van Huis, Floor van Leeuwen, Dennis Molendijk, Jonathan Offereins, Bart van Rosmalen, Floris Siekman, Anneke Tonen, Harmen van Twillert a.o.
5. In 2016, for example, conversations took place in Brussels, Riga, Groningen, Eindhoven, Utrecht, Zagreb, Terni, Den Bosch, Poznan, Amsterdam, Norwich, Kortrijk, Purmerend, Rotterdam and Heerlen.
6. This is the reason why I deliberately call the conversations by Building Conversation conversational practices/performances, using the '/' to denote the ambivalence.
7. I invited Peter Aers a first time at Ghent University during the Schone Week, an annual initiative by the Arts Department, seeking to bring the students in contact with artists and their practice. From 1 to 5 April 2019, Peter Aers facilitated several conversations with students in the City

Hall of Ledeberg, a small town in the Ghent surroundings (https://sch oneweek.wordpress.com/makers/peter-aers-ding/). For a report of this long-term residency, see the portfolio in *Documenta* (2019). I invited Peter Aers again for a series of conversational practices, culminating in the conversational performance *Parliament of Things* during the Summer School *Climate Change and Solutions*, organized from 20 until 25 September 2019. (https://www.ugent.be/nl/univgent/waarvoor-staatugent/duurzaamheidsbeleid/onderwijsstudent/summerschoolklimaat) In January 2020, Building Conversation was an artist in residence at the Academy of Architecture in Amsterdam. For ten days, 130 master students from 37 different countries took part in a winter school, doing conversational practice on the topic of inclusive design. (https://www.buildingc onversation.nl/en/#over).

8. Peter Aers is a member of Building Conversation, with a conversational art practice of his own. *On Future, Crime and Punishment, The Pain of Others* and *Against Interpretation* are three conversational practices and dialogues by Peter Aers, as part of the series *Everything Depends on How a Thing is Thought*. These three different subjects "explore how the individual and the community are related and how the community influences the individual and vice versa. (...). They are a co-construction with other artists and/or philosophers, psychiatrists, psychologists and other people involved in the topics" (https://everythingdepends.be/en/).
9. I borrow the term "resurgence" from Anna Tsing (2015, 179–192). She describes "persistent resurgence" as "regeneration" (179), "moving away from "nostalgia-driven reconstructions" (187). To resurge is an intransitive verb: it is characterized by not having or containing a direct object. One can only undergo a resurgence. I deliberately (mis)use the verb to resurge in an active way, acknowledging agency in interconnected matter, especially in processes of resurgence.
10. In case you are looking for the meaning of the word 'conker': it is not only the name for the seed of the horse chestnut tree. 'Conkers' also refers to the name for a traditional children's game, in which two players alternately try to strike each other's conker until it breaks. The conkers are threaded onto a piece of string.
11. 70 per cent of the words in Potawatomi are verbs, in comparison to 30 per cent in English (Kimmerer 2013, 53).
12. Or, as Kimmerer put it, it "teeters on extinction" (2013, 57).
13. "The mycorrhizal symbiosis enables the fungi to forage for mineral nutrients in the soil and deliver them to the tree in exchange for carbohydrates" (Kimmerer 2013, 20).
14. Macfarlane draws on Suzanne Simard's research when he observes that following "forest wisdom" in a "forest ecology", "some older trees

even 'nurture' smaller trees that they recognize as their 'kin', acting as 'mother'" (Macfarlane 2019, 91).
15. Anna Tsing observed the extreme resilience of the mushroom; they were amongst the first living things to emerge in the blast landscape in Hiroshima (2015, 3).
16. I participated in the conversational practice/performance *Thinking Together – an Experiment* on 5 April 2019, as a presentation of the weeklong artist-in-residency of Peter Aers during the Schone Week at the Arts Department of Ghent University.
17. This number of participants is based on the concept of the micro-culture as developed by the English psychiatrist Patrick de Mare, who proposed that "a sampling of an entire culture can exist in a group of twenty or more people, thereby charging it with multiple views and value systems" (Bohm 1996, x).
18. The Rights of Nature were ratified by referendum by the people of Ecuador in September 2008. It was published in the Official Register on October 20, 2009.
19. When they enforced on the State of New Zealand the Awa Tupua Act (Whanganui River Claims Settlement) in 2017, the resulting environmental "stewardship" (Kimmerer 2013, 190; Argyrou and Hummels 2019, 752) had a positive impact not only on the well-being of the river, but also on the living conditions of the Māori. This Earth jurisprudence or wild law (Thomas Berry) also provided other indigenous communities with tools for legal action. In May 2019, hundreds of Waorami people travelled to the city of Quito and called upon the authorities to protect part of the Amazon rainforest from further oil drilling, and with success.
20. The North Sea Embassy is an initiative of the Parliament of Things and is being built by Stroom Den Haag, De Noordzee Foundation, Building Conversation, The Ponies and Waag Society, with support from Creative Industries Fund NL, Mondriaan Fund and Bank Giro Loterij Fund and collaboration of Daan 't Sas, Tjallien Walma van der Molen, Studio Alloy, Jasper van den Berg, Partizan Publik, Andrea Simmelink and Jasmine De Bruycker. (https://theparliamentofthings.org/noordzee/ambassade-van-de-noordzee/) In the context of the awarding of the Spinozalens to Bruno Latour, the educational and public programme *Welcome to the Parliament of Things*, was launched 18–27 November 2020 at various locations (www.parlementvandedingen.nl).
21. The entanglement of empire, colonialism and the rise of botanical science in the early modern world has been outlined by Londa Schiebinger and Claudia Swan in *Colonial Botany* (2005). Latour also outlined the entanglement of colonialism and ecocide in the West (1993, 9).
22. In his extraordinary book *Flight Ways. Life at the Edge of Extinction* (2014) ecological philosopher and ethnographer Thom van Dooren

considers extinction as 'suitable' for mourning, as "extinction is a protracted slow death that unravels great tissues of ways of going on in the world for many species, including historically situated people" (in Haraway 2016, 38). Deborah Bird Rose even calls it "a double death", as it is a killing of generations, "an undoing of the tissues of ongoingness" (in Haraway 2016, 177, vn 24).
23. Following Arendt's political philosophy in *The Human Condition*, this simple activity of talking to each other, this human interaction through speech, is a space for politics, and, ultimately, for freedom, as it holds "the spontaneous beginning of something new", expanding "the predetermined net of relationships" (243).
24. Obiozo Ukpabi calls herself a facilitator, analyst, strategist, creative consultant and project manager in the areas of peacebuilding, inclusive transitions and transformative justice.

REFERENCES

Abram, David. 1996. *The Spell of the Sensuous. Perception and Language in a More-then-Human-World*. New York: Pantheon Books.
Arendt, Hannah. 1958. *The Human Condition*. Chicago: The University of Chicago Press, 2019.
Argyrou, Aikaterini, and Harry Hummels. 2019 "Legal Personality and Economic Livelihood of the Whanganui River: A Call for Community Entrepreneurship." *Water International* 44, nos. 6–7: 752–768.
Arons, Wendy, and Theresa J. May. 2012. "Introduction." In *Readings in Performance and Ecology*, edited by Wendy Arons and Theresa J. May, 1–10. New York: Palgrave Macmillan.
Atwood, Margaret, et al. 2015. "Authors' Letter to the Oxford University Press." *Caught by the River*, 15 January. Accessed February 18, 2020. https://www.caughtbytheriver.net/2015/01/letter-oxford-university-press-atwood-macfarlane/
Bohm, David. 1996. *On Dialogue*. London: Routledge.
Code, Lorraine. 2006. *Ecological Thinking. The Politics of Epistemic Location*. Oxford: Oxford University Press.
"Constitution of the Republic of Ecuador." 2008. Political Database of the Americas, October 20. Accessed February 18, 2020. https://pdba.georgetown.edu/Constitutions/Ecuador/english08.html.
Ferdinand, Malcolm. 2019. *Pour une écologie décoloniale. Penser l'écologie depuis le monde caribéen*. Paris: Editions du Seuil.
Forde, Patricia. 2018. *The Wordsmith*. Dublin: Little Island.
Ghosh, Amitav. 2016. *The Great Derangement. Climate Change and the Unthinkable*. Chicago: The University of Chicago Press.

Haraway, Donna J. 2016. *Staying with the Trouble. Making Kin in the Chthulucene*. Durham: Duke University Press.
Ingold, Tim. 2007. *Lines. A Brief History*. London: Routledge, 2016.
Kimmerer, Robin Wall. 2013. *Braiding Sweetgrass. Indigenous Wisdom, Scientific Knowledge and the Teaching of Plants*. Minneapolis, MN: Milkweed Editions.
Latour, Bruno. 1991. *We Have Never Been Modern*. Translated by Catherine Porter. Cambridge: Harvard University Press, 1993.
Latour, Bruno. 2004. *Politics of Nature. How To Bring the Sciences into Democracy*. Translated by Catherine Porter. Cambridge, MA: Harvard University Press.
Latour, Bruno. 2007. *Reassembling the Social. An Introduction to Actor-Network Theory*. Oxford: Oxford University Press.
Macfarlane, Robert, and Jackie Morris. 2017. *The Lost Words*. London: Penguin Books.
Macfarlane, Robert. 2019. *Underland. A Deep Time Journey*. London: Penguin Random House.
Margulis, Lynn,ed. 1991. *Symbiosis as a Source of Evolutionary Innovation. Speciation and Morphogenesis*. Boston: MIT Press.
Morton, Timothy. 2012. *The Ecological Thought*. Cambridge, MA: Harvard University Press.
Morton, Timothy. 2013. *Hyperobjects. Philosophy and Ecology After the End of the World*. Minneapolis, MN: The University of Minnesota Press.
Mouffe, Chantal. 2005. *On the Political*. London: Routledge.
Mouffe, Chantal. 2013. *Agonistics. Thinking the World Politically*. New York: Verso.
Rose, Deborah Bird. 2004. *Reports from a Wild Country. Ethics for Decolonisation*. Sydney: University of New South Wales Press.
Schiebinger, Londa L., and Claudia Swan. 2005. *Colonial Botany. Science, Commerce and Politics in the Early Modern World*. Philadelphia, PA: University of Pennsylvania Press.
Sheldrake, Merlin. 2020. *Entangled Life. How Fungi Make Our Worlds, Change Our Minds and Shape Our Futures*. London: Penguin Random House.
Stalpaert, Christel. 2018. "Cultivating Survival with Maria Lucia Cruz Correia: Towards an Ecology of Agential Realism". *Performance Research* 23, no. 3: 48–55.
Stalpaert, Christel. 2019a. "Maria Lucia Cruz Correia's *Urban Action Clinic GARDEN*. A Political Ecology with Diplomats of Dissensus and Composite Bodies Engaged in Intra-Actions." In *The Routledge Companion to Theatre and Politics*, edited by Peter Eckersall and Helena Grehan, 203–206. London: Routledge.
Stalpaert, Christel. 2019b. "This Body is in Danger! On Ecology, Protest, and Artistic Activism in Benjamin Verdonck's *Bara/Ke* (2000)". In *Emerging*

Affinities: Possible Futures of Performative Arts, edited by Malgorzata Sugiera, Mateusz Borowski, and Mateusz Chaberski. Transcript Verlag, 211–236.
Students Arts Studies and Theatre, Ghent University. 2019. "Schone Week. VIJF DAGEN TINGELN EN DAN - " *Documenta: tijdschrift voor theater* 37, no. 1: 236–271.
Tsing, Anna Lowenhaupt. 2015. *The Mushroom at the End of the World. On the Possibility of Life in Capitalist Ruins*. Princeton: Princeton University Press.
Van Dooren, Thom. 2014. *Flight Ways. Life at the Edge of Extinction*. New York: Columbia University Press.

Posthuman Epistemologies: The Politics of Knowledge Transmission

The Point of the Matter: Performativity in Scientific Practices

Maaike Bleeker and Jean Paul Van Bendegem

INTRODUCTION

Laura Karreman

The conference *Does it Matter? Composite Bodies and Posthuman Prototypes in Contemporary Performing Arts* (Ghent University, 2015) featured a 'keynote dialogue' between performance scholar and philosopher Maaike Bleeker (Utrecht University) and mathematician and philosopher of science Jean Paul Van Bendegem (Free University of Brussels). Speaking from their respective areas of interest and expertise, Bleeker and Van Bendegem discussed various examples of scientific processes that exposed performative mechanisms resulting from the entanglement of technological tools and human agency—a dynamic that is a characteristic feature of scientific practices.

M. Bleeker (✉)
Utrecht University, Utrecht, The Netherlands
e-mail: M.A.Bleeker@uu.nl

J. P. Van Bendegem
Vrije Universiteit Brussel, Ixelles, Belgium
e-mail: jean-paul.van.bendegem@vub.be

© The Author(s), under exclusive license to Springer Nature Switzerland AG 2021
C. Stalpaert et al. (eds.), *Performance and Posthumanism*,
https://Doi.org/10.1007/978-3-030-74745-9_12

The dialogue of Bleeker and Van Bendegem was enriched by the fact that both scholars share a special interest in the other's research area. Bleeker's curiosity about performative processes of the scientific domain is reflected in the analysis of the 'hunt for Higgs' (Bleeker and Van der Tuin 2014), which shows how the Higgs particle was 'made to perform' in a scientific practice that involves types of both human and non-human agency. Van Bendegem's interest in drawing connections between mathematics and performing arts practices has led him to engage with prominent figures in this field, such as Belgian choreographer Anne Teresa De Keersmaeker and theatre maker Kris Verdonck. Inspired by these and other interactions he is concerned with exploring new avenues of thought, by looking at possible parallels that may be drawn between practices of knowledge transmission in the arts and sciences.

The way in which Bleeker and Van Bendegem's dialogue has taken shape in this chapter is the result of a thought experiment, which was designed specifically for this volume. The aim of this experiment was to enable an in-depth exploration of the three main topics that surfaced in Bleeker and Van Bendegem's original dialogue at the conference, which related to knowledge production, knowledge transmission and the impact of specific practices in artistic and scientific domains. In the set-up of the thought experiment, the format of a dialogue was maintained, for this volume, the dialogue was shifted from the oral domain to the realm of writing. Both philosophers wrote three individual reflections, in which they demonstrated how the three aforementioned epistemological topics come alive in their respective areas of critical inquiry. In the final stage of this extended written exchange, each of them presented some closing thoughts in response to their interlocutor's reflections.

The outcome of this thought experiment materializes here in two parts. In the first part Bleeker and Van Bendegem individually relate to the three topics: knowledge production, knowledge transmission and the complex collaboration of technological and human agents in scientific and artistic practices. The second part of the text consists of their closing reflections, in which they respond to each other. The resulting dialogue is a dynamic exploration of thought and practice in philosophy, sciences and the humanities. Time and again in this dialogue, it becomes apparent how one thought inspires another to unfold. A surprising reciprocity between these two thinkers emerges in the process.

The Problem of Knowledge Production: Finding or Constructing Proof

Jean Paul Van Bendegem

Philosophy of science has undergone some major changes in the twentieth century. No one will disagree with this near-tautological statement. Instead of focusing on the results—theories, laws, predictions (seen as logical derivations), machines…—the whole scientific process came into view, which introduced a vocabulary of revolutions (Thomas Kuhn 1962), incommensurability (Paul Feyerabend 1975), logic(s) of discovery (Tom Nickles 1980), social determinants (David Bloor 1976; Barry Barnes 1977) and scientific practices (Andrew Pickering 1995). One particular set of practices concerns the gathering of evidence and/or the construction of proof. As to the former, we can no longer speak of collecting the facts, whatever they are, assuming that they are out there waiting to be found by us. And, as to the latter, proof in terms of final, objective justifications is no longer defensible in the fields of logic and mathematics, as they have undergone similar changes as the philosophy of science. Let me elaborate on this a bit further.

"We found evidence that …" seems quite an innocent start of a phrase but it carries with it a world view that accepts (at least) that (i) there are things to be found, (ii) they somehow draw our attention, (iii) we register them, and, most importantly, (iv) they do not involve us. The last point needs clarification. What I mean is that whatever is found is not influenced by us in any way—we are here, what is to be found is over there—and, by consequence, it does not matter who finds it. It is objective in (at least) this particular sense. Perhaps in a small set of cases we can act as if this is the whole story (or, should I say, the whole truth). Take any handbook of classical mechanics. Look for the chapter on collisions. The pictures do seem to depict the world as we find it (sorry for the cheap Wittgensteinian-*Tractarian* reference!): two masses collide, one does this, the other one does that (and they are determined to do so). That is precisely what textbooks are supposed to do: to let us believe that what works for the small set works for the whole. But does it?

"We have found evidence that the Higgs boson exists". Have we? Firstly, we constructed a machine of staggering complexity, the L(arge) H(adron) C(ollider), that involves nearly the whole of physics, mathematics and computer science, that involves a community of technicians, scientists and managers to maintain the instrument, to "keep it alive"—I dare use these terms because, after a check-up, the LHC is "activated" again—and that requires an environment where it can "survive", economically, socially and politically. Secondly, experiments are performed and "performance" seems to be the right term, in the sense that what happens is partially ritualized, often codified, and it takes place on a particular stage, in this case, an underground laboratory. There is nothing to be seen; only the dials and the digits inform us that something has happened and that it has been measured by the LHC. Note that the plural is correct: we do not talk about a single experiment but millions of them. Thirdly, all this "raw" material—is that still an appropriate term?—is sent through the "grid", a network of computers worldwide, making use of existing networks, to perform the most amazing calculations of a statistical nature (more about mathematics in the next section), and then to return to Geneva to produce graphics on screens. Fourthly, these drawings, for that is what they are, need to be interpreted, basically, "meaningful" spikes in the picture need to be traced. If at the "right" location, the spike "becomes" a trace of a Higgs boson and we proudly claim: "We have found it!" Have we really? We made it, we constructed it, we manufactured it, we created an environment where it could manifest itself... All these Latourian phrases seem more appropriate.

"Ah yes, but we can prove that it is the Higgs boson". Better still: "We can prove it with mathematical certainty!" Why? Because mathematical proof is the best you can imagine. Why? Because each and every step in the reasoning process has been made explicit and can be checked by everyone, even computers can do it. Except that proofs of such high quality are not what mathematicians produce, at least when the level of complexity is sufficiently high. The "real" proofs contain gaps, make large jumps, rely on the reader's background knowledge and often leave the logical principles implicit. Gottlob Frege, Bertrand Russell and Alfred North Whitehead, the Bourbaki group, all had a go at a complete version of (the language of) the mathematical universe. They encountered the same problem that Esperanto did: any language that is too universal is spoken by no one in particular. If statistics become involved, then the matter becomes even more difficult, for now we have to interpret probability statements. Of course, it is certain that an "honest" (really?) die has a chance of 1 out of 6 to produce a 3. (Unless someone with a hammer is present.) This still leaves us with the question: But how are proofs found?

Certainly not in this world of ours, so where then? Our imagination? But is that a "place" where things are "found"?

THE PROBLEM OF KNOWLEDGE PRODUCTION: MAKING MATTER PERFORM

Maaike Bleeker

The hunt for the Higgs particle presents a most interesting example indeed of how to prove something is a performance, or actually a constellation of performances, by humans as well as by their instruments and matter. At the press conference announcing CERN's success in proving Higgs' theory, Rolf-Dieter Heuer, the director of CERN, announced the discovery of the Higgs particle by saying: "As a layman I would now say, I think we have it, do you agree?" His announcement followed an explanation of the complex probability calculations that form the basis for this statement. It is a remarkable and complicated statement, for what is actually being confirmed, or negated, by Heuer's speech act? Framing his statement by saying "As a layman I would say" is ironic. Obviously, the director of CERN is not a layman. At the same time, his statement could be understood as a way of reaching out to an audience of non-specialists, explaining that the probability calculations are physics' way of saying: "I think we have it".

These probability calculations require capacities that exceed those of humans and can only be performed by extensive networks of computers on the basis of data captured by sensors sensing what humans cannot perceive. These sensors and computers open up what media theorist Mark Hansen calls "an expanded domain of sensibility that can enhance human experience" (2015, 4). To access this domain of sensibility, "humans must rely on technologies to perform operations to which they have absolutely no direct access whatsoever and that correlate to no already existent human faculty or capacity" (2015, 4–5). This performance of technology is the basis for Heuer's claim that "As a layman I would now say, I think we have it. Do you agree?"

Peter Higgs, sitting on the front row, sheds a tear. Fifty years and billions of money have been spent to produce the proof of the theory he penned down as a still relatively young and unknown scientist. And now the proof is there. Or is it not? For, what is Heuer actually saying? As a scientist these calculations convince him to the point that as a layman he would say: "I think we have it". But apparently this is not enough for him as a scientist, for it is followed by a question directed to his audience of fellow scientists present at the presentation: "Do you agree?" Their applause confirms his statement and the validity of the claim expressed in it. The existence of the Higgs particle is thus presented as a matter of probability that requires an additional performance, namely that of intersubjective confirmation, to be acknowledged and accepted as truth. With their applause, the community of scientists not only expresses its participation in this moment of celebration; it also performs the confirmation of the validity of the decades-long process of producing this 'proof' of Higgs' theory.

The calculations that are thus confirmed to be proof demonstrate the probability of the success of another performance of technology, namely that of the Large Hadron Collider, to produce a particle that performs according to the parameters predicted by Higgs' theory. Proving Higgs' theory meant literally to make matter perform in the way that Higgs had predicted the particle named after him would. This was not a matter of detecting the existence of the particle 'out there' but to first produce the particle and then detect the traces of it having existed. The proof of Higgs' theory thus demonstrates the inseparability of scientific apparatus and the phenomenon observed, as theorized by Karen Barad (2007) after Niels Bohr. Bohr's philosophy of quantum physics challenges the assumption that processes of measurement are transparent and that measurements reveal the pre-existing values or properties of independently existing objects as separate from the measuring apparatus and the observing agencies.

Demonstrating the truth of Higgs' theory meant to design an experiment in which the Higgs particle—"the missing piece in the Standard Model puzzle", as the press release of the Royal Swedish Academy of Sciences announcing the Nobel Prize in Physics for 2013 puts it[1]— is challenged forth as matter (even though its ultra-short existence can only be detected after the fact by detecting the traces of its decay). This challenging forth happens by means of apparatuses constructed to make matter perform while at the same time it is within this performance that the Higgs particle is supposed to materialize. In the collider, nature is made to perform and made to perform in such a way as to produce the proof of Higgs' theory, which is also the proof of the collider's intended efficiency. In order for the experiment to be successful, the Higgs particle therefore has to perform too. It has, to use performance theorist Jon

McKenzie's (2001) felicitous expression, to "perform, or else" it does not exist. And it has to perform within the parameters according to which the detectors are designed to detect its traces.

Bohr's insights have important epistemological as well as far-reaching ontological implications. "What he is calling into question is an entire tradition in the history of metaphysics: the belief that the world is populated with individual things with their own set of determinate properties" (Barad 2007, 19). Moreover, Barad shows how Bohr's ideas also challenge traditional humanist accounts of knowledge and of knowing as something done by a self-contained rational human subject. Rather, she argues, "Knowing is a distributed practice that includes the larger material arrangement. To the extent that humans participate in scientific or other practices of knowing, they do so as part of the larger material configuration of the world and its ongoing open-ended articulation" (379).

Large-scale highly technological research projects such as the hunt for Higgs at CERN involve complex constellations of scientists and their instruments in which human researchers are literally nodes in networks that operate on a scale and in cognitive modes that exceed human understanding. These 'agencies of observation' (another Baradian term) do not perform on their own. Rather, groups of humans and technology form complex assemblages of actors (human–machine-matter-data) intra-acting with one another in various ways. Barad uses the term 'intra-actions' rather than 'inter-actions' because the latter would suggest something happening in between already existing entities and her point is that these intra-actions precede the existence of what they relate. It is through intra-actions that things come to matter. Understanding the implications of this inseparability requires a radical posthumanist performative approach that takes into account the performance of humans as well as of instruments and matter, and the complex intra-actions between them.

Re-Imagining Knowledge Transmission: From One-Way Channels to Open-Endedness

Jean Paul Van Bendegem

Transmitting knowledge: How to imagine this? Should we keep life simple and accept the sender – channel – receiver (S – C – R) model and calculate, as Claude Shannon has done, the informational entropy of the message so as to reduce the errors where error means any syntactical difference between the sign(al)s at S compared to the sign(al)s at R? I am not downplaying the importance of this model, for it allows us to get a signal on the iPhone as it is enhanced by electronic means (hence the metallic sound) to be understandable. It also allows us to enjoy that CD, although it contains a high number of errors in its digital code. But even under the most classical (= analytical) definition of knowledge as *justified, true belief*, this does not fit the model. So, how to imagine this?

A teacher teaches a pupil (a bit of) mathematics, say the Pythagorean theorem, the infamous $a^2 + b^2 = c^2$. Why? The teacher is a trained mathematician who has a set of beliefs, among them the conviction that it is vital that everyone has some mathematical knowledge and hence the next generation should know this, so the teacher has a preconceived, possibly if not likely a biased, conception of the pupil. He or she has been trained to use certain procedures, ways of doing and practices to transmit this knowledge. Usually these procedures operate both sequentially and in parallel: body language, spoken words and signs, written words and signs... These procedures should create understanding and meaning in the pupil's head. The pupil may or may not have a clue why this piece of information is important as he or she is not a mathematician and has a different set of beliefs, including the belief that the teacher knows what he or she is talking about. Nevertheless, the pupil is supposed to be willing, "wanting" to learn. The innocent phrase "Consider a right-handed triangle" betrays a world of intricate language games: how is one supposed to do "the considering", will any right-handed triangle do? (If the figure on the blackboard has to be manipulated it cannot be any size, likewise a triangle consisting of the North Pole and two points on the equator ninety degrees apart will not do because it is curved, assuming, by the way, that the Earth is a perfect sphere, which it is not.) Is the labelling a, b and c necessary, ...? These considerations are not figments of my imagination as I have been able to show (in the context of an exhibition on mathematics and art, titled *0/10²*) what happens when one or more of these background conditions are violated. What happens if the teacher is incompetent? What happens if the teacher is a sex worker? What happens if other signs (musical signs, choreographic patterns, real objects such as people and chairs...) are used? The results are often humorous because expectations are violated and "damage" the mathematical proof. It ceases to be "convincing".

Let us resist the temptation to make the model more complex although it is an obvious strategy. We should take into account the model in the minds of S and R of the whole process, thus introducing a form of reflexivity because how they view the transmission process influences that very process. We could continue and defend that a knowledge transmission channel is never uniform, thereby allowing us to see it as just one unique channel, so rather we have a heterogeneous series of channels operating in parallel. All too soon we will be writing down expressions such as

$$S_{S'-C'-R'} - (C_1|C_2\ldots|C_n) - R_{S''-C''-R''}$$

that look like an improvement but now error-correcting codes are not of much help. Getting a message faithfully from S to R appears now as something close to a miracle. Or, if you prefer, most messages are distorted one way or another. But what should we do then? Let us start again.

Transmitting knowledge: How to imagine this? The expression "transmitting knowledge" suggests a direction (from S to R in the simple model) and is quite passive, as what is transmitted is supposed to remain unchanged. So, if instead of "transmitting" we emphasize the two-way direction, then terms such as "sharing", "creating together", "experiencing together"…come to mind and, rejecting passivity, terms such as "constructed meanings", "collective practices"…pop up, and how different is the sound of "creating collective practices together" or "sharing constructed meanings"? And now the real drama can begin. The collective meaning creation in a group of scientists will differ from that among scientists and "ordinary" citizens and will differ in turn from that among citizens and scientists-as-citizens, and among this and the next generation and … Perhaps "drama" is not the right choice of words (for "drama" suggests a beginning and an end, maybe even an unfolding, and this need not be the case). Is not "open-ended" a better choice? It resists both a genesis as a comforting and explanatory device and it also resists an end-goal to be reached no matter what, which dictates the (preferably unique) road to follow. That sounds familiar: not knowing where you came from, not knowing (not even wanting to know) where you will arrive, is that not simply called wandering from passage to passage, through the arcades, Benjamin-like (also unfinished)?

RE-IMAGINING KNOWLEDGE TRANSMISSION: RE-ENACTMENT AS A NON-REPRESENTATIONAL APPROACH

Maaike Bleeker

In his *The Idea of History* (originally published in 1945), philosopher of history Robin Collingwood proposes re-enactment as a perspective on sharing thoughts and ideas. With re-enactment he does not refer to redoing past events, like re-enactments of historical battles or the redoing of performances from the past created by performance and dance makers. Rather, re-enactment is part of his speculative approach to possibilities of understanding the choices and decisions made by historical agents and how these have resulted in history as we "know" it. To this end, he argues, historians must envision the situation with which the historical agent was trying to deal and then imagine the reasons for choosing one course of action rather than another, and thus go through, or re-enact, the process the historical agent went through in deciding on a particular course.

Collingwood has been criticized for mixing up the ideas of the historian re-enacting the situation from the past with those of the historical agent involved in the historical situation. And indeed some of his examples do suggest precisely that. Other examples, however, allow for a different reading, one that is surprisingly close to contemporary enactive approaches to perceptual cognition. One of these examples is that of Archimedes and his insight into the law of special gravity. Getting the idea of gravity, Collingwood explains, involves grasping the relationships observed by Archimedes between mass and volume of an object, an insight that, history tells us, occurred to Archimedes while taking a bath (Collingwood 1993, 287, 444–446). Getting the idea of gravity thus involves a kind of re-enactment of grasping this set of connections perceived by Archimedes as a result of which we 'get' his idea. This does not require taking a bath, nor is it about getting a better understanding of the historical person Archimedes and his situation. Rather, it is a matter of grasping the logic perceived by Archimedes and in this sense re-enacting his idea.

Re-enactment thus understood presents a non-representational approach to the transmission of knowledge and ideas, in which transmission is not a matter of transporting some independently existing entity from one person to the next but rather the result of a grasping, or what Whitehead (1978) describes as a prehending of, the logic also grasped by someone else. In such grasping, the idea is re-actualized. From the perspective of such a non-representational approach, the transmission of ideas is a matter of organizing the conditions for them to be triggered in someone else and thus be rearticulated. This is, one might argue, what Jean Paul Van Bendegem experiments with in his exhibition project *0/10* mentioned above, in which he explores the effects of changing the conditions of transmitting the Pythagorean theorem.

Re-enactment as a perspective on knowledge transmission shifts attention from representation to enactment: to what happens in the doing, to embodiment and materiality. How such doing is constitutive of grasping even highly abstract principles is the subject of Gilles Châtelet's *Figuring Space: philosophy, mathematics, and physics* (2000), Elisabeth de Freitas and Nathalie Sinclair's *Mathematics and the Body* (2014) as well as Brian Rotman's reflections on research into the transmission of mathematical insights by Nemirovsky and Ferrara. Rotman describes how:

> by tracking the moment-to-moment eye movements (saccade gestures) of a group of mathematics students arguing about, notating, and engaging with real and imagined diagrams, Nemirovsky and Ferrara found the students' thinking to encompass 'parallel streams of bodily activity' manifest as a 'coordinated activity among hands, eyes, and talk in the process of expanding, or bringing into the open, aspects of visual meaning' (2004), an organic notion that leads them to concur with the thesis that 'children's thinking' and hence human thinking in general, 'is more akin to an ecology of ideas, co-existing and competing with each other for use, than like monolithic changes from one stage to the next'. (Rotman 2008, 34)

Bodily engagement and movement, this research into cognition suggests, is not only part of how we understand what other people are doing and feeling but also of grasping highly abstract ideas. It is part of how we participate in processes of producing and sharing knowledge by navigating ecologies of ideas with and through our bodies.

Knowledge Production in Practice: What Mathematicians Do

Jean Paul Van Bendegem

Any mathematics handbook will have problems in the exercises section that start with "Show that ..." or "Prove that ..." An example: "Show that the sum of the first hundred natural numbers 1, 2, 3, ..., 100 is equal to 5050". There is an easy way to solve the problem: do the actual counting (and the answer will be yes, it is equal). There is another way, just by looking at this figure:

```
  1   2   3   ...       ... 98  99  100
100  99  98   ...       ...  3   2    1
101 101 101   ...       ...101 101  101
```

On the second line the numbers are written in descending order and if the sum is made for each pair in the first and second line, the answer is always 101. So we have counted 101 a hundred times so that is 10100 but we have counted the required sum twice, so divided by two, hence $10100/2 = 5050$. (This "proof" is claimed to have been found by Carl Friedrich Gauss, a young boy at the time, who thus "proved" his mathematical talent.)

If the handbook is on number theory, very likely the next exercise will be: "Generalize the previous result and prove that $1 + 2 + 3 + \ldots + (n-1) + n = n.(n + 1)/2$". Would one not be tempted to simply generalize the scheme above?

```
  1     2     3    ...       ... n-2   n-1    n
  n    n-1   n-2   ...       ...  3     2     1
 n+1   n+1   n+1   ...       ...n+1   n+1   n+1
```

So n times $n + 1$, but we double counted, therefore, $n.(n + 1)/2$.

But is that what mathematicians do? It depends on the handbook. Some of them will insist that a "clear" method of proof should be used such as *mathematical induction* and that produces a curious kind of reasoning that goes like this: if I can prove that the claim holds for $n = 1$, and if I can prove that if the result holds for n, then it also holds for $n + 1$, then I can conclude that it holds for all numbers n. The proof now looks like this:

1. For $n = 1$, we see that $1 = 1.(1 + 1)/2$ and that is correct.
2. Assume $1 + 2 + 3 + \ldots + (n-1) + n = n.(n + 1)/2$. Add $n + 1$ to both sides, to find $1 + 2 + 3 + \ldots + (n-1) + n + (n + 1) = n.(n + 1)/2 + (n + 1)$. The expression on the right is equal to $(n + 1).(n/2 + 1) = (n + 1).(n + 2)/2 = (n + 1).((n + 1) + 1)/2$ and that is the same expression as before but with $n + 1$ in the place of n.

So it holds for all n. QED.
Do note that in (1) we did not sum anything; there is only the number 1 (how do you add one number unless you are a Taoist, while clapping your hands?) and nothing else. Is it meaningful then to talk about the sum of so and so many numbers? Would you not at least expect there to be two numbers? And do note that in (2) we have done something entirely different from what Gauss did and what a simple but long-winded calculation would show. And do note in general that the above is considered to be elementary mathematics. Is not the complexity at this stage already overwhelming? Questions come easily: (a) Why is mathematical induction a reliable proof method? (b) What exactly does the symbol "n" mean that we use (d) it so freely? (c) Is this really meant to be convincing? Conversely, the answers do not come easily at all. Ad (a): philosophers of mathematics are still discussing the matter because any justification of the method creates vicious circles. Ad (b): it would be better to use the plural because we indeed use "n" in different ways in the proof but at the same time it is crucial to distinguish n from $n + 1$. Ad (c): it surely is convincing to mathematicians, among other reasons because they are familiar with the method and have seen the wonderful stuff one can do with it. In summary: What a curious rhetorical process is manifesting itself here! May I repeat that we are still on the level of elementary mathematics?

What happens when we move to full-scale academic research mathematics is staggering. In a single phrase (and referring back to the first question): a mathematical proof is no less complex than a Higgs boson. The innocent-sounding message "Andrew Wiles proves Fermat's Last Theorem"—in *Tractarian* fashion we have a fact, establishing the connection "to prove" between objects, named "Wiles" and "Fermat's Last Theorem"—when deconstructed transforms into a complex multi-faceted set of pictures of mathematical communities, implicitly deciding what problems are interesting, sharing methods, sharing strategies to "find" proofs, arguing about the correctness of a result, re-examining accepted proofs because of doubts... No wonder, really, that the applicability of mathematics to the "real" world out there has become a mystery (and for the moment remains so) and then I have not said the first word about the most curious mathematical invention of all times: infinity.

Knowledge Production in Practice: Collaborations Between Technological and Human Agents

Maaike Bleeker

In large-scale research projects, like, for example, the Large Hadron Collider at CERN, human researchers and machines function as nodes in large interactive networks that operate on a scale and in cognitive modes that exceed individuals and exceed human modes of thinking and understanding. It was human intelligence that built the machines. However, being the product of complex collaborations of large groups of experts, the capacities of the machines nor the measurements produced by them can be understood as being controlled by individual human agency. Furthermore, a large amount of interpretations needs to have already been made by the machines before human agency is able to engage with the data and in processes that exceed human capacities. This raises questions concerning the relationship between human agency and technology and of technology as itself endowed with agency. Here it seems that explorations from the field of theatre and dance could contribute to further understanding the relationship between human and technological agents in the production of new, posthuman modes of knowing.

Over past decades, a considerable number of theatre and dance makers have experimented with outsourcing agency and making technology an active agent in creative processes. John McCormick's project *Emergence* (presented at the conference *Does it Matter? Composite Bodies and Posthuman Prototypes in Contemporary Performing Arts*) features collaborations between a human dancer and an artificially intelligent performing agent. The agent is not explicitly programmed with set behaviours, as in more traditional software programming. Instead, its capabilities originate in the unsupervised learning process and have the inter-dependent relationship with the dancer embedded in that learning.

Several decades ago already, Merce Cunningham began to use the computer programme *Life Forms* to create choreographies. More recently, the British choreographer Wayne McGregor's *Choreographic Language Agent* and the *Enhancing Choreographic Objects*, as well as the Croatia-based dance and performance collective BADco.'s *Whatever Dance Toolbox*, similarly aims to provide technological tools that can act as active agents in creative processes and become co-creators (see Bleeker [2017]). New York-based artist Annie Dorsen investigates the potential of algorithm as a creative agent. In *Hello Hi There* (2010), she staged a dialogue between two autonomous chat bots, using the famous television debate between Michel Foucault and Noam Chomsky as inspiration and material. In *A Piece of Work* (2013), algorithms create an on the spot re-interpretation and rewriting of *Hamlet* and instruct a performer to execute the performance.

Art projects such as McGregor's, Dorsen's, BADco.'s and McCormick's (and there are many more) continue a longer history of theatre and dance artists devising ways of working that aim to diminish their control over the creative outcome and to distribute agency, for example by means of chance procedures (throwing the dice, using I Ching) or by means of various improvisation techniques. Different from these historical predecessors, however, is how they explore the possibilities and implications of technology becoming an active agent in creating. This is also what distinguishes their work from many other explorations of the use of new technologies on stage, in which technology appears as merely a means used by a human agent to give shape to her or his creation.

In projects like these, technology is not merely something used by a creative agent, but is itself an agent in the creation process. Technological agents create differently than the artists do. This difference is precisely the reason for artists to invest in these ways of working and in the development of technological agents. An important reason for these artists to develop these technological agents and to collaborate with them is how this opens up possibilities for moving beyond the subjective perspective of the artist and even, one might argue, beyond human modes of imagining and creating. In this respect we might understand these projects as contributions to the development of new, posthuman perspectives, where posthuman does not mean the absence or doing away with the human, but refers to a decentring of human agency, and to acknowledging the implications of such decentring. In dance and performance, the aim is to generate artistic creation. In science projects, the aim is to generate knowledge. This is an important difference. This difference might be productive, however, precisely in how the artistic projects invite different ways of understanding the agency of technology and of the potential of collaboration between human and technological agents. Their work demonstrates an understanding of agency as, to speak with Karen Barad, not something that someone or something has, but as a distributed phenomenon that is enacted, and that can be enacted by humans as well as by technology.

SOME FURTHER THOUGHTS, RATHER RANDOM, YET ORGANIZED

Jean Paul Van Bendegem

After reading Maaike Bleeker's responses (MB for short from now on) to the three questions put before us, I was deeply and happily struck by the similarities and affinities between our responses. In fact, I experienced them as an invitation to reconsider and revisit 'old' themes in my thinking about logic, philosophy of science and of mathematics in particular. Let me briefly present some comments on each of these themes and then end with a conclusion that refuses to conclude.

Theme 1 from logic: there has been (and to a certain extent there still is) a current in logical research where the game of questions and answers is being modelled. Jaakko Hintikka has been the strongest promotor of this so-called (dialogical) game semantics where two players are involved (see for an overview Hodges [2013]). The dialogue enters into the game because both players have to question the other. A special type of game is that where one of the players is 'Mother Nature' herself (and that game is therefore supposed to model scientific enquiry). Actually, I am not inventing this label here and now, it has a long tradition. It goes together with a powerful (gender-biased) picture of nature as reluctant to provide answers, who therefore has to be 'seduced', but with no guarantee at all that the forthcoming answers are correct (or 'true'). For what do we expect from '*Das Weibliche*', to make the gender-bias more explicit ? Should one be amazed that Sherlock Holmes often appears in these texts, the great misogynist who only accepted one woman as worthwhile, hence labelled 'The Woman'? Seen from this perspective, logic itself becomes a culturally thoroughly embedded game of its own or, in Baradian terms, it confirms the inseparability. Even the most formal and abstract of logical rules cannot 'escape' its embedding. For sure, cognitive anthropologists know this, logicians themselves as far as I know do not.

Theme 2 from philosophy of science: obviously 're-enactment' is a powerful concept that, at first sight, seems to be lacking in the philosophy of science and hence one could be tempted to think that here we find an important difference between scientific and artistic practices. This need not be the case because in the philosophy of science there are (at least) two important concepts that are definitely quite distinct from re-enactment, but that have many elements in common, namely 'reconstruction' and 'intervening'. I do know that reconstruction has acquired a bad reputation if it is considered as 'rational' reconstruction, as has been suggested by Imre Lakatos (see Lakatos [1971]); what one aims for is for a history 'retold' such that we come to understand the 'messy', 'real' and 'actual' history. That being said, it does invite us to consider the attempt of reconstruction as a form of justification or of understanding. Ironically this does require, first of all, a deep immersion into the 'messiness' itself. In addition, if one now includes the concept of 'intervening', as has been suggested by Ian Hacking in his seminal book *Representing and Intervening* (1983), then the 'outsider' position is blocked and one has to understand how 'Mother Nature' was dealt with. (The combination of 'Mother Nature' and interventions invites us to consider the importance of aggression and violence—what is the ecological impact of a nuclear explosion in vivo?) The Archimedes example in MB's answers shows, I think, what is at stake: the re-enactment in order to grasp Archimedes' logic requires an understanding of why, so to speak, this one particular bath he took was different to all those that he took before (and we have to leave open what taking a bath meant to him afterwards). Making the connection between mass and volume already presupposes that there are such *distinct* notions as mass and volume. Or for that matter, did we separate them first only to be confronted with the question whether they are connected or not? This brings me almost automatically to the third theme because the same questions and challenges pose themselves if we look at mathematics, including Archimedes' contributions themselves.

Theme 3 from philosophy of mathematics: as I had indicated in my responses to the three questions, mathematics is not to be excluded from the above considerations. Here too re-enactment, intervention and grasping are present and are needed to understand what happens when Archimedes proves in *On the Sphere and the Cylinder* that the volume of a sphere is $(4/3).\pi.r^3$, where r is its radius and, of course, π is that mysterious number that started out as 'merely' the proportion of the circumference of a circle and its diameter to become over the centuries one of the most enigmatic numbers we know (or to have been constructed?). This 'starting out' is of extreme importance because it shows mathematics as embedded in everyday life and hence as being part of practices of human embodied beings. It was therefore a most pleasant surprise to see MB mention the work of Brian Rotman as he has been an important source of inspiration in my thinking about the finite, the infinite and the human bodily existence. (See the review [1996] that I wrote of Rotman's book on infinity.) And, of course, I must include technology here as well for, if we now 'know' π up to 22,459,157,718,361 decimals (state of the art, November 2016, computation by Peter Trueb), this is due to not only an increase in computing power but also due to 'clever' theorems that speed up the calculations. So in mathematics too we can have a discussion about where the 'centre' is to be located and furthermore how these practices relate to artistic practices. As Merce Cunningham is mentioned by MB, a composer from the same period came to mind immediately: Iannis Xenakis. In a sense, in compositions such as *Pithoprakta* (1955–1956) he 'outsourced' part of the creative process to a computer through the use of statistical methods. Macro-properties such as density (is there an Archimedian echo here?) of the sounds produced and average intensity are in his hands, the micro-properties are in the 'hands' of the computer.

In form of a conclusion there is a final and more general comment that concerns the opening sentence of the final paragraph of MB's answer to the third question: "In dance and performance, the aim is to generate artistic creation. In science projects, the aim is to generate knowledge. This is an important difference". One must agree but at the same time differences can be generated through an underlying common structure and I do believe there is one. It is, using perhaps words too grand, all about possibilities, potentialities and their explorations. And here is the absolutely nice thing about possibility: it is a perfectly (at least) two-faced concept. On the one hand, adding possibilities complicates and complexifies matters by extending the space of potentialities, on the other hand, we can only understand what *is* through what *could have been*. How else could one understand this statement: "If I were to throw this ball at you, it would hit you"? Especially if I am not holding a ball at all and I am standing in front of a mirror.

More Thoughts Again, Rather Abstract and One After Another

Maaike Bleeker

At the very beginning of this text, Jean Paul Van Bendegem (JPVB for short) observes that philosophy of science has undergone major changes in the twentieth century. These changes have foregrounded the performativity of scientific practices of knowledge production and transmission and how knowledge production and transmission are grounded in social material practices. They are, as Donna Haraway (1988) puts it, 'situated'. How the world, and the universe, come to be known is a correlate of the (organic and inorganic) bodies involved in practices of perceiving and understanding, and the social, cultural, technical and other specificities of these bodies, practices and circumstances. JPVB's own explorations with knowledge transmission (in his various 'stagings' of transmitting the Pythagorean theorem in the exhibition *0/10*) draw attention to this correlation and also to the complexity of understanding the nature of this correlation. His experiments with knowledge transmission demonstrate that not all bodily practices and not all social material circumstances will do, and also that which is transmitted (the theorem) cannot be reduced to any of the material circumstances. Or to return to Archimedes once more: his Eureka moment was directly correlated with him taking a bath, yet the insight that occurred to him is not reducible to these corporeal circumstances. Rather, his Eureka moment is the result of his capacity to observe relationships and connections, and in doing so, to abstract the theorem out of the event of him taking a bath and the constellation of elements involved in that event.

Perhaps we could think of this correlation between bodies and knowledge in terms of what Michel Foucault describes as incorporeal materialism. Foucault introduces this notion in "Discourse on Language", a lecture that has been published as an appendix to *The Archaeology of Knowledge*. In this lecture, Foucault argues that we should conceive of discourse not in terms of consciousness and continuity, nor of sign and structure, but as ensembles of discursive events. Understanding how discourse operates as event requires acknowledging that events are material yet incorporeal, Foucault observes, because.

an event is neither substance, nor accident, nor quality nor process; events are not corporeal. And yet, an event is certainly not immaterial; it takes effect, becomes effect, always on the level of materiality. Events have their place; they consist in relation to, coexistence with, dispersion of, the cross-checking accumulation and the selection of material elements; it occurs as an effect of, and in, material dispersion. (230–231).

Grasping the nature of an event, therefore, requires that we "advance in the direction, at first sight paradoxical, of an incorporeal materialism" (231). Knowledge production and transmission likewise have their place and consist in relation to the cross-checking accumulation and the selection of material elements. They occur as effect of, and in, material dispersion. Yet, they are not themselves substance, accident, quality or process. They are events in which humans and other elements participate and as events they are material yet incorporeal.

In the introduction to *Parables for the Virtual* (2002) philosopher Brian Massumi refers to Foucault's incorporeal materialism as part of reflections on how to think movement. Movements take effect on the level of the very materiality of the body moving, yet as events movements cannot be located in or reduced to the body. "When a body is in motion, it does not coincide with itself. It coincides with its own variation. The range of variations it can be implicated in is not present in any given moment, much less in any position it passes through" (4). To think the body in movement therefore "means accepting the paradox that there is an incorporeal dimension *of the body*. Of it, but not it. Real, material, but incorporeal" (5). Thinking movement requires grasping movement as dynamic unity that, like an event, is only present in passing.

This incorporeal dimension is abstract, yet not in a detached and cold way, as abstraction has come to be understood in Marxist analyses of capitalism. The abstract nature of movements and other events is not imposed on matter, but given in the relational dimension of their occurring as dynamic unity, and in the capacity of bodies to grasp and live these relations and thus participate in their unfolding. Massumi refers to Deleuze's real-but-abstract, where "abstract means: never present in position, only ever in passing. This is an abstractness pertaining to the transitional immediacy of a real relation—that of a body to its own indeterminacy (its openness to an elsewhere and otherwise than it is, in any here and now)" (5). In *Semblance and Event* Massumi further elaborates on this abstractness and terms it 'lived abstraction' (2011, 15–17).

Could lived abstraction provide a perspective on a common structure that, JPVB observes, might be underlying the arts and sciences? When watching a dance performance, philosopher Susanne Langer observes "one does not see people running around; one sees the dance driving this way, drawn that way, gathering here, spreading there—fleeing, resting, rising, and so forth; and all the motion seems to spring from powers beyond the performers" (1953, 175). Similarly, when listening to a musical composition, one does not hear individual sounds made by instruments but melodies, developments, an internal logic of relations of similarity and difference, even when the choreographer or composer explicitly avoids providing a preconceived composition. The choreography or the musical composition transmitted by the performance is given in the relational dimension of occurrences as dynamic unity, and in the capacity of bodies to grasp and live these relations and thus to participate in their unfolding. Could we conceive of Nemirovsky and Ferrara's students in mathematics (referred to above) as similarly involved in grasping and living the relationships proposed by mathematical theorems? Could we conceive of the object of knowledge as that which choreographer William Forsythe calls a 'choreographic object', a choreographic idea or set of ideas that materializes in (usually) moving bodies but cannot be reduced to these materializations? From the perspective of lived abstraction, "what we call objects, considered in the ontogenetic fullness of process, are lived relations between subjective forms of occasions abstractly nesting themselves in each other as passed-on potentials" (*Semblance and Event*, 15). Grasping the object means enacting the relationships that produce the object as lived abstraction.

These relationships between abstraction, movement and the ways in which bodies grasp what they encounter as lived relations—as observed by Massumi after Deleuze and Whitehead—are also recognized by enactive approaches to perception and cognition. Sensory inputs are multiple, manifold, ambiguous, staggered over time, they do not cover the same range of velocities, and they are often fuzzy and incomplete. This is what Alain Berthoz describes as the fundamental problem of perception, which is unity (2000, 90). Enactive approaches to perception point to the repertoire of sensorimotor schemas (Berthoz) or sensorimotor skills (Noë) as key to how bodies are capable of doing so as a result of practical knowledge of the ways movement gives rise to changes in sensory stimulation (Noë 2004, 8). The kind of implicit knowledge, for example, that movement of the eyes to the left produces movement across the visual field.

Or the kind of implicit knowledge that, when in the dark, or with our eyes closed, we touch different sides of a box, we feel not only a succession of surfaces, but grasp their spatial relationships as different sides of the same box. The impression of the different sides of the box on our fingers alone cannot explain how we are capable of perceiving a box as a three-dimensional object in space that we can pick up, turn around and open. Actually, it is the other way around: because of our experience with the effects of moving around boxes and other objects as well as moving objects around, we are capable of grasping the connection between simultaneous and successive impressions and thus abstracting objects out of multitudes of impressions. "[T]o perceive (…) is to perceive structure in sensorimotor contingencies", Noë observes (2004, 105). Perceiving is not merely to have sensory impressions but rather to *make sense of* sensory impressions and this is a matter of how our sensorimotor skills afford grasping relationships between impressions, and thus afford us to abstract the box out of the multitude of impressions. What we perceive—the box—is an abstraction that consists of a set of lived relations. Furthermore, Noë argues, our sensorimotor skills are not only that which allows us to perceive a box rather than a blur of sensory impressions; they are also the root of our ability to grasp more complex abstractions such as a musical composition, a choreography or the Pythagorean theorem.

Notes

1. https://www.kva.se/en/pressroom/Press-releases-2013/The-Nobel-Prize-in-Physics-2013/, last accessed on 8 March 2014.
2. In 2011 I was invited by the department of cultural activities of the Free University Brussels to set up a small-scale exhibition on the relations between mathematics and art. Rather than going down the well-trodden road of Escher-like exhibits, I opted for a different approach: is there art in mathematics itself? The result was a set of nine videos, average time around eight minutes, each one illustrating what happens when a vital condition for transmission of mathematical knowledge is violated. My personal favourite is a translation of a proof of Pythagoras' theorem in a musical performance (by setting up code).

REFERENCES

Barad, Karen. 2007. *Meeting the Universe Halfway. Quantum Physics and the Entanglement of Matter and Meaning*. Durham and London: Duke University Press.
Barnes, Barry. 1977. *Interests and the Growth of Knowledge*. London: RKP.
Berthoz, Alain. 2000. *The Brain's Sense of Movement*. Cambridge, MA: Harvard University Press.
Bleeker, Maaike, and Iris van der Tuin. 2014. "Science in the Performance Stratum: Hunting for Higgs and Nature as Performance." *International Journal of Performance Arts and Digital Media* 10, no. 2: 232–245. In special issue "Hybridity: The Intersections between Performing Arts and Science," edited by Eirini Nedelkopoulou and Mary Oliver.
Bleeker, Maaike, ed. 2017. *Transmission in Motion. The Technologizing of Dance*. New York and London: Routledge.
Bloor, David. 1976. *Knowledge and Social Imagery*. London: RKP.
Châtelet, Gilles. 2000. *Figuring Space: Philosophy, Mathematics, and Physics*. Dordrecht: Kluwer.
Collingwood, Robin G. 1993. *The Idea of History*. Oxford: Oxford University Press.
De Freitas, Elisabeth, and Nathalie Sinclair. 2014. *Mathematics and the Body. Material Entanglements in the Classroom*. Cambridge: Cambridge University Press.
Feyerabend, Paul. 1975. *Against Method*. London: New Left Books.
Forsythe, William. n.d. "Choreographic Objects." *Williamforsythe.com*. Accessed March 27, 2017. https://www.williamforsythe.de/essay.html.
Foucault, Michel. 1972. *The Archaeology of Knowledge & Discourse on Language*. New York: Pantheon Books.
Hacking, Ian. 1983. *Representing and Intervening*. Cambridge: Cambridge University Press.
Hansen, Mark B.N. 2015. *Feed Forward. On the Future of Twenty-First Century Media*. Chicago and London: University of Chicago Press.
Haraway, Donna. 1988. "Situated Knowledges: The Science Question in Feminism and the Privilege of Partial Perspective." *Feminist Studies* 14, no. 3: 575–599.
Hodges, Wilfrid. 2013. "Logic and Games". In *The Stanford Encyclopedia of Philosophy*, edited by Edward N. Zalta. https://plato.stanford.edu/archives/spr2013/entries/logic-games/.
Kuhn, Thomas. 1962. *The Structure of Scientific Revolutions*. Chicago: University of Chicago Press.
Lakatos, Imre. 1971. "History of Science and Its Rational Reconstructions." In *PSA 1970: Boston Studies in the Philosophy of Science* 8, edited by Roger C. Buck and Robert S. Cohen, 91–135. Dordrecht: Reidel.

Langer, Susanne K. 1953. *Feeling and Form. A Theory of Art*. New York: Charles Scribner's Sons.
Massumi, Brian. 2002. *Parables for the Virtual. Movement, Affect, Sensation*. Durham and London: Duke University Press.
Massumi, Brian. 2011. *Semblance and Event. Activist Philosophy and the Occurrent Arts*. Cambridge, MA: The MIT Press.
McKenzie, Jon. 2001. *Perform or Else. From Discipline to Performance*. New York: Routledge.
Nickles, Thomas, ed. 1980. *Scientific Discovery, Logic, and Rationality*. Dordrecht: Reidel.
Noë, Alva. 2004. *Action in Perception*. Cambridge Massachusetts: The MIT Press.
Pickering, Andrew. 1995. *The Mangle of Practice. Time, Agency, & Science*. Chicago: Chicago University Press.
Rotman, Brian. 2008. *Becoming Beside Ourselves: The Alphabet, Ghosts, and Distributed Human Being*. Durham and London: Duke University Press.
Van Bendegem, Jean Paul. 1996. "Review article: The strange case of the missing body of mathematics. Review of Brian Rotman's 'Ad Infinitum: The Ghost in Turing's Machine. Taking God out of Mathematics and Putting the Body Back In.'" *Semiotica* 112, no. 3/4: 403–413.
Whitehead, Alfred North. 1978. *Process and Reality*, edited by David Ray Griffin and Donald W. Sherburne. New York: The Free Press.

Music Notation and Distributed Creativity: The Textility of Score Annotation

Emily Payne and Floris Schuiling

One of the most important developments in recent music scholarship has been a turn towards performance as the defining element of music, afforded by a deconstruction of the notion of the musical "work" and its questioning of the centrality of notation in musicology (Goehr 2007). The traditional work-centred approach locates music in the text rather

---

This chapter is a revised version of an article that originally appeared in *Music & Letters* (Payne and Schuiling 2017). In this amended version, we have rewritten the text for a wider audience, drawing a parallel between musicological research on musicians' score annotations and recent research on annotations in the notebooks of theatre directors. We have also embedded our discussion in a broader context of media studies, exploring the paradigm shift of the transmission of knowledge in a digital era and by explaining technical musicological terms.

E. Payne (✉)
University of Leeds, Leeds, UK
e-mail: e.l.payne@leeds.ac.uk

F. Schuiling
Utrecht University, Utrecht, The Netherlands
e-mail: f.j.schuiling@uu.nl

© The Author(s), under exclusive license to Springer Nature Switzerland AG 2021
C. Stalpaert et al. (eds.), *Performance and Posthumanism*,
https://doi.org/10.1007/978-3-030-74745-9_13

than in the interactive and creative processes of performance, and has led to discourse and practice being dominated by, in Nicholas Cook's words (2004, 21), the "ocularcentric identification of the score with what the music is". Alongside the questions of ontology to which Cook refers,[1] the work-centred approach suggests a hierarchy in which the composer is seen as the primary creative agent rather than the performer, in which as Georgina Born (2005, 34) writes: "the composer-hero stands over the interpreter, conductor over instrumentalist, interpreter over listener, just as the work ideal authorises and supervises the score, which supervises performance, which supervises reception".

In this regard, musicology (like several other disciplines) has attempted to negotiate what David Bleich (2013, 11) calls the "sacralisation of texts" that has characterized the transmission of knowledge since the medieval university, or the modern "purification" of scientific knowledge diagnosed by Bruno Latour (1993, 11). Scores have been understood as objective representations of music, and consequently "music" has come to be conceptualized in terms of those elements that have a more direct relationship to notation (i.e. pitch and rhythm) rather than less "tangible" attributes such as timbre (see, e.g., Doğantan-Dack 2011), or indeed the creative skills and interaction of musicians. As Gary Tomlinson (2012) has shown, this distinction between the "specifically musical" and the physical, emotional and social qualities of musical practice was part of a late eighteenth-century discourse about Western exclusivity, wherein alphabetism was taken as a sign of Western progress, and similarly, the specificity of a culture's notation system was seen as a sign of its musical sophistication.

An approach that saw the musical text as a form of technology rather than a transparent representation of an abstract, ideal object would be more compatible with the performance-oriented scholarship proposed by Cook, while simultaneously troubling the problematic relation between writing and humanism as signalled by Tomlinson. In recent work in comparative literature and media studies, the influence of post-humanist philosophy has meant that such associations of writing with human rationality are being reconsidered. The material qualities of written communication are no longer seen to be accidental to its content, but crucial for understanding the way it informs and constructs reading practices, which are consequently no longer conceptualized as purely cognitive acts, but as embodied and social activities.[2] N. Katherine Hayles, one of the foremost authors on literature and posthumanism, argues that for too long "print literature was widely regarded as not having a body, only a speaking mind" and that "literary theory and criticism have been imbued with assumptions specific to print" (2002, 32–33). In the wake of such arguments, various scholars have addressed what Tore Rye Andersen (2015, 122) calls the "body language" of texts, and in such work particular editions or versions have come to be regarded as *performances* in their own right rather than derivations of an ideal original.

Music notation, with its double life as both a description of sound and a prescription for action (Kanno 2007), makes this reconsideration of the nature of texts particularly apposite. Not only is a score itself a performance of musical ideas (apropos Andersen's definition), but its purpose is also to give rise to new performances. Its material qualities do not just influence the musical ideas expressed *to performers*, but also the creative, social and embodied processes whereby these musical ideas are expressed *in performance*. Music, as an art form "between process and product" (Cook 2001), thus draws attention to the processes of remediation and distribution by which it comes into existence, and rather than a text *or* an act emerges as a "paradigmatic multiply-mediated, immaterial and material, fluid quasi-object, in which subjects and objects collide and intermingle" (Born 2005, 7).

This chapter investigates how *annotations* play a role in creative processes in rehearsal and performance in two apparently contrasting musical practices. It is rare to find a performer's part that does not contain annotation in some form, and performers spend varying degrees of time working with their scores, contributing additional markings, cues and amendments, sometimes so much so that their working parts become "elaborate hybrids" (Bayley and Heyde 2017, 83) that bear little resemblance to the original text. Through score annotation performers continually make new versions or "performances" of their scores in preparation for their own performance, suggesting that the relation between text and act is one of fluidity rather than opposition.

Our argument thus reconsiders the role of the score, not as the representation of an abstract structure but as a concrete material object, to move beyond a paradigm that opposes notated permanence to performed and/or improvised transience. Is it possible to describe how scores can function as sources of creative knowledge for performers, while avoiding the discourse of "reproduction" and its associated "idea that performance means bringing out something that is already there in the score, composed into it and just waiting to be released by the performer" (Cook

2013, 338)? Moreover, can notation be understood not just as an object of cognition, but as an integral element of the forms of social and creative interactions that are now seen to characterize performance?

We present case study material from our respective research projects: Payne's (2015) investigation of the creative processes of performance undertaken with clarinettists and their collaborators; and Schuiling's (2018) work with improvising collective the Instant Composers Pool Orchestra. Both studies employed observational methods drawn from ethnography to investigate the "real-world" contexts and attributes of live music-making. The former case study is an example of contemporary Western art music, where performers are often highly specialized in certain instruments and techniques, and in which it is common to work together with composers in the genesis and preparation of a piece. The latter represents a different tradition, in which performers with a background in unprepared and improvised music have started to use composed elements for the sake of stylistic diversity and to create novel creative possibilities. In these two practices, the relationship between notation and performance is very different, as is the nature of rehearsal and preparation. In one, performers use notation as a basis for preparing a more or less "definitive" version of that piece, while in the other a piece might be introduced into a variety of musical situations already taking place, and its performance might take very different forms in different circumstances. The differences between the two practices should not be exaggerated, however, since our comparison of a "score-based" performance practice with an "improvisatory" one is partly intended to complicate the assumptions that underpin these terms.

Most importantly, we suggest that annotations are not just additions to already existing and finished "works", but an integral part of the creative process itself. Timmy De Laet, Edith Cassiers and Luk van den Dries (2015) take a similar position in their research on the notebooks of theatre directors Jan Fabre and Jan Lauwers, showing how annotation combines imaginative, interpretive and pragmatic concerns in the process proceeding "from the realm of imagination to the reality of the stage" (De Laet et al. 2015, 43). Crucially, they argue that a focus on annotation might serve as a reconsideration of the role of texts as technologies in the "post-dramatic theatre" in which the dramatic text "no longer functions as the primary resource for theatrical creation" (44). Rather, they embed annotation in the processes of externalization that philosopher Andy Clark

(2008) has described as necessary components of cognition in his hypothesis of the "extended mind", whereby cognition is not restrained to the workings of the brain, but distributed across the reciprocal relationship between an organism and its environment. In music scholarship, too, there is a growing body of research in a similar direction, investigating the multi-layered forms of social and distributed creativity inherent in the practical processes of performance.[3]

Attending to the distributed nature of music-making bears not only on ontological matters, but also on concepts of musical creativity. In a paper entitled "The Textility of Making", anthropologist Tim Ingold (2010) criticizes the *hylomorphism* inherent in much thinking about creativity: the idea that to produce means to apply an already existing form to shapeless matter. The work-concept in musicology is a prime example of hylomorphic thinking, as it detaches and hypostasizes musical form from its materials. To challenge this understanding of material engagement, Ingold invokes the practice of weaving: the weaver does not shape threads into a pre-established form, but lets this form emerge by binding together separate threads. That is to say, even with a pre-established design, the process of making is not so much a matter of "moulding" the material into shape, but of negotiating the motion and the tension of the threads, the various elements of the loom and the particular characteristics of the fabric. What Ingold calls the "textility" of creative practice is meant to shift attention to the *materials* used in creative work, and the "tactile and sensuous knowledge of line and surface" (2010, 92) that comes with handling them.

In this contribution, we propose an approach in which musical notation is not understood primarily as a formal model but as one of the materials with which musicians work. As a prime example of the change that the score can undergo in the creative process, a study of annotation will allow for a consideration of notation in its *textility* rather than its *textuality*. An important thread running through our discussion is the tension, briefly alluded to above, between the descriptive and prescriptive functions of music notation (Kanno 2007), each associated with their own respective ontology of music in terms of either product or process. The annotations that performers make frequently intervene in the descriptive aspect of notation, and it is this physical and tactile engagement with the descriptive side of music that reveals what the textility of music notation signifies. Cook has referred to the two functions and their ontologies as "two sides of the musical fabric" (1990, 122) and "complementary strands of the twisted braid we call performance" (2001, 20). Performers' annotations, then, may rightly be considered as weaving one into the other.

Case Study 1: *To My Father for Clarinet and Piano*

Annotations can serve as material[4] traces of the collaborative processes of composers and performers. While performers may consider most of their annotations as negotiations of "technical" issues (such as fingering or bowing indications) unrelated to the "compositional" decisions of the composer, our following discussion suggests that this distinction between composer and "executant" is somewhat artificial, and that these technical considerations are in reality part of the fluid and reciprocal relationships between composers, performers, instruments and scores, that constitute the creative process of music-making. Technical and conceptual additions to the score can thus be understood as a way in which performers develop an intimacy with their material and temporarily take ownership of the music. In this way, they create the musical meaning in performance rather than bringing out a meaning already contained in the score.

The focus of this case study is the preparation, by clarinettists Lucy Downer and Margaret Archibald, of a suite of five pieces called *To My Father* for basset clarinet and piano (2014) composed by Nick Planas.[5] Downer and Planas' collaboration was documented from a first workshop meeting in October 2013, where Downer experimented with techniques for Planas, to the three rehearsals and premiere of the piece in March 2014. A second perspective is provided by Archibald, who performed movements from the piece at around the same time as Downer. A particular point of focus in this discussion is the reciprocal relationship between musician, score and instrument: the basset clarinet is a relatively uncommon instrument, a variation on the standard soprano clarinet extended with a slightly lower range. This alteration presents first-time performers of the instrument with an unfamiliar interface, to which they must adapt their practical skills—indeed, Downer had not played the instrument before. The supplementary keywork that operates the lower range, moreover, is not uniform across different basset clarinets, and so performers cannot necessarily rely on previously acquired fingering configurations. In this particular case study then, the basset clarinet's agentic capacity was rendered more explicit than if a more commonplace instrument had been used.

Downer described her role in the collaboration as being largely practically directed, in terms of "technically *how* to create what Nick wanted on the clarinet, rather than actually *what* to create in the first place".[6] Planas' view seemed to correspond with Downer's, in that he came to their workshop seeking to find out "What was doable and what wasn't"[7] rather than inviting Downer to contribute her own compositional material. Planas has composed for the clarinet on a number of occasions in the past, but nevertheless, he expressed his reliance on Downer's knowledge of extended instrumental techniques for the movement "Clouds" in particular, stating "I know what I want to get but I don't know how to get it. So it'll be more a case of Lucy sitting in here going 'Well I could do this, or I could do that' and me saying 'Yes I like that. No I don't like that'".[8] As a consequence, their workshop was composer-led and focussed largely on considerations of technical detail. Planas sent Downer a "trial sheet" for the movement, which presented working ideas for "Clouds". Downer's interactions with this material open up questions of creative ownership within the collaboration, with the instrument itself also playing a crucial role. Before the workshop, she had worked through the sheet and recorded her choices of microtonal fingerings for each note. An extract from her copy is shown in Example 1 (Fig. 1).

The trial sheet served two functions: first as a tool, both to ascertain whether Planas' sonic aim could be produced effectively and to act as a "key" to learning the passages (Downer remarked that notating the fingerings helped her to remember them); it could also be understood as fulfilling the role of "workbench", with the notation becoming an object of negotiation between performer and composer in the collaborative process, and a means through which material was worked and reworked into a more "complete" state.

Downer's annotations in Example 1 map her technical relationship to the material at the initial stages of preparing the piece for performance. Interestingly, later on in the workshop she advised Planas to omit fingering suggestions, saying "Usually you'd expect to find them yourself. ... The chances are someone else is going to look at that fingering and say 'Oh that doesn't work for me' and ignore it anyway".[9] As well as emphasizing the contingency of such techniques on the particular affordances of the instrument and the individual practice of the performer, her suggestion that the fingering indications should be left out so that other performers may find their own ways of realizing the music assumes the performer's creative agency from the outset of interacting with a score,

Fig. 1 Example 1: Trial sheet for "Clouds" (bb. 11–14), from "For my Father", by Nick Planas

which Downer seemed to regard as a totally obvious and unproblematic aspect of the performance process. In the example above, the notation was left open in the final version of the score so that each performer could interact with the score on his or her own terms.

This creative engagement between Downer and Planas shows the agency that annotations may have in the shaping of compositional material. But annotations may also be a means of problem-solving, for trying to understand the score's conceptual ambiguities and its implications for the performer's physical relationship to his or her instrument. This is where the aforementioned unfamiliar keywork comes in. As noted above, Downer had not played the basset clarinet before and neither she nor Planas had access to an instrument until the second rehearsal, which took place two days before the premiere. The primary performative challenges that Downer encountered in preparing *To My Father* related to the instrument's mechanism. Downer articulated the difficulties of having to "unlearn" her conventional fingering patterns because of the problems that the keywork presented:

I suppose the obvious [technical challenge] would be all the extra notes, ... because I didn't know where they were going to be on the instrument. They weren't quite the same as on my bass [clarinet] and I didn't have the alternatives that I'm used to on my bass either. So having to learn where they were, so when I went for c sharp I was accidentally getting c [natural] because I was used to that being where it was.[10]

For Downer, it was not so much a case of having to learn new notes, but that her physical perception of where the notes—or perhaps more importantly, *combinations* of notes—lay on the instrument had been obscured. What David Sudnow (1979, 17) has described as the expert performer's sense of "perfect familiarity" with his or her instrument was disrupted, and Downer had to adapt her embodied patterns of fingerings, acquired and internalized over years of practice, to this new and less ergonomic performance situation. Consequently, she had to direct more conscious attention to the actions of her fingers in order to develop new movements with which she was less familiar.

Downer's adaptation of her skilled practice in response to the basset clarinet's anatomy is made visible by her annotations in response to instances of problematic little finger combinations occurring in "Clouds".[11] She annotated her part with "R" and "L" as reminders of which notes were to be played by which little finger. These served to negotiate challenging fingering configurations, such as the jump performed by her right-hand little finger in the middle of a phrase which needed to be executed with an increase in tempo, or *accelerando* (indicated by the asymmetrical beaming over the notes), as shown in Example 2 (Fig. 2).

Here, Downer's solution prioritized the execution of the notes at the expense of phrasing and tempo, rearticulating the notes that were operated by the same finger, which, while breaking the phrasing that Planas has indicated (the curved line along the bottom of the notes indicates that the notes should be played without separation), allowed her to execute the note more "cleanly". Downer's annotated arrows correspond to her decision to manipulate the tempo of the phrase in order to execute it more effectively: the reversed arrow reminds her to delay the *accelerando* until she has achieved the particularly awkward jump in the middle of the phrase.

In considering the relationship between a performer and a less familiar instrument interface, Archibald's perspective on performing the pieces

Fig. 2 Example 2: Downer's annotations in response to problematic fingering combinations, section I, "Clouds" (basset clarinet part), from "For my Father", by Nick Planas

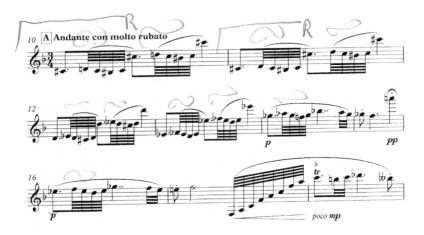

Fig. 3 Example 3: "Czardas" (bb. 10–18), from "For my Father", by Nick Planas, with Archibald's annotations (basset clarinet part)

provides further insights. Her pencilled-in figurations on her part of "Czardas" (Example 3) are gestural reinterpretations of the musical material (Fig. 3).

Here Planas' notated turns[12] have been transcribed graphically as tildes, with the "R" acting as a reminder to Archibald to place her little finger on the right key in order to achieve a smooth transition to the upper register of the instrument in the rapidly rising phrases she has to play. For Archibald, illustrating the turn in this way communicated the required gesture more effectively than reading the original notation, and allowed her to direct her focus to the physicality of shaping the turns without needing to read the individual pitches. In this way, the visual dimension of the score influenced her temporal shaping of the figures. Indeed, she commented to Planas that "If it were written as a turn, you'd play it faster. ... It's because you think 'Oh my god I've got to get all of those notes in', so visually it looks as if it ought to be slower".[13]

Like Downer, Archibald indicated the required coordination of the right- and left-hand little fingers in passages such as bar 61 of the "Czardas" movement as the melody swoops down to the lower register of the instrument, but she also included arrows as reminders of the direction her fingers needed to move in, prompts that she described as "sat nav stuff" to assist with navigating the "geography" of the instrument's keywork.[14] Archibald described the arrows as reminding her:

> That my right finger has to go up there and my left finger has to go down there! [*Laughter*] In a word, it's a map! And this [curved arrow] means, "Tuck your little finger round to the far right- and left-hand bottom corner you twit!" ... This [key] is much further away ..., so I always miss it. Unless I've recently practised it I always hit one of these, and I need *that* one![15]

The arrows that Archibald describes are another instance of a gestural reinterpretation of the visual relation to musical notation. These kinds of indications will be familiar to most musicians, but while they might be a widespread and everyday aspect of a performer's practice, they point towards the highly refined physical relationship between performers and their instruments, which is usually taken for granted. Although it is likely that Downer and Archibald's annotations became redundant by the point of public performance, they illustrate the ways in which they both grappled with the less familiar properties of their basset clarinets, negotiating their musical knowledge and their embodied relationships to the "geographies" of their instruments. Comparison of the experiences of Downer and Archibald shows that performance involves not merely engaging with the material properties of one's tools in a habitual manner, but continually adapting embodied knowledge according to the challenges that arise in the moment of performing *with* the instrument. In sum then, Downer and Archibald's annotations can be understood as making explicit the implicit, or "tacit", forms of knowledge that constitute music-making: both the negotiations of territory between composers and performers, and the bodily negotiations of instrumental interaction.

CASE STUDY 2: THE INSTANT COMPOSERS POOL ORCHESTRA

The kinds of annotations discussed in the first case study are a familiar part of the preparation of composed material in the Western art music tradition. The use of notations in the context of improvised music, however, especially their particular use by the Instant Composers Pool (ICP) Orchestra, presents a rather different situation. The ICP Orchestra is based in Amsterdam and was founded in 1967 by pianist and composer Misha Mengelberg, drummer Han Bennink, and reed player and composer Willem Breuker. The latter left the group in 1973, after which the ICP developed from a loose collective of musicians into the ICP Orchestra, although line-ups continued to change.[16] The group still exists and performs regularly, making them one of the longest consistently performing groups in improvised music, and one of the central groups in the genre. The term "instant composition" expresses Mengelberg's conviction that improvisation and composition involve the same forms of musical thinking and that only the production process differs.

As this definition of improvisation in terms of "instant composition" suggests, a central aspect of their musical aesthetic outlook is the questioning of the distinction between composition and improvisation. Part of this questioning is the use of a repertoire of stylistically varied compositions, mainly composed by Mengelberg, that use different notational strategies and compositional indeterminacies to explore different kinds of opportunities for improvisation. The duo of Mengelberg and Bennink became famous for alternating various stylistic idioms in the course of an improvisation. Moreover, their musical interaction was not always geared towards collaboration, but could equally be antagonistic, as the negotiation of such idioms included the subversion or sabotage by one musician of what the other was playing. For the ICP Orchestra, Mengelberg wrote a large repertoire that enabled a performance practice that was similar to the iconoclastic practice of the ICP duo, but which would be suitable for a larger group of musicians. Hence, the ICP musicians may start a new piece at any point, juxtapose and combine different pieces, and freely improvise transitions between them.

As such, the ICP's practice subverts the assumption that the notation is a fixing and dominating force that constrains the performers' creativity—a common assumption in improvised music, where improvisation is often described in terms of the musician's freedom and autonomy.[17] ICP Orchestra's saxophonist Tobias Delius argues instead that a free improvisation may get stuck in a particular idiom and that the notated pieces allow for more diversity:

> Many people say that improvisation can be too chaotic and then there is the "guiding hand" of the composer or a piece to bring some sense of structure, but I think it's the other way around. The purpose of the written material is to disrupt a "nice flow" of improvisation. It can create more anarchy than improvisation sometimes. ... The compositions play their own part.[18]

Delius points out the importance of constraints in the creative process, of being challenged when a "flow"[19] encounters some form of resistance, and he suggests that the pieces in the repertoire play an important role in this group dynamic, as they afford the disruption of the direction of a musical situation.

Shortly before each set, a set list is made, containing a selection of this repertoire. The ideal for a set is to play it in its entirety, improvising transitions between items, thus creating an improvised collage of pieces. This way of working requires a conception of the pieces as fluid rather than static objects. Trumpeter Thomas Heberer describes them as follows:

> Quite a few of Misha's pieces ... are often very interesting ... because on the surface they look very... not demanding and simplistic but then there's ... all sorts of options internally which make them fantastic vehicles for improvisation because they are almost like a modular machine, you can see them from so many angles.[20]

Heberer's reference to modular machines, a programming term for software that uses interchangeable parts rather than a single, inflexible monolithic system, implies that these pieces fulfil multiple purposes and adapt to a particular environment. Just like Delius' suggestion that the pieces may be used to create stylistic diversity by disrupting the musical situation, Heberer describes them not as "models" that structure and homogenize a performance, but, corresponding to our earlier discussion of the textility as opposed to the textuality of notation, as more flexible materials that contribute to the heterogeneity of creative possibilities.

As Heberer mentions, most of the compositions are quite easy to play from a technical point of view. This fact, coupled with the fact that the musicians are not working towards a definitive version for performance, means that there are comparatively few marginalia in their scores. Still, the ICP's repertoire is central to their way of working and to the forms of creativity inherent in their performance practice, albeit in a very different way than seen in the previous case study. Similarly to the previous case study, the annotations found in the ICP's scores are indicative of their particular ways of working. A closer look at some of them will make this clear.

Example 4 shows the score of *Kneushoorn* ("Krhinoceros" [sic]). In this piece, each part stands more or less on its own, and the musicians can start and stop playing their lines as it progresses, creating different instrumentations and textures. The musicians also often play with the rhythm of the piece, cueing each other to play irregular entries of their parts. In this way, the seemingly closed form becomes a tool for the musicians to play with and challenge each other, by disassembling and assembling the "modules" of the score in the course of performance. This applies not just to the context of performance itself, but also to the longer term as pieces change over time: most obviously, the group's line-up has changed since the piece was composed; not only is there an additional violist, but the trumpet part on the second stave (the main melody of the piece) was given to Wolter Wierbos to play on trombone at some point and Heberer, the current trumpeter who joined the group only later, plays along with the accompaniment in staves three and four instead of playing the melody that was originally assigned to the trumpet.

This brief history shows that ICP's repertoire has a "social life" (Appadurai 1988) of its own that develops in tandem with the group's changing personnel (on the concept of repertoire see also Faulkner and Becker 2009). This can present new challenges in performance, since trombone and trumpet parts are notated differently, and the trumpet part is thus notated in an unfamiliar way for Wierbos. Because of this, Wierbos wrote "begin F" on his copy, making it possible for him to play the rest of this simple melody by ear without having to actually read and translate the trumpet part. This is particularly useful in such a context where it is important to be able quickly to play a new phrase yet where the concentration of musicians cannot be overly focussed on the score. Hence, although this particular marking may seem insignificant, it indicates how the scores function in the ICP's practice, and how Wierbos' engagement with the score can be characterized as a process of "weaving" the piece into practice (Fig. 4).

A second example shows a more elaborate annotation, and one that explicitly involves the role of the instrument in this "weaving" process. Example 5 shows Wierbos' part for an arrangement by Michael Moore of Brooks Bowman's *East of the Sun (West of the Moon)*, with position markings added to the score by Wierbos indicating how to physically play a note, comparable to the fingerings discussed in the first case study of this contribution. Wierbos did this more frequently; when Schuiling was discussing a piece by Ab Baars where Wierbos had made similar markings, Baars said: "Is this Wolter's part? Oh... funny, I see all these things here that I hadn't expected from him...!" When asked what he meant, he

Fig. 4 Example 4: Instant Composers Pool Orchestra, *Kneushoorn*, Wierbos' copy with "Begin F" in the margins

half-jokingly replied "that's none of your business!"[21] Clearly, such scribbling has a degree of intimacy about it—that is not to say that Wierbos' annotations are very dear to him, but simply that they are a way of personally negotiating with this material. Example 5 has positions indicated over every single note (indeed, although this excerpt shows just one stave, they are indicated over all the notes in the piece). When asked about this, Wierbos explained:

> I don't like sharps.
> FS: Yes, it's in B major.
> Well, that doesn't mean much to me. I just have difficulty reading lots of sharps and there are four… no five here. … So if I just notate the slide positions it saves me the trouble. Also, I seem to remember Michael wrote this arrangement because somebody requested it, and we only had one brief play-through, not even a rehearsal so I had to make sure I was able to play it quickly. I was quite thorough with it though![22]

Wierbos, together with Bennink, is one of two current ICP musicians who never had any formal training in music, and the knowledge of his slide positions is more obvious to him than the more abstract theoretical concept of "being in B major". The positions, read in combination with the written notes, allow him to sight-read the piece without having to worry about the alterations. As such, the markings suggest his thinking about the connection between his embodied knowledge of his instrument and the more abstract representation of these notes on the page. Interestingly, he has marked every note in the score like this, even if a note had already appeared a number of times before. At some point, it seems, these position markings were no longer solutions to a problem, but an exercise undertaken for its own sake to gain a familiarity with his part as well as his instrument—or rather, of negotiating the relation between them (Fig. 5).

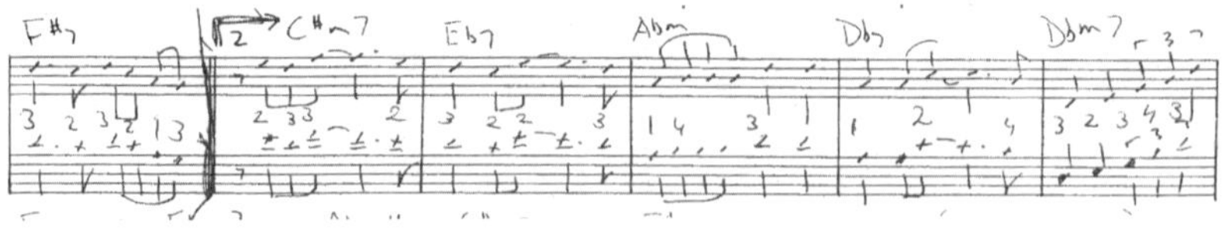

Fig. 5 Example 5: Instant Composers Pool Orchestra, *East of the Sun (West of the Moon)* with trombone positions added by Wierbos

The above examples show how Wierbos' annotations serve to gain familiarity with this repertoire in rehearsal. However, the notion of the score as a dynamic material rather than a representation of a static, abstract object also plays a role during performances, as the musicians frequently intervene in the notated score during the performance. Example 6 shows the score of *Kehang* ("Kallpaper" [sic]) as used by the ICP today. This particular version is again written for an older line-up of the group, and the main annotation is a part that transcribes the original viola part for trumpet, once underneath the viola part and again at the bottom of the page.

Additional markings like these do not just reflect changing instrumentations, but are frequently used as a source of musical ideas in performance, especially when the group improvises a transition from one piece to another. The motif in x-shaped note heads in the box at the bottom of the score of *Kehang* is usually used to enter the piece. Musicians can start repeating this rhythmic idea, which is clearly recognizable, to signal to the others to make a transition from whatever they are playing into *Kehang*. The others can then join in with repeating this riff, and the piece may then start on cue. Over the course of time, however, the musicians have learned more extensive and playful ways of making such improvised transitions. At one performance in Antwerp on 18 February 2012, the horn section played this rhythmic idea once, which signalled the start of a transition, but they did not start repeating the phrase right away (Fig. 6).

While the other musicians were improvising, Baars pointed to the wavy lines in the box just right of the middle of the score, and the horns interpreted this marking "graphically" by playing "wavy" trills. Baars then pointed to the downward arrow below this box, and the horns interpreted this idea graphically too, playing a downward *glissando* (chromatic slide through a series of pitches). Baars then pointed to the first three notes of the annotated transcribed trumpet part, slowly waving his hand up and down to indicate to the other horn players to play these notes softly and slowly. Then the horn section started repeating the main motif and on a cue started playing *Kehang*.

By extending this improvised transition, the horn section allowed the other musicians more time to adjust to the transition to the next piece, but they also created a sense of expectation and ambiguity. Such interaction and collaborative creation of musical shape and expectation requires very close concentration, trust and an almost telepathic sense of each

Fig. 6 Example 6: Instant Composers Pool Orchestra, *Kehang*

other's intentions. Some of the musicians in the horn section—Wierbos, Baars and Moore—have been playing together in this band for over thirty years and are very attuned to one another. This last example shows how this particular constellation of annotations, markings, non-diastematic symbols and regular notation allows the musicians to explore new creative possibilities in performance, radically reinterpreting the signifying potential of markings on the score. It may be thought that these examples are very particular to the practice of the ICP. To indicate how the two case studies shed light on the role of music notation in performance more generally, we conclude this chapter with a brief comparison of them.

ITINERARY (AN)NOTATION

Although the examples presented here are drawn from two distinctive performance traditions with notations of varying "specificity", annotations function in both as traces of the complex and reciprocal relationships that performers develop with their materials. Most obviously, both cases show how annotation plays a role in allowing performers to develop musical relationships in a number of ways: negotiating their musical knowledge, their embodied relationship to their instrument and their own creative agency and (co-)ownership of the music. More than merely being the expression of a performer's structural understanding of a piece, or even of a demonstration of a performer's understanding of how to play such structures, annotations are ways of imaginatively negotiating the variety of practical considerations that form part of the creative process, a bodily engagement with the body language of notations.

We wish to draw attention to three of these considerations in particular. First, the externalization of ideas is part of the creative process—this is a basic element of the concept of distributed creativity. Certain notational ambiguities in *To My Father* such as those in the trial sheet (Example 1) became a source of interaction between performer and composer during the workshop. The performer's personal relationship to and sense of ownership over the material is clearly visible in Downer's assertion that Planas' fingering indications might not be suitable for other performers, who will need to spend time working with the material in order to develop their own relationships with it. In the case of *Kehang*, the changes in the score are indicative of long-term developments (the changing line-ups that made it necessary to create an extra trumpet part) and short-term developments (the reinterpretation of various parts of the score to find improvisatory ways into the piece) in the ICP's creative practice. Annotation, then, is not a process of *iteration*, the repeated application of the same idea in a number of instances, but of *itineration* (Ingold 2010, 97). That is to say, it is not defined by the individual points but by the movement between them. The markings do not just "reflect" the cognitive process but may in turn stimulate new ideas. Furthermore, this process of itineration is not just an individual process, but also a matter of developing social relations. In *Kehang*, for example, the reinterpretation of certain signs mediates the interaction between the horns and simultaneously gives them a way to take control of the musical situation by guiding the transition into a new piece. In the case of "Clouds", Downer's annotations interrogate the material and assert her creative authority, while also tracing her embodied relationship with her instrument, suggesting that part of a performer's sense of ownership over the music is achieved through finding one's own gestural relationship, both to the notation and to the instrument. The reciprocity inherent in performance emphasizes its itineracy, with form emerging from a continuous process of growth and discovery, thus bringing its textility into sharp relief.

Second, this point about the importance of externalizing creative ideas raises questions about the nature of problem-solving. Wierbos' trombone position indications (Examples 5 and 6) are only partly evidence of solving problems in an explicit sense. However, the amount of markings he has made is well beyond that necessary to solve the "problem" of reading the five sharps and many of his markings are thus redundant, suggesting that making them was also in order to develop through them an intimacy with his material. Problem-solving has been a dominant focus within creativity research, but recent work suggests that problem-*finding* is an equally important aspect of creative work (Kozbelt et al. 2010; Sawyer 2003). Richard Sennett (2008) has suggested that an integral element of a practitioner's engagement with material is the ability to problem-find as well as to problem-solve through a "dialogue between concrete practices and thinking" (9). For Sennett, solving and finding are inextricable. Sometimes on encountering a problem, practitioners might explore their material, getting to know all its details ("identifying with it") in order to solve it, but sometimes practitioners seek problems *in order* to develop a closer relationship to their material (214–231). Creative processes of performance share aspects of both of these activities, and they are evident in several of the examples above. Downer's negotiation of fingering problems turns the score into a kind of "workbench": a means through which composer and performer interact. *Kehang* has a similar kind of "workbench" function, only during performance and among performers, as the musicians deconstruct and reinterpret aspects of the score as part of their improvisatory practice. Both examples show how annotation can afford performers a co-creative role, engaging with the material on their own terms, according to the circumstances of performance.

Our final point concerns the dual function of notation as a *description* of sound and a *prescription* for its production by musicians. At the beginning of the first case study, we mentioned that markings serving to negotiate "technical" considerations are not wholly distinct from compositional decisions, but can be inextricably intertwined with aesthetic considerations, and can thus be considered as parts of the creative process. The continuity of the descriptive and prescriptive aspects of notation is particularly apparent in two examples discussed above. Archibald's markings in "Czardas" (Example 3) serve to simplify Planas' notation and make it more immediately legible. There are two points to draw from this: first, the turns are primarily a gesture, with their pitches and intervals functioning as secondary considerations; what is more, the movement that defines these turns is not just apparent in the experience of these sounds, but also relates directly to Archibald's physical experience of playing them. This is even more apparent in her "sat nav" arrows, which serve to navigate her finger movements on her clarinet keys. Archibald's description of these markings as a "map" illustrates their dual function as visualizations and prescriptions for physical behaviour. In the ICP case study, the interpretation of various aspects of the notation as "graphic scores" similarly exemplifies the blurred boundary between description and prescription: Baars uses a hand gesture to indicate tempo and dynamics to his fellow performers, and there is no categorical difference between such a gesture and the interpretation of the downward line as a downward *glissando*. Such examples underscore and make tangible the idea of the "body language" of texts described by Andersen (2015), and show that the idea of the materiality of writing and reading is crucial for understanding the function of music notation.

Conclusion

To conclude, these observations lead to the question of how working with a score does not just build a familiarity with it, but is also a process of personal development and acquiring a sense of ownership. The score becomes a territory on which the performer's markings are evidence of a tightening up of ownership over the piece. Notation is limited: an extra "layer" of labour on the part of the performer is needed in order to clarify or to realize the music. Performers can have extraordinarily intimate, fruitful, and perhaps most importantly, *reciprocal* relationships with their materials. Nevertheless, it is important not to over-emphasize the ubiquity of annotation. Some musicians choose not to annotate their manuscripts, which we do not suggest demonstrates a lack of creative engagement on their part. Indeed, annotations are just one manifestation of itineracy that musicians exercise. The itinerative character of musical performance is embodied in performers' attentive engagements with their materials and fellow musicians, for example, in the fine-tuning of the relationship between body and instrument to achieve the necessary fluency to execute a complex musical phrase, or in the learning of new musical and professional roles in playing in various formations over the course of a musical career. These practices are necessarily textile, that is, enmeshed within the tangled relationships between bodies, instruments, materials and the environment. The musical result of such entanglements can never be guaranteed and will vary—either minutely, or more radically—each time, and as a consequence, no work is ever finished: itineracy lies in the *processes* of performance rather than the outcome.

Notes

1. Schuiling (forthcoming) discusses the ontological functions of music notation in greater detail.
2. See Andersen (2015), Clarke and Rossini (2017), Hayles (2002), Hayles and Pressman (2013), Kirschenbaum (2016), McDonald (2006), and Starre (2015).
3. See, e.g., the activities of the AHRC Centre for Musical Performance as Creative Practice, www.cmpcp.ac.uk; Born (2005), Clarke and Doffman (2018), Clarke et al. (2013), Clarke et al. (2016), Cook (2013), and Sawyer and DeZutter (2009).
4. While the musicians in this particular case study worked with paper scores, "material" includes the digitally material, as musicians increasingly perform from, and annotate, digital technologies such as tablets. For a detailed account of rehearsing and performing music with tablet technology, see Roche (2013).
5. The titles of each movement are: "Pastorale", "Romance", "Czardas", "Clouds" and "Calypso Finale". The suite was composed in memory

of Planas' father, the clarinettist and instrument maker Edward "Ted" Planas (1924–1992), who played a significant role in developing the basset clarinet during the sixties.
6. Interview with Lucy Downer, 20 March 2014.
7. Interview with Nick Planas, 26 March 2014.
8. Interview with Nick Planas, 25 July 2013.
9. Workshop, 29 October 2013.
10. Interview with Lucy Downer, 20 March 2014.
11. The dynamic nature of skilled practice in musical performance is explored in greater detail in Payne 2018.
12. A turn is a musical embellishment comprising the note above the one indicated, the note itself, the note below the one indicated, and the note itself again. It is usually indicated by a tilde-like symbol.
13. Interview with Margaret Archibald, 14 April 2014.
14. Ibid.
15. Ibid.
16. During Schuiling's fieldwork, the group consisted of Misha Mengelberg, Han Bennink, Ernst Glerum (bass), Tristan Honsinger (cello), Mary Oliver (violin and viola), Wolter Wierbos (trombone), Ab Baars (tenor saxophone and clarinet), Tobias Delius (tenor saxophone and clarinet), Michael Moore (alto saxophone and clarinet) and Thomas Heberer (trumpet). For a more detailed history of the group's personnel, see Schuiling (2018).
17. This embrace of compositional elements has a particular significance because of the ICP's cultural position between free jazz and contemporary art music, and also because of their involvement in the countercultural politics in Dutch music around 1970. See Adlington (2013).
18. Interview with Tobias Delius, 31 January 2013.
19. For discussions of flow in various domains, see Csikszentmihályi (1996) and Sawyer (2003).
20. Interview with Thomas Heberer, 1 February 2013.
21. Interview with Ab Baars, 4 January 2013.
22. Personal communication from Wolter Wierbos, 28 May 2016.

References

Adlington, Robert. 2013. *Composing Dissent: Avant-garde Music in 1960s Amsterdam.* New York: Oxford University Press.

Andersen, Tore Rye. 2015. "'Black Box' in Flux: Locating the Literary Work Between Media." *Northern Lights: Film & Media Studies Yearbook* 13: 121–136.

Appadurai, Arjun. 1988. *The Social Life of Things: Commodities in Cultural Perspective.* Cambridge: Cambridge University Press.

Bayley, Amanda, and Neil Heyde. 2017. "Communicating Through Notation: Michael Finnissy's Second String Quartet from Composition to Performance." *Music Performance Research* 8: 80–97.

Bleich, David. 2013. *The Materiality of Language: Gender, Politics, and the University.* Bloomington: Indiana University Press.

Born, Georgina. 2005. "On Musical Mediation: Ontology, Technology and Creativity." *Twentieth-Century Music* 2: 7–36.

Clark, Andy. 2008. *Supersizing the Mind: Embodiment, Action, and Cognitive Extension.* Oxford and New York: Oxford University Press.

Clarke, Bruce, and Manuela Rossini, eds. 2017. *The Cambridge Companion to Literature and the Posthuman.* Cambridge: Cambridge University Press.

Clarke, Eric, and Mark Doffman, eds. 2018. *Distributed Creativity: Collaboration and Improvisation in Contemporary Music.* New York: Oxford University Press.

Clarke, Eric, Mark Doffman, and Liza Lim. 2013. "Distributed Creativity and Ecological Dynamics: A Case Study of Liza Lim's *Tongue of the Invisible.*" *Music & Letters* 94: 628–663.

Clarke, Eric, Mark Doffman, and Renee Timmers. 2016. "Creativity, Collaboration and Development in Jeremy Thurlow's *Ouija* for Peter Sheppard Skærved." *Journal of the Royal Musical Association* 141: 113–165.

Cook, Nicholas. 1990. *Music, Imagination and Culture.* Oxford: Oxford University Press.

Cook, Nicholas. 2001. "Between Process and Product: Music and/as Performance." *Music Theory Online* 7. Accessed November 1, 2014. https://www.mtosmt.org/issues/mto.01.7.2/mto.01.7.2.cook.html.

Cook, Nicholas. 2004. "Making Music Together, or Improvisation and Its Others." *The Source: Challenging Jazz Criticism* 1: 5–25.

Cook, Nicholas. 2013. *Beyond the Score: Music as Performance.* New York and Oxford: Oxford University Press.

Csikszentmihályi, Mihályi. 1996. *Creativity: Flow and the Psychology of Discovery and Invention.* New York: Harper Collins.

De Laet, Timmy, Edith Cassiers, and Luk Van Den Dries. 2015. "Creating by Annotating: The Director's Notebooks of Jan Fabre and Jan Lauwers." *Performance Research* 20: 43–52.

Doğantan-Dack, Mine. 2011. "In the Beginning Was Gesture: Piano Touch and the Phenomenology of the Performing Body." In *New Perspectives on Music and Gesture*, edited by Anthony Gritten and Elaine King, 243–265. Abingdon: Ashgate.

Faulkner, Robert, and Howard S. Becker. 2009. *Do You Know...? The Jazz Repertoire in Action.* Chicago: University of Chicago Press.

Goehr, Lydia. 2007. *The Imaginary Museum of Musical Works: An Essay in the Philosophy of Music*. Rev. ed. Oxford: Oxford University Press.
Hayles, N. Katherine. 2002. *Writing Machines*. Cambridge and London: MIT Press.
Hayles, N. Katherine, and Jessica Pressman, eds. 2013. *Comparative Textual Media: Transforming the Humanities in the Postprint Era*. Minneapolis: University of Minnesota Press.
Ingold, Tim. 2010. "The Textility of Making." *Cambridge Journal of Economics* 34: 1–102.
Kanno, Mieko. 2007. "Prescriptive Notation: Limits and Challenges." *Contemporary Music Review* 26: 231–254.
Kirschenbaum, Matthew G. 2016. *Track Changes: A Literary History of Word Processing*. Cambridge: The Belknap Press of Harvard University Press.
Kozbelt, Aaron, Ronald A. Beghetto, and Mark A. Runco. 2010. "Theories of Creativity." In *The Cambridge Handbook of Creativity*, edited by James C. Kaufman and Robert J. Sternberg, 20–47. Cambridge: Cambridge University Press.
Latour, Bruno. 1993. *We Have Never Been Modern*. Cambridge: Harvard University Press.
McDonald, Peter D. 2006. "Ideas of the Book and Histories of Literature: After Theory?" *PMLA* 121: 214–228.
Payne, Emily. 2015. "The Creative Process in Performance: A Study of Clarinettists." PhD diss., University of Oxford.
Payne, Emily. 2018. "The Craft of Musical Performance: Skilled Practice in Collaboration." *Cultural Geographies* 25: 107–122.
Payne, Emily, and Floris Schuiling. 2017. "The Textility of Marking: Performers' Annotations as Indicators of the Creative Process in Performance." *Music & Letters* 98: 438–464.
Planas, Nick. 2014. *To My Father for Basset Clarinet and Piano*. Brackley: Self-Published Score.
Roche, Heather. 2013. "Why iPad?" *Heather Roche*, December 3. Accessed July 30, 2018. https://heatherroche.net/2013/06/08/why-ipad/.
Sawyer, Keith. 2003. *Group Creativity: Music, Theater, Collaboration*. Mahwah: Lawrence Erlbaum Associates.
Sawyer, Keith and Stacy DeZutter. 2009. "Distributed Creativity: How Collective Creations Emerge From Collaboration." *Psychology of Aesthetics Creativity and the Arts* 3: 81–92.
Schuiling, Floris. Forthcoming. "Notation Cultures: Towards an Ethnomusicology of Notation." *Journal of the Royal Musical Association*.
Schuiling, Floris. 2018. *The Instant Composers Pool and Improvisation Beyond Jazz*. New York: Routledge.
Sennett, Richard. 2008. *The Craftsman*. London: Penguin.

Starre, Alexander. 2015. *Metamedia: American Book Fictions and Literary Print Culture After Digitization.* Iowa City: University of Iowa Press.

Sudnow, David. 1979. *Talk's Body: A Meditation Between Two Keyboards.* New York: Knopf.

Tomlinson, Gary. 2012. "Musicology, Anthropology, History." In *The Cultural Study of Music: A Critical Introduction,* edited by Martin Clayton, Trevor Herbert, and Richard Middleton, 2nd Edition, 59–72. New York: Routledge.

Spectators in the Laboratory: Between Theatre and Technoscience

Mateusz Borowski, Mateusz Chaberski, and Małgorzata Sugiera

The emergence of performance art in the late 1960s and the early 1970s called into question the received notion of the spectator as merely the beholder of an artefact. Richard Schechner's environmental theatre and Richard Serra's site-specific sculptures among others explored different performative strategies of engaging spectators as co-creators in the artistic process. With reference to these developments, Josephine Machon observed how performance art blurred the boundaries between

---

The article has been written as an outcome of a research project "Artificial Bodies / Living Machines in the Laboratory of Performing Arts" supported by the Polish National Science Centre (ID 264316).

M. Borowski (✉) · M. Chaberski · M. Sugiera
Department for Performativity Studies, Jagiellonian University, Kraków, Poland
e-mail: mateusz.borowski@uj.edu.pl

M. Chaberski
e-mail: mateusz.chaberski@uj.edu.pl

M. Sugiera
e-mail: malgorzata.sugiera@uj.edu.pl

© The Author(s), under exclusive license to Springer Nature Switzerland AG 2021
C. Stalpaert et al. (eds.), *Performance and Posthumanism*,
https://doi.org/10.1007/978-3-030-74745-9_14

art as making sense and art as a *sense*-making experience (2009, 16–19). Performance art of the sixties and seventies was premised on the assumption that it provides participants with an unmediated experience of reality (through inter-human relations, the body or the materiality of the object) within an aesthetic framework. This concept of performance art has undergone significant and necessary modifications in the face of recent performative practices, drawing, as we would like to posit here, on the seventeenth-century model of laboratory in order to conduct experiments on and with spectators. Those contemporary practices directly address social imaginaries of their audiences in order to blend their aesthetically, physically and technologically mediated experiences, manifestly undermining the division between arts and sciences. Crossing this division is also germane to what Rosi Braidotti terms "Critical PostHumanities" (Braidotti 2019, 100). Those are both heterogeneous theories and hybrid creative practices that go beyond the study of cultural and social phenomena as a purely human domain. Countering the hitherto accepted anthropocentric ways of knowing and being, they seek to demonstrate productive entanglements of human and more-than-human agents in producing not only the actual worlds, but also worlds to come. According to Braidotti, both science-fictional fabulations and popular culture as well as the developments in Science and Technology Studies introduced recently by such scholars as Bruno Latour and Donna Haraway have been seminal in producing such "posthuman knowledge" (2019, 4) by blurring the boundaries between social practices and nature, between the observer and the observed. Taking this concept of posthumanism as our starting point, in the present paper we investigate the performative potential of contemporary arts as a laboratory where new types of affective and cognitive (post) human experiences that challenge the binaries of the material versus the virtual on the one hand and subject versus its environment on the other. We also suggest a genealogy of this kind of performance art, by drawing on the tradition of Brechtian *Lehrstücke* (the learning plays).

To this aim, we will take a closer look at three interrelated aspects of contemporary performative arts which meet "technoscience". These new participatory formats thrive on performance art's experimental character in the way they link various media and arts. In order to connect arts with sciences, more and more artists have started using mixed genres, combining various artistic media and conventions, as well as participatory strategies. Starting with an analysis of ORLAN's bioart project *Harlequin Coat* (2007) we will first discuss the still problematic cooperation between artists and scientists after many years of division between the two domains. Then, scrutinizing performative strategies in Rimini Protokoll's interactive installation *Situation Rooms* (2013), we will suggest a new definition of spectatorial experience as *expérience* related to contemporary performing arts meeting technoscience. Finally, the discussion of Rabih Mroué's performative lecture *The Pixelated Revolution* (2012) will allow us to conclude with problematizing the current notion of participation with Heiner Müller's idea of theatre as a "laboratory of social imagination", which already in the 1980s problematized the category of aesthetic experience.

Artists and/or Scientists

The phrase "spectators in the laboratory" in the title of our article may sound quite paradoxical, since contemporary laboratories remain shut for those who would like to observe scientists at work, not only for ordinary viewers but also for fellow scientists working in the same field. One can even argue that this is one of the long-term consequences of the birth of the institution of the laboratory in the mid-seventeenth century, when, for the first time, science was separated from the wide cultural field in such a clear-cut way. The historical studies on Robert Boyle's first laboratory (Schaffer and Shapin 1985) and the scientific practices in the Netherlands of that era (Kooijmans 2010) indicate that the laboratory space and the dramaturgy of experiments, conducted together with fellow scientists and curious onlookers (who fulfilled most probably the role of witnesses vouching for the probity of the experiment), ran parallel with the conventions of the seventeenth-century theatre. Moreover, the rules of authentication worked out in the theatre were used to evoke a reality effect in the case of scientific research, at the same time sanctioning the results of an examination. In *An Inquiry into Modes of Existence* (2013), Bruno Latour has demonstrated the process of purification, critical to the functioning of laboratories, where phenomena under investigation were separated from their natural environment and studied in technologically controlled circumstances. The dependence of knowledge-making on highly specialist procedures led, then, to the closure of the laboratory for the interested viewers, severing for three centuries all the links with the theatre and its rules of authentication. Only when studying purified objects, substances and phenomena could science become plausible and verifiable on its own terms, at the same time becoming more and more self-contained, comprehensible only for the "initiated".

As Latour testifies in *Laboratory Life* (1979), written together with Steve Woolgar, the laboratories remained tightly closed in the mid-seventies, and it was only by courtesy of professor Roger Guillemin and his team that Latour could undertake field research in the laboratories of Salk Institute in California. After two years of observing the production of scientific facts, he presented the results of his research in *Laboratory Life*. Admittedly, the last two decades have brought about significant changes in this respect. Increasingly, scientists cooperate with artists, opening the door to their laboratories, patiently explaining the intricacies of their research. As artists look for new inspiration and territories to be explored, scientists try to spread and explain the discoveries that an outsider might not immediately understand. The mutual benefits of such a cooperation have been emphasized, for example, by David Weinberg, a professor of astronomy at Ohio State University. In 2004, he prepared the installation *Island Universe* together with trained glass-blower Josiah McElheny. It was shown in prestigious galleries around the world (Miller 2014, 132–135). The installation comprises five glass and chrome starburst sculptures, each representing a different scientifically accurate model of the cosmos and other potential universes. Although Weinberg sincerely admits that his collaboration with McElheny hardly influenced the research carried out at that time, he is certain of its wider impact: "More people saw *Island Universe* in one day in Madrid than ever read my *Astrophysical Journal* articles" (in Miller 2014, 135). Small wonder that nowadays scientists—from astrophysicists to data analysts and neurosurgeons—expect artists to render visible and understandable that which for many of us is abstract and invisible when written about in academic terms; which is too small or too big to be looked at with our own eyes. There is no doubt that in these projects the artistic performance is supposed to provide a visual and palpable representation of phenomena which could otherwise be studied only in a laboratory environment. In this respect, the role of art is to provide a framework counteracting the purification principle—the installation provided alternative ways to access the scientific methods of investigating natural phenomena. The installation did not impose any way of looking at the sculptures, which could just as well be appreciated purely for their aesthetic qualities, without the awareness of their relationship to scientific notions, natural and technological processes. However, in the following we would like to depart from this concept of art as vehicle for science to turn to contemporary projects which model participation of the spectators on various types of laboratories, to question the very act of viewing and making sense of what is seen.

One of such projects, called *Harlequin's Coat*, was carried out by ORLAN in 2007 at the SymbioticA laboratory at Western Australia University in Perth, where artists cooperate with biologists. *Harlequin Coat* hardly qualifies as body art, which the French artist has hitherto been said to represent. During her carnal art period, she twisted and re-appropriated aesthetic surgery, by undergoing various (real and virtual) procedures, having her own body transformed. ORLAN's strategies are usually interpreted, mainly by popular media, as ordinary plastic surgeries whereby the artist aims to achieve the ideal of female beauty reminiscent of Boticelli's Venus and Mona Lisa. However, contrary to those widespread accounts, the artist painstakingly explains (ORLAN and Sayey 2016) that her aim is actually the opposite. She distorts and criticizes that idealized image as a product of a male artist. The critical gesture becomes evident if we look closely at the features ORLAN's body gained in those surgeries. For example, the by now iconic two bumps on her forehead are clearly a disruption of the idealized body image, but due to their intriguing, almost seductive character, cannot be easily subsumed under another classical category—the monstrous. Rather, ORLAN's carnal art introduces a striking tension between "beauty" and abjection. However in the latter phase of her work she departed from a direct concern with the practices of re-appropriating the body and subversion of the dominant ideal of beauty, to move towards problems of contemporary technoscience. In the first decade of the new millennium, ORLAN became particularly interested in the immortality of cancer cells, which was proven by the famous line of HeLA cells, taken at Johns Hopkins University from a patient who died sixty years earlier.[1] She designed her harlequin's coat as a patchwork of different types of skin. She used her own skin cells, and mixed them with cells from a twelve-year-old female foetus of African origin collected in a biopsy, muscle cells from a marsupial, human blood cells, goldfish neurons and so on. The cells were cultivated in petri dishes set inside diamond-shaped Perspex, a plexiglass plate of different colours that together formed the patchy coat. The installation evolved unceasingly as the living material gradually replaced the dead cells in the petri dishes. However, this process was barely visible, because the tempo of cell development is too slow for the human eye to perceive it. Thus, those looking at *Harlequin's Coat* were put in a position in which they had to question the received viewing habits and frames of reference, on which they relied when confronted with a work of art. In this case they had to do with a living artefact which changed continually and whose materiality never reached the ultimate shape, posing a challenge to the viewing abilities of human eye.

ORLAN herself described this particular art project as "caught between the folly of wanting to see and the impossibility of seeing" (Miller 2014, 207). This tension generated through the invisibility of the ongoing processes raises the question of what can be seen only with the help of various technological instruments, which mediate, influence or even distort our vision. Thus they performatively produce a given view of the world. In this respect *Harlequin's Coat* differed significantly from the above-mentioned project of Weinberg and McElheny, who tried to give a perceptible and palpable shape to phenomena which evade human perception and could otherwise be seen only through specialized equipment in laboratory conditions. Contrary to facilitating access to the imperceptible, ORLAN complicated the relationship between the viewer and that which was seen. Instead of playing the role of an obedient and reliable intermediary, she chose to subvert common perceptual schemata to question their role in producing knowledge and disseminating scientific facts.

ORLAN was fully aware of the interdependencies between mediation and knowledge-making, as she explained the rationale of her project in the following way: "Biotechnology is taken out of the laboratory and turned into a spectacle through the *commedia dell'arte* character of Harlequin and ORLAN's cells which play an actor's role, in both the theatrical and the linguistic sense of the word" (Miller 2014, 208). Clearly, it is not enough to transpose the procedures of establishing scientific facts, objects of study or its results from the laboratory to the outside world and make them available to viewers without reflecting on the new framework and the context of exposition. To explain the connections and interactions designed by ORLAN between the spectators and the object under scrutiny, the eponymous coat, it is useful to draw on the concept of "polyphonic assemblage" introduced by the anthropologist Anna Löwenhaupt-Tsing (2015, 22–24). Admittedly, she coined the term in a context different from the one we address in the present paper: she investigated the relationship between capitalist destruction and collaborative survival within multispecies landscapes in order to grasp different stories and temporalities that every single element of a given assemblage has brought with it. Her concept of "polyphonic assemblage" refers to heterogeneous and dynamically developing compounds made up of humans and non-humans, organic and inorganic elements, organisms and technologies, stories and ideologies, as well as economic and scientific notions which simultaneously interact with each other to produce momentary and ever-changing orders.

ORLAN created such an assemblage, putting together a variety of evolving living organisms, and creating a situation in which aesthetic and scientific frames of reference collide. In *Harlequin's Coat* there are two crucial actors in the polyphonic assemblage: ORLAN's own cells and the figure of the Harlequin, borrowed from *commedia dell'arte*. The latter deserves particular attention, because its presence in the project's title can be read as a self-reflexive comment on the function of art, particularly theatre as a specific viewing apparatus. After all, *commedia dell'arte* is the most renowned exponent of the type of theatre born before the onset of the box stage that became prototypical of our thinking about theatre as bourgeois art. As Hannah Arendt argued in her *Human Condition*, "the theatre is the political art par excellence; only there is the political sphere of human life transposed into art. By the same token, it is the only art whose sole subject is man in his relationship to others" (Arendt 1998, 188). The basic gesture of theatre-makers of the bourgeois theatre in the Enlightenment period was to clearly narrow down the scope of its interests to human interactions, in order to purify the stage not only of all metaphysical elements, but also of all non-human agents. ORLAN counters this purification procedure, by creating a heterogeneous "polyphonic assemblage" within which human spectators are but one among many interacting elements. They are made acutely aware that what and how they see and comprehend is conditioned by all the dynamically changing actants involved in this project.

Even if today's artists, theatre directors and performers transpose scientific practices into the theatre or the gallery, demonstrating the agency of human and non-human actors where it remained invisible before, in most cases they resort to participatory strategies taken from performative arts, which violated the stage-audience contract in a bourgeois theatre. Otherwise, the artists would not be able to demonstrate the performativity of scientific experiments, and their power to produce knowledge and an understanding of the world. In these artworks, which thrive on scientific knowledge, another aesthetics is at work. The new meaning of the term "aesthetics" has recently been suggested by Peter Weibel, a performance and media artist, and chairman and CEO of Zentrum für Kunst und Medientechnologie in Karlsruhe. He pointed at the etymological roots of the word "aesthetics" to indicate that it is not only concerned with "beauty" (Miller 2014, 334). The Greek *aisthomai* means "I perceive, feel, see", and refers to information, images of the world and its phenomena that our mind constructs from the complex interplay of our senses, which make sense of the world around us. As he posited, this definition of aesthetics is applicable to the most significant developments in arts and science at the turn of the century, particularly those—such as *Harlequin's Coat*—in which the agency of human and non-human actors is made visible in order to shed light on the cognitive and epistemological aspects of aesthetics.

This redefined concept of aesthetics applies particularly to those developments in the field of performative arts which, as we argue, employ a laboratory format in order to redefine the principles of participation and reception. In this context, a crucial difference should be emphasized between two types of laboratories which can be identified in the field of aesthetic experimentation. The notion has been used in the metaphorical sense by those practitioners who, active outside of the mainstream institutional theatre, tried to work out new forms, acting styles or approaches to the text. In this context, the name "laboratory" appeared by analogy with industry and new technologies, created in autonomous places, where different rules operate than those at the assembly line or in everyday life. Such a laboratory was supposed to be a place of artistic independence. The laboratory character of the work of these artists resulted from the need to unify means of expression that were recognized as belonging to other arts and by the same token to work out a specific stage aesthetics. The most prominent example of this type of performative practice is Jerzy Grotowski's Theatre Laboratorium, in which the director and the performers together tried, tested and combined a variety of theatre techniques, partly borrowed from other cultures, partly invented for the purposes of each staging. By the same token a metaphorical laboratory is mainly concerned with the process of artistic creation and the experimentation with innovative means of expression, combining various styles and conventions. In contradistinction to that, the metonymic laboratory can be derived from the earlier practice of the naturalist theatre-makers, notably Émile Zola. In this case, laboratory was not a metaphor, but rather a metonymy, theatre becoming a place of scientific investigation, focused mainly on the processes of biological and social conditioning of an individual. In this case the fictional situation on stage, in *Thérèse Raquin* (1868) for instance, provided an opportunity for a collective analysis of the motivations and behaviours of characters as representative of more general biological or social principles operating outside the theatre. This understanding of theatre in the age of science provided the naturalist theatre-makers with analytical tools to dissect social processes, which gave their analyses a necessary sanction that the aesthetics as such could not have assured. Most significantly in the context of our paper, the metonymic understanding of laboratory differs from the metaphorical one in the sense that the former provides a format for the stage situation in which the audience is invited not only to observe stage events, but also to take active part in their analysis.

Admittedly, it is difficult to find a more adamant critic of naturalism than Bertolt Brecht, who criticized the late nineteenth-century theatre for over-reliance on melodramatic effects and the inefficiency in activating the spectators into political thinking. However, he also conceived of his theatre theory and practice as firmly rooted in the scientific paradigm of the era. In this respect his theatre practice can be regarded as continuing the tradition of metonymic "laboratory". This observation is particularly pertinent to the artistic practice he called *Lehrstücke* (learning plays). In relation to the practice, he spoke about theatre in the scientific age and the scientific character of the theatre was linked to playwrights' and directors' ambitions to analyse the vast field of social interactions, economy and politics. Only then can theatre present the spectators with reliable (i.e. scientifically proven) knowledge about the world, and gain the same status as economy or political sciences. Brecht designed his *Lehrstücke* as collective exercises in dialectical thinking, according to the principles that he introduced in *The Messingkauf Dialogues* (1985). There, he described the workings of the epic theatre by means of an example of a street scene in which all the eye-witnesses of an accident give an account of what they saw. In the epic theatre, this scene is recounted by each of the participants from their own standpoint, instead of being narrated from one point of view only. This strategy not only demonstrates to all participants that the meaning of a given event is relative to the situation from which it is being recounted. Moreover, a social conflict played out in such a format foregrounds the very workings of the institutions that govern the everyday life of society. In this sense, *Lehrstück* was not a typical didactic play, used for spreading the typically Marxist ideology of dialectical materialism. As Fredric Jameson rightly points out in his ingenious reading of the concept of the epic theatre (1998), Brecht wanted to teach the participants in his *Lehrstücke* basic analytical methods used by dialectical materialists. In other words, he provided them with a laboratory situation to try out fictional social conflicts so that they could learn to react to concrete situations and find their way out in the rapidly changing social circumstances. In his *Lehrstücke* Brecht did not leave room for free invention of the performers, who were provided the entire script of the performance. However, he encouraged role-changing and cross-casting as typically epic strategies. Not only did they allow for a critical distance and eliminated the danger of emotional identification with the character, they also enabled the participants to enter different roles within one performance, if it was repeated (or rehearsed) several times. Thus, he subversively employed the typical procedures of bourgeois theatre so that the participants taking part in a fictional plot could see the problem under discussion from different points of view.

What is particularly interesting in Brecht's metonymic approach to the theatre as laboratory is that he also introduced non-human agents as actors in his texts and theatre productions. This can be seen in *Der Ozeanflug*, which Brecht wrote together with Kurt Weill for the Baden-Baden Music Festival in 1929 (Brecht 1980). Brecht was inspired by an event that made headlines at the time: the first transatlantic flight from New York to Paris in 1927. However, *Der Ozeanflug* does not document Charles Lindbergh's achievement, although in a series of dialogues it takes up the topic of the confrontation of the human with the powers of nature and state-of-the-art technology. The centrepiece of the play is an airplane, a symbol of scientific progress in the first half of the century, and a major success of technoscientific development. Brecht, however, was not so much concerned with celebrating this technological achievement, and even if he used it to attract spectators, his main concern was to assure their participation in the process of co-creating a specific performative event. Significantly, the protagonist of the play is a collective entity called *Flieger* (Aviators, Pilots).[2] Thus, all members of the audience were supposed to become co-creators, something that was hardly possible in the theatre of the time.

However, the most significant innovation which Brecht introduced to assure the participation of the spectators was concerned with modifying the perceptual habits of the audience, schooled in traditional, proscenium-arch theatre. Brecht intended his play to be mediated by the radio, a technology that he wanted to employ in order to call into question the principles of theatrical reception. After all, the main object of his attacks, the late nineteenth-century theatre, was essentially a viewing machine which imposed a fixed point of view on every spectator and made any change of perspective literally impossible. This fixity of point of view seriously impeded any activity on the part of viewers. To counter this format of reception, Brecht proposed an ingenious way of staging his *Der Ozeanflug*, in which the perceptual acts of the participants and the workings of mediation would come to the foreground. He suggested that the "listeners" sit in front of a radio wearing headphones, each of them as lonely as Lindbergh, and in a dispersed but harmonious chorus say their lines, written for them by Brecht. His aim was not merely to prove that radio can connect people across distance, or even to make a production of a theatre play possible. His *Radiolehrstück* problematizes the way the sense of hearing functions as the second (after sight) of the "clear senses", that is, as one of those human cognitive capacities that is more susceptible to cultural conditioning than other capacities. When codified and learned, the perceptual schemata of seeing and hearing become naturalized. As a consequence, we fail to notice the difference between "crude" perceptions and seeing/hearing as recognition and meaning-attribution. It is the difference between the reception of stimuli through the sense of hearing and hearing itself that became the central problem of the *Radiolehrstück*. Significantly, it was through programming this type of mediated participation that Brecht involved the participants in a laboratory-like situation, which, however, was quite different from the one ORLAN designed for her audience. The listeners/readers/pilots taking part in *Der Ozeanflug* form together an assemblage in which participants have a chance to become laboratory analysts who primarily and self-reflexively direct their gaze towards the processes of perception and the way they condition communication between humans and non-humans.

In *Der Ozeanflug*, radio listeners in the role of Pilots talk with the Voice of Fog, Snowstorm and a Dream that torments them, then with the Voice of the Ocean, the Working Engine and the Crowd gathered at the airport near Paris. Significantly, only the first three voices use articulate language. The other three reach the listeners-Pilots' ears as an incomprehensible hum and noise. The participants-listeners can observe and literally experience the functioning of perceptual schemata that separate the meaningful from the meaningless, that is, that which has not been codified. Hum and noise in the ears of the listeners-Pilots, described in the text as the voice of the waves, engine and crowd, appears at a significant juncture in the text, right after the Pilots, as fearless colonizers of the "wild" nature, have delivered a speech entitled "Ideology". The text can be read as proof of the negative influence of the anthropocentric vision on the world, which gives (articulate) voice only and exclusively to human beings, and not to non-human agents. Following this analysis we can call *Der Ozeanflug* an interface in the sense which W. B. Worthen provided, in order to explain the function of a text for the stage in a theatrical context. Interface, a term originally denoting the visual structure mediating between binary data flows and the computer user, has been employed in the context of dramatic writing to highlight the performative aspects of the text when it meets its active recipient in a given context: "This interface between drama and theatre, writing as fictive representation and writing as equipment for doing, is where the engaging 'ambiguities' of drama 'necessarily arise'" (Worthen 2010, 25). By deliberately involving listeners/readers/pilots in co-creating those ambiguities, Brecht makes the participants in *Der Ozeanflug* focus on possible glitches, stammers and obstacles in communication. In this respect his play can be read as a parable about the agency of the non-human: both nature and modern technology, the latter particularly emphasized by the form of a radio play.

It should be emphasized that we have just presented an ideal performance of Brecht's play. As the few photographs from the 1929 performance in Baden-Baden testify, there was only one Pilot/Listener on stage, in front of a big orchestra conducted by Kurt Weill. The Pilot/Listener sat at his radio with the headphones on his head, and the audience, placed vis-à-vis the stage, watched him as in a traditional theatre. In this constellation, Brecht's *Der Ozeanflug* becomes an example of the theatre as a laboratory in the metonymic sense of the word. Nevertheless, Brecht's *Lehrstück* could be rightly recognized as a starting point of a genealogy of contemporary theatre which by that time began to seek inspiration in the sciences in order to become a place of not only "universal" and "timeless", but also historical and socially valuable aesthetic experiences. But to do that, it had to redefine the basic relationship between the stage and the audience, and depart from the basic principle of theatre communication to focus on the aural experience of the participants.

Experiments and Experiences

In his latest work, *Alien Agency. Experimental Encounters with Art in the Making,* Chris Salter identifies the parallel between experience and laboratory by referring to the French term *expérience* which, unlike the English term *experience,* has a double meaning: "that of experiment or speculation and that of experience, of something that happens to us" (2015, 241). In other words, every experiment performed in the laboratory is to some extent experiential. When using the French word, we intend to accentuate this double meaning, crucial for contemporary performance. However, Salter claims that "science seeks to stabilize its agencies—make them predictable, reproducible, repeatable" (2015, 241). As the history of science testifies, this is only true in the context of the post-Enlightenment scientific practices aimed to produce so-called objective knowledge. This generalizing reference to the history of science entails a binary opposition between what becomes then conservative science and progressive contemporary performance practice which is "the affective and improvisatory assemblage of conditions that operates on and transforms us (...). It destabilizes both the phenomena and its perception/affection—keeping things moving, unsettled" (2015, 241). Although Salter's assertions seemingly fit into the context of contemporary performance, his binary hierarchy, prioritizing artistic practice over scientific experiment, is highly problematic as the history of science, especially in the seventeenth century, demonstrates a constant interplay between practices of stabilizing and destabilizing the subject's experience of reality.

In the context of the tension between stabilization and destabilization of experience, seventeenth-century science becomes a rich field of *expériences* which constantly negotiate the hitherto accepted modes of perceiving reality. This is due to the intrinsically social character of the new model of laboratory created by natural philosophers, primarily Robert Boyle and Robert Hooke. According to Steven Shapin and Simon Schaffer, Boyle and Hooke contributed to creating a scientific procedure according to which "[e]xperimental performances and their products had to be attested by the testimony of eye witnesses. Many phenomena, and particularly those alleged by the alchemists, were difficult to accept by those adhering to the corpuscular and mechanical philosophies" (Shapin and Schaffer 1985, 56). To this effect, seventeenth-century scientists employed a plethora of strictly conducted performative techniques in order to allow others to experience the results of their experiments, thereby rendering them believable. For example, the Royal Society's early experiments performed in front of various audiences ranging from the *virtuosi*, that is, the seventeenth-century aristocratic connoisseurs of science, to servants that were supposedly the first to witness Boyle's discovery of bioluminescent qualities of rotten meat.

Yet, the experiential aspect of such performances often led to producing conflicting perceptions of reality rather than establishing definite forms of knowledge. This was the case for Dutch physicist Reiner de Graaf, who in 1665 argued for the acidic nature of pancreatic juice. In order to prove his argument he invited three *virtuosi* to his laboratory; they were to taste the juice extracted from a living dog's pancreas. De Graaf also provided them with technical details of the extraction. However, as Luuc Kooijmans points out, the spectators were not unanimous as to the flavour of the liquid, as most of them did not find it sour (Kooijmans 2010, 107). This was not only incongruent with the well-established theory of digestion but also ran counter to the medical practice of the time. Thus, the gustatory *expérience* organized by de Graaf resulted in an epistemological dissonance among its spectators rather than contributed to grounding a firm scientific system. Although, with the institutional support of the University of Leiden, de Graaf successfully defended his dissertation on the pancreatic juice, the public experiment itself clearly destabilized the spectators' perception of the phenomenon under scrutiny. The example of de Graaf's experiment indicates that scientific practices taking place in seventeenth-century open laboratories were characterized by the tension between the need to stabilize a particular vision of the world and a subversive potential of the experience, which was supposed to support it. This tension must be also taken into consideration when analysing contemporary performances as laboratories, as they also involve different kinds of spectatorial experiences.

From the perspective of this double nature of *expérience*, we would like to analyse the 2013 performance *Situation Rooms* by Rimini Protokoll, in which spectators experientially tested the boundaries of the virtual and the material by interacting with Augmented Reality (AR) technology. The structure of the event resembles that of a laboratory experiment. At the beginning of the performance each of the twenty spectators is assigned a tablet and headphones, which are displayed on a big table before them. They are told to follow the instructions that appear on the screen as they move through a series of rooms built in a vast performance hall. If they get lost, a member of the staff would help them to get back "on track". As promotional materials for the performance suggest, fulfilling the instructions may enable the spectators to literally step into the shoes of the so-called experts of the everyday, that is, people whose interactions with *Situation Rooms* were previously recorded on the tablets. Among the experts, for instance, is a German sniper working at a shooting range and the owner of a canteen in a Russian military facility. Each spectator is guided by a number of experts who then interact with one another, which results in the interaction between the spectators. Therefore, they do not only hear the experts' testimonials but also, via the tablets, they can actually experience their way of perceiving the world. Rimini Protokoll clearly invites the spectators to literally step into the shoes of their experts and thus reflect on the personal dimension of contemporary warfare.

However, the whole performance is based on the idea of stimulating a controlled interaction between the spectator, the environment of the rooms built by the artists and the digital image generated by technology, which in AR nomenclature is referred to as Hand-Held Display. Thus, Rimini Protokoll's performance can be read along the lines of the findings of the Canadian art historian Christine Ross who claims that "Augmented Reality means in fact a new spectatorial paradigm" (Ross 2010, 19). Put in another way, the *expérience* devised in *Situation Rooms* also aims at investigating the impact of contemporary technological advancements on the spectator's perception of reality.

In this context, the performance negotiates the relations between digitally generated AR technology on tablets and the physically felt environment in which the spectators are immersed. Therefore, Rimini Protokoll critically examines the realistic paradigm underlying the creation of AR in 1960, which manifests itself in the words of one of its pioneers, Ivan Sutherland. He claimed that "the ultimate display would, of course, be a room within which the computer can control the existence of matter. A chair displayed in such a room would be good enough to sit in" (in Bimber and Raskar 2005, 2). We can see here that the ultimate aim of AR is to bring the virtual so close to the material that it would gradually acquire its physical properties. Sutherland's designed experience of AR is therefore still based on the traditional paradigm of reality defined by its sensually felt materiality. *Situation Rooms* significantly complicates this model of experience by accentuating the distance between the digitally generated image on screen and that which happens to spectators in contact with other spectators and the environment. This distance can be analysed by scrutinizing the spectatorial experience of the space as it is augmented by the tablets.

The experience is based on a clear boundary between what the spectators see on screen and what is situated behind it. Due to its materiality, the Hand-Held Display becomes a sort of framing device constantly raising the spectator's awareness of the division between the virtual and the real. Thus, inadvertently, the spectator begins to look for differences between the digital representation and its material counterpart. Often during the performance, the images are discrepant with one another. For instance, people shown by the tablets are different than those standing in a particular place in the actual event. Moreover, sometimes the expert tells us to shake hands with another expert whereas in the real situation there is no one there, as one of the spectators is absent from the scenario devised by the artists. Both the felt presence of the frame and the discrepancy between the screen and the real create a clearly Brechtian *Verfremdungseffekt* rather than blurring the boundaries between virtuality and materiality, as Ivan Sutherland would have it.

What is the spectatorial experience in the face of the distancing strategies employed in *Situation Rooms*? As Christine Ross points out, the most important element of AR experience is the physical contact between the spectator and technology. The spectator-technology connection explored by Rimini Protokoll is worth taking a closer look at. The spectators hold their tablets in one hand by means of a wooden handle. Although in some sequences of the event they leave the device on a stand, which enables them to use both their hands, the tablet becomes a kind of prosthetic replacement for the hand. This often leads to sudden sensory confusion, especially when the spectator fails to follow the expert's instructions. This techno-human set-up resembles the one employed in the famous psycho-neurological experiment referred to as the rubber hand test. The participant puts one hand on a table whereas the other hand is replaced by a fake one. The researcher gently touches the rubber hand with a brush or a feather. After a few seconds the participant begins to feel tactile experiences in the artificial object. The experiment ends abruptly as the researcher suddenly hits the rubber hand with a hammer, which causes pain-like experience of the participant also known as the phantom experience.

In his work *Ghosts in the Brain* (1998), contemporary American neuroscientist Vilayanur Ramachandran argues that phantom experiences do not only arise after amputation, as traditional neurological theory would have it. They can be experimentally generated in a laboratory by means of multisensory stimulation of participants. Ramachandran claims that "with a few seconds of the right type of sensory stimulation, you can make your nose three feet long or project your hand onto a table" (1998, 247). Such phantom experiences are neither illusory nor purely sensual in nature. They are the result of destabilizing the body image transferred to the brain through the senses, which clashes with the inherent genetic body image located in the frontal lobe of the brain. Yet, Ramachandran's experimental practice suggests that laboratory practice may also reverse the effect. He has formulated a method of treating phantom pain in disabled patients, which he called virtual reality box. As using actual virtual reality technology was too expensive, Ramachandran used a mirror, which helped his patients restore the stability of their body image. The mirror created an illusion of the missing limb, which relieved the phantom pain they felt in their non-existent limbs.

In the context of phantom experience as defined by Ramachandran, the *expérience* devised in *Situation Rooms* turns out to recreate the destabilizing/stabilizing effect of sensory stimulation in an AR environment, generating phantom experiences among the spectators. As in Ramachandran's laboratory, the performance produces an overwhelming assemblage of sensory experiences, further intensified by the kinaesthetic aspect of the spectators' involvement in the performance. This manifests itself especially in the sequence led by the German sniper. The expert tells the spectator to lie down on her belly in a room resembling a shooting range. He gives instructions as to the correct shooting position: the spectator is told to keep a specific distance between her legs for the whole duration of this sequence. Next, the spectator raises the tablet, which displays the barrel of a gun and aims at a target situated across the room. The sequence lasts a couple of minutes in order to make the spectator actually feel the physical effort of holding a gun displayed on the tablet. The experience is even further reinforced by the uncomfortable position of the spectator. Then, suddenly, the gun on screen fires, which causes the spectator to flinch in the same way as the participant of the rubber hand test does when unexpectedly hit by the hammer. In line with Ramachandran's findings, *Situation Rooms* stimulates multisensory experiences of the spectator in order to destabilize her perception. This creates a condition in which the tablet held by the spectators can perform the function of both the rubber hand and Ramachandran's virtual box. It produces strong phantom experiences and enables them to disappear.

To follow the mechanisms behind the *expérience* devised in *Situation Rooms*, we will refer to one of the sequences of the performance in which the spectator is guided by a Swiss engineer who demonstrates complicated measurements crucial for the construction of a new type of weapon. Using devices provided by Rimini Protokoll, the participant is asked to follow the engineer's actions displayed on the tablet. As the participant looks at the virtual hand on screen in place of her own hand, she instantly attempts to synchronize movements with the digital image as if it was her own hand. The phantom experience intensifies as she fails to perform the precise movements of the expert. However, gradually the participant becomes more efficient and the physical movements adhere to the digital image. Then, the experience—as in Ramachandran's virtual reality box—weakens and eventually vanishes.

This analysis of Rimini Protokoll's performance has indicated that the laboratory as a model for contemporary performative practice serves to forge new types of experience based on the interplay of destabilizing/stabilizing the spectators' perception of the world. In this respect the group can be regarded as the descendants of the tradition of *Lehrstück* as a form that simultaneously thwarts the perceptual habits of the audience and takes them up as its subject. Similarly to *Der Ozeanflug*, *Situation Rooms* takes up the problem of the perceptual patterns conditioned by modern digital media and technological advancements. Consequently, the phantom experiences generated here provide the spectators with ample material for an analysis of their own perceptual habits. The spectators' phantom experiences are ones that surpass the binary opposition of what is real and what is virtual, for the phantom experience generated in the course of the interaction between spectators and tablets is both extremely tangible and highly illusionary. In fact, the *expérience* devised by Rimini Protokoll becomes an illustration for Ramachandran's assertion that "[y]our own body is a phantom, one that your brain has temporarily constructed purely for convenience" (1998, 58). In other words, *Situation Rooms* experimentally and experientially proves that what we call the body is just an effect of efficient cooperation between the senses and the brain, which may be easily destabilized, opening up space for new models of subjectivity to emerge.

Laboratory of Social Imagination

When artists become intermediaries in demonstrating the scientific discoveries of our era, giving them a material, sensual shape, they have to face some practical problems: they have to come up with such structures and conventions that would communicate often extremely complex theoretical issues to larger audiences composed of mainly non-experts. Historical studies on the birth of the scientific paradigm prove that this conundrum is not new to those who sought the cooperation of a large community in the production of scientific facts.

The presence of artistic conventions of representation at the heart of the laboratory set-up has been identified by Steven Shapin to be situated as early as in seventeenth-century science. Shapin, one of the co-authors of the seminal book *Leviathan and the Air-Pump* (1985), analysed the process of knowledge production in a broader context of the organization of scientific community around laboratory experimentation, in an article called "Pump and Circumstance. Robert Boyle's Literary Technology" (1984). As Shapin argues, one of the problems faced by Boyle upon the invention of modern laboratory practices was how to gain recognition within the larger community of scientists. After all, this common and unanimous recognition was to guarantee that true scientists were considered more trustworthy than the alchemists who relied only on their personal testimony as a means of spreading the results of their research.

At this point the basic problem of the media of scientific popularization emerged. Boyle was well aware of the fact that in order to produce undeniable and universal facts, he had to do more than just inform his fellow scientists of his discoveries. He proposed that "matters of facts be generated by multiplication of witnessing experience" (Shapin 1984, 483), therefore it was not enough to just inform his peers about his discoveries. He had to make it possible for them to conduct the experiment for themselves and verify the validity of his claims themselves. One practical problem, however, thwarted his efforts: the technology needed to conduct his experiments with the air pump was very expensive and available only in a handful of places all over Europe. Therefore, the problem of building a scientific community proved to be a problem of communication, of "making things common" (Shapin 1984, 482), at the same time sharing and seeking approval, turning a single experiment into a demonstration of undeniable and universal facts. Therefore, Boyle invented a scientific protocol; a convention that made possible "virtual witnessing"

(Shapin 1984, 490), seeing the experiment in the mind's eye. For this reason he not only provided the account of how he conducted consecutive segments of the experiment, but also included a detailed description of the technology, together with explanatory drawings. He produced a DIY kit with all the necessary tools and procedures to relive the experiment and take active part in it. The protocol was used as a means of popularization of scientific discoveries by way of, as Shapin calls it, "the extension of experience from the few to the many" (Shapin 1984, 481). These conventions, that is, the forms of constructing the protocols together with all rhetorical devices that guarantee the cooperation and attention of the spectators, played a crucial role as one of three technologies of producing science invented in the seventeenth century: material, literary and social technologies connected into one complex machine producing undeniable facts.

From this point of view, the means and forms of communication as the tools of creating a scientific community turned out to be instrumental in the process of closing off laboratories for non-experts and opening them anew in the twentieth century. Partly, this opening up has taken place in the era of mass media communication, notably the Internet, which has expanded the possibility of virtual witnessing even more. In their use of digital media, contemporary artists found new tools for spreading knowledge and assuring the participation of the spectators in the act of producing facts. However, a number of the representatives of bio art present their works in quite traditional forms, either solely in a gallery (like *Harlequin's Coat*) with the accompanying description, or on the Internet, in the form of extensive reports illustrated with pictures or film footage (as in the case of Eduardo Kac's projects, such as *Genesis* from 1999). Such a format of display obviously prevents the audiences from verifying the veracity and scientific character of those experiments which become merely representations of possible, virtual laboratory experiences. Other artists, however, have sought to solve the problem of validation by involving their audiences in a laboratory experiment, by turning them into both the observers and the basic material upon which the experiment is performed.

This solution to the problem of how to communicate to an audience the experiences which are utterly unfamiliar to them is hardly new in the field of performative arts and we would like to argue that one of the forerunners of this type of laboratory is the concept of theatre of the German playwright Heiner Müller, who openly described his project of performative practice as a "laboratory of social imagination" (Friedman 2007, 21). This formula significantly departed from the understanding of Brecht's concept of theatre in the scientific age, particularly his *Lehrstücke*, which was a major point of reference for Müller. Müller took issue with the all too rational nature of Brecht's theatre and his over-reliance on logical argumentation. His idea of a "laboratory of social imagination" had more to do with bringing back the cathartic impact of theatre as a place in which the experience of productive dissonance leads to a shock that might lead the audience to an unexpected discovery. "The leap drives experience, not the step" ("Shakespeare a Difference" 1988, p. 1), wrote Müller, commenting on his rewritings of Shakespeare's plays and the desired impact of his plays on the spectators. However, his strategy of introducing dissonance for inciting thought had little to do with the naturalists' use of violent scenes to shock the audience and exert on them an emotional impact in the name of moral engagement. Rather, he invented such structures of the text that were to turn the gaze of the spectators towards themselves and towards the cognitive processes typical of the "naturalist" theatre reception. There is one crucial aspect which in Müller's work is much more salient than in the case of the laboratory projects which we have dealt with so far. *Harlequin's Coat*, *Der Ozeanflug* and *Situation Rooms* were concentrated primarily on the cognitive functions of human perception, the ability to discern aspects of reality and endow them with meaning. Müller's theatre was a laboratory of social imagination, but unlike Brecht he did not seek a rational, cognitive appeal to the audience. Instead in his texts and his concept of the stage he provided a model for the functioning of human affects, on both an individual and collective level. In this laboratory the spectators and their own affects, awoken through the stage production, primarily the text, were to become the basic material for observation and dissection. Müller conceived this laboratory as a place where social conflicts can be played out and perhaps resolved.

In this respect, Müller's plays were meant to be structures that mediated the experience of the few actors onto numerous audience members, involving them in a laboratory situation. The example of such a structure is Müller's *Description of a Picture* (1984, also known in English as *Explosion of a Memory*), a text composed of a single sentence stretching across eight pages. Indeed, this short piece presents a description of a picture provided by an anonymous voice that does not even have any anthropomorphic characteristics. It would be more accurate to say that language in this case registers the experience of looking at an immobile, two-dimensional scene, and the movement of the eye through a painted landscape with a man, a woman and a bird. The onlooker sketches different imaginable connections and relationships between the elements of the scene. It is this gaze that brings the figures to life, arranging them in constellations, each of which is more and more violent and bloody. Therefore, it is the series of cognitive acts of looking, recognizing and meaning-making that occupies the central place in Müller's play in which we literally witness how imagination works to bring about interpretations of a given state of affairs. In this sense Müller designs a laboratory experiment, reverting the established hierarchy in which the objects are looked upon and observed by onlookers. In *Description of a Picture* it is the onlooker that becomes a laboratory animal, when he/she is confronted with a depicted scene which sets in motion the mechanism of recognition and meaning-making. Müller very clearly shows that it is the gaze that channels violence to the picture, when the speaking voice presents increasingly cruel explanations of the relationship between the painted figures.

In this context one can clearly see the basic difference between Müller's and Brecht's concept of a laboratory. Müller did not intend to provide the spectators with an opportunity to gain reliable knowledge about the relationship between seemingly unrelated aspects of their everyday experience and the shortcomings of the anthropocentric perspective. He was rather interested in provoking such a response from the audience that would make manifest the tensions and conflicts that might pass unnoticed in everyday life, but clearly could lead to an explosion in the least desirable moment. This, however, should not be identified with a purely therapeutic function of the theatre. Rather, Müller wanted to turn theatre into a laboratory of affects, emotions and bodily reactions that Brecht was less interested in, treating them as remnants of the age-old melodramatic tradition.

In this laboratory human affects and bodily reactions are observed and tested with the recipients as the providers of the material for laboratory analysis, which they themselves have a chance to carry out, in order to better understand the social relationships in which they are involved. From this point of view, we would like to take a closer look at one more recent example of such a laboratory situation, in order to demonstrate not only the means of its construction, but also its impact on the audience. In 2012, Rabih Mroué conducted his lecture performance *The*

Pixelated Revolution, a laboratory dissection of social imagination. This was similar to the one that Müller undertook in *Description of a Picture* (1989), although Mroué used the form of a performative lecture. The most obvious similarity with Müller's work lies in the fact that Mroué also carries out a description of pictures that he found in the vast archives of the cyberspace. In his lecture, his voice sounds like the voice speaking in *The Description of a Picture*—Mroué demonstrates his method of looking at images, reading them and pondering on their construction and their impact on the onlooker. In a sense, the abstract cycle of violence that Müller demonstrated in his text becomes historically and geo-politically concrete in *The Pixelated Revolution*, since the images that Mroué analyses were taken during the civil war in Syria that broke out anew in 2011. They were made by rebels and civilians, mainly with cell phones, and they were spread on the Internet as proofs of the violence of the ruling regime. These pictures had a clearly political function to fulfil, since they were to help garner the support for the revolution on the international arena. However, Mroué, who in his performance is far from passing any judgements, presents the materials in a quite unexpected way, asking the question what guaranteed the immense affective impact of those images on the viewers.

Significantly, Mroué quotes the list of rules that were spread among the rebellious citizens to dictate very clearly how to shoot and frame the images from the battlefield, whose faces to show and how to register movement so as to mediate the turbulent emotions and physical exhaustion of the cameramen. He juxtaposes this list with the manifesto of the Dogma filmmakers, who introduced documentary and amateur techniques of filming to the mainstream cinema in order to achieve a heightened reality effect and an emotional impact on the spectators. By showing exemplary pictures and film footage on a big screen, Mroué dissects the construction of those images and proves their unexpected affinity with other cinematic images that show other military conflicts. The images of revolution in Syria feature, for example, the barrels of guns aiming at the person standing behind the camera, which creates the impression that it is the viewers who found themselves in the line of fire. The blackout that followed after the shot, when the bullet hits the phone (and therefore also the person holding it), exerts a much stronger affective impact than the actual images of suffering bodies.

The message that Mroué wanted to put across in his lecture was quite straightforward: the viewers of those images and media reports from the war became participants in the conflict, by watching these images and allowing them to exert their affective impact. By choosing the form of a performative lecture, Mroué put the spectators in the double role as both the recipients of images and distant analysts who had to question the perceptual schemes, receptive mechanisms and affects occasioned by these images. In this sense, *The Pixelated Revolution* shows an act of communication through images as a process that involves not only rational thinking, but is also able to exert a sensual and affective impact on the level of emotions and bodily reactions. Clearly, Mroué's lecture performance is an example of a laboratory of imagination, because he directs the spectators' attention to their own cognitive involvement in the construction of images, catches them in the act of participating in the production of knowledge about current political affairs, assuring their involvement in the domestic conflict. At the same time, this example demonstrates another aspect of the contemporary laboratory experimentation in the field of art, namely its dependence on existing communication technologies, both on the level of topics and forms of addressing the audience.

Mroué's projects can be treated as descendants of Müller's idea of the "laboratory of social imagination" in that they aim at turning the audience into a group of co-operating participants, but also at turning their attention towards the media that serve as the tools used to create and validate the image of reality. Therefore, it is an example of metonymic laboratories in which the simulation of cognitive processes and affects demonstrates the functioning of media and their role in the production of images that pass as representations of objective knowledge. In those laboratories, which come into being at a crossroads of various social practices, the new technologies serve to question the process of mediation, and to show in what way it is used as a means of political mobilization.

Conclusion

To conclude, we have to return to the mid-seventeenth century, when the first laboratory was constructed as a self-contained and self-organized environment, which started to become more and more distant from history and politics. As it has already been demonstrated by many scholars, such a separation was a strictly political decision. In such a way the different sciences were born, each of them forming a closed system with specific rules and language, capable of reproducing and maintaining itself.

The same happened around the same time to the arts and many other modes of existence, according to Latour. The mixed genres of the last two decades that are popping up at the crossroads between (techno) sciences and the arts testify that the Modern construction has begun to topple. Not only do artists help scientists demonstrate the historical character of their work and its vital connectedness to other systems of situated knowledge, its "symbiopoiesis" (Löwenhaupt Tsing 2015, 142), instead of autopoiesis, which was the model that was successfully maintained for three centuries. For their part, artists draw on scientific insights to demonstrate that art could be political not only in the sense that it engages directly in revolutions and protests, as in the case of the recent Arab Spring or antiterrorist movements. Art of this kind gains political character when taking up such seemingly "safe" and universally valid topics as knowledge production—the procedures of observation and validation which are typical of laboratories as places where the dominant understanding of the world is being forged. And it could have deeper and longer-lasting repercussions than direct action of engaged and/or engaging theatre.

This problem is closely related to another issue critical for the development of new mixed genres. Together with the re-emergence of laboratory as a site where sciences meet arts, the question of audience participation needs to be posed anew. Most of the projects mentioned here testify to the fact that the laboratory not only provides a model of viewing and interacting with other participants, but also redefines experience and agency as such. In this context, the notion of experiment no longer applies to the formal aesthetic complexity typical of high modernism. Even if it goes back to the original seventeenth-century meaning, it does so in order to subvert the divisions imposed at the time when the paradigm of science was set up. The experiments of contemporary mixed genres analysed above provide a carefully designed framework within which boundaries between watching and being watched, the observer and the object of study, effectively collapse. In most cases it is the participants themselves, their bodies, affects and cognitive involvement that become the object of study in the circumstances designed by the artist/scientist. As a result, in the laboratory experiment, the spectator becomes both the analyst and the site where situated knowledge is being performatively produced. The knowledge is not only intellectually but also physically experienced as participants smell, hear, taste, see and touch. In this way the mixed genres lay bare the processes of division that lead to the establishment of a commonly shared vision of reality. Perhaps it is these mixed genres that can lead to the emergence of new aesthetic paradigms, more congruent with contemporary social and medial practices as well as collective and individual experiences.

NOTES

1. In her book on DNA as a cultural icon of the twentieth century, Dorothy Nelkin posits that there even exists a special current of the contemporary art, which she calls DNA-art (see Nelkin and Lindee 1995).
2. It is important to underline that Brecht wanted the name in plural as, for instance, in the only Polish version of the play, the original version of the name was "corrected", most probably by the translator, and the more traditional singular was introduced.

REFERENCES

Arendt, Hannah. 1958. *The Human Condition*. Chicago and London: The University of Chicago Press, 1998.
Bimber, Oliver, and Ramesh Raskar. 2005. *Spatial Augmented Reality. Merging Real and Virtual Worlds*. Natick, MA: A.K. Peters.
Braidotti, Rosi. 2019. *Posthuman Knowledge*. Cambridge and Medford, MA: Polity Press.
Brecht, Bertolt. 1980. "Der Ozeanflug." In *Der Ozeanflug. Die Horatier und die Kuriatier. Die Maßnahme*, 7–27. Frankfurt am Main: Suhrkamp Verlag..
Brecht, Bertolt. 1985. *The Messingkauf Dialogues*. Translated by John Willett. London: Methuen.
Friedman, Dan. 2007. *The Cultural Politics of Heiner Müller*. Cambridge: Cambridge Scholars Publishing.
Jameson, Frederic. 1998. *Brecht and Method*. London: Verso.
Kooijmans, Luuc. 2010. *Niebezpieczna wiedza: Wizje i lęki w czasach Jana Swammerdama*. Warszawa: Wydawnictwo Aletheia.
Latour, Bruno. 2013. *An Inquiry onto Modes of Existence. An Anthropology of the Moderns*. Translated by Catherine Porter. Cambridge, MA: Harvard University Press.
Latour, Bruno, and Steve Woolgar. 1979. *Laboratory Life: The Construction of Scientific Facts*. Beverly Hills: Sage.
Löwenhaupt Tsing, Anna. 2015. *The Mushroom at the End of the World: On the Possibility of Life in Capitalist Ruins*. Princeton, NJ: Princeton University Press.

Machon, Josephine. 2009. *(Syn)aesthetics. Redefining Visceral Performance*. New York and London: Palgrave Macmillan.
Miller, Arthur I. 2014. *Colliding Worlds. How Cutting-Edge Science Is Redefining Contemporary Art*. New York and London: W.W. Norton.
Müller, Heiner. "Shakespeare a Difference." Translated by Dennis Redmond. Speech at Shakespeare festival in Weimar, 23 April 1988, pp. 1–2. Accessed 20 February 2020. http://theater.augent.be/file/14.
Müller, Heiner. 1989. *Explosion of a Memory / Description of a Picture*. Translated by Carl Weber. New York: PAJ Publications.
Nelkin, Dorothy, and Susan Lindee. 1995. *The DNA Mystique. The Gene as a Cultural Icon*. New York: W. H. Freeman.
ORLAN, and Nadja Sayey. 2016. *ORLAN: "I Walked a Long Way for Women"*. Accessed 19 November 2020, https://www.theguardian.com/artanddesign/2016/jan/15/orlan-i-walked-a-long-way-for-women.
Ross, Christine. 2010. "Spacial Poetics. The (Non)destinations of Augmented Reality Art." *Afterimage. The Journal of Media Arts and Cultural Criticism*, no. 2: 19–24.
Salter, Chris. 2015. *Alien Agency. Experimental Encounters with Art in the Making*. Cambridge: MIT Press.
Schaffer, Simon, and Steven Shapin. 1985. *Leviathan and the Air-Pump: Hobbes, Boyle, and the Experimental Life*. Princeton: Princeton University Press.
Shapin, Steven. 1984. "Pump and Circumstance. Robert Boyle's Literary Technology." *Social Studies of Science* 14, no. 4: 481–520.
Ramachandran, Vilayanur Subramanian. 1998. *Ghosts in the Brain*. New York: William Morrow.
Worthen, W.B. 2010. *Drama: Between Poetry and Performance*. Wiley-Blackwell.

A Hybrid Device to Choreograph the Gaze: Embodying Vision Through a Historical Discourse on Optics in Benjamin Vandewalle's *Peri-Sphere*

Dieter Brusselaers and Helena Julian

In 1836, the American transcendentalist author Ralph Waldo Emerson published his now-classical essay *Nature*, a celebration of the titular subject and the spiritual elevation it could elicit. Sadly enough, Emerson admits, that kind of exhilaration could only befall those who knew how to visually experience the landscape, for "[t]o speak truly, few adult persons can see nature. Most persons do not see the sun. At least they have a very superficial seeing" (11). He laments this lack of visual refinement in his contemporaries in such a way that betrays an anthropomorphic, theatrical way of thinking about visual relationships between mankind and nature: "If the stars should appear one night in a thousand years, how would men believe and adore (...)! But every night come out these preachers of beauty, and light the universe with their admonishing smile" (9–10). The (astronomical) stars come out every night to perform, as it were from behind the curtain, in a similar fashion to the (human) stars of the theatrical stage. Like their human counterparts, the performers in

---

D. Brusselaers (✉) · H. Julian
Antwerp, Belgium

© The Author(s), under exclusive license to Springer Nature Switzerland AG 2021
C. Stalpaert et al. (eds.), *Performance and Posthumanism*,
https://doi.org/10.1007/978-3-030-74745-9_15

the spectacle of nature require a knowledgeable and distinguishing audience in order to be fully appreciated. For the visual vanguard led by Emerson, able to develop their sensorium beyond a "superficial seeing", the reward is great. "Standing on the bare ground,—my head bathed by the blithe air, and uplifted into infinite space,—all mean egotism vanishes", a sensation Emerson proceeds to describe (in)famously as "I become a transparent eye-ball [sic]". Soaring assertions about a unity with both nature and the supernatural conclude the passage: "I am nothing. I see all. The currents of the Universal Being circulate through me; I am part or particle of God" (13).

Disregarding the final leap into divinity, the spectatorial ecstasy Emerson formulates before the show of nature in the *theatrum mundi* could be considered a prototypical immersive experience: a totalizing sensation in which the sum of his sensorial and kinaesthetic[1] capacities are engaged, described as simultaneously reaching out to the far ends of his body (his feet and his head). However, despite the momentarily holistic character of Emerson's descriptions, his experiential rapture seems to be emanating first and foremost from the eyes and return there when he himself is turned into a transparent eyeball. Vision is so predominant of a sense it ends up undoing his corporeality, reducing him to pure sight. In Emerson's anthropomorphic theatre of nature, this should not come as a surprise to us: after all, "[t]raditionally in Western theatre, the eyes and to some degree the ears are where theatricality is experienced" (Schechner 2001, 27). By proposing a human spectator and an anthropomorphic performing object for that spectator's gaze, Emerson's discourse intuitively mimics what theatre studies would later accept as a defining condition for precisely that Western theatre tradition: the bodily co-presence of (human) performers and spectators (Fischer-Lichte 2008). As a result, looking at nature—or any predetermined object, for that matter—comes to resemble watching a traditional theatrical performance, and the corporeality of the spectator, who is experiencing primarily through vision, is similarly obfuscated.

However, this text is not a critique of Emerson's anthropomorphic, theatrical understanding of vision and its limitations. Rather, Emerson's text exemplifies the historically predominant discourse on vision and optics that informed *Peri-Sphere*, an exploratory research project we (Dieter Brusselaers and Helena Julian) embarked on with Brussels-based dancer and choreographer Benjamin Vandewalle in January 2015. In it, we retraced a range of historical cases (both performative and discursive)

Fig. 1 *Peri-Sphere*, Benjamin Vandewalle, Dieter Brusselaers and Helena Julian (© Paul McGee)

in which the understanding of vision deviated from its traditional invisibility as a corporeal process due to its dominance in Western culture. As artistic researchers on the project, we processed and shared pieces of historical discourse that covered a range of topics such as the emergence of embodied vision as a disciplinary tool in nineteenth-century optics or as a fixture in the visual arts with the rise of Minimalism. Simultaneously, Vandewalle worked on the construction of a mobile, performer-operated installation which was informed by the historical discourse laid bare by us, so as to deconstruct through performance the reduction of the spectator to an incorporeal, transparent eyeball (Fig. 1).

Superficially, there appears to be a kinship between the kind of visual immersion recorded in Emerson's *Nature* and the kind experienced by participants in the performative installation first presented as part of the ongoing research project *Peri-Sphere* at the *Working Title Situation*[2] festival in Brussels, June 2015.[3] One by one, participants would take place in the mobile encasement, lying down on their backs while being moved through the space by a performer, their gazes continuously displaced in the space through a mechanical constellation of mirrors and levers. The mechanisms of the installation were designed after the technological set-up of a fundamentally pragmatic technological instrument: the reflective mirrors that constitute the insides of a periscope, and account for its usefulness in displacing the peripheral vision of the user. At times, the viewpoints employed by the installation made the participants look back on their own bodies, eliciting something like an out-of-body experience, or placed their gaze in direct proximity to their bodies (e.g. underneath them) without making them visible, thus potentially creating an illusion of literal bodily transparency or even incorporeality. Offered a fully embodied experience thanks to the mobility of the installation, these participants may have felt that they were aware on a kinaesthetic level. Nevertheless, their gazes may have simultaneously seemed paradoxically disembodied to them because of the viewpoints that were impossible for the human eye to embody without an external apparatus.

However, we find it reductive to describe *Peri-Sphere* in terms of the participant's experience—not only because we are hesitant to tread upon the perilous territory of defining a unified, idealized audience experience (and thereby implying an equally unified and ideal spectatorial body), but also because the sum of the participants' experiences does simply not add up to the whole of the *Peri-Sphere* project. *Peri-Sphere* was pitched as a process, not as a product, and the choice to focus on an idealized or real experience would imply that both the research conducted in the context of the project, and the installation as its material component, only serve as the means to a specific end: the recreation of an experience that approximates the one described above. Rather, we consider *Peri-Sphere* to be a continuous reformulation of tentative answers to these questions: *Can we choreograph not for, but with an audience's gaze? In other words, can we access an audience's vision as the raw material for a performance without the employment of predetermined external objects (such as human performers) to direct it?* As such questions warrant a methodology to answer them (rather than an object or a performance), that is exactly what *Peri-Sphere* turned out to be (Fig. 2).

Investigating Vision

Yet, why would we want to choreograph with an (objectless) gaze? What prompted us to start developing the experimental artistic methodology of *Peri-Sphere* in the first place? What makes investigating vision so worthwhile? Let us begin with the simple observation that the modalities of

Fig. 2 *Peri-Sphere*, Benjamin Vandewalle, Dieter Brusselaers and Helena Julian (© Paul McGee)

seeing have been objects of scrutiny and fascination long before *Peri-Sphere* in contemporary Belgian performance, at the very least in the oeuvre of our artistic collaborator Benjamin Vandewalle. During his final year at Brussels-based Modern Dance Master's programme P.A.R.T.S. in 2006, Vandewalle created *Théâtre de la Guillotine*, a micro-theatre installation for one spectator, which he later developed into *Inter-View* in 2014. During *Inter-View* the participant experiences a one-on-one encounter with a performer, who, in absence of a script, reduces the reciprocal process of observing and being observed to the profound action of locking eyes. In *One/Zero* (2009), a collaboration with Belgian visual artist Erki De Vries, the performance made palpable how we experience time and movement. The performance unfolded much like a film montage, where the dancers only changed position during the dark intervals between two flashes of light. In *Birdwatching 4x4* (2012), an outdoor mobile installation was created where participants could take place and be driven through a cityscape in which dancers would infiltrate the daily urban routines while performing choreographies, turning the installation into a black box theatre on wheels. In short, Vandewalle's performative oeuvre is profoundly preoccupied with vision, and could even be read as an ongoing quest for its audience's visual perception. In his artistic experiments prior to *Peri-Sphere*, he resorted to a plethora of performative means (including technological objects as well as the corporeality of performers and spectators) and visual references in order to investigate vision itself. His perpetual preoccupation with vision betrays an awareness that the vivisection of sight through performance is relevant as a subject of public discourse, yet simultaneously elusive enough to permit repeated efforts. These qualities are the result of broader cultural concepts of seeing that inevitably serve as premises for *Peri-Sphere*.

Firstly, vision is generally considered central to Western society and history, both of which are often deemed "ocularcentric", that is, "'dominated' by vision" (Jay 1993, 3). If not the entirety of the Western timeline is branded as such, at the very least modernity is understood to be visually biased (Jay 1988, 3). The importance of visual metaphors in our language (Jay 1993, 2–3) and the way our thinking is tethered to seeing by such concepts as that of the mental image (8) prove the pervasiveness of vision in our culture, and, indeed, in our very own culturally conditioned bodies and minds. This in itself is sufficient reason for it to become a valuable object of research. Its central symbolic and practical significance makes vision an important site of investigation to our inquiry in this project.

However, there is more at stake here, as vision's status as the most dominant of the senses in a Western context also renders it as it were "near-invisible" because of its omnipresence. Vision is strongly naturalized in everyday life, and we generally do not "look into" it. Yet, as a determining yet routinely unacknowledged factor in Western thought and culture, it begs investigation, if only to be exposed as an object of scrutiny. At the very least, we need the awareness that examining vision is a possibility. This awareness matters because, to an important extent, vision is a societal construct rather than a given of the human condition. However naturalized, vision is not "natural" in the sense of "non-cultural": quite on the contrary, it is steeped in historical and contextual parameters. This inevitably entails that vision is not only omnipresent, but also laden with ideological meaning. By accepting our own, culturally specific way of seeing as "natural", we therefore run the risk of similarly naturalizing the judgement that its ideological determinants would exercise on the objects of our gaze. This is a second reason for investigating it.

In fact, Emerson already displayed an awareness of ideology's attachment to vision when he reproached his contemporaries for their defective understanding of nature. The flaw in their way of seeing, apparently, was the fact that they let their cultural preconceptions clutter the unfettered functioning of their visual organs. He writes: "Our age is retrospective. It builds the sepulchres of the fathers. It writes biographies, histories, and criticism. The foregoing generations beheld God and nature face to face; we, through their eyes. Why should not we also enjoy an original relation to the universe?" (1836, 5) In other words, cultural codes are deeply engrained in seeing, but they can be circumvented by anyone aware of them. While recognizing the coding of vision as a traditional default in his society, the Romantic Emerson nevertheless did not question the existence of what the art critic John Ruskin would call "the innocent eye" two decades later. This was supposedly a childlike, transparent way of seeing, devoid of interpretations or societal conventions—a version of vision that was generally lost in adult individuals, but which those educated in the arts could (and, according to Ruskin, should) reacquire (Varnelis 1998, 212). Discerning a seemingly similar intent in the work of Maurice Merleau-Ponty, contemporary Dutch arts and media scholar Renée van de Vall (2008, 15) dismisses the quest for the naturalized innocent eye in a poignant formulation for the present age: "It is a wish that will hardly appeal to an intellectual era that has learnt to live with the denial of all *dehors texte*".

This type of awareness about the fundamental historicity and cultural conditioning operative in our eyesight engenders radically different approaches to vision than cataloguing sight as part of nature does. As such, the belief in the (non-)existence of the innocent eye bears important methodological consequences for *Peri-Sphere*. A revealing passage in Susan Sontag's *On Photography* about Emerson's close friend and transcendentalist disciple Henry David Thoreau (1817–1862) provides an account of how the increasing societal importance of mediation in the realm of the visual gave rise to the awareness that the innocent eye is a myth. According to Sontag, Thoreau, who lived in a predominantly pre-photographic society, did not consider seeing as an activity separate from the other senses, or separate from "the context he called Nature". In sharp contrast to later, image-flooded societies, there was no stark separation between the act of seeing and the object seen: they were both part of the same "polysensual" realm. Therefore, Thoreau logically considered vision to be "linked to certain presuppositions about what he thought was worth seeing": the adjacency of the two was immediate. Whether or not Sontag was right in attributing the altered perspective of later generations to the photographic camera, she definitely described accurately what happened to vision when it was moved out of the context of the natural(ized) and, as it were, became "visible" itself. In the place of the transcendentalists', Ruskin's and others' strife for an innocent and transparent view of the world, came "another attitude towards the sensorium: the didactic cultivation of perception, independent of notions about what is worth perceiving, which animates all modernist movements in the arts" (1977, 93).

Peri-Sphere takes place in this current age of technological images rather than on Thoreau's polysensual, unified plane of existence, which is a third reason to direct our research interest towards *how* is seen rather than to *what* is seen. Once the modalities of seeing are no longer taken for granted, the question becomes how to highlight those very modalities—hence our desire to choreograph an audience's gaze without the use of predetermined objects to guide it (such as the bodies of performers). Providing no such objects means sidestepping notions about what is worth seeing for a naturalized, innocent eye and thereby avoiding the aggressive transition of naturalized vision to naturalized judgement. Indeed, a persistent aggressive connotation clings to the conjoined acts of seeing/judging in Western culture. The idea that a gaze can be violently inflicted upon its objects is well-documented: think of the ancient superstition of the evil eye (Jay 1993, 28), or the psychoanalytic associations between voyeurism and sadism that pop up in the work of feminist film critic Laura Mulvey (1999, 840). In this line of thinking, even a detached, investigative gaze violates the integrity of its objects by subjecting them to judgement.

This becomes apparent by looking, for instance, at the writings of German theatre reformer Bertolt Brecht (1898–1956), whose appeal to his contemporaries as "children of the scientific age" (1964, 183) conveyed a preference for detached visual probing in the theatre. While Brecht may be generally known for his very vocal advocacy of political depictions of social issues onstage, it could be argued that he did not have a special interest in the peculiarities of the sensorium and his work therefore cannot be validly compared to our project. While the sensory process of seeing as such is seldom deemed one of Brecht's primary points of interest, a closer inspection of his "Short Organum for the Theatre" of 1948 reveals him to be profoundly visually biased. Part of this visual bias inevitably stems from his living in ocularcentric Western culture, which infused his language with visual metaphors—for example when he asks us to keep the impermanence of social structures "before our eyes" (190).[4] Similarly, when Brecht resorts to storytelling, many of his dramatic turning points are visual moments: he has mankind "[looking] about himself with a new vision" when entering the scientific age, and describes how in times of war, "the mothers of every nation, with their children pressed to them, scan the skies in horror for the deadly inventions of science" (184–185).

On a deeper level, Brecht's understanding of the dramatic stage appears to be fully dependent on the visual: he invites us to "go into one of these [theatre] houses and observe" the spectators, diagnosing that all of them "look at the stage as in a trance" (187). What Brecht sets out to alter is, fundamentally, this entranced way of *looking*—and little wonder, as he believes in such a thing as a "stage image" (191), and the actor in Brecht's own aesthetic ideal is described in terms of lifting a veil, showing, making visible, working with illustrations and patterns (194). The visual also permeates acting: "[o]bservation is a major part of acting" and "the choice of viewpoint is also a major part of the actor's art" (196). If done deftly, audience and performers will be participating in an exchange in which the performers hand over their representations to them, both parties having their "eyes fully open" instead of glaring away in a state of trance. This sort of critical distance is necessary, for as another visual simile of Brecht has it, "[i]f art reflects life it does so with special mirrors" (204).[5]

Martin Jay (1988, 3–5) has formulated the idea that visual subcultures can simultaneously exist with a dominant way of seeing or "scopic regime" in a particular historical period, while other visual subcultures simultaneously co-exist. Within any given scopic regime an act as simple as observation submits the observer to a set of "tacit cultural rules" (1993, 9), and from Brecht's text speaks a clear disagreement with the tacit scopic rules of both theatre-going conventions and everyday observation. However, it appears that he expects to achieve a distanced observation only by altering the object that is seen—and in doing so, he inadvertently backs away from inspecting the peculiarities of the gaze within the scopic regime itself to begin with. In *Peri-Sphere*, by taking away the definable object which guides the gaze through the choreography, the parameters of perception offer themselves up for scrutinizing, ultimately opening into the possibility of what Jay calls a "multiplicity of scopic regimes" (1988, 20).

Exploring Parameters of Perception

While eliminating predetermined objects from the performance was an important step, *merely* taking them away would not allow the gaze to be choreographed: we did not want to direct the participants' eyesight to a particular event, body or inanimate object as the focus of attention, but still we had to develop several steps to access their embodied vision. We developed a two-pronged approach. Firstly, there was a *discursive* component: drawing on Jay's suggestion of multiple scopic regimes, we would trace historical practices that bore witness to different examples of those regimes or pointed to their potentiality. This discursive component was process-oriented and open-ended: the three of us would share and discuss these historical practices in live sessions, or in to-and-fro recordings we shared digitally. However, it also included the discursive output of *Peri-Sphere* at various points in our project's timeline: we presented academic lectures on *Peri-Sphere* on multiple occasions[6] and provided an audio lecture that was integrated in the performance at its first presentation during *Working Title Situation* (audience members were given headphones while they queued for the performance, and witnessed the previous participant experience it as an onlooker). This very text is, as a matter of fact, the most recent addition to this open-ended discursive component of the project. Secondly, there was the *technological* aspect of the project: the material installation built by Benjamin Vandewalle, created with a sensitivity towards the historical case studies we integrated. This allowed us to conceive of *Peri-Sphere* as an experiment that had not yet been conducted, but that is already contributing to a historical discourse that has not yet been fully developed.

We retrace that historical discourse to the heavily visual era of modernity. Charney and Schwartz (1996, 2) recount how "perception in modern life became a mobile activity and the modern individual body the subject of both experimentation and new discourses". In other words, ever since modernity, there have been myriad attempts of mapping the (history of the) (visually) perceiving body, either discursively or theoretically. Here, Jay's multiplicity of visual subcultures kick in, providing a contrast for the dominant scopic regime.[7] That regime is what he elsewhere calls "Cartesian perspectivalism", a conceptual approach to visual perception that entails a double reduction of the perceiver's body due to two widespread features of mainstream Western culture. On the artistic plane, linear perspective had propagated the idea that sight originated from an abstract point of view rather than from an embodied entity in pictorial representation. On the philosophical plane, the influence of René Descartes led to further abstraction of the embodied aspects of seeing, downplaying the role of the seeing I's body in vision (1993, 54–82).

As Jonathan Crary (1988) recounts in his now-classical text "Techniques of the Observer", this limited awareness of corporeal vision was somewhat thwarted by the advent of the titular "observer" in the early nineteenth century.[8] The bearer of the gaze was reconceptualized as someone in possession of a particular body that determined his or her subjective vision, emerging in this era in parallel with its scientific interest in optical experimentation. Cutting-edge research on optics spawned a number of popular optical devices exploiting recently spread knowledge on retinal afterimages, the persistence of vision and binocular vision, resulting in a multitude of what we usually call pre-cinematic toys: phenakistoscopes, kaleidoscopes, stereoscopes and their ilk. Crary remarks that these were all devices which contained a disciplinary element. They all entailed the position of an immobile spectator in relationship to a (usually mobile) device, and subjected him or her to an implied agenda of norm and deviance: for example, not seeing the moving images of the phenakistoscope illusion implied a bodily pathology (14–23). So while subjective vision vested in the body was being discovered, it was simultaneously seized as an opportunity to improve upon it and to standardize the flaw-ridden subjective aspect of the corporeal eye. Or, as Iwan Rhys Morus (2012, 49) puts it, nineteenth-century discourse held that "[t]o be reliable, the eye needed to be trained. Audiences needed to learn how to see spectacle; and spectacles themselves needed particular kinds of discipline to deliver vision".

Examining these discourses on optical experimentation gave us an insight in subjective observation in its earliest nineteenth-century occurrence, but the observations were not particularly illuminating when it comes to defining the parameters operative when that kind of observation is no longer directed at predetermined objects such as a particular event or body. Not immediately finding a historical situation equivalent to the *Peri-Sphere* that we could recreate ourselves, we went on to investigate a similar process taking place in the realm of the visual arts: an observation of predetermined objects that had lost their predetermined meanings as representations.

When pictorial illusionism was subverted and subsequently eliminated in the late 1950s, both the status of the object of art and the address of the observing subject became unhinged, paving the way for experimental practices in visual and performative arts from the 1950s onwards. As Hal Foster writes in relation to Roland Barthes' famous 1967 essay, the disruption signifies: "[a] "death of the author" that is at the same time a birth of the viewer" (50). Similarly, André Lepecki (2012, 19) describes a shift in priorities for the arts, as: "[t]o experiment became to animate the body's capacities and potencies beyond and besides formations of the 'human' as a general category for subjectivity. To experiment was to open up the body to new areas of the sensible, the perceptible and the meaningful, of affects and sensations as moving and mobilizing corporal assemblages". Freed from the final formalist demands of Modernism, where a "normative examination" governs the scope and capabilities of the art object, the artwork could now be recognized through a "functional analysis": "[t]he object of whose investigation would be social effect (function) of a work and a sociologically definable public within an already existing institutional frame"(Bürger 1984, 87). The encounter with a work of art now takes place in an "expanded situation", where the observer finds himself engaging with the conditional parameters of this encounter, both sensorial and contextual, identifying himself as a participant within the concrete conditions of where, when and how the viewing of the work takes place. The fundamental phenomenological reorientation that Minimalism introduces confronts the subject with objects that seem mere objects, no longer imbued by a representation that lies beyond them. Their significance unfolds only through a reflexive inquiry rooted in the conditions that govern both subject and object in their shared reality. Robert Morris (1968) would describe the significance of this development and the conception of his *gestalts* in 1966 as: "It is in some way more reflexive, because one's awareness of oneself existing in the same space as the work is stronger than in previous work, with its many internal relationships. One is more aware than before that he himself is establishing relationships as he apprehends the object from various positions and under varying conditions of light and space" (232).

It is noteworthy that Morris works towards the formulation of his gestalts both from his practice of sculpture and his meaningful involvement with the experiments of postmodern dance by his contemporaries. Morris emphasizes that, contrary to the visual arts, the practice of sculpture has never been involved with the concerns of illusionism. He describes the nascence of his gestalts as a clearer articulation of the nature of the values of sculpture: "The sculptural facts of space, light, and materials have always functioned concretely and literally" (223). Other than the perceptual conditions above, Morris distinguishes two other corporeal phenomena as essential qualities of the encounter with sculpture, namely the conditioning of gravity and the awareness of scale. As a profound corporal process, experiencing scale then becomes a realization of one's own bodily conditions as a constant, in comparison with the endless variations of sizes in its surroundings. The attachment of qualities such as intimacy or publicness is, Morris writes, essentially imbedded in the recognition of scale.

Ranging in size between a monument and an ornament, it is no wonder that the objects proposed in Minimalism have been experienced as resembling the presence of a "surrogate person"(Fried 1998, 156): "In fact, being distanced by such objects is not, I suggest, entirely unlike being distanced, or crowded, by the silent presence of another person" (156). Michael Fried would further address his concern for these objects' body-like presence by describing the apparent hollowness of these so-called gestalts: "The quality of having an inside – is almost blatantly anthropomorphic" (156). A similar remark can be found in the writings of Rosalind Krauss, who recognizes "a latent kind of Cartesianism" (Kraus 1973, 50) in the presence of the gestalts of Morris. "The gestalt seems to be interpreted as an immutable, ideal unit that persists beyond the particularities of experience, becoming through its very persistence the ground for all experience. Yet this is to ignore the most rudimentary notions of Gestalt theory, in which the properties of the 'good Gestalt' are demonstrated to be entirely context-dependent".

Considering these notions, let us once more recall Morris' memorable and frequently examined[9] *Column*, a seven-minute performance that was presented at the Living Theatre in New York in 1962. The recollection of the performance is one of minimal means: the curtains opened to reveal a column, plywood, painted grey, two feet by eight feet, that was placed upright on stage. After three and a half minutes, the column toppled and subsequently fell down on the stage, where it remained horizontal for the remaining three and a half minutes. Initially the column was devised as a hollow shell to contain Morris' own body. The dramatic action of the column would then be initiated by the weight of Morris' own body, pressing on one side of the column until the column would topple. During the rehearsal of the piece, Morris was injured by *his/their/the* fall and he decided to retreat from the stage, subsequently causing the column to fall by pulling on piece of string attached to the object. During the performance, the column showed itself as an object shrouded in duality; no longer containing the body of the performer, but devised precisely in correspondence with the scale of his body and bound to its author in the offstage. The withdrawal of Morris from the column is significant, rendering *Column* a performerless performance, while remaining profoundly imbued with the parameters of corporeal presence. Unintentionally, *their/the* fall demonstrated the consequences of the deeply rooted alliance of the object and the subject. There are a few other remarkable instances by Morris' contemporaries where performative objects are cast that contain traces of the subject's longing of *becoming-object*; always in some way referential, even indexical to the body of its author. We are reminded here, for instance, of Lygia Pape's *Neoconcreto Ballet 1* (1958)[10] in which the theatrical space displayed cylindrical and rectangular columns, embodied by performers who would perform a geometric choreography, and Franz Erhard Walther's various textile *Werksatz* (1963–1969), which he continues to demonstrate during numerous variations of the *Werkvorführung*.

The significance of Morris' corporeal referentiality resurfaces in the performance of *Peri-Sphere*, in which (the corporeality of) Vandewalle as a performer is both present and offstage. The design of the installation seems to be fitted to the limits of the body. The L-shape of the installation consists of two planes of just over two meters: a body standing up and a body lying down. During the performance the presence of the performer's body is filtered out through the series of consecutive angles that are accessible as an analogue montage of points of view embodied by the participant. Through the fragmented mirroring surfaces, the gaze of the viewer is directed to the reflection of their own body in motion, its own conditions in space and time, and the parameters of his or her own perception. No longer the focal point of the performance, the body of the performer is consequently freed from the constraints of representation. Vandewalle's choreography is both a set of manoeuvres to perform the mechanics of the installation, and an improvisation in the conditions of the space where the performance takes place; neither are meaningful beyond their use in the concrete time and space of the performance. The participant might notice fragments of the performer's body as glimpses of a body in movement through the cracks of the assemblage of mirrors, or experience a certain "nearness" to the performer. As *Peri-Sphere* is presented in situations where the one-on-one performance takes place in essentially public spaces, such as the entrance hall of a theatre, an exhibition space of a modern art museum, or surrounded by the outdoor cityscape of cities such as Brussels and Amsterdam, the bodily presence of the performer will remain a body amongst other bodies in the concrete surroundings of the performance, not once confirming its signification or representation as performer. And yet, witnessing the performance as an onlooker outside of the installation, the true encounter of Vandewalle as a performer with the object becomes apparent; as Vandewalle exhausts his physical capacities to manoeuvre the installation through the space, assembling the points of view manually.

Different Angles

Although adopting the part of the onlooker could be construed as a legitimate part of the aesthetic experience of the *Peri-Sphere* prototype—onlookers, more often than not, were people awaiting the opportunity to participate themselves—the crux of this project resides in the utopian quest of internalizing a choreography as an unfolding of a visual structure. When we think of *Peri-Sphere* as a "choreography of the gaze", we think of a gaze that is no longer directed through the body of the other, as a moving target on stage embodying the limits of the aesthetic experience. The performance attempts to structure potentialities and limits, a choreography, between object and participant. A choreography would now set out the conditions for a visual experience and implement them not in the body of the performer, but in the gaze of the viewer.

This enterprise entails some risk, as the spectre of pathologist optics still haunts contemporary performances that place a special focus on embodied experience: Keren Zaiontz's (2014) concept of narcissistic spectatorship may very well be its most recent incarnation. Looking into immersive and one-on-one performances, Zaiontz notices a competitive, exclusive strain in its audience's attitudes:

> Their use of more than one sense organ (such as sight or hearing) not only enables a more fulsome artistic encounter, but it also demonstrates just how good they are at steering their own course and consuming the performance. It is a marker of distinction that announces: *Hey, look, I produced a completely unique artistic experience for myself!* (408; emphasis in original)

Zaiontz remarks how in some cases, this leads to an uneven spectatorship, where a "conflation between mobility and ability" takes place: those immersants with a physical capacity that deviates from the norm[11] will have a different experience. While this difference is cherished as part of the "one-on-one" aspect of these performances, there is nonetheless often a tacit agreement that certain ways of experiencing are preferable to others (411–413), which in turn leads to a denigration and disciplining of observation that is not wholly unlike the one introduced by Crary's optical toys. But audiovisual performance, insofar that it is sensory, cannot completely forego the fact that it will always be reliant on the sensorial capacities of its audience—and therefore, be reliant on their limitations as well.

That realization, in turn, brings us to the utter limits of removing the predetermined objects for an audience's gaze to see. We have taken into account these historical attempts of stripping representation of the object, the choreography from the dancer. A choreography would then become present as a structure that is not implemented in the body of the performer, nor in objects that in some way and even in their most rigid forms are unable to escape their representation of a human-like presence or a human scale. The choreography is internalized in the gaze of the viewer and works with both the raw material of the gaze as with the concrete, ever changing, ever dynamic parameters and conditions of the subject. Some degree of human scaling is inevitable, as the bodily qualities of the participant themselves are ultimately irreducible—and therefore, we realized our methodology should draw from a historical example that positively valued the incorporation of the body in performance rather than to develop a methodology that stands in sharp contrast with the rigidity of the optical toys of the nineteenth century or the dualistic appearance of the objects in minimalism.

We found this kind of approach in Elizabeth Carlson's (2011) proposal to connect the emergence of the subjective spectator in the nineteenth century to the era's obsession with mirrors, which were manufactured on an industrial scale and used in popular attractions. In her description of mirror palaces that redoubled and multiplied their own interiors like a larger-than-life kaleidoscope, to great spectatorial delight, we found one of those rare instances of historical artistic practices where the corporeality of vision was unapologetically explicit. In a mirror palace, the observer's body became part of the kaleidoscopic spectacle—it was, indeed, visibly reflected in the very object of marvel, thus firmly grounding visual perception in a corporeal perceiver (26). Carlson quickly became a key reference for *Peri-Sphere*. Inspired by her approach to the materiality of mirror palaces, which she distinguished as consisting of both *technological objects* (mirrors) and *bodies* (spectators), we came to regard our participant's body as a part of the choreography. We even went as far as to consider it the finishing technical piece to our installations. And while mirrors were to be part of the installation from its earliest design (periscopes worked with mirrors, after all), now we discovered the virtues of literally mirroring the gaze back to the participant's body. Describing Morris' *Four Mirrored Cubes* (1965), Seth Kim-Cohen observes another occurrence of objects in Minimalism that contain the body of the subject and their shared situation, and is reminded by this process of the art historical trope of the *mise en abyme* (2008, 12). The use of mirroring surfaces seems to be a more literal, although potent measure to compose the body and the object. Integrating the bodily presence of the subject in the work through the mirroring surface, the objects now mirrored the interaction of contemplative and concrete space.[12]

While we cannot practically overcome the limitations that bind vision to the body, through our insistence on the uncovering of multiple versions of vision we try to deconstruct the authority of a singular scopic regime, even if that scopic regime is one installed by the coded conventions of performance itself. In that way our mode of performativity holds a potential for scrutinizing the relationship between vision and what we call "world orientation", the connection between a literal and metaphorical "outlook" on life. Accepting this connection, or even setting out to investigate it, implies essentially a multiplicity of viewpoints, both metaphorical and literal, and therefore a multiplicity of "correct" or at least legitimate existent visions. To proclaim a singular line of vision to be more "pure" correlates with an ideological choice—where a more reasonably objective description would relate to the multitude of possible angles. The idealistic concept of the innocent eye of the human infant is then supplanted by the compound eye of the insect—or, to do away completely with the idea of a naturalistic and spontaneous vision, by a multi-angular technological object: a kaleidoscope, a hall of mirrors, or indeed, an adjustable periscope.

The *Peri-Sphere* choreography is a series of consecutive angles without a fixed focal point, and with a very minimal arc—a most bare version of visual montage that highlights the raw confrontation of different points of view itself. The installation shows itself as a flayed apparatus: cords and wheels are not hidden nor disguised as trickery. When we discursively juxtapose different angles on a theatrical experience within subjective vision, a composite of bodily perception arises.

In this sense, the installation could be perceived as a theoretical automaton, a philosophical materialization of the "montage ideal" of dialectical thinking represented in such works as Walter Benjamin's *Arcades Project*. "I needn't say anything", Benjamin wrote, "Merely show" (1999, 460). Repudiating a more analytical discourse in this fabled example of "literary montage", he supposedly expressed with this statement his belief that by merely juxtaposing certain discursive fragments on a certain subject—scraps from literature, criticism or even advertisements and other sources—he could elicit a philosophical insight in an audience. As Benjamin's literary montage cheerfully steered past the necessity of explicit theoretical reflection by merely juxtaposing different points of view on a certain matter, our visual montage steers past the necessity of an explicit content. It could be said to evoke insight by the bare succession of different angles—were it not for the fact that the montage aspect encompasses theory: theory and practice both become modular elements of the same technological construct. Continuously implementing research and reflection into a point of view, *Peri-Sphere* turns into one hybrid discursive/experiential device.

In our viewing machine, the body of the participant functions as a necessary cogwheel—and so a relationship of mirroring and reflection arises between the participant and the installation, exposing the cog work of a reciprocal theatrical relation of what is being viewed and under which conditions it is viewed. Important aspects of a metaphorical "outlook" on the world, such as ideology, then become a matter of technological reconfiguration—political conscience, the outcome of an artificially redefined literal point of view. As this article shows, *Peri-Sphere* is an apparatus engrossed in historical discourse. The set-up of the performance is used to give a participant access to a point of view that alternates from their regular, ideology-laden way of seeing—offering an equally ideologically compromised but nevertheless *different* angle. In this manner, *Peri-Sphere* presents itself as an archive of perspectives, a database of viewpoints, assembled into one.

NOTES

1. Çelik (2006, 159) sums up kinaesthesia as "those unclassifiable sensations that could not be traced to one of the five known sense organs, but seemed to originate from the undifferentiated mass of the viscera".
2. The *Working Title Situation* festival was organized by Workspacebrussels, a Brussels-based laboratory for performing arts.
3. Earlier prototypes of this installation were presented at the conferences *Does It Matter? Composite Bodies and Posthuman Prototypes in Contemporary Performing Arts* (Ghent University, 17–19 March 2015) and at *Play/Perform/Participate* (Utrecht University, 16–18 April, 2015).
4. For the sake of clarity, we have opted to quote from an English-language translation of Brecht's text. Therefore, we have as much as possible avoided what seemed purely linguistic expressions containing visual imagery.
5. It could also be argued that Brecht's "dialectical materialism" is in and of itself a visually imbued philosophical practice—at least, that is what Susan Buck-Morss (1989) appeared to be implying when she titled her classic study of Walter Benjamin and *his* exercise in dialectical materialism *The Dialectics of Seeing*. Benjamin himself compared Brecht's epic theatre to the visual medium of a film strip (1998, 21).
6. Lectures about the process of *Peri-Sphere* were presented at the conferences *Does It Matter? Composite Bodies and Posthuman Prototypes in Contemporary Performing Arts* (Ghent University, 17–19 March 2015), *Play/Perform/Participate* (Utrecht University, 16–18 April, 2015) and *Bodies On Stage: Acting Confronted by Technology* (Sorbonne Nouvelle, 3–5 June 2015).
7. It must be noted that Jay's concept of modernity stretches back to what is more commonly designated as "early modernity", including events from the Italian Renaissance. "Cartesian perspectivalism" develops and rises to dominance throughout this period. In addition to the pages cited here, Jay's text "Scopic Regimes of Modernity" (1988) also contains an account of Cartesian perspectivalism. A concise summary of Jay's ideas on the subject can be found in van de Vall (2008, 17–21).
8. Crary later published a monograph on the same subject, likewise entitled *Techniques of the Observer* (1990).
9. For reference, see André Lepecki (2014, 121–122) and Rosalind Krauss (1994).
10. For a more elaborate discussion of Pape's *Neoconcreto Ballet 1*, see Lepecki (2014, 110–118).
11. Zaiontz' own example is the performance *Sleep No More* (premiered 2011) by Punchdrunk, in which audience members were encouraged to follow around performers at high speed in order to understand the storyline

presented in the performance. She elaborates that an audience member's "individual mobility within the performance is linked to her personal ability to access and piece together the event through relentless pursuit" (411–412). She refers briefly to a visually impaired audience member in a footnote (413), implying that a similar point could be made about sensory disabilities.

12. Here we are also reminded of the mirroring surfaces we perceive in the installations of Larry Bell, which he introduced in his work in the late 1960s, or the mirroring sculptures and pavilions that Dan Graham integrated in the public sphere from the 1980s on.

REFERENCES

Benjamin, Walter. 1998. *Understanding Brecht*. Translated by Anna Bostock. London: Verso.

Benjamin, Walter. 1999. *The Arcades Project*. Edited by Rolf Tiedemann. Translated by Howard Eiland and Kevin McLaughlin. Cambridge: Belknap Press of Harvard University Press.

Brecht, Bertolt. 1964. "A Short Organum for the Theatre." In *Brecht on Theatre: The Development of an Aesthetic*, edited and translated by John Willet. New York: Hill and Wang.

Buck-Morss, Susan. 1989. *The Dialectics of Seeing: Walter Benjamin and the Arcades Project*. Cambridge, MA: MIT Press.

Bürger, Peter. 1984. *Theory of the Avant-Garde*. Translated by Michael Shaw. Minneapolis: University of Minnesota Press.

Carlson, Elizabeth. 2011. "Reflections to Projections: The Mirror as a Proto-Cinematic Technology." *Early Popular Visual Culture* 9, no. 1: 15–35. https://doi.org/10.1080/17460654.2011.544111.

Çelik, Zeynep. 2006. "Kinaesthesia." In *Sensorium: Embodied Experience, Technology and Contemporary Art*, edited by Caroline A. Jones, 159–162. Cambridge, MA: MIT Press.

Charney, Leo, and Vanessa R. Schwartz. 1996. "Introduction to *Cinema and the Invention of Modern Life, 1–14*." Edited by Leo Charney and Vanessa R. Schwartz. Berkeley: University of California Press.

Crary, Jonathan. 1988. "Techniques of the Observer." *October* 45: 3–35.

Crary, Jonathan. 1990. *Techniques of the Observer: On Vision and Modernity in the Nineteenth Century*. Cambridge, MA: MIT Press.

Emerson, Ralph Waldo. 1836. *Nature*. Boston: James Munroe and Company.

Fischer-Lichte, Erika. 2008. *The Transformative Power of Performance: A New Aesthetics*. Abingdon: Routledge.

Foster, Hal. 1996. *The Return of the Real*. Cambridge, MA: MIT Press.

Fried, Michael. 1998. *Art and Objecthood*. Chicago: University of Chicago Press.
Jay, Martin. 1988. "Scopic Regimes of Modernity." In *Vision and Visuality*, edited by Hal Foster, 3–23. Seattle: Bay.
Jay, Martin. 1993. *Downcast Eyes: The Denigration of Vision in Twentieth-Century French Thought*. Berkeley: University of California Press.
Kim-Cohen, Seth. 2008. "Sculpture in the Reduced Field: Robert Morris and Minimalism Beyond Phenomenology." Self-published, PDF file.
Krauss, Rosalind. 1973. "Sense and Sensibility: Reflection on Post 60's Sculpture." *Artforum* 12, no. 3:43–53.
Krauss, Rosalind. 1994. "The Mind/ Body Problem: Robert Morris in Series." In *Robert Morris: The Mind/ Body Problem*, edited by Anthony Calnek, 2–17. New York: Guggenheim Museum.
Lepecki, André. 2012. "Moving as Thing: Choreographic Critiques of the Object." *October* 140: 75–90.
Lepecki, André. 2014. "From Objectacts to Dancethings: 'Transcreation' in the work of Robert Morris, Hélio Oiticica and Lygia Pape." In *Regionality/ Mondiality: Perspectives on Art, Aesthetics and Globalization*, edited by Charlotte Bydler and Cecilia Sjöholm, 105–129. Södertörn: Södertörn University Press.
Morris, Robert. 1968. "Notes on Sculpture Part I & Part II". In *Minimal Art: A Critical Anthology*, edited by Gregory Battcock, 222–235. Berkeley: University of California Press.
Morus, Iwan Rhys. 2012. "Illuminating Illusions, or, The Victorian Art of Seeing Things." *Early Popular Visual Culture* 10, no. 1: 37–50. https://doi.org/10.1080/17460654.2012.638806.
Mulvey, Laura. 1999. "Visual Pleasure and Narrative Cinema." In *Film Theory and Criticism: Introductory Readings*, edited by Leo Braudy and Marshall Cohen, 833–844. New York: Oxford University Press.
Schechner, Richard. 2001. "Rasaesthetics." *TDR* 45, no. 3: 27–50. https://doi.org/10.1162/10542040152587105.
Sontag, Susan. 1977. *On Photography*. London: Penguin.
van de Vall, Renée. 2008. *At the Edges of Vision: A Phenomenological Aesthetics of Contemporary Spectatorship*. Aldershot: Ashgate.
Varnelis, Kazys. 1998. "The Education of the Innocent Eye." *Journal of Architectural Education* 51, 4: 212–233. http://www.jstor.org/stable/1425477.
Zaiontz, Keren. 2014. "Narcissistic Spectatorship in Immersive and One-on-One Performance." *Theatre Journal* 6, 3: 405–425. https://doi.org/10.1353/tj.2014.0084.

Index

A
Aboutness, 94–97, 99, 104, 105, 107
Abram, David, 12
Abramović, Marina, 22, 84, 85, 88
 Rhythm 0, 22, 84
activator, 22, 88, 90
activism, 30, 31, 197, 225
Actor Networks, 6
actor-network theory, 77
Adlington, Robert, 283
Aers, Peter (Building Conversation), 30, 195, 199, 200, 212, 213, 219, 221
aesthetics, 8, 13–16, 23, 26, 52, 58, 95–98, 104, 106, 107, 122, 123, 138, 156, 176, 272, 281, 288–291, 293–295, 298, 311, 312, 323, 329
Agamben, Giorgio, 5, 13, 16, 19, 20, 52–55
agencies of observation, 243
agency, distributed, 16, 251
agency, human, 32, 34, 35, 89, 237, 250, 251
agency, non-human, 21, 238
agential realism, 7, 33, 102, 178, 186
agent, technological, 250–252
Agonistic Conversation (Building Conversation), 198, 199
Aït-Touati, Frédérique
algorithm (algorithmic), 4, 32, 251
alienation, 119, 120, 122, 185
alienation effect. *See* Verfremdungseffekt
alphabetism, 262
Alÿs, Francis, 89
Amélia (Édouard Lock), 133
Andersen, Tore Rye, 37, 263, 281
animacy, 204, 205, 207, 209
animacy, a grammar of, 30, 196, 200, 205, 206, 209, 215, 227
annotation, itinerary, 279
Anthology of optimism (Pieter De Buysser and Jacob Wren), 95
Anthropocene, the, 2, 17, 22, 103–105, 149, 201, 203, 205, 218
anthropocentrism (anthropocentric), 2, 9, 12, 15, 16, 20, 22, 28, 62,

© The Editor(s) (if applicable) and The Author(s) 2021
C. Stalpaert et al. (eds.), *Performance and Posthumanism*,
https://doi.org/10.1007/978-3-030-74745-9

65, 70, 76, 88, 99, 138, 215, 298, 308
Anthropogenic, the, 2, 5
anthropology, 63, 103
anthropomorphism (anthropomorphic), 9, 70, 74, 307, 315, 316, 327
A Piece of Work (Annie Dorsen), 251
apparatus, 5, 13, 19–21, 24, 34, 39, 40, 52–55, 57, 58, 69, 73, 97–103, 106–108, 142, 162, 186, 189, 242, 293, 318, 331, 332
apparatus, desubjectifying
Arab Spring, 311
Archibald, Margaret, 36, 266, 269–272, 281, 283
Archimedes, 33, 246, 253, 255
Arendt, Hannah, 29, 30, 197, 225, 293
Aristotle (Aristotelian), 15–17
Arons, Wendy, 220
Ars Industrialis, 27
Artaud, Antonin, 167
artificially intelligence (artificially intelligent) (AI), 35, 250
art-science-activist worlding, 30, 33, 195–197, 200, 225, 228
Assange, Julian, 157
assemblage, 23, 34, 39, 40, 68–70, 112, 137, 138, 140, 141, 143–147, 149, 150, 177, 179, 186, 189, 243, 293, 297, 299, 303, 326, 328
atomic bomb, 2, 113
Atwood, Margaret, 200
Augmented Reality (AR), 38, 40, 300–303
Auslander, Philip, 166
avatar, 27, 128, 130–133, 160, 161

B
Baars, Ab, 275, 277, 279, 281
BADCo, 35, 251
  Whatever Dance Toolbox, 251
Badmington, Neil, 3
Bailie, Joanna, 18
  C.O. Journeys, 57
Ballard, J.G., 5
Bal, Mieke, 11
Balthazar(David Weber-Krebs), 9, 23, 25, 61, 62, 66, 70, 77
Barad, Karen, 7, 24, 33, 36, 41, 88, 90, 98, 102, 105, 178, 179, 181, 183, 186, 188, 189, 242, 243, 252
Barnes, Barry, 239
Barthes, Roland, 326
Bayan Obo mine, 173, 181, 183
Bayley, Amanda, 263
Bazelon, Emily, 165
Becker, Howard D., 274
Beckett, Samuel, 122, 123, 139
becoming-animal, 22, 56
becoming-fungi, 23
becoming-object, 39, 328
becoming-thingly (becoming-thing), 19, 21, 55, 56
becoming-virtual, 130
becoming with (becoming-with), 4, 6–8, 10, 16, 22, 43, 225
Beghetto, Ronald A.
being-in-a-more-than-human-world, 12
being-in-the-world, 12, 16, 43
Bell, Larry, 334
Benjamin, Walter, 66, 332
Bennett, Jane, 7, 12, 102, 112, 174
Bennink, Han, 272, 276, 283
Benoit, Mylène
  Effet Papillon, 128, 129, 131, 132, 134–136
  ICI, 128

INDEX 339

La chair du monde, 128
Benso, Silva, 25, 55
Bergson, Henri, 7, 12, 73
Berthoz, Alain, 257
Bimber, Oliver, 301
bio-art, 306
biography of things, the, 181, 182
biotechnology, 292
Birdwatching 4x4, 319
Bishop, Claire
Blanchot, Maurice, 139
Blanga Gubbay, Daniel, 16, 21, 22, 24, 25, 41
Bleeker, Maaike, 32, 34–38, 40, 42, 237, 238, 251, 252, 255
Bleich, David, 37, 262
Bloor, David, 239
body language (of texts) (Tore Rye Andersen), 37, 244, 263, 279, 281
Bohm, David, 197, 198, 209–214, 225–227
Bohr, Niels, 102, 103, 242, 243
Born, Georgina, 262, 263
Borowski, Mateusz, 32, 37, 38, 41
bouleverser (Debord, Guy), 87
Bourbaki group, the, 240
bourgeois theatre, 293, 296
Bowman, Brooks, 275
East of the Sun (West of the Moon), 275
BOX (Kris Verdonck), 113, 118
Boyle, Robert, 33, 289, 299, 300, 305
Braidotti, Rosi, 7, 11, 25, 41, 42, 137, 147, 154, 288
Brassier, Ray, 7
Brecht, Bertolt, 37, 39, 295–298, 307, 308, 322, 323
Der Ozeanflug, 37, 296–298, 304, 307
Flieger, 296

Bresson, Robert, 66
Breuker, Willem, 272
Brusselaers, Dieter, 32, 39–41, 316
Peri-Sphere, 39, 40, 316–325, 328, 329, 331, 332
Buck-Morss, Susan, 333
Building Conversation
 Agonistic Conversation, 198, 199
 General Assembly, 198, 199
 Impossible Conversation, 196–199, 203, 204, 221, 223, 225, 227
 Parliament of Things, 30, 195–200, 215–223, 225, 227
 Thinking Together—An Experiment, 196–198, 209, 210, 212–214, 225, 227
 Time Loop, 198, 199
Bürger, Peter, 326
Burroughs, William, 140, 144

C
Caillieu, Barbara, 130
camera obscura, 57, 102
Capitalocene, 23, 104
capture, 35, 52, 54, 57, 144, 179, 241
Carels, Edwin, 10
Carlson, Elizabeth, 39, 330
Cartesian perspectivalism, 40, 324
Cassiers, Edith, 37, 264
Causey, Matthew, 28
Çelik, Zeynep, 333
CERN, 34, 241, 243, 250
Césaire, Aimé
Chaberski, Mateusz, 32, 37, 38, 41
chair du monde, La (Mylène Benoit), 128
Chapman, Michael J.
Charmatz, Boris, 20, 56
Charney, Leo, 324
Châtelet, Gilles, 247

Chaudhuri, Una, 203
child abuse, 28
Chomsky, Noam, 251
Choreographic Language Agent (Wayne McGregor), 251
choreographic object, 257
Choreography of Taylorism, 185
choreography of the gaze, 40, 329
Chthulucene, 105
Clark, Andy, 264
Clarke, Bruce, 282
Clarke, Eric, 282
climate, 30, 195, 199, 200, 203, 208, 217, 218
climate change, 2, 29–31, 93–96, 107, 114, 148–150, 176, 195, 203, 204, 212, 213
co-creation, 11, 14, 17, 22, 105, 107
co-creator, 26, 105, 251, 287, 296
Code, Lorraine, 6, 33
C.O. Journeys (Joanna Bailie & Christoph Ragg), 57
Colebrook, Claire, 149
Collingwood, Robin, 246
colonialism, 30, 55, 97, 180, 197, 222, 223, 227, 230
Column (Robert Morris), 39, 327, 328
commedia dell'arte, 292, 293
commodity, commodity fetishism, 53–56, 58, 158, 186
composite, 8–10, 43, 112, 189, 332
composite bodies (composite body), 8–10, 17, 20, 111, 112
com-post, 23
contamination, 105, 128, 133, 135, 172
Contour Progressif, 132
conversational performances, 30, 195, 198–200, 215, 223, 227
Cook, Nicholas, 37, 262, 263, 265, 282

Copernicus, Nicolaus, 3
coronavirus crisis, 43
corporeality, 39, 128, 135, 316, 320, 328, 330
corporeal referentiality, 39, 328
cosmic webs, 6
cosmology, 62, 75–77
CPAI (Child Physical Abuse Images), 163
Crary, Jonathan, 39, 40, 325, 330
Critchley, Simon, 74
Croft, Lara, 128, 132, 133
Crutzen, Paul, 2
CSAI (Child Sexual Abuse Images), 156, 157, 163, 165
Csikszentmihályi, Mihályi, 283
cultivation, 67, 101, 106, 322
Cunningham, Merce, 251, 254
Curie, Marie, 176
cybernetics (cybernetic), 4
cyborg, 5, 6

D

Darwin, Charles, 3, 4, 7
data-double(s), 153–155
data-subjectivity, 154
data-subject(s), 153–155, 157, 159, 164, 165, 167
Davies, Kate (Unknown Fields Division), 171
Daydream House (Laurent Liefooghe), 18, 19, 25, 26
Debaise, Didier, 17
Debord, Guy, 22, 41, 53, 54, 82, 84–88
De Buysser, Pieter, 95
  Anthology of Optimism, 95
decolonization, 30, 197
defocalization, 138, 141
de Freitas, Elisabeth, 247
de Graaf, Reiner, 300

INDEX   341

De Keersmaeker, Anne Teresa, 238
De Laet, Timmy, 37, 264
Deleuze, Gilles, 3, 5, 7, 10, 12, 15, 16, 23, 24, 27, 43, 70, 71, 138, 140–147, 149, 150, 177, 256, 257
Delius, Tobias, 273, 283
Dempster, Beth M., 6
De Mul, Jos, 2
Der Ozeanflug (Bertolt Brecht), 37, 296–298, 304, 307
Derrida, Jacques, 3, 64, 167
Descartes, René, 63, 69, 76, 78, 325
Description of a Picture (Heiner Müller), 38, 307–309
deterritorialization, 28, 144–146
Despret, Vinciane
detonator, 85, 86, 90
De Vries, Erki, 319
  One/Zero, 319
DeZutter, Stacy, 282
Dibble, Julian, 160
Diedericksen, Diederick
digital surveillance, 153
digital swarm, 155
dispositivo. See apparatus
dispossession, 54, 58
distributed agency, 16, 251
distributed creativity, 41, 265, 279
Does it Matter? Composite Bodies and Posthuman Prototypes in Contemporary Performing Arts (Conference, Ghent University 2015), 8, 10, 112, 237, 250, 333
Doffman, Mark, 282
Doğantan-Dack, Mine, 262
Dogma manifesto, 309
domestication, 106, 107
donkey, 9, 23, 25, 61, 62, 66, 70–73, 77
Dorsen, Annie, 35, 251
  A Piece of Work, 251

Hello Hi There, 251
Downer, Lucy, 36, 266–272, 279, 280, 283
dramatic theatre, 13, 16
dramaturgy (dramaturgical, dramaturgies), 11, 14, 21, 22, 24, 27, 32, 43, 62, 66, 71, 72, 111, 117, 121, 122, 131, 289
dramaturgy, new, 14, 15
dramaturgy, new media, 21
dramaturgy of simulacra, a, 131
dramaturgy, posthuman, 14
droit à l'oubli (right to be forgotten), 157, 159
dystopia, 24, 114

E
Earth, the, 2, 105, 145–150, 184, 190, 201, 244
East of the Sun (West of the Moon) (Brooks Bowman), 275, 276
Eckersall, Peter, 9, 20, 21, 43, 111, 112, 114, 115, 117–119, 122, 123
ecocritical, 7
ecology (ecological), 3, 14, 28–31, 42, 94, 97, 148, 171, 172, 179, 180, 183, 188, 192, 195, 197, 200, 203, 204, 207, 208, 220, 222, 227, 230, 247, 253
ecosophy, 177
Effet Papillon (Mylène Benoit), 128, 129, 131, 132, 134–136
Eibeler, Thorsten, 93, 98, 99, 101, 102, 104
elaborate hybrids, 263
embodied knowledge, 272, 276
emergence, 4, 33, 39, 53, 87–89, 142, 177, 287, 312, 317, 330
Emergence (John McCormick), 34, 35, 250

Emerson, Ralph Waldo, 39, 315–317, 320, 321
empathy, 24, 65, 69, 74, 119, 134
END (Kris Verdonck), 9, 20, 117
Enhancing Choreographic Objects (Wayne McGregor), 251
enlightenment, 33, 94, 97, 103
entanglement, 5, 6, 24, 32, 100, 105, 107, 176, 179, 183, 188, 212, 220, 223, 225, 227, 230, 237, 282, 288
epic theatre, 295, 296, 333
epistemologies, posthuman, 14, 31
epistemology (epistemological), 7, 38, 64, 238, 243, 294, 300
ethnography (ethnographic), 36, 41, 264
ethology, 70
expérience, 38, 289, 299–301, 303, 304
extraction, 172, 173, 187, 190, 300

F
Fabre, Jan, 37, 264
fabulation, 5, 23, 99, 151, 288
failure, 89, 99, 107, 123, 148, 203
Faulkner, Robert, 274
Federici, Silvia, 97
feedback loop, 68
Ferdinand, Malcolm, 222
Ferrara, Francesca, 247, 257
Feyerabend, Paul, 239
figure(s), 5, 9, 20–22, 66, 88, 89, 99, 111, 118, 133, 137, 145, 147, 149, 160, 182, 186, 191, 214, 215, 238, 244, 271, 293, 308
figurine(s), 133
Fischer-Lichte, Erika, 316
Flieger (Bertolt Brecht), 296
flora, 30, 197, 223
flow, 4, 11, 159, 174, 177, 178, 186, 220, 273, 283, 298

Folkers, Andreas, 177, 178
foraging, 106, 108
Foster, Hal, 326
Foucault, Michel, 3, 36, 139, 251, 255, 256
Four Mirrored Cubes (Robert Morris), 331
Francis Alÿs, 89
Franko, Mark, 56
Frege, Gottlob, 240
Freud, Sigmund, 3
Friedman, Dan, 307
Fried, Michael, 39, 327
Fuchs, Elinor, 8
fungus, 3, 64, 108

G
gamification, 27
Gauss, Carl Friedrich, 248, 249
gaze, choreography of the, 40, 329
General Assembly (Building Conversation), 198, 199
Genesis (Eduardo Kac), 306
gestalts (Robert Morris), 39, 326, 327
gesturality (gesture), 19, 83, 128, 144, 160, 271, 281, 291, 293
Ghosh, Amitav, 203
Gibson, William, 5
Gilbreth, Fred, 184
Gilbreth, Lillian Moller, 185
global transformation, 2
Goebbels, Heiner, 28, 139, 140, 142, 144, 148
Stifters Dinge, 28, 139, 140, 144–150
Goehr, Lydia, 261
Goldstein, Kurt, 67, 68
Goodman, Nelson, 95, 136
government (to govern), 93
Graham, Dan, 334
grammar of animacy, 30, 196, 200, 204, 206, 209, 215, 227

graphic scores, 281
Grehan, Helena, 21
Grosz, Elizabeth, 7, 69
Grotowski, Jerzy, 294
GTA (video game), 128, 132
Guattari, Félix, 3, 7, 24, 27, 70, 138–147, 149, 150, 177
Guillemin, Roger, 290
Guisgand, Philippe, 27, 132

H
Haas, Maximilian, 9, 22, 23, 25, 62, 67
Hacking, Ian, 253
Hamdani, Haidar, 202, 209
Han, Byung-Chul, 155
Hand-Held-Display, 38, 301, 302
Hansen, Mark, 241
Haraway, Donna J., 2, 4–7, 12, 17, 21–24, 26, 27, 29–31, 33, 42, 66, 78, 99, 105, 106, 137, 147, 176, 178–181, 187, 189, 190, 195, 197, 200, 208, 214, 221, 223, 225–228, 231, 255, 288
Harlequin Coat (ORLAN), 38, 289, 291
Harman, Graham, 7, 12, 85
Hassan, Ihab, 1, 6
Hayles, N. Katherine, 6, 8, 82, 262, 282
Heberer, Thomas, 273, 274, 283
Heidegger, Martin, 12, 56
Hello Hi There (Annie Dorsen), 251
Heuer, Rolf-Dieter, 241
Heyde, Neil, 263
Higgs boson (Higgs particle), 34, 40, 238–242, 249
Higgs, Peter, 241
Hijikata, 56
Hintikka, Jaakko, 252
historical materialism, 112

Hobbes, Thomas, 33
Hodges, Wilfrid, 252
Hölderlin, Friedrich, 145
Höller, Carsten, 90
The Baudouin Experiment, 90
Holocene, the, 2
Honsinger, Tristan, 283
Hooke, Robert, 299
human actant, 15, 106
human-animal divide, 63, 64, 78
human-as-humus, 12
humanism (humanist), 2, 3, 5, 7, 8, 13, 31, 33, 63, 64, 137, 141, 150, 243, 262
Hustak, Carla, 4
Hutchison, Steph, 34, 35
hylomorphism, 265
hyperobject, 29, 175–177

I
I/II/III/IIII (Kris Verdonck), 20
ICI (Mylène Benoit), 128
ICP. *See* Instant Composers Pool (ICP) Orchestra
identification, 37, 73–75, 162, 296
Iglesias, Marc, 121
immersive experience, 316
Impossible Conversation (Building Conversation), 196–199, 203, 204, 221, 223, 225, 227
incorporeality, 318
incorporeal materialism, 36, 255, 256
indeterminacy, 87, 256
index(es), 56, 143
Ingold, Tim, 9, 30, 36, 184, 222, 265, 280
innocent eye, the, 321, 331
inorganic, 53, 55, 154, 155, 189, 255, 293
installation, 18, 26, 28, 39, 56, 58, 101, 111, 121, 131, 160,

289–291, 317–319, 324, 328, 329, 331–334
Instant Composers Pool (ICP) Orchestra, 36, 264, 272, 276, 278
Kehang ("Kallpaper"), 277, 279–281
Kneushoorn ("Krhinoceros"), 274, 275
interconnectedness, 4
interdependence, 4, 106
internet of things, 18
interspecies interaction (interspecies collaboration), 70, 72, 106
interspecies performance, 71, 72
Inter-View (Benjamin Vandewalle), 319
intimacy, 4, 117, 266, 276, 280, 327
intra-action, 7, 33, 36, 41, 103, 105, 178, 183, 186–188, 221, 243
IN VOID (Kris Verdonck), 118, 119
In-der-Welt-Sein. See being-in-the-world
Irigaray, Luce, 7
Island Universe, 290
itineracy, 280, 282
itinerary (an)notation, 279
itineration, 36, 280

J
0/10 (Jean Paul Van Bendegem), 34, 244, 247, 255
Jameson, Frederic, 295
Janmaat, Joost, 216
Jay, Martin, 39, 320, 322–324, 333
Johnson, Barbara
Julian, Helena, 32, 39–41, 316
   Peri-Sphere, 39, 40, 316–325, 328, 329, 331, 332

K
Kac, Eduardo, 306
   Genesis, 306
Kafka, Franz, 122, 123
Kanno, Mieko, 263, 265
Kant, Immanuel, 63, 69, 76, 78
Kantor, Tadeusz, 13
Karreman, Laura, 11, 31, 35
Kehang ("Kallpaper") (Instant Composers Pool Orchestra), 277, 279, 281
Kharms, Daniil, 122, 123
Kim-Cohen, Seth, 331
Kimmerer, Robin Wall, 30, 196, 200, 201, 205–207, 209, 215, 227, 229, 230
kin, 5, 42, 230
kinaesthetic empathy, 135
kinaesthetics (kinaesthetic), 135, 303, 316, 318
Kirschenbaum, Matthew G., 282
Klee, Paul, 146
Kluge, Alexander, 123
Kneushoorn ("Krhinoceros") (Instant Composers Pool Orchestra), 274, 275
knowledge, politics of, 11, 31, 33
knowledge transmission, 11, 31, 32, 34, 238, 245, 247, 255
Kooijmans, Luuc, 289, 300
Kozbelt, Aaron, 280
Krauss, Rosalind, 57, 327, 333
Krishan, K. Cha, 9
Kuhn, Thomas, 239

L
laboratory, 4, 30, 32, 33, 37, 38, 101, 102, 173, 181, 197, 221, 240, 288–290, 292, 294–296, 298–300, 303–311, 333
laboratory of social imagination, 38, 289, 307, 310

Lakatos, Imre, 253
landscape, 22–24, 27, 29, 65, 82–86, 88, 89, 103, 134, 141, 144, 171, 172, 181, 187, 230, 292, 308, 315
landscape-play, 138, 150
Langer, Susanne, 257
Large Hadron Collider (LHC), 34, 240, 242, 250
latent performances, 21, 22, 84, 85, 88–90
Latour, Bruno, 6, 12, 18, 29–31, 33, 77, 78, 151, 190, 195, 197–200, 204, 215, 216, 218, 219, 221, 226, 227, 230, 262, 288–290, 311
Lauwers, Jan, 37, 264
Lazzarato, Maurizio, 112
Leach, James, 31
learning plays (Brecht). See *Lehrstücke*
Lehmann, Hans-Thies, 8, 13, 14, 18, 25, 138, 141, 142
Lehrstücke, 288, 295, 296, 307
Lehrstücke, 37
Lepecki, André, 13, 16–20, 25, 326, 333
Le Roy, Xavier, 20
Lévi-Strauss, Claude, 140, 144
Liefooghe, Laurent, 18, 19, 25, 26, 56
  Daydream House, 18, 19, 25, 26
  LivingMachine, 18, 26
Life Forms, 251
Lim, Liza, 282
Lindbergh, Charles, 296, 297
Lindee, Susan, 312
lived abstraction, 36, 256, 257
Live-in-room (Lilia Mestre), 57
LivingMachine (Laurent Liefooghe), 18, 26
lockdown, 42
Lock, Édouard

Amélia, 133
logical research, 37, 252
Lucretius (Titus Lucretius Carius), 177

M
Macfarlane, Robert, 200–202, 205, 207–209, 215, 220, 221, 230
machine, 4, 5, 8, 10, 13, 18, 20, 28, 40, 69, 73, 74, 98, 100, 102, 111–120, 122, 128, 144, 147, 161, 162, 187, 209, 239, 250, 297, 332
machinic opera, 28, 144
Machon, Josephine, 287
Malcolm X
Manning, Chelsea, 157, 158, 165, 167
Manning, Private First Class Bradley Edward, 157
Mantero, Vera, 20, 56
Margulis, Lynn, 3, 23, 208
Martin, John, 135
Marx, Karl, 3, 53, 97, 117, 183
Massumi, Brian, 25, 36, 87, 256, 257
mastery, 2, 4, 16, 106, 150
  allure of, 7
  ethos of, 6
material-discursive contextures, 183
mathematical induction, 248, 249
Matsutake, 103
May, Theresa J., 220
McCormick, John, 34, 35, 250, 251
  Emergence, 34, 35, 250
McDonald, Peter D., 282
McElheny, Josiah, 290, 292
  Island Universe, 290
McGregor, Wayne, 35, 251
  Choreographic Language Agent, 251
  Enhancing Choreographic Objects, 251

McIntosh, Kate, 102
McKenzie, Jon, 243
McNamara, Lauren, 157
medianatures, 187
Meillassoux, Quentin, 7
Mengelberg, Misha, 272, 283
Merleau-Ponty, Maurice, 321
Mestre, Lilia, 18, 57, 58
　Live-in-room, 57
　Moving by you, 58
metakinesis, 135
metaphysics, 243, 293
metonymic laboratories, 294, 310
Middeldorp, Thijs, 216, 217
Mignolo, Walter, 14
Miller, Arthur, 290, 292, 294
mimesis, 135
mimetic gesture, 136
Minimalism, 39, 317, 326, 327, 330, 331
mirror, 39, 40, 88, 117, 201, 205, 254, 303, 317, 318, 323, 328, 330–332
mirror neurons, 135
mirror palace, 330, 331
mise en abyme, 331
Mitrović, Sanja, 18, 19
modernism, modernity, 11, 14, 22, 52, 65, 86, 222, 311, 320, 324, 326
modular machine, 273
Moore, Michael, 275, 283
Morris, Jackie, 202
Morris, Robert
　Column, 39, 327, 328
　Four Mirrored Cubes, 331
　gestalts, 39, 326, 327
Morton, Timothy, 3, 7, 29, 175, 176, 180
Moten, Fred, 54
Mother Nature, 252, 253
Motion, Andrew, 200

motion capture, 32, 35
movement-image, 15
Moving by you (Lilia Mestre), 58
Mroué, Rabih, 38, 289, 308–310
　The Pixelated Revolution, 38, 289, 309, 310
Müller, Heiner, 38, 122, 123, 139, 289, 306–310
　Description of a Picture, 38, 307–309
Mulvey, Laura, 39, 322
music notation, 36, 263, 265, 279, 281
mycorrhiza, 23, 24, 97, 100, 101, 103–108, 207, 208
Myers, Laure, 130
Myers, Natasha, 4
My Great Grandfather's Portfolio (Adalbert Stifters), 140

N
narcissistic spectatorship, 329
Natal, the, 145, 146
Nelkin, Dorothy, 312
Nemirovsky, Ricardo, 247, 257
Neoconcreto Ballet 1 (Lygia Pape), 328
neo-Darwinian evolution, 3
new dramaturgy, 14, 15
New Materialism, 7, 29, 33, 107, 177, 178
New Media Dramaturgy (NMD), 20, 21
Nickles, Thomas, 239
Nietzsche, Friedrich, 3
Noë, Alva, 257, 258
non-binary constellation, 8
non-human, 8, 9, 12, 23, 29, 38, 64, 65, 69, 70, 72, 75, 77, 84, 87, 101, 112, 176–179, 181, 184, 186, 189, 205, 218, 293, 294, 296–298
non-human agency, 21

INDEX   347

non-human agent, 77
nonhuman philosophy, 7
non-representational approach, 246, 247
Normand, Olivier, 128
North Sea Embassy, 216, 230
notation, the textility of, 265
Novati, Gabriella Calchi, 161

O
object-oriented ontology, 7, 29, 175
ocularcentric, 262, 320, 322
Oliver, Mary, 283
ongoingness, 17, 28, 231
ORLAN, 38, 288, 291–293, 297
   Harlequin Coat, 38, 289, 291

P
pandemic, 42
Pape, Lygia, 328
   Neoconcreto Ballet 1, 328
Parikka, Jussi, 187, 188
parliament of lines, 30, 222
Parliament of Things (Building Conversation), 30, 195–200, 215–223, 225, 227
participatory thought, 197, 198, 209, 212–214, 225–227
Partizan Public, 216, 217
Pavis, Patrice, 15, 21, 22
Payne, Emily, 32, 36, 37, 41, 42, 264
perceptual schemata, 292, 297
perfect familiarity, 269
performance art, 53, 58, 61, 88, 137, 287, 288
performativity of scientific practices, 32, 34, 255
performativity (performative), 13, 17, 19, 26, 32, 41, 53, 56, 84, 88, 105, 154, 166, 293, 331
Perniola, Mario, 56, 58

Persia, Prince of, 128
personhood (persona), 20, 56, 71, 112
phantom experience, 302–304
pharmacology (pharmacological), 27
pharmakon, 27
Phelan, Peggy, 166, 167
phylogenesis, 129
physical distancing, 42
Pickering, Andrew, 239
pixel(ization), 130
place, vexed, 29, 30, 197, 223
Planas, Nick, 36, 266–269, 271, 279, 281
   To My Father, 266, 268, 279
poisoned light, 29, 175
polyphonic assemblage, 38, 292, 293
positivism (positivist), 6, 70, 71
postanthropocentrism (postanthropocentric), 18, 27, 42, 138, 140–142, 146, 147
postdramatic theatre (postdramatic), 264
posthuman condition, 12, 42
posthuman dramaturgy (dramaturgies), 14
posthuman epistemologies, 14, 31
posthumanism (posthuman), 1–12, 14, 15, 18, 21, 23, 25, 26, 28, 31–33, 35, 36, 41, 42, 137–139, 144, 147–150, 155, 156, 207, 250, 251, 262, 288
posthumanization, 43
posthuman prototypes (posthuman prototype), 8
presence, 12, 18, 21, 26, 33, 39, 40, 52, 56–58, 83, 86, 112, 117, 118, 153, 154, 156, 158, 159, 161, 163, 166, 212, 219, 222, 225, 293, 302, 305, 327–331
pre-situationists, 88, 90
Prince of Persia (video game), 132

problem-finding, 280
problem-solving, 36, 268, 280
projection, 73, 118, 119, 123, 128, 139, 144, 156
proof, mathematical, 34, 240, 244, 249
proof, theatre of, 33, 197, 221
proof, the construction of, 239
props, 13, 21, 26, 57
prototype, 8, 10, 40, 111, 329
prototype, posthuman, 8
Prynne, Jeremy, 209
Punchdrunk, 333
  Sleep No More, 333
Pythagorean theorem, 34, 244, 247, 255, 258

Q
quantum physics, 7, 242
quarantine, 42
quasi-objects, 218–220, 263

R
radioactivity, 29, 173–175, 181
Ragg, Christoph, 18
  C.O. Journeys, 57
Ramachandran, Vilayanur, 302–304
Rare Earthenware (Unknown Fields Division), 29, 171, 172, 174, 175, 179, 181, 182, 184, 185, 188
Raskar, Ramesh, 301
real-but-abstract, 256
re-enactment, 36, 246, 247, 253
refrain, 27, 28, 138, 140, 141, 143, 145, 148, 211
regime of visibility, 56
relational aesthetics, 104
response-ability, 11, 14, 17, 20, 25, 27–29, 197
resurgent world, 31

rhizome ontology, 10
Rhys Morus, Iwan, 325
Rhythm O (Marina Abramović), 22, 84
Rimini Protokoll, 38, 289, 300–302, 304
  Situation Rooms, 38, 289, 300–304, 307
Rizzolatti, Giacomo, 135
Robert, Lilou, 130
robot, 25, 118, 119
Roche, Heather, 282
Rodney King riots, Los Angeles, 159
Ross, Christine, 38, 301, 302
Rossini, Manuela, 282
Rotman, Brian, 36, 247, 254
Rousseau, Jean-Jacques, 139
RP (Revenge Porn), 156, 157, 164, 165
rubber hand test, the, 302, 303
Ruhsam, Martina, 29, 191
Runco, Mark A.
Ruskin, John, 39, 321, 322
Russell, Bertrand, 240

S
sacralisation of texts, 37, 262
Sagan, Dorian
Salter, Chris, 38, 299
Sartre, Jean-Paul, 83
Sawyer, Keith, 280, 282, 283
scenopoïetes, 142, 143, 150
Schaffer, Simon, 289, 299
Schechner, Richard, 287, 316
Scheer, Edward, 21
Schouten, Matthijs, 226
Schuiling, Floris, 32, 36, 37, 41, 42, 264, 275, 282, 283
Schwartz, Vanessa R., 324
science and technology studies (STS), 6, 11, 78, 288

science art worldings, 4, 228
science fiction (sci-fi), 5, 29, 108, 171, 180
scopic regime, 40, 323, 324, 331
score, 32, 36, 37, 41, 42, 87, 88, 107, 262, 263, 265, 266, 268, 271, 274–277, 279–282
score annotation, 36, 261, 263
Scruton, Roger, 226
Sennett, Richard, 280
sensorimotor schemas, 257
sensorimotor skills, 257, 258
sensory-motor scheme, 15–17, 23
sensory partnership, 4
Serra, Richard, 287
Serres, Michel, 2, 177
Shakespeare, William, 307
Shannon, Claude, 243
Shaolin, 133
Shapin, Steven, 289, 299, 305, 306
Sheldrake, Merlin, 207, 208
Silberg, Joyanna, 165
Simard, Suzanne, 207, 208, 215, 229
Sinclair, Nathalie, 247
Situationism (situation), 15, 24, 25, 55, 58, 66, 71, 73, 74, 76, 82, 84–90, 93, 97, 101, 102, 105, 114, 116, 119, 121, 137, 155, 158, 164, 166, 167, 246, 264, 269, 272–274, 280, 293, 295–297, 307, 308, 325, 328, 331
Situationist International, 22, 82
Situation Rooms (Rimini Protokoll), 38, 289, 300–304, 307
Sleep No More (Punchdrunk), 333
slow revolt, 226
Snowden, Edward, 158
social life, 53, 274
Society of Spectacle (Debord), 4, 86
Sontag, Susan, 321
Spångberg, Mårten, 87

species, 2, 3, 42, 62, 68, 70, 71, 101, 104, 106, 113, 116, 117, 137, 143, 144, 147, 148, 150, 202, 206, 208, 220, 222, 223, 231
spectatorial ecstasy, 40, 316
speculative gestures, 17
Speculative Realism, 7, 177
Spinoza, Benedictus de, 9, 70
stagemaker, 142, 143
Stalpaert, Christel, 7, 10, 11, 15, 16, 20, 30, 33, 119, 203, 221
Starre, Alexander, 282
Star Trek, 133
Stein, Gertrude, 138, 139
Stengers, Isabelle, 17
Stiegler, Bernard, 27, 161, 162
Stifters, Adalbert, 139
    My Great Grandfather's Portfolio, 140
Stifters Dinge (Heiner Goebbels), 28, 139, 140, 144–150
Stoermer, Eugene, 2
string figures, 5, 6, 20
Stuart, Meg, 136
subjectivation (subjectivity), 16, 52–55, 69, 70, 112, 119, 147, 154–156, 178, 304, 326
Sudnow, David, 269
Sugiera, Małgorzata, 32, 37, 38, 41
surrogate person, 39, 327
surveillance technologies, 5, 42
suspension, 210, 211, 214
sustainability, 24, 96, 97, 99, 217
Sutherland, Ivan, 301, 302
symbiopoiesis, 311
symbiosis, 3, 105, 207, 229
sympoesis, 6

T

tacit knowledge, 214
Taylor, Frederick, 185

Taylorism, Choreography of, 185
techno-human, 302
technology, 1, 2, 4, 5, 7–10, 13, 14, 18, 20, 27, 31, 32, 34, 37, 38, 40–42, 105, 112, 114, 115, 127, 156, 163, 166, 179, 187, 189, 198, 207, 241–243, 250–252, 254, 262, 264, 282, 293, 294, 296, 298, 301–303, 305, 306, 310
techno-memory, 160
technoscience, 288, 289, 291
tentacular thinking, 30, 197, 200, 214, 215, 227, 228
tentacular thinking-with-things, 30, 197, 215, 216, 221, 227
territory, 27, 28, 64, 67, 131, 138–147, 150, 272, 282, 290, 318
textilic practices, 282. *See also* textility
textility, 36, 265, 274, 280. *See also* textilic practices
Théâtre de la Guillotine (Benjamin Vandewalle), 319
Theatre Laboratorium (Jerzy Grotowski), 294
theatre of proof, 33, 197, 221
theatrum mundi, 316
The Baudouin Experiment (Carsten Höller), 90
theoretical automaton, 40, 332
The Pixelated Revolution (Rabih Mroué), 38, 289, 309, 310
Thérèse Raquin (Émile Zola), 295
thingliness, 17, 18, 21, 57, 58
thingly variations, 14, 22, 25
thing-power, 12, 13, 15, 18, 26
things as mediators, 30, 31, 33, 197, 200, 215, 221
Thinking Together

An Experiment (Building Conversation), 197, 209, 210, 212–214, 225, 227
Thoreau, Henry David, 321, 322
Time Loop (Building Conversation), 198, 199
Timmers, Renee, 282
Tomb Raider (video game), 132
Tomlinson, Gary, 262
To My Father (Nick Planas), 266, 268, 279
tragedy, 15, 117
transformation, 13, 53, 54, 67, 82, 118, 119, 183, 186, 208, 213
transmitting knowledge. *See* knowledge transmission
trauma, 153, 154, 156, 163, 166
trauma (traumatizing), 28, 97
Tree That Owns Itself, The, 217, 218
Tret'iakov, Sergei, 182, 183, 191
Tsing, Anna Löwenhaupt, 23, 38, 103, 105, 292, 311
Turpin, Etienne, 25, 82, 85, 86

U
Uexküll, Jakob von, 23, 24, 68–71
Ullian, Joseph, 95
Umwelt, 67, 68
Umwelt, 24
uncanny, 111, 150, 155
uncertainty, 22, 41, 62, 86–88, 149, 196, 204
Unknown Fields Division
 Earthenware, 191
 Rare Earthenware, 29, 171, 172, 174, 179, 181, 184, 185, 188–191
UNTITLED (Kris Verdonck), 20, 119, 121, 122
use-value, 19, 54
utility, 16, 54, 88

V

Valéry, Paul, 139
van Baarle, Kristof, 11, 18, 20, 111, 119
Van Bendegem, Jean Paul, 32, 34, 36–38, 40, 42, 237, 238, 243, 247, 248, 255
   0/10, 34, 244, 247, 255
van den Berg, Lotte (Building Conversation), 199, 215, 224, 228
van den Dries, Luk, 37, 264
van der Tuin, Iris, 238
van de Vall, Renée, 321, 333
Vandewalle, Benjamin, 39, 316, 317, 319, 324, 328, 329
   Birdwatching 4x4, 319
   Inter-View, 319
   One/Zero, 319
   Peri-Sphere, 39, 40, 316–325, 328, 329, 331, 332
   Théâtre de la Guillotine, 319
Van Dooren, Thom, 28, 223, 228, 230
Van Kerkhoven, Marianne, 14, 20, 26, 111, 117, 123
Varnelis, Kazys, 321
Vazquez, Rolando, 14
VCR, 135
Verdonck, Kris
   BOX, 113, 118
   DANCER #3, 116, 118, 119
   END, 9, 20, 117
   I/II/III/IIII, 20
   IN VOID, 118, 119
   UNTITLED, 20, 119–122
Verfremdungseffekt, 302
vibrant matter, 102
virtual reality, 5, 131, 303
virtual, the, 130, 132–134, 155–158, 160–162, 166, 202, 288, 300–302, 304
virtuosi, 300
virtuosity, 19, 20, 135
virus, 42, 226
vital materialism, 12
Vivat dance festival, Armentières, 132
Von Kleist, Heinrich, 122

W

Wagner, Richard, 146
Walther, Franz Erhard
   Werksatz, 328
weaving, 36, 266, 275
Weber-Krebs, David, 25
   Balthazar, 9, 23, 25, 61, 62, 66, 70, 77
Weibel, Peter, 293
Weill, Kurt, 296, 298
Weinberg, David, 290, 292
   Island Universe, 290
Weiner, Anthony, 159
Wenner, Stefanie, 23, 24, 93, 98, 104
Werksatz (Franz Erhard Walther), 328
Whanganui River Claims Settlement, 216
Whatever Dance Toolbox (BADCo), 251
Whitehead, Alfred North, 23, 62, 75–77, 240, 246, 257
Wiame, Eline, 27, 28, 151
Wiener, William
Wierbos, Wolter, 274–276, 279, 280, 283
WikiLeaks, 157–159
withdrawal, 22, 88–90, 182
Witzgall, Suzanne, 177, 189
Wood, Jason W.
Wood Wide Web, 100, 101, 207
Woolgar, Steve, 290
Working Title Situation festival, 333
worlding, 178, 228
world-object, 2

world orientation, 331
Worthen, W.B., 298
Wren, Jacob, 95
   Anthology of Optimism, 95

X
Xenakis, Iannis, 254

Y
Yablo, Stephen, 94, 95
Young, Liam (Unknown Fields Division), 171, 172, 176, 180, 183, 184, 187

Z
Zaiontz, Keren, 329, 330, 333
Zola, Émile, 37, 294
   Thérèse Raquin, 295

Printed in the United States
by Baker & Taylor Publisher Services